INTRODUCTION TO EU COMPETITION LAW

INTRODUCTION TO EU COMPETITION LAW

EDITED BY

PETER WILLIS

|L|L|P|

LONDON SINGAPORE
2005

Informa Professional
(a trading division of T&F Informa (UK) Ltd)
Mortimer House
37–41 Mortimer Street
London W1T 3JH
professional.enquiries@informa.com

EAST ASIA
Informa Professional Asia
No. 1 Grange Road
#08–02 Orchard Building
Singapore 239693
professional.asia@informa.com

British Library Cataloguing in Publication Data
A catalogue record for this book
is available from the
British Library

ISBN 1–84311–4356

Text set in 10/12 Plantin and Helvetica
by Interactive Sciences Ltd, Gloucester
Printed in Great Britain by
MPG Books
Bodmin, Cornwall

PREFACE

This book provides an introductory but thorough guide to EU competition law, covering the underlying economics, and the key substantive areas of anti-competitive agreements (Article 81), abuses of dominance (Article 82), the application to the most common types of commercial agreement, state aids, state measures limiting competition and mergers. It also examines the procedures under which the relevant competition authorities apply the rules, private enforcement of the rules before the courts, and minimising risk by implementing a compliance programme.

Publication of a new introductory book on EU competition law in 2005 seems particularly timely: 2004 saw a number of major developments, including an entirely new approach to competition enforcement under Regulation 1/2003, a revised Merger Regulation introducing not only a new substantive test but also new procedures, and new rules for technology transfer agreements.

The emphasis is practical rather than theoretical: the authors are practitioners in the field of competition law and economics, with many years' individual and collective experience in the area. One of the advantages of a work like this is that it offers a number of perspectives of the same issue. Other than editing to ensure consistency throughout the book, the chapters therefore reflect the individual style of the authors.

Although the chapters reflect the state of the law at the end of February 2005, it was possible to include major developments at proof stage in June 2005.

I am grateful to my fellow-authors for their enthusiasm for this project, for contributing a series of excellent chapters and for working to a tight publication timetable.

Peter R Willis
Taylor Wessing, London
July 2005

LIST OF FIGURES AND TABLES

Figures

Tables

AUTHORS' BIOGRAPHIES

PETER WILLIS (EDITOR)

Peter is a partner in Taylor Wessing's competition, regulation and trade group. He advises UK and international clients, particulary in the IT and communications sectors, on their dealings with UK and EU competition and regulatory authorities in the context of mergers, notifications, complaints and investigations. He is acknowledged as an expert on the UK Competition Act 1998 and is the author of *The Competition Act 1998—A Guide for Business* (2nd edition, Informa Professional, February 2001). He was seconded to the Office of Fair Trading for six months to assist in the development of its procedures.

Peter is a member of the advisory board of the *Competition Law Journal* and is recommended for his competition expertise in *The Legal 500*. He is the author of a number of articles on competition law and is a regular commentator on competition issues.

SEAN-PAUL BRANKIN

At the time of writing, Sean-Paul was a senior associate in Lovells' EU, competition and trade group based in London. He has since become a director in the legal department of the OFT, on the competition enforcement side.

Before becoming a regulator, Sean-Paul had extensive experience of representing clients before the European Commission, courts and OFT in sectors including credit cards, video games, aircraft manufacture and chemicals. He qualified as a barrister in 1993 and gained experience in Brussels and Paris, including a period in the Commission's Merger Task Force, before moving to London.

HELEN JENKINS

Helen is a director of Oxera with responsibility for the competition policy practice area. Her areas of expertise are competition policy, financial services (including payment systems), the communications sector, and econometric analysis. She has carried out work on market definition and the assessment of competitiveness in a number of industries, including banking, telecoms, broadcasting, pharmaceuticals, airlines, and energy supply. She has also worked with a range of clients on anti-competitive practices and the economic issues that underlie the application of the relevant competition legislation in the UK, Europe, Australia and the Middle East. Helen has advised retail banks and payment schemes in the UK, Europe and the Middle East on economics issues pertaining to agreements, abuse of dominance and the regulation of credit.

Authors' Biographies

BEATRIZ YEMAIL

Beatriz is a member of competition and communications teams at Oxera. She has provided advice to regulators, the Commission, and public and private companies on market definition, the existence of market power, the effect of practices alleged to have hindered the competitive development of markets, and the evaluation of the effects of regulation. She has worked in several sectors including telecoms, food, drinks and sports in the UK, Europe, Hong Kong and Latin America.

VANESSA TURNER

Vanessa has been a partner in Freshfields Bruckhaus Deringer's anti-trust, competition and trade group since 2000 and works in Brussels and Düsseldorf. She specialises in competition/anti-trust and merger control law. She has advised a broad range of international clients before the Commission, European courts and national authorities in relation to inquiries under Article 81 and 82 of the EC Treaty into anti-competitive practices, including many international cartel investigations, merger cases (first and second phase) and general EU competition law matters.

MARC REYSEN

Marc has been a partner in Freshfields Bruckhaus Deringer's anti-trust, competition and trade group since 2001 and works in Brussels. He specialises in merger control, general competition and state aid law. He has advised a broad range of clients before the Commission and the German *Bundeskartellamt* as well as national and EU courts in relation to inquiries under Article 81 and 82 of the EC Treaty, the ECMR and German competition law.

PAT TREACY

Pat is a partner in, and heads, the competition law team at Bristows. She advises on the competition law aspects of agreements and commercial conduct, particularly in the context of high-technology industries such as IT, biotechnology and pharmaceuticals. She has also advised on all aspects of the rules on free movement of goods and parallel trade. She has expertise in advising clients in dealings with the Commission under both Article 81 and Article 82 and has represented clients throughout EU proceedings up to and including the Court of First Instance and European Court of Justice in Luxembourg. Pat also has considerable experience in working with the national competition authorities in the UK.

She has specialised in competition law since qualifying in 1986 and is a member of the Competition Law Association and of the British Institute of International and Comparative Law.

LAURA ANDERSON

Laura is a partner at Bristows in the intellectual property department. She specialises in non-contentious IP matters and has experience of a broad range of commercial transactions relating to IP rights and their development and exploitation. Her practice covers a number of industry sectors, including pharmaceuticals and biotechnology, IT and branded goods.

She also advises in respect of the competition law aspects of commercial IP agreements and has spent time working in Brussels, both at the Council of Ministers of the European Union and in private practice.

SOPHIE LAWRANCE

Sophie is an associate solicitor in Bristows' competition department. She advises regularly on the competition issues that arise from distribution and licensing agreements, and on the behavioural issues that affect companies with larger market shares. Her experience spans both transactional and contentious aspects of competition law.

MARTIN BAKER

Martin is a partner at Taylor Wessing and is head of its competition regulation and trade group in London. He advises organisations in a broad spectrum of industries on a range of competition, public procurement, trade and other EU and UK regulatory matters, particularly in the life sciences and consumer goods sectors. The structuring of mergers, strategic alliances and distribution arrangements in order to maximise commercial benefit is also a key element of Martin's practice.

He is recommended for his competition expertise in *The Legal 500* and is a frequent commentator on competition issues in the press and broadcast media.

CHRIS BRIGHT

Chris is a partner at Shearman & Sterling LLP, where his practice covers EU and UK competition law issues arising in transactions, commercial agreements and disputes. He is a non-executive director of the Jersey Competition Regulatory Authority and has been appointed to the UK Competition Commission. He is a CEDR-accredited mediator.

JOHN SCHMIDT

John is counsel in Shearman & Sterling LLP's competition group in London. He studied law at Edinburgh University and is dual-qualified as a Scottish solicitor and a German *Rechtsanwalt*.

He has extensive experience of major cross-border merger and acquisition transactions and joint ventures in a variety of industrial sectors, including pharmaceuticals, energy, mining and consumer goods, as well as financial services. He has represented clients before the Commission, the OFT and Competition Commission as well as the German *Bundeskartellamt*, and has advised in various merger and non-merger proceedings before other national competition authorities.

STEPHEN WISKING

Stephen is a partner at Herbert Smith. He practices in all areas of competition law both in the EU and UK. He has worked in Brussels and London and is qualified as a solicitor advocate. He is also qualified as a barrister and solicitor in Australia.

Stephen has particular experience in relation to mergers, regulatory investigations, competition litigation and broadcasting regulation. Significant mergers have included: Price Waterhouse/Coopers & Lybrand; Chevron/Texaco; Group 4/Securicor. His clients operate in the media, IT, pharmaceutical, professional services and oil and gas sectors.

GIULIO FEDERICO

Giulio is a principal at Charles River Associates. He has advised clients on competition matters in sectors ranging from electricity and gas to telecoms, media, Pay TV and security exchanges. He has worked on several EU mergers —including Oracle/PeopleSoft (for Oracle)—as well as various Article 81 and 82 cases. He holds a PhD in economics from the University of Oxford, and has published several papers on competition issues in energy markets.

DIANA JACKSON

Diana is a principal at Charles River Associates. Since joining Lexecon (as it was then) in 1998 she has had particular experience in Commission merger investigations, having worked on Andersen/Ernst & Young, GE/Honeywell and Airtours/First Choice (both at the Commission stage and in the Court of First Instance appeal), as well as cases before the Competition Commission (Centrica/Dynegy) and *Bundeskartellamt* (BP/E.ON), among others. This work has involved collective dominance, unilateral effects, portfolio and "failing firm" issues.

ANDREW MACNAB

Andrew was called to the Bar in 1986. He has been a member of Monckton Chambers since 1989. He acts in both litigious and non-litigious EU and UK competition law matters. He acted for the claimant in *Network Multimedia Television Ltd v. Jobserve* [2001] UKCLR 814, [2002] UKCLR 184 (the first case in which an interim injunction was granted to restrain a threatened infringement of the Chapter II prohibition) and, most recently, represented the Consumers' Association in *Burgess* v. *OFT* (the first case in which the Consumers' Association has intervened in the Competition Appeal Tribunal).

JANE WHITTAKER

Jane is a partner in Macfarlanes and head of its competition law group. She has extensive experience in all aspects of competition law work.

She acts for major international groups on regulatory matters particularly in the advertising, technology and retail sectors, representing them before the UK and EU authorities. She also successfully advised IBA Health on the first appeal of an OFT merger clearance decision under the Enterprise Act. She writes and lectures regularly on competition legislation and practice.

MARTIN BALLANTYNE

Martin is a senior solicitor in Macfarlanes' competition law group. He advises on a wide range of both transactional and behavioural competition issues and has particular experience in cartel and price-fixing cases, and related leniency considerations, under both the UK and EU regimes.

He is a member of the *Studienvereinigung Kartellrecht*, a leading discussion forum on competition law in Germany and the EU. He regularly contributes to legal journals.

TABLE OF CONTENTS

TABLE OF CASES

Table of Cases

Table of Cases

TABLE OF LEGISLATION

Table of Legislation

STATUTORY INSTRUMENTS

CHAPTER 1

INTRODUCTION

Sean-Paul Brankin, Lovells

1.1 WHY READ THE INTRODUCTION?

In many areas of law it is easy to understand why the rules are the way they are. You do not need to be an expert in criminal law to understand that murder is wrong, or an expert in contract law to understand that you ought to deliver on commitments you have agreed to and been paid for. The legal rules in these areas make sense because they embody principles of morality and fairness that we are all familiar with.

Competition law is different. It is not about fairness or morality (at least not directly). The rules of competition law reflect economic, not ethical, principles. And, as a result, competition law will sometimes permit behaviour that seems very unfair—like charging different customers different prices for the same product. Worse, it will sometimes prohibit and sometimes permit exactly the same behaviour—for example, refusing to supply a customer—depending on the economic background. All of this can make competition law very difficult to understand.

The problem is exacerbated by the language of competition law. The competition rules in the EC Treaty prohibit the "abuse" of a "dominant position" (in Article 82) and agreements that "have as their object or effect the prevention, restriction or distortion of competition" (in Article 81). On its face, this language is pretty meaningless. In order to understand it, you need to have some idea of what it is trying to achieve. And in order to do that, you need to have some understanding of the kind of problems that competition law is intended to address—or, in other words, why we have competition law in the first place.

This introduction is intended to give readers a basic understanding of what the rules of competition law are by exploring the type of problems that competition law is trying to address and how that is reflected in the rules themselves.

1.2 WHY DO WE HAVE COMPETITION LAW?

EU competition law can usefully be thought of as having two objectives. The first is to deal the problems that can arise when an undertaking (or coordinated group of undertakings) exercises a significant degree of market power.

In relation to this first objective, EU competition law is just like competition law in other jurisdictions such as the US, the UK or Germany.

The second is the creation of a single market within the EU. This second objective is arguably separate from the first, and it is specific to EU competition law.

1.2.1 The first objective: dealing with market power

"Market power" is an economic concept. An undertaking has market power if it can make a profit by raising its prices above the level that would exist on a competitive market. Any undertaking can raise its prices. However, most will simply lose customers—and money—if they raise their prices higher than their competitors. Most undertakings do not, therefore, have market power.

The circumstances in which market power may exist, and why it can be a problem, are best illustrated with an example, as follows.

1.2.1.1 Opec's 1973 oil price rise

On 4 November 1973, the member countries of Opec (the Organisation of Oil Producing and Exporting Countries)—who at that time represented around 55 per cent of world crude oil production—announced that they would reduce their production of crude oil by 25 per cent with immediate effect and by a further 5 per cent that December.

This had a massive impact on the price of crude oil: it jumped to four times its previous level. The profits of Opec members also jumped. Although Opec members were selling less oil (in principle, 30 per cent less) they were selling it at four times the previous price.

This is a nice example of the exercise of market power. By cooperating rather than competing, Opec members were able to raise the price of their product above the previous market level and to make a (very large) profit in the process.

1.2.1.2 Why oil prices rose

Why did Opec's actions have this effect? Two factors were of particular importance. First, the position of Opec's members in the market meant they were able to significantly reduce the total world supply of crude oil. Together they represented a 55 per cent of world production. Their competitors—the producers of the remaining 45 per cent of world supply—were unable to increase their own oil production to make up for the substantial reduction in supplies from Opec.[1]

Second, there were no good substitutes for crude oil and the products derived from it. Oil refineries, power stations, chemicals plants and cars could

1. After a certain point, increasing oil production is not straightforward and may involve drilling new wells or even finding new oil fields.

not easily be converted to run on alternative fuels like coal or gas. If the owners of these assets wished to make use of them, they had to buy oil. And when the quantity of oil on the world market fell, they bidded the price up trying to obtain a share of the reduced supply.

If either of these factors had not been present, Opec's strategy might not have worked. If other oil producers had been able to increase production in response to Opec's action, customers would not have needed to bid up prices. Similarly, if customers could easily have switched to other fuels, they would have done so rather than pay the new high prices for oil. As we will see, both the availability of alternative products and the market position of the companies involved are key issues in determining whether a competition law problem exists.

1.2.1.3 The problem: welfare loss

The increase in the price of crude oil was not the only effect of Opec's actions. Much more importantly, they had a hugely damaging effect on the world economy. In the 23 years prior to Opec's announcement, between 1950 and 1973, the economies of the countries belonging to the OECD[2]—in effect, the economies of the developed world—grew by an average of between 3 per cent and 4 per cent per year. In the 12 years following the announcement, from 1973 to 1985, average annual growth in these economies slowed to just over 1.5 per cent per year. The oil price shock caused by Opec's behaviour was a major factor in this slowdown. In other words, Opec's behaviour contributed to a halving of economic growth in the developed world for more than a decade.

The reason for this is fairly simple. Less oil was being produced, and there were no effective alternatives. As a result, some owners of chemical plants, power stations, etc were unable to obtain the supplies of oil they needed—or at least were unable to pay the increased price of crude and still turn a profit. They had no choice but to allow their assets to lie idle. The wealth those assets could have created, if used, was never generated—and the world economy suffered (and slowed) as a result. This effect is referred to by economists as "welfare loss".

This is obviously an extreme example of welfare loss. Oil is central to the operation of modern economies. Cartels in other industries—beer, for example—would have less dramatic consequences. However, the principle is of general application. Companies with market power have by definition the ability to raise the prices of their products to super-competitive levels, and the effect is a welfare loss suffered by society as a whole. This is the primary problem that the rules of competition law seek to address.

2. The Organisation for Economic Cooperation and Development.

1.2.2 The second objective: market integration

A particularly hostile attitude is taken under EU competition law to behaviour that affects inter-state trade in the EU—such as provisions in agreements that prohibit the export of goods between Member States. It is generally accepted that what lies behind this is the (economically dubious) view that behaviour which interferes directly with the free flow of products between EU Member States is inconsistent with the creation of a single market within the EU.

It is unclear to what extent EU competition law prohibits behaviour under this secondary "market integration" objective where no market power issues arise. The better view is probably that it cannot do so. The remainder of this Chapter will therefore deal exclusively with EU competition law's primary "market power" objective.

1.3 HOW EU COMPETITION LAW DEALS WITH MARKET POWER

Since the problem that competition law seeks to address is the welfare loss that occurs where market power is exercised, competition law might be expected simply to prohibit the holding of market power.[3] However, there would be problems with such a straightforward ban.

First, a company may obtain market power "honestly"—ie as a natural result of competition on the market. This may occur because a company's products are so much better (or cheaper) than those of its competitors that customers choose not to buy anything else. In such cases, the company's competitors may go out of business. But that is no bad thing; it simply reflects the better service customers are getting from the successful company. Equally, the threat of going out of business is a powerful incentive for competing companies not to fall too far behind each other in terms of their products or prices. Alternatively, it may occur if customers in a market obtain greater benefits if they all buy products from a single supplier—for example, where customers benefit more if the products they buy are compatible (think of Microsoft's word processing software or the battle between Betamax and VHS video recorders). In markets like this, a single supplier may emerge naturally as a result of customer choice. Arguably, this is how Microsoft achieved its monopoly position: its products were good and its customers benefited from all using the same software since this allowed them to exchange documents easily or work together in other ways. It would be counterproductive to make success of this type unlawful. That would reduce the incentive for undertakings to produce products if they might be "too successful" and could deprive customers of the benefits of better or cheaper products.

3. Particularly as a company with market power can be expected to charge super-competitive prices (thereby limiting sales and causing a welfare loss), since—by definition—it can increase its profits by doing so.

Second, once a company has achieved a position of market power—even if it has not done so "honestly"—the cost of putting an end to that situation may outweigh the benefits of doing so. The only remedy may be to break up the company with market power into smaller units. This will often be costly and disruptive. Moreover, the smaller units may be less efficient than the original company and may produce more expensive and poorer products as a result.

Given these problems, it should come as no surprise that EU competition law does not prohibit simply having market power or obtaining it "honestly"—ie by normal competitive means such as producing better or less costly products. However, short of that, EU competition law can and does prohibit behaviour that seeks, by means other than normal competition, to:

— establish new positions of market power or increase the level of existing market power;[4]
— entrench existing market power—ie protect or defend an existing position of market power from competitive attack; or
— exploit market power—eg through increased prices.

Identifying whether the effect of an agreement, a merger or the behaviour of a dominant company may have the effect of establishing, exploiting or entrenching market power goes a long way towards identifying whether it may infringe competition law.

1.4 HOW THE STRUCTURE OF COMPETITION LAW REFLECTS ITS PRIMARY OBJECTIVE

EU competition law operates through three central legal provisions. These are:

— Article 82 of the EC Treaty, which prohibits the abuse of positions of market dominance;
— Article 81 of the EC Treaty, which prohibits anti-competitive agreements; and
— the EC Merger Regulation ("ECMR"), which prohibits anti-competitive mergers, acquisitions and joint ventures.

These three provisions, and the three prohibitions they create, each seek to prevent behaviour that (i) establishes, (ii) entrenches, or (iii) exploits, market power. However, each provision does so in a slightly different context. The following sections describe how this works in more detail.

4. On one level there is a clear distinction between establishing a new position of market power and increasing existing market power. However, in each case, the effect will be achieved by reducing existing competitive constraints on the relevant undertaking(s). It is therefore helpful to think of these two categories of behaviour together.

1.5 ARTICLE 82: ABUSE OF DOMINANCE

For an infringement of Article 82 of the EC Treaty to exist, an undertaking must both:

— hold a dominant position; and
— abuse that position.

These two concepts—"dominance" and "abuse"—are explored further below.

1.5.1 Dominance

The legal definition of a dominant position has been established by the European Court of Justice ("ECJ") as:

"a position of economic strength enjoyed by an undertaking which enables it to hinder the maintenance of effective competition on the relevant market by allowing it to behave to an appreciable extent independently of its competitors and customers and ultimately of consumers."[5]

At the heart of this rather cumbersome definition is the concept that an undertaking will hold a dominant position if it has sufficient economic strength to act independently of its customers and competitors to a significant extent. That is exactly the kind of independence enjoyed by entities with significant market power, like the Opec members in our example. As we saw, Opec members were able to make a profit by forcing up the price of oil only because:

— their position on the market was so strong that their competitors could not supply enough oil to make up for Opec's reduced production; and
— customers had no choice but to continue to purchase oil when the price went up, because there were no good alternatives to oil.

Indeed, it is generally agreed that the concept of dominance is close—if not identical—to that of significant market power.

That is fine in theory. But in practice, how does one identify a dominant position? Following the ECJ definition, lawyers tend to examine two key factors:

— the "relevant market"; and
— the relevant undertaking's "position of economic strength" on that market.

Very broadly, the relevant market may be thought of in terms of the extent to which an undertaking is potentially independent of its customers, and the

5. Case 322/81, *Michelin v. Commission* [1983] ECR 3461.

undertaking's position on that market may be thought of in terms of the extent to which it is independent of its competitors.

1.5.1.1 The relevant market

The term "relevant market" is a technical legal one. It refers to the market in which the dominant undertaking operates *for the purposes of competition law.* That may have very little to do with what the average person—or even the management of the undertaking—would think of as the market.

The process of identifying the relevant market is generally referred to as "market definition". The purpose of identifying (or "defining") the relevant market is to identify the scope of potential competitive constraints on the undertaking alleged to be dominant. In other words, the purpose is ultimately to identify who that undertaking's competitors are. As the European Commission states puts it in its Notice on market definition:

> "Market definition is a tool to identify and define the boundaries of competition between firms."[6]

Relevant markets are generally thought of as having two aspects:

- the "relevant product market"—ie the relevant range of competing products; and
- the "relevant geographic market"—ie the geographic area within which competition takes place.

In deciding which products and geographic areas are relevant for these purposes, the starting point is to look at the options open to customers. However, issues of market definition are frequently complex and technical. In larger cases, this is often an area in which professional economists are deeply involved. The sections below give a brief introduction to the concepts of the relevant product and geographic market.

1.5.1.1.1 The relevant product market

The relevant product market comprises all the products that customers regard as good substitutes for those of the potentially dominant undertaking. In its Notice on market definition, the European Commission states:

> "a relevant product market comprises all those products and/or services which are regarded as interchangeable or substitutable by the consumer, by reason of the products' characteristics, their prices and their intended use".[7]

Substitute products of this type are important because they are the alternatives that customers will turn to if the allegedly dominant undertaking seeks to

6. Commission Notice on the definition of relevant markets for the purposes of Community competition law (the "Market Definition Notice"), 1997 OJ C 372, p 5, para 2.

7. *Ibid*, para 7.

reduce its production or raise its prices. Only if the range of alternatives is limited is an undertaking likely to have market power.

In the Opec example, the problem customers faced was that there were no effective substitutes for oil: they could not switch to coal or gas to keep their oil refineries, chemical plants or cars running. As a result, they had no choice but to pay more for oil. Opec members' profits rose because although they were selling substantially less oil, they were selling it at a much higher price. If suitable alternatives had been available, Opec's customers would have switched to those alternatives rather than pay the higher prices for oil and Opec's members would have lost money.

The relevant product market may also include products that are not direct substitutes. This will be the case if companies that manufacture products which are not good substitutes from the point of view of customers could switch relatively simply and quickly into manufacturing products that are.[8] For example, one size of bottle cap may not be substitutable for another for a customer that uses a particular type of bottle, but the cap manufacturer may be able to produce all the different sizes of cap fairly easily on the same machine. Such switching by manufactures is referred to as "supply-side substitution"; in contrast, switching by customers is referred to as "demand-side substitution".

1.5.1.1.2 The relevant geographic market

The relevant geographic market comprises the geographic area in which the relevant undertaking and its competitors compete. The Commission's Notice on market definition defines it as:

> "the area in which the undertakings concerned are involved in the supply and demand of products or services, in which the conditions of competition are sufficiently homogeneous and which can be distinguished from neighbouring areas because the conditions of competition are appreciably different in those areas."[9]

The concept is relatively simple. The process of identifying the relevant geographic market in practice often is not.

1.5.1.2 Market position

Having defined the relevant market, the next step in assessing dominance is to assess the strength of the relevant undertaking's position on that market; in other words, to assess the degree to which the relevant undertaking can act independently of—or is, to the contrary, constrained by—its competitors.

A complete assessment of the strength of an undertaking's market position involves the examination of a wide range of factors. However, a good starting point—and in practice often the key factor in the legal analysis—is the market

8. See *ibid*, paras 20–23.
9. *Ibid*, para 8.

share held by the relevant undertaking. Simply put, the larger an undertaking's market share (and the smaller those of its competitors), the more likely it is to hold a dominant position.

The following market share thresholds are often used a rough guide to assessing dominance:

- *less than 40 per cent*: an undertaking with a market share of less than 40 per cent is unlikely to be found to hold a dominant position;[10]
- *more than 50 per cent*: the ECJ has held that an undertaking with a stable market share in excess of 50 per cent will be presumed dominant, provided that an examination of other relevant factors does not indicate that it is not;[11]
- *more than 75 per cent*: an undertaking with a market share in excess of 75 per cent may, according to the ECJ, be found dominant on the basis of its market share alone.[12]

Note, however, that these thresholds are guidelines rather than absolute rules. Other factors generally need to be examined before concluding that an undertaking is dominant. In particular, market share data is valueless unless the relevant market has been correctly defined. Equally, high market shares are only meaningful if they are stable over time. A market in which certain undertakings have high market shares for one or two years but then lose them to other undertakings is likely to be highly competitive. The ECJ has held that holding a high market share for a period of over three years is sufficient to be considered relevant.[13]

1.5.1.3 Joint or collective dominance

Article 82 refers to abuse of dominance by "one or more undertakings". It is now clear that a group of undertakings may hold a joint or "collective" dominant position.[14] The analysis of dominance in a case where a group of undertakings are alleged to dominate a market is more complex than where the allegation is that a single undertaking holds a dominant position, and therefore beyond the scope of this introductory Chapter. However, the underlying issue—ie whether the relevant group of undertakings have significant market power—remains the same.

10. In *Virgin/British Airways*, 2000 OJ L 30, p 1, the Commission found that BA held a dominant position on the basis of a market share that varied between 46.3 per cent and 39.7 per cent between 1992 and 1998. This is at the very bottom end of the Commission's findings of dominance in terms of market share.

11. Case C-62/86, *Akzo v. Commission* [1991] ECR I 3359.

12. Case 85/76, *Hoffmann-La Roche v. Commission* [1979] ECR 461.

13. See *Akzo* and *Hoffmann-La Roche* nn 11 and 12 above.

14. See, eg, Cases T-24/93 etc, *Compagnie Maritime Belge v. Commission* [1996] ECR II 1201.

1.5.2 Abuse

An undertaking does not infringe Article 82 simply by holding a dominant position: it must also abuse that position. This reflects the fact that, as discussed above, it would not be good policy for competition law to prohibit simply holding a position of market power.

So what constitutes an abuse of dominance? The first thing to say is that normal competition—ie seeking to satisfy customer demand for better or cheaper products—is not an abuse. The ECJ refers to "methods different from those which condition normal competition".[15] But that only gets us so far. If normal competition is not an abuse of dominance, what is? For the most part, the European courts have not sought to give a general definition of abuse. Instead, they have focused on identifying, on a case-by-case basis, whether particular behaviour is abusive or not. However, going back to the goals of competition law described above, it is possible to suggest three general categories of abuse:

— *behaviour establishing or increasing market power*: ie behaviour on the part of an undertaking that increases its existing level of dominance or uses its existing dominance in one market to establish a new position of dominance in another market;
— *behaviour entrenching market power*: ie behaviour on the part of a dominant undertaking intended to protect its existing position of dominance from competitive challenge, eg by placing barriers in the way of new competitors seeking to enter the market; and
— *behaviour exploiting market power*: ie using dominance to drive prices above the level that would prevail on a competitive market.

Details of the various types of behaviour that have, to date, been identified by the European courts as abusive are set out in later Chapters. Nonetheless, the following examples illustrate the kinds of behaviour that fall into each of these categories of abuse.

1.5.2.1 Behaviour that establishes or increases market power

The classic example of an abuse that seeks to establish or increase dominance is what competition lawyers refer to as "predatory pricing". Put simply, predatory pricing is artificially low pricing by a dominant company which is designed to drive its competitors out of business. The objective of such pricing is to reduce the competitive constraints on the dominant company—and thereby increase its dominance—by eliminating its competitors. In other words, the objective is to increase the undertaking's market power. Once that has been achieved, the dominant company may be able to make profits by raising prices (further) above the competitive level.

15. *Hoffmann-La Roche*, n 11 above, at para 91.

1.5.2.2 Behaviour that entrenches market power

A simple example of behaviour that may "entrench"—ie protect—market power is that of a dominant company offering so-called "loyalty bonuses". These are discounts offered to customers on condition that they purchase all or a substantial proportion of their total requirements for a particular product from the dominant undertaking over a significant period of time, eg a year. Such discounts may tie customers to the dominant company, since customers will lose the discount if they buy products from the dominant company's competitors. It follows that, in order to lure customers away from the dominant company, its competitors may be obliged not only to offer lower prices or better products, but also compensation for the loss of the loyalty bonus. The effect of loyalty discounts may therefore be to protect existing dominance. As a result, the European courts have held that the use of loyalty bonuses may constitute an abuse for the purposes of Article 82.

1.5.2.3 Behaviour that exploits market power

The simplest example of abusive behaviour that exploits market power is so-called "excessive pricing", ie charging prices significantly higher than those that would exist on a competitive market. In theory, the price of a product on a competitive market will be close to the costs of producing that product. The ECJ has defined the abuse of excessive pricing as "charging a price which is excessive because it has no reasonable relation to the economic value of the product supplied".[16] Although this is potentially a rather vague test, it is generally understood that a key issue is whether the prices charged by the dominant undertaking are significantly above those that would prevail in a competitive market—ie prices at or close to cost.

1.6 ARTICLE 81: ANTI-COMPETITIVE AGREEMENTS

Article 81 of the EC Treaty has two key paragraphs:

- Article 81(1), which contains a broad prohibition on anti-competitive agreements; and
- Article 81(3), which provides that agreements may escape that prohibition if certain specified conditions are met. In essence, Article 81(3) allows agreements to escape prohibition if they offer benefits that justify their anti-competitive effects.

Overall, therefore, Article 81 sets up a structure in which a broad prohibition on anti-competitive agreements is balanced by an escape clause for agreements that can be shown to have positive benefits.

16. Case 27/76, *United Brands v. Commission* [1978] ECR 207.

1.6.1 Introduction

1.6.1 Article 81(1)—the prohibition

For an agreement to infringe the Article 81(1) prohibition it must:

— prevent, restrict or distort competition; and
— do so to an appreciable extent.

As discussed further below, these two requirements are related to the requirements for, respectively, abuse and dominance under Article 82.

1.6.1.1 Prevention, restriction and distortion of competition

The text of the Article 81(1) prohibition refers to agreements that may have as their object or effect the "prevention, restriction or distortion" of competition. No clear-cut legal distinction is made between the concepts of "prevention", "restriction" and "distortion". What is required for Article 81(1) to apply is the potential for a negative impact on competition. As a result, EC competition lawyers often refer generically to agreements that "restrict competition".

In determining whether an agreement restricts competition for the purposes of Article 81(1), a (very) rough rule of thumb is that it may be at risk if it includes provisions that limit the ability of one or more of the contracting parties to buy from, sell to, or otherwise trade with, third parties. The analysis cannot, however, stop there. Not all agreements that are caught by Article 81(1) include express terms of that type. For example, as will be discussed in later Chapters, an agreement between competitors to share information about their customer prices is likely to be caught by Article 81, but need not contain any express contractual restrictions. Equally, not all agreements that do include such terms are caught by Article 81(1).

A more accurate method for identifying whether an agreement should be considered restrictive is to think in terms of the goals of competition law identified above—in other words, to adopt an analysis similar to that suggested above in relation to abuse of dominance, ie does the agreement seek to:

— establish or increase market power;
— entrench market power; or
— exploit market power?

The following examples illustrate the point:

1.6.1.1.1 Agreements that may establish market power

One way for competing undertakings to cooperate to establish positions of market power may be to enter into what are known as "market-sharing" agreements. Under such arrangements, competitors divide up a market—for example, into distinct geographic areas—and share it out between themselves, each agreeing not to compete in any area allocated to someone else. A simple example would be where two major chemicals companies, one based in the

UK and the other in France, agree to divide the UK and French markets between them with only the UK company making sales in the UK and only the French company making sales in France. If the two companies are sufficiently powerful, this may result in two separate positions of market power: one in France and one in the UK.

1.6.1.1.2 Agreements that may entrench market power

A simple example of the type of agreement that may entrench market power is a long-term exclusive supply agreement between a powerful company and its key customers. An example from the European Commission's case law is the NutraSweet case. NutraSweet, the world's largest producer of the sweetener aspartame, entered into agreements with both the Coca-Cola Company and PepsiCo Inc, the maker of Pepsi-Cola. Under these agreements, both Coca-Cola and PepsiCo agreed to purchase aspartame exclusively from NutraSweet for a period of at least two years. Coca-Cola and PepsiCo were, at the time, the largest and second largest purchasers of sweeteners in Europe. The Commission had concerns that, since the two largest potential customers were already tied in to NutraSweet, new competitors might be prevented from entering the market for aspartame. The Commission therefore persuaded NutraSweet to remove the exclusive purchasing obligations from the agreements.

1.6.1.1.3 Agreements that may exploit market power

Agreements may exploit market power more or less directly. A very direct example would be a price-fixing cartel between all the competitors in a market. By collectively agreeing the prices they charge to customers, the cartel members can eliminate price competition and can use the resulting collective market power to set price levels above those that would exist on a competitive market. Alternatively, a powerful manufacturer may exploit its market power more indirectly, by using terms in its contracts with distributors that prevent them from selling below a fixed price (so-called "resale price maintenance" provisions) to support a higher price for its products than would exist if its distributors were allowed to compete freely with one another.

1.6.1.1.4 The distinction between "horizontal" and "vertical" agreements

In examining whether an agreement restricts competition, it is helpful to adopt a distinction made by economists between "horizontal" and "vertical" agreements. Horizontal agreements are those between competitors or potential competitors: an agreement between Coca-Cola and Pepsi, for example, would be considered horizontal. Vertical agreements are those between parties that do not compete but operate at different levels in the supply chain: for example, the distribution agreements in place between car manufacturers like Ford and their branded dealers.

1.6.1 Introduction

The distinction is important for the following reason: since they are competitors, the parties to a horizontal agreement can reduce the competitive constraints on one another by agreeing to cooperate rather than compete. If they are able to reduce those constraints significantly, they may be able in effect to operate (collectively) like a single dominant company. In other words they may be able to establish a (collective) position of market power. In contrast, since the parties to a vertical agreement are not competitors they cannot, by cooperating, create new market power where none existed before. However, a vertical agreement may be a means by which an existing position of market power is entrenched or exploited.

1.6.1.2 Appreciable extent

As mentioned above, to be caught by the Article 81(1) prohibition an agreement must not only restrict competition, it must also do so to an appreciable extent. The reason for this is as follows. As illustrated by the examples given in the previous section, agreements may restrict competition if they have the potential to establish, entrench or exploit market power. However, such agreements will only actually have this effect if the parties already have market power or can create it through the agreement. Like the requirement for dominance under Article 82, the requirement for appreciable effects under Article 81(1) is, in effect, a market power test.

The means of identifying market power in the context of Article 81(1) is similar, but not identical, to that under Article 82. As under Article 82, the first step is to identify the relevant market. The second step is to identify whether the position of the parties on the relevant market is sufficiently strong to give rise to market power. In this latter regard, the European Commission has issued a Notice which, in essence, sets minimum market share thresholds that must be met if an agreement is to have an appreciable effect on competition.[17] Below these thresholds, most types of agreement will not be considered to restrict competition sufficiently to be caught by the Article 81(1) prohibition.[18] As in the case of Article 82, these thresholds are only meaningful if applied in the context of a properly defined relevant market. The thresholds set out in the Notice are:

- — for horizontal agreements, that the parties have a combined market share of at least 10 per cent; and
- — for vertical agreements, that at least one of the parties has a market share of at least 15 per cent.

17. Commission Notice on agreements of minor importance which do not appreciably restrict competition under Article 81(1), 2001 OJ C 368, p 13.

18. The market share thresholds set out in the Commission's Notice are subject to certain exceptions. In particular, agreements containing certain "hardcore" restrictions—including most price-fixing, resale price maintenance, export and market-sharing restrictions—may have appreciable effects even where the parties' market shares fall below these levels.

These thresholds are clearly much lower than the indicative thresholds for dominance under Article 82 discussed above, which start at around 40 per cent. This may reflect the fact that Article 81(3) provides an escape route from the prohibition under Article 81(1) for agreements whose beneficial effects justify any restrictions in them. Article 82 has no such escape clause. As a result, it may be that the Commission considers it appropriate to apply the Article 81(1) prohibition in relation to much lower levels of market power than those dealt with under Article 82.

1.6.2 Article 81(3): the escape clause

Article 81(3) provides, in essence, that an agreement which would otherwise be caught by Article 81(1) will escape prohibition if it has benefits that that justify its anti-competitive effects. This might apply, for example, to a joint research agreement between two competing pharmaceutical companies that will allow them to develop a new treatment faster than either one of them could working independently. Assuming that both companies could ultimately produce effective treatments working separately, the agreement will restrict competition. But the benefits of obtaining a treatment faster may well be considered sufficient to justify any restriction.

Although the concept is simple, assessing the application of Article 81(3) in an individual case will often be complex, since the effect of an agreement may vary considerably depending on the nature of the market affected.

1.7 THE EC MERGER REGULATION

1.7.1 The scope of the ECMR

The ECMR is intended to deal with transactions that create changes in the structure of competition in markets in the EU. It therefore applies to mergers, acquisitions and certain structural joint ventures;[19] these three classes of transaction are referred to collectively under the ECMR as "concentrations".

Once completed, concentrations are difficult and expensive to undo. The ECMR therefore requires that, where certain jurisdictional thresholds are met, concentrations are notified to the Commission for clearance prior to completion.

The relevant jurisdictional thresholds and procedures for clearance fall outside the scope of this introduction. The following sections deal briefly with

19. The ECMR applies to so-called "full-function" joint ventures. A joint venture will be considered "full-function" if it is intended to perform all the functions of an autonomous economic entity on a lasting basis.

the substantive tests applied by the Commission in assessing concentrations under the ECMR.

1.7.2 Prohibited transactions

The ECMR requires the European Commission to prohibit concentrations that are likely to significantly impede effective competition, in particular by creating or strengthening a dominant position.[20] This may seem like a very broad prohibition—in particular, there is no requirement for "abuse" as under Article 82. However, it reflects two factors. First, if a concentration creates a new position of dominance (ie significant market power) this will not be the result of normal competition on the market reflecting customer choice. Instead, it will be the result of a decision by one company to merge with, acquire or enter a joint venture with another. Prohibiting the creation of significant market power through concentrations does not, therefore, present the same policy problems as an absolute prohibition on market power under Article 82. Second, prohibition is sensible since, as we have seen, an undertaking that acquires significant market power as the result of a concentration will—by definition—have a profit incentive to exploit it by charging super-competitive prices.

Because the ECMR focuses on structural changes in a market that may create market power, the analysis of problematic concentrations is, in principle, simpler than that under Article 81 or 82. Only two questions need to be asked in relation to a concentration:

- will it establish a new market power or increase existing market power? and/or
- will it entrench an existing position of market power?

The question whether a concentration may exploit market power does not arise, in effect because the ECMR assumes that market power will be exploited once it exists.

As in the case of anti-competitive agreements—and for the same reasons—it is useful to distinguish between horizontal concentrations, where the merging parties are competitors, and vertical concentrations, where they are not. As in the case of horizontal agreements, horizontal concentrations have the potential to establish new market power or to increase existing market power; vertical concentrations do not.

As a result, in the case of most horizontal concentrations the competition issue is simply whether the concentration establishes a new position of market power or increases existing market power. In cases where the concern is that the new entity created by the transaction—the merged undertakings or the

20. ECMR, Art 2(3): note that in practice, the Commission will frequently avoid applying the prohibition by allowing parties to modify a notified transaction so as to remove the risk that it will significantly impede effective competition.

joint venture—will hold a position of market power, the analysis is similar to that in an Article 82 case.[21] As in an Article 82 case, the starting points are identification of the relevant market and an assessment of the new entities' market share. In ECMR cases the following market share thresholds have historically represented fair rules of thumb:

- *less than 40 per cent*: little chance of the concentration being prohibited;[22]
- *40 per cent to 50 per cent*: some risk of prohibition or, more likely, of the Commission requiring changes to the transaction to remove the risk of creating or strengthening dominance;
- *50 per cent to 70 per cent*: a real risk of prohibition or changes being required; and
- *more than 75 per cent*: the concentration is not likely to be cleared without changes being required and there is a substantial risk that it will be prohibited.

In contrast, vertical concentrations—where the parties are not competitors but operate upstream or downstream of one another in the chain of production and distribution—are not capable of creating new positions of market power or directly increasing market power. The potential issue of concern is therefore a narrow one: does the concentration entrench existing market power? In particular, the concern will generally be whether an undertaking that already has some degree of market power as a result of its strong position on the market is seeking to protect that position by acquiring a key customer or a key supplier, thereby preventing its competitors from having access to that customer or supplier.

1.8 SUMMARY

The three basic rules of EU competition law are:

(a) Article 82 of the EC Treaty, which prohibits the abuse of a position of market dominance;
(b) Article 81 of the EC Treaty, which prohibitions restrictive agreements that affect trade; and

21. Less frequently, the concern will be not that the merged entity will itself hold a dominant position, but that the merger will create a position of joint or collective dominance between the merged entity and its closest competitors on the market. The analysis in such cases will be substantially more complex.

22. In its Guidelines on the assessment of horizontal mergers, the Commission states (at para 17) that "in some cases" market shares below 40 per cent may lead to the creation or strengthening of a dominant position and cites two cases where it has found this to be the case: Case IV/M 1221, *Revel/Mein* and Case COMP/M 2337, *Nestlé/Ralston Purina*. The Commission adds (at para 18) that mergers "where the market share of the undertakings concerned does not exceed 25 per cent" are unlikely to give rise to problems. The two cases cited by the Commission are, however, exceptional and the 40 per cent threshold remains a reasonable guide. The 25 per cent threshold may be regarded as a very safe harbour.

(c) the ECMR, which prohibits anti-competitive concentrations.

Each of these rules applies in different circumstances: Article 82 to individual behaviour; Article 81 to agreements; and the ECMR to mergers, acquisitions and certain joint ventures. But the purpose of each one is the same: to prevent the problem of welfare loss that can arise when an undertaking or a coordinated group of undertakings exercise market power. To achieve that, each of these rules seeks, in its different context, to prevent behaviour whose objective is—by means other than normal competition—to:

(a) establish a new position of market power or increase existing market power;
(b) entrench existing market power; or
(c) exploit market power.

CHAPTER 2

ECONOMICS AT THE HEART OF COMPETITION POLICY

*Helen Jenkins and Beatriz Yemail, Oxera**

2.1 INTRODUCTION

Economic concepts are inextricably bound into competition law. A good understanding of the purpose and application of such law requires an understanding of the economic logic that lies behind the legal framework. Judicial precedent in this area can be seen to develop in line with economic theory and practice, illustrating the central role economics plays in this realm.[1]

Adam Smith and his "invisible hand"—the self interest that guides the most efficient use of resources—underpin the paradigm that dominates modern neo-classical economics: that of a perfectly competitive market. In a market for a homogeneous product where there are many consumers and many suppliers, with no barriers to entry and exit and with good information, each participant, working towards their own self-interest, will help deliver the optimal solution from society's perspective. Here, optimality means that scarce resources are allocated to produce the highest collective utility. Rivalry between the many producers (and consumers) drives out inefficiencies, and signals which products have the highest value to consumers.

In reality, markets do not conform to these theoretical constructs and this may provide a justification for governments to intervene. The breadth and nature of such state intervention when markets "fail" is the subject of extensive political debate and will not be canvassed here; suffice to say that competition law is part of this intervention. It is predicated on protecting an ideal of market interaction and is concerned that, when unconstrained by rivalry, businesses would seek to behave in ways that are considered socially undesirable.

The four main elements of competition law and policy can be described in this way:

— *Prohibition of anti-competitive agreements*: in the simplest form of such agreements, firms in a rivalrous position seek to dampen that rivalry by agreement on prices and/or output.

* The author would like to thank Gunnar Niels for helpful comments.

1. See Kovacic and Shapiro, "Antitrust Policy: A Century of Economic and Legal Thinking", *Journal of Economic Perspectives* 14:1, Winter 2000, 43–60.

— *Prohibition of abuse of dominance*: once a firm is sufficiently large that it is not hampered by rivalry from its competitors or from the behaviour of its customers, its self-interest will dictate that it behaves in a way that no longer benefits consumers, ie by seeking to exclude competitors or exploit customers.
— *Merger control*: as an extension of concerns about agreements, the result of one company buying another firm may be the dampening of rivalry. To prevent market structures arising where firms do not compete effectively, competition policy can prohibit certain mergers and acquisitions.
— *Market investigations*: these focus on the behaviour arising from the informal interaction of market participants, whereby structures or practices that hinder rivalry may have evolved without any specific abuse of dominance necessarily taking place.

In this chapter we explore how economics is at the heart of these statutes. The rationale for their existence is the protection of means of delivering economic efficiency. The key aspect of analysis is the economic concept of rivalry; the main tools for conducting this scrutiny arise from economics.

The chapter is structured as follows. Section 2.2 examines efficiency concepts, highlighting why competition is seen to be desirable. These are linked to the types of rivalry and competition that are observed—indicating that, in the real world, identifying undesirable market behaviour is not always straightforward. This section also outlines the concept of market power, which is a crucial element of many anti-trust investigations.

Section 3 looks in more detail at three areas where economic analysis has strongly influenced the development of legal guidance and precedence: market definition, the analysis of anti-competitive agreements and the analysis of abuse of dominance. Chapter 8 below, by Giulio Federico and Diana Jackson, gives another detailed example of this interrelationship ie, merger control. Indeed, from assessing market power to quantifying damages, economic tools can be fruitfully applied to any competition policy question.

2.2 WHY COMPETITION?

The rationale for promoting and protecting competitive forces relates to theoretical results that show that competitive markets make efficient use of resources.[2] At its heart, competition law promotes rivalry, seeing this as the ultimate driver of economic progress. This rivalry can manifest itself in many

2. These considerations are often described as "positive" in that the analysis arguably focuses on achieving aims that are clearly beneficial—in this case how to maximise an economy's output given the resources available. "Normative" aspects focus on issues that arise in determining optimal distribution.

ways and, by exploring this complexity, the intricacies of applying competition law come to the fore. Before outlining these, first we define the underlying benchmark: the perfectly competitive market.

2.2.1 Perfect competition

Figure 1 shows the interaction of demand for a product (which declines with price) with supply of a product (which is constant at a price that reflects the underlying costs of the product). Imagine that this is a market for apples. The result of rivalry between consumers wishing to purchase apples and suppliers wishing to sell (for example, at a farmers' market) is that output Q* is produced and sold at price P*. This is the price and output combination such that the quantity of output supplied by producers is equal to the quantity that consumers demand. There are no more customers willing to buy at this price and no suppliers willing to offer a lower price to increase sales. This is known as a market equilibrium.

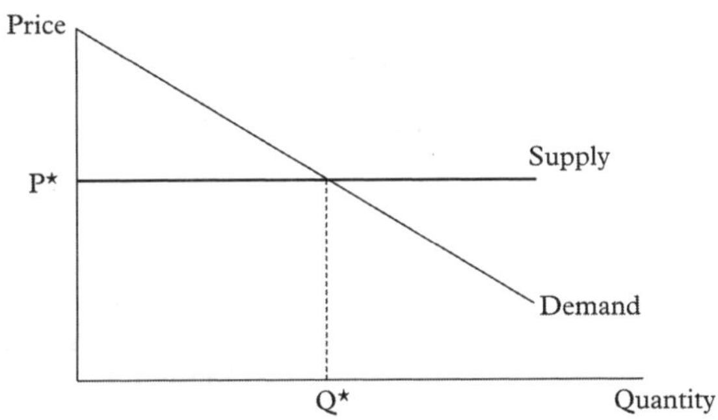

Figure 1: Perfectly competitive market

It is the line indicating supply (the "supply curve") here that embodies the assumptions on market interactions. The product is homogeneous (all apples are the same); information is good, so firms know when another firm has introduced a more advanced technology (eg, better fertiliser) and can imitate. There are no barriers to entry or exit (orchards can be rented easily). The result is that there is an unending supply of producers available to offer the desired good at the price P*. If one producer sought to increase its price, it would lose all business because customers would have no incentive to choose anything but the lowest-price product, and other suppliers would be able to expand to meet demand.

The other extreme is a market where there is a monopolist. Figure 2 illustrates.

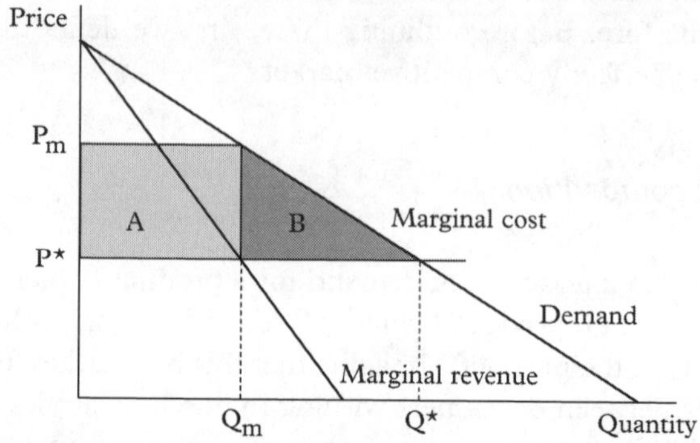

Figure 2: Social cost of monopoly

Here the demand curve is as in Figure 1, but there is now no supply curve, as there is only one supplier. As in Figure 1, the underlying costs of producing the good are shown to be constant at P*. However, the competitive equilibrium is not reached. The monopolist can decide how many apples to send to the market each day. Restricting supply to Q_m, at which quantity consumers are willing to pay P_m, the monopolist makes above-normal profits (the area marked A), given that the price is well above the cost of producing the apples. The monopolist will choose the amount of output that maximises the size of these profits.

The consequence of this decision is social costs (represented by the triangle marked B in the figure), known as "deadweight losses". This reflects that there are a number of consumers who would be willing to purchase the product at a price sufficiently high to cover the costs of production, but who are not given that opportunity. This is a lost opportunity to society.

The reason why monopoly is regarded as damaging is because of the social loss rather than the high pricing as such. If the issue were only one of transfer between monopolist and consumers (area A), this could in principle be rectified by distributional policies (eg high corporate taxes). If the social deadweight loss cannot be offset, these opportunities are lost.

2.2.2 Assessing market power

Competition statutes are based on defending rivalry as an ideal of market interaction. The concern of competition authorities is that, in the absence of vibrant rivalry, socially undesirable behaviour will ensue. The reason that this is considered undesirable is reflected in Figure 2 above as the deadweight social loss. The dampening of rivalry results in the firm having market power, and it is this that is at the heart of most interventions by competition authorities.

The essence of market power is the ability to restrict output and raise prices. A firm with this power is not fully constrained by its rivals and customers. Significant market power, or dominance, refers to firms that can behave independently of economic pressures in the market. Such market power may allow the firm to maintain prices above the competitive level, or to engage in other forms of anti-competitive conduct that affect the process of competition, such as pricing behaviour designed either to exclude competitors from the market or to constrain the growth of competitors already present in the market.

To assess dominance in a relevant anti-trust market, a competition authority would usually consider a range of structural and performance matters to ascertain the state of competition. These again are linked closely to the underlying economic theory of the desirable characteristics of a competitive market.

The assessment of market power can examine whether the market delivers the outcome predicted under the perfect competition paradigm (ie whether prices equal some measure of costs), and/or whether the key assumptions of the perfect competition paradigm (ie no entry or exit barriers, homogeneous goods, perfect information) hold. This translates into examining three types of information—the first addresses whether the market is delivering competitive outcomes; the other two examine the central assumptions of the paradigm:

— Direct assessment of evidence that prices are above costs.
— Indicators of market structure (eg market shares; entry, exit, and barriers to entry and exit; and consumer switching).
— Unilateral pricing power of the firm in question.

Examination of guidelines and case law on market power illustrates that these are the key elements of any investigation. Again, it is the underlying economic theory that gives the framework for the analytic approach.[3]

2.2.3 Other means of competition

Firms can compete over a number of dimensions. The simplest formulation of competition, described above, has firms competing only on price. In reality, firms also usually compete on the following.

— *Quantity*: there may be cases where capacity is constrained; for example, if the decision on number of trees to plant (and hence apple yield) is made one year in advance. As compared with the perfect competition model, entry is restricted and when one supplier seeks to raise

3. It is beyond the scope of this introductory chapter to cover in detail all these elements of market power assessments. For more detail, see OFT, "Assessment of market power. Understanding competition law", Competition Law Guideline, 2004.

prices, other suppliers cannot respond quickly. In this model, firms will choose the capacity in which to invest each year and will compete on this.[4]

— *Product characteristics*: individual consumers may not consider all apples to be the same. Some may prefer sweet red apples to crisp green ones and *vice versa*. In this type of market, firms can compete on differentiating their products to match the various demand niches. By so doing, again price competition is dampened, because consumers do not see a rival supplier's product as a close enough substitute and will be prepared to spend more on their preferred option.[5] Advertising is seen as expenditure that facilitates product differentiation. The underlying product may be very similar to its rivals, but advertising can enable one firm to extract higher prices because of the brand value or perception of quality that is developed.

— *Research and development ("R&D")*: in some markets, the main competition that occurs is through innovation, competing to be the firm that finds the next successful product (or process). Pharmaceuticals and computer games are examples of this. Firms must choose how much to invest in R&D in order to have a chance to "win"—that is, develop the product that is preferred by customers. Whichever is successful then has a pseudo-monopoly until the next innovation attracts consumers away. Indeed, without some prospect of the high returns associated with winning the market, firms would have little incentive to undertake risky R&D. As a result, society allows firms to protect any such innovation (through intellectual property rights "IP rights") to ensure that other firms cannot simply imitate and free-ride on the first company's investment. Depending on the innovation cycle, this pricing power may last a few months or many years. Increasingly, IP rights and competition law are coming into conflict.

2.2.4 Efficiency concepts

There are three central aspects of efficiency that underpin efficient resource allocation:

4. Cournot oligopoly models describe the outcomes in these types of markets; see Carlton and Perloff (2000), *Modern Industrial Organization*, 3rd edn, 2000.

5. Models of monopolistic competition explore the market outcomes in this context (based on Chamberlin, "Duopoly: Value Where Sellers are Few", *Quarterly Journal of Economics* 43, (1929), 63–100). The best-known model of differentiated products is the Hotelling model, where identical ice-cream sellers locate themselves along a beach, thereby capturing a proportion of the market and being able to price higher, reflecting the consumers' lack of desire to walk to buy an ice cream.

— allocative efficiency;
— productive efficiency;
— dynamic efficiency.

All these concepts relate to how scarce resources are used in the economy. The first describes how well the economy is matching the needs of consumers; the second and third on how well the economy is producing the products demanded. These latter two relate to the layperson's view of efficiency—making more output out of the same amount of input.

Allocative efficiency is achieved when prices reflect the underlying costs of producing the good, including an appropriate return on capital invested in the process. Market prices are signals from marginal consumers of the value they receive from the product, showing their willingness to pay. As more is supplied, prices fall, since the valuation of the new marginal consumer is lower. An efficient allocation means this price reflects the cost of producing the good. If all markets in the economy exhibit this, resources cannot be allocated differently to make any consumers better off without making someone else worse off.

Productive efficiency reflects the economy being technically efficient whereby all producers are using the best available technology. This ensures no wastage of resources.

Dynamic efficiency refers to incentives to innovate. It occurs when the economy has the right incentives to develop new, more efficient ways of production.

These efficiency benchmarks are affected by the different levels of competition. Allocative efficiency is achieved by strong price competition and the presence of aggressive rivals producing similar products. It is this that delivers clear consumer welfare gains in the immediate term. Productive efficiency is also enhanced by strong price competition, coupled with financial market competition. Firms that are not on the efficiency frontier will find that they cannot compete with the more efficient firms and at the same time adequately reward their investors. Those investors will seek cost savings, or will cease to invest. Competition through takeovers also enhances this type of efficiency. Dynamic efficiency is facilitated by strong incentives to invest in R&D, and where competition is *for* the market rather than *in* the market.

As may be clear, there are tensions between the different types of efficiency and competition. The strongest friction is between allocative and dynamic efficiency. To develop better ways of production, firms must invest. As described above, competition in this investment can lead to firms making large-scale, risky, investments. If they win the race and develop the best new technology, they may have a very strong position, which is protected through IP rights. Without this protection, innovation might not be forthcoming because of the risk of other firms rapidly imitating a rival's innovation, leading to prices that do not deliver a return on the initial investment. With this protection, a firm may price away from the cost of producing the good, leading to allocative efficiency. Balancing these interests is a difficult task.

2.3 AREAS OF COMPETITION POLICY IN THE EU INFLUENCED BY ECONOMIC THOUGHT

Economics has greatly influenced the development of competition policy and law in the areas of market definition, anti-competitive agreements and abuse of dominance. Without a clear framework, market definition often relied on product characteristics or the characteristics of the consumers (eg age).[6] The current approach of competition law to market definition relies on the notion that a market is the set of products or geographic areas that closely compete with each other in terms of prices, the product's characteristics or its intended use. The ability and willingness of consumers and producers to switch between products and geographic areas in response to price changes is the source of competition.

In the area of anti-competitive agreements, both horizontal and vertical, economic theory suggests that, under certain circumstances, agreements between companies operating at the same or different levels of the production chain may improve efficiency, correct market failures and increase welfare. Therefore, such agreements are not anti-competitive *per se*. This view has, for example, been incorporated into European and UK competition law, where the approach to horizontal and vertical restraints has shifted from a careful scrutiny of all agreements to an evaluation of only those that are more likely to hinder competition.

Economic thought has also been one of the engines of the current debate on whether more economic thinking could benefit legal decision-making in the area of Article 82 of the EC Treaty, which relates to firms with market power. In EU competition law, practices of a dominant firm that could be abusive are mainly evaluated in terms of the form of the abuse, rather than its effects on efficiency or consumer welfare.

This section describes the economic rationale behind the current definition of the relevant market in competition law, as well as the approach to horizontal and vertical restraints. The economics of abuse of dominance is discussed and some common practices, such as margin squeeze, predation and barriers to entry, are also analysed before discussing the current approach of EU law on the area.

2.3.1 Market definition

Before determining whether a firm's conduct, or an agreement between firms, hinders competition, it is necessary to define the market where the firm or

6. See, for example, *United Brands v. EC Commission* [1978] ECR 207, [1978] 1 CMLR 429.

firms under investigation is or are active. The market share that a company is perceived to have will automatically change depending on how broadly the market is defined. In general, firms with a small market share do not have market power—the other firms in that market will restrain prices. Thus, agreements between such firms are unlikely to damage other market participants (other than in cases of so-called "hardcore" price fixing and market-sharing agreements), and their lack of market power precludes them from being able to undertake exploitative practices. The higher the market share of a company, the more likely it is that it is found to have market power. This explains why market definition is often the decisive—and therefore the most disputed—issue in competition inquiries.

Economic principles have helped to develop a powerful and simple analytical tool that is one of the primary elements used in competition law for defining the relevant market: the "hypothetical monopolist" test. This is also known as the "SSNIP"—or Small but Significant Non-transitory Increase in Price—test, which was developed for the analysis of merger cases.[7]

The SSNIP test follows an iterative process in which all the products and regions that provide a significant competitive constraint on a small set of products and regions are identified.[8] In practice, a series of steps are followed. First, a narrow set of products in a geographic area is identified. Second, it is determined whether a *hypothetical* profit-maximising monopolist with control over *all* the products in the area identified in the previous step would be able to raise prices profitably by 5–10 per cent for a period of time of around one year.

Third, if the answer to the question formulated in the second step is "no", an additional set of products and regions should be added and the SSNIP test carried out again until the set of products that is worth monopolising is identified.

In practice, a firm's ability to raise prices depends on the degree of responsiveness of customers and of other producers to price changes. A price increase will therefore not be profitable if an important proportion of the hypothetical monopolist's clients switch to cheaper products or products with similar characteristics (eg blue rather than red mouse pads), or that can be used for the same purpose (eg two different brands of hair dryer). This is called "demand-side substitution". Furthermore, a price increase will not be profitable if existing companies already supplying similar products (or the same

7. The SSNIP test was developed by the US competition authorities in their 1992 Horizontal Merger Guidelines, and has been endorsed in the EU with some modifications. See European Commission, "Notice on the Definition of Relevant Market for the Purposes of Community Competition Law", OJ C 372/03, 9 December 1997; OFT, "Market Definition", OFT 403, March 1999; and OFT, "The Role of Market Definition in Monopoly and Dominance Inquiries", OFT 342, July 2001.

8. In addition to the basic product and geographic dimensions, markets can also have a time dimension (peak times versus off-peak), a type-of-buyer dimension (residential versus business telephony customers), or can be segmented according to the distribution channel (distribution of beer in pubs, bars and restaurants ("on-trade") or through supermarkets or general and specialised shops ("off-trade")).

product but in neighbouring geographic areas) readily switch to supplying the product in question (ie "supply-side substitution").

For example, take the market for bottled still water in the UK. Consider whether a hypothetical single supplier would find it profitable to raise prices by more than 5–10 per cent. On the one hand, it might be the case that a proportion of consumers would not be willing to pay the extra price and therefore start consuming other products that they consider substitutes for still water, such as sparkling water (ie demand-side substitution). On the other hand, companies producing sparkling water could also start producing still water without having to make relatively significant investments in their plants or incurring high risks (ie supply-side substitution). If this is the case, the market must be defined more widely and include an additional product: sparkling water.

Applying a complete hypothetical monopolist test is difficult. Ideally, it would require modelling some general demand system, and then econometrically estimating all the own- and cross-price elasticities of demand on the basis of empirical price and sales data. As a result, competition authorities often resort to other quantitative tests, such as price correlations over time, or to qualitative tests, such as consumer surveys. For example, a marketing study may ask customers directly whether they would switch from still water to sparkling water in the event of a price increase. This test is clearly less rigorous than a quantitative assessment.[9]

The SSNIP test has some problems when defining a market where market power may already exist, because there is doubt over the competitive benchmark. In dominance cases, the market might already be a monopoly and an increase in the current level of prices might induce customers to switch to other products that would not necessarily be substitutes under competitive conditions (eg lower-quality products). This is referred to as the "cellophane fallacy" after the *Du Pont* case.[10] Under these circumstances, the use of the SSNIP test would result in very wide market definition leading to underestimation of the market share of the firm under investigation and (potentially) to its degree of market power. One solution is to use the "competitive" price level instead of the "prevailing" price level as the starting point for applying the SSNIP test, but this itself may be difficult to determine in practice.

9. For examples of cases where the Competition Commission has relied on survey evidence, see Competition Commission, "FirstGroup plc and the Scottish Passenger Rail Franchise: A Report on the Proposed Acquisition by FirstGroup plc of the Scottish Passenger Rail Franchise Currently Operated by ScotRail Railways Limited", June 2004. See also Competition Commission, "National Express Group plc and the Greater Anglia Franchise: A Report on the Acquisition by National Express Group plc of the Greater Anglia Franchise", November 2004.

10. Du Pont argued that cellophane was in the same market as flexible packaging materials (eg aluminium foil, wax paper and polythene). However, Du Pont was the only producer of cellophane and was likely to have already raised prices to a point where an additional increase would be unprofitable, as consumers would switch to other products. The US Supreme Court failed to recognise that a high own-price elasticity and the identification of effective substitutes at the prevailing prices may mean that the firm already had market power. See *United States v. EI Du Pont de Nemours & Co*, 351 US 377; 76 S Ct 994; L Ed 1264 (1956).

Despite the shortfalls of the SSNIP test, it is a simple tool that has improved the process of identifying the markets that are relevant for competition investigations.

2.3.2 Horizontal and vertical agreements

There are essentially two types of agreement between firms: "horizontal" and "vertical". The former are agreements between two or more companies operating in the same market (eg an agreement between mobile phone operators), and include practices such as price-fixing, division of retail markets among suppliers and joint selling agreements.

Vertical agreements involve companies operating at different stages of the supply chain, such as an agreement between a mobile phone operator and a handset producer. They include agreements:

— for maintaining a fixed retail price—also known as resale price maintenance ("RPM") (eg the retail book market in the UK);
— for obtaining exclusivity over geographic areas—eg only one brand of breakfast cereals sold in England and another in Scotland and Wales; or
— for obtaining exclusivity over retailers—eg the retailer is not allowed to sell products other than petrol.

Although agreements can harm competition at a horizontal and/or a vertical level, economic theory and practice have showed that, under certain circumstances, these practices promote efficiency and can have pro-competitive effects. These issues are discussed further below.

2.3.2.1 Horizontal agreements

Agreements between rival firms to fix prices and/or output are usually considered harmful to consumers. Such "hardcore" restrictions generally occur where firms collude to restrict output and raise prices to a level higher than if competition were not distorted—known as a "cartel". In addition to paying higher prices, consumers are hurt by cartels because, by artificially limiting competition, firms might avoid the pressures that lead them to innovate in terms of novel or significantly improved products and production processes.

Economic literature, has established that there are some price-fixing, market division and joint selling agreements that can make productive activity more efficient. This happens when the elimination of rivalry also involves the integration of productive activities and therefore has the potential of creating efficiencies. For example, the way in which lawyers cooperate in a partnership is an example of a joint selling agreement that is likely to improve welfare.[11]

11. Bork, *The Antitrust Paradox*, 1978, pp 261–279.

2.3.2 Economics at the Heart of Competition Policy

A law firm is typically composed of lawyers who could compete with one another but who have instead eliminated rivalry and integrated activities in the interest of a more effective operation. In such a partnership, partners may agree on the fees to be charged for the partnership's services (price-fixing), and typically operate on a certain understanding about fields of specialisation and primary responsibility for particular clients (both of which are instances of market division). The objective of such a partnership is not to restrict output or increase fees; in practice, the agreement could result in efficiencies. One function of the agreement is to prevent the 'free-rider' problem. If lawyers work together and contribute to the partnership activities but are free to compete with each other, there is a risk that partners could appropriate for personal profit the contributions made by other partners. For example, if a client comes to one partner as a result of the reputation of the law firm, and the partner is able to charge the client directly, that partner could be seen to be free-riding to some extent on the other partners' efforts to build up the reputation of the firm. If this occurs, or is suspected to be occurring, the other partners may decrease or discontinue their contributions to the partnership activity. In other words, the agreement to cooperate works only if it is complemented by a selling agreement (ie market division).

From an economic perspective, cooperation between companies and its ancillary restraints (including price-fixing and market division) can be beneficial when three conditions are met:[12]

- the agreement to fix prices or divide markets is ancillary to a contract integration—ie the parties must be cooperating in an economic activity other than the elimination of rivalry, and the agreement must be capable of increasing the effectiveness of that cooperation and must not be broader than necessary for that purpose;
- the collective market share of the parties does not make the restriction of output a realistic danger (judged by horizontal merger standards); and
- the parties must not have demonstrated a primary purpose or intent to restrict output.

The EU legal framework under Article 81(1) does provide some scope for assessing horizontal agreements in a more economics-based manner, as opposed to prohibiting them *per se*.[13] Some categories of agreement do not fall under Article 81(1) because of their nature—for example, a cooperation agreement that does not imply a coordination of the parties' competitive behaviour in the market. This can be exemplified by cooperation between

12. See Bork, *op cit*, n 11 above.

13. European Commission "Guidelines on the Applicability of Article 81 of the EC Treaty to Horizontal Co-operation Agreements", 2001 OJ C3 p 2. See also 4.3 below.

competing companies that cannot carry out the project or activity without cooperating (eg development of a gas field).[14]

Additionally, agreements of companies with low market shares do not fall under Article 81(1). However, the guidelines do not give a clear market-share threshold, which varies depending on the type of agreement and its effect. The guidelines also state that price-fixing agreements almost always fall under Article 81(1), although this may, exceptionally, not apply to a production joint venture.[15] Finally, even if the agreement falls under Article 81(1), it can still be granted an exemption if it meets the criteria specified in Article 81(3).

2.3.2.2 Vertical agreements

As in the case of horizontal agreements, economic theory suggests that no vertical restraint is anti-competitive *per se*, and that in some cases they can correct certain market failures. In addition, before reaching a conclusion, it is necessary to make an assessment of the structure of the "upstream" and "downstream" markets. Consider the case of an upstream supplier and a downstream retailer, each being dominant in their respective markets. Both firms would charge the profit-maximising monopolist price. A double mark-up would be charged to the final customer, as the wholesale (input) price set by the upstream supplier would be above the marginal cost of production, and the downstream firm would set a second mark-up over the wholesale price. A vertical agreement prohibiting the retailer from marking up over the wholesale price would provide incentives to the upstream supplier to price the input below monopoly level. In this case the "double marginalisation" problem will be overcome as retail prices are lowered, and the demand for the product will be maximised. As a result, total welfare will increase.[16]

Vertical agreements can also be welfare-enhancing when there is fierce competition between retailers stocking the same products, and when some retailers free-ride on the promotional activities and pre-sale support of a rival. In the first case, competition might squeeze profit margins to a point where it becomes unprofitable to stay in the market. As a result, the number of retailers stocking a manufacturer's product might fall below the optimal level. In the second case, retailers engaging in promotional activities cannot ensure that customers buy the products from other retailers that do not make such investments and can therefore charge a lower price. If discounters exist, other retailers would be deterred from engaging in promotional activities and the overall level of advertising and pre-sale support would be sub-optimal. In both

14. See para 87 of the European Commission Guidelines (see n 13 above). For a detailed explanation of the efficiency gains derived from cooperation in the operation and selling of gas, see Oxera Consulting, "Competing ideas: are all cartels bad?", March 2004, at www.oxera.com.

15. See footnote 18 in the European Commission Guidelines.

16. However, under certain circumstances vertical agreements might reduce competition between rival brands, or foreclose the market. For a technical discussion, see P Rey, and J Tirole, "A Primer in Foreclosure", in Armstrong and Porter (eds), *Handbook of Industrial Organisation* (forthcoming).

cases, the solution for the manufacturer is to impose RPM, or exclusive or selective selling. This will benefit both the upstream retailer (eg by normalising profit margins) and the downstream manufacturer (through having an optimal number of retailers or higher level of advertising that leads to an increased output level).

Economic theory in this area has influenced, to a large extent, European and UK competition law. Article 81(1) of the EC Treaty prohibits vertical agreements with the object or effect of restricting competition. Vertical agreements that infringe Article 81(1) are void under Article 82(2), unless they benefit from an individual exemption under Article 81(3) or a block exemption. In 2000, a new block exemption came into force specifying that, under certain conditions, some types of vertical agreements are exempted from the prohibition.[17] In particular, it stipulates that a vertical agreement is exempted from prohibition if does not include hardcore restraints such as price-fixing, and if the supplier's market share does not exceed 30 per cent.[18] If market share does exceed 30 per cent, an individual assessment of the pro- and anti-competitive effects of the agreement is required.

The UK jurisdiction exempts all vertical agreements (with the exception of RPM) from the Chapter I prohibition in the Competition Act 1998. However, vertical agreements can still be assessed under the Enterprise Act 2002, and if the company is dominant under Article 81 and/or the Chapter II prohibition of the Competition Act 1998.[19]

It is important to note that, although the hardcore vertical restraints identified by the Commission could qualify for an exemption under Article 81(3), the EU Guidelines state that: "individual exemption of vertical agreements containing such hardcore restrictions is also unlikely".[20] This position could undermine practices such as those described above, where vertical agreements not only benefit the parties that enter into the agreement but also final consumers through expanded output.

2.3.3 Abuse of dominance

Dominance can be abused in two key ways: exploitation of customers and exclusion of rivals. Exploitation arises from the charging of excessive prices.

17. Commission Regulation (EC) 2790/1999 of 22 December 1999 on the application of Article 81(3) of the Treaty to categories of vertical agreements and concerted practices. See 4.1 below.

18. In addition to price-fixing, there are four hardcore restrictions that have the effect of taking vertical agreement outside the scope of the block exemption. These include restrictions concerning the territory into which, or the customers to whom, the buyer may sell; restrictions on sales to end users by authorised retail distributors in a selective distribution system; restrictions on authorised distributors in a selective distribution system selling or purchasing from other members of the network; and restrictions on the sale of components as spare parts by the manufacturer of the component to end users, independent repairers and service providers.

19. For the application of competition law to vertical restraints in the UK jurisdiction, see OFT, "Vertical Agreements: Understanding Competition Law", Competition Law, December 2004.

20. Commission Regulation 2790/1999, para 46.

More attention has been given to exclusionary business practices aimed directly at rivals, which might then also affect final consumers.[21]

2.3.3.1 Excessive pricing

In EU and UK competition law, excessive pricing is addressed under the abuse of dominance provisions. In its 1978 *United Brands* decision, the European Court of Justice ("ECJ") determined that "charging a price which is excessive because it has no reasonable relation to the economic value of the product supplied . . . is an abuse".[22] Under the Competition Act 1998 (Chapter II, s. 18), "directly or indirectly imposing unfair purchase or selling prices or other unfair trading conditions may constitute an abuse of a dominant position". This contrasts with the position of US anti-trust law, which is not concerned with exploitative abuses such as excessive pricing.

The differences between the European and US approaches are explained by the time frame considered for the analysis of the excessive pricing. Excessive pricing creates allocative inefficiency in the form of a deadweight welfare loss to society—ie prices are too high and output is too low compared with the competitive market outcome. However, from a longer-term perspective, prohibiting excessive pricing under competition law might be counterproductive. While allocative efficiency may be improved, dynamic or productive efficiency could be affected. The very prospect of profits is what drives firms to reduce costs and introduce new products and technologies in order to become the market leader. The prospect of those profits being regulated once a dominant position is obtained may distort these incentives.

Furthermore, over time, dominant positions tend to be eroded by new entry into the market. Again, the high profit made by the incumbent is precisely what attracts entrants. Regulatory control of those profits may distort the efficient "market-signalling" function of excessive pricing, and may actually slow down the process of erosion of market power.

However, the presence of barriers to entry—discussed in more detail below—might prevent new firms from entering the market or delay the decision to enter. If this is the case, it might take a long time before other firms can enter the market and put pressure on the incumbent's high prices. Therefore, in practice, the crucial question that needs to be answered in order to assess the impact of excessive pricing on welfare is whether new competitors are indeed likely to enter the market, and in what time frame.

2.3.3.2 Exclusionary conduct

Several types of practice are considered under this category, including refusal to supply, tying, leverage, low pricing and targeted discounting. Here, we look in more detail at three specific practices:

21. See Chapter 5.
22. Case 27 *United Brands v. Commission* [1978] ECR 207; [1978] 1 CMLR 429.

— predatory pricing;
— margin squeeze; and
— bundling.

Predatory pricing is the most familiar form of unfair low pricing, and involves a *dominant* firm *deliberately* incurring short-term losses in order to eliminate its competitors, so as to be able to charge monopolistic prices in the long term. This requires prices to be below cost, and entry barriers to be high, so that the future monopolistic prices can be sustained long enough to recoup the short-term losses. The appropriate definition of costs has proved to be controversial, and a wide variety of cost benchmarks have been used to determine whether a firm has engaged in predatory pricing, including the average variable cost ("AVC"), the average total cost ("ATC"), the long-run incremental cost ("LRIC") and the avoidable cost.[23]

Margin squeeze can arise when a vertically integrated firm dominates the market for an input to a downstream product that is important not only for itself but for other rival firms in the downstream market. The vertically integrated firm lowers its downstream price or raises the price of the input. These actions, either on their own, or together, have a similar effect: lowering the *margin* earned by its downstream rivals such that they cannot profitably compete or are forced out of the market. This will enhance the dominant position of the firm in the downstream market. There are an increasing number of cases upholding an allegation of margin squeeze as an abuse of dominance, including, for example, *Deutsche Telekom*, on the price of unbundled access to local telecommunications loops,[24] and *Genzyme*, on the downstream market for the drug, Cerezyme, and its associated home delivery service.[25]

Bundling consists of selling two products (for example, a TV sport channel and a TV movie channel) together at a price below their individual purchase prices.[26] Pure bundling is where the products are only supplied together; mixed bundling is where the products are also available individually.

Bundling is a practice that can hinder a rival's ability to compete in a market. Suppose that a firm has market power in both the sport channel and movie channel markets. New entrants might be forced to offer both channels,

23. The EU predatory pricing standards were established in the ECJ's *ECS/Akzo* decision in 1985 OJ L 374/1, [1986] 3 CMLR 273; and Case C-62/86 [1991] ECR I 3359: [1993] 5 CMLR 215). In this case, the court determined that prices below AVC should be presumed to be predatory. Prices in the range between AVC and ATC are predatory if set in the context of a plan aimed at eliminating a competitor. Prices above ATC do not normally indicate predation. However, subsequent European Commission and OFT decisions have taken different cost benchmarks into account, such as the LRIC and the avoidable cost. See 5.5.9 below.

24. Commission of the European Communities *Deutsche Telekom AG* 2003 OJ L263 p 9. See 5.5.8 below.

25. Competition Appeal Tribunal, *Genzyme Limited v. Office of Fair Trading* [2004] CAT 4.

26. Tying is a special case of bundling. Suppose that there are two products (eg sport and movie channels). The movie channel is "tied" to the sport channel if a broadcaster refuses to sell the sports channel (the "tying" good), unless the customer also purchases the movie channel (the "tied" good). See 5.5.13.2 below.

and might therefore find it difficult to offer either the sport or the movie channel to attract subscribers. Furthermore, if the two channels are complementary for a significant proportion of viewers, the activities of smaller channel broadcasters might be significantly constrained when they are unable to offer the same package. Hence, bundling is therefore more likely to distort competition when existing rivals and new entrants are prevented from offering a competing bundle.[27]

2.3.3.3 A *per se* approach or an effects-based approach to abuses?

Article 82 of the EC Treaty deals with abuse of firms with market power. Currently there is a debate on whether more economic thinking could benefit legal decision-making in this area. EU case law on abuse of dominance has established a two-step approach, where dominance is first determined and then the practice is assessed mainly on the basis of its form rather than on its economic effects. The current approach therefore seems to classify allegedly anti-competitive abuses under a certain category based on descriptions of a type of unlawful behaviour (eg predatory pricing), regardless of their actual and potential effects on competition and consumer welfare.

Effects-based considerations are already taken into account to some degree in decision-making. Take the example of the OFT's decision in *BSkyB* to approve a bundled price structure for premium channels. Despite the fact that this bundling was a hindrance to the growth of independent channel providers, the OFT considered that this negative effect was outweighed by the positive benefits to consumers from the practice.[28]

Several economists and lawyers have recommended more use of tests that examine the economic effects of an allegedly anti-competitive action rather than focusing on *per se* abuses, particularly where the alleged abuse results in lower prices for consumers.[29] In these cases, there is a trade-off between the reduction in the level of competition between firms and consumer welfare.

US anti-trust law follows an effects-based approach, following the ideas of the so-called "Chicago School" of the 1970s. In the area of abuse of dominance, one of the main principles is that competition policy should protect competition as a whole in the relevant market, not individual competitors. Efficiencies should therefore be welcomed because they benefit consumers, even if they harm competitors. This derives from the idea that the ultimate

27. For a detailed analysis of bundling, see Majumdar, "Mixed bundling, economic analysis and BSkyB", *Competition Law Journal 2003* Vol 2, issue 2, pp 135–145.

28. See Office of Fair Trading, "Decision of the Director General of Fair Trading, BSkyB investigation: alleged infringement of the Chapter II prohibition: No CA 98/20/2002, 17.12.2002.

29. See, for example, Vickers, Speech to the 31st conference of the European Association for Research in Industrial Economics, Berlin 2004; and Competition Law Forum's Article 82 Review Group, "The Reform of Article 82: recommendations on key policy objectives" (2005).

goal of competition policy is to protect consumer welfare, with competition being only an intermediate aim.[30]

Virgin v. British Airways illustrates that an effects-based approach to abuse of dominance might result in a different outcome from a form-based approach.[31] In 1993 Virgin lodged a complaint before the European Commission, and in 1994 before a US court, claiming that British Airways ("BA") had used incentive schemes to foreclose the market and impede Virgin's growth.[32] Using an economic effects approach, the US appeals court concluded that BA's discount schemes had not harmed other businesses. The opposite conclusion was reached by the Commission, which focused the analysis on the structure of the schemes—ie the *form* of the abuse and its *potential* effects on competition.

Under the schemes, travel agents could qualify for "performance rewards" and other bonuses, and for funds from BA for marketing and staff training courses. The schemes were generally linked to the yearly growth of ticket sales of BA by the travel agent, and were structured to pay rewards retroactively on all ticket sales once the performance target was met, and not just on the incremental sales above the target. In 1997, BA held 40 per cent of Heathrow Airport's slots and operated around 60 per cent of all international routes from the airport. Virgin was a smaller operator, with 2 per cent of slots at the same airport and 5.5 per cent of airline sales in the UK.

In the US, the case was appealed after the lower court had rejected the complaint. As regards to Section I of the Sherman Act (restraint of trade), according to the court Virgin failed to demonstrate that BA's behaviour had harmed overall competition. The court also stated that BA's discounts had not prevented Virgin from becoming a successful airline that had even become the leader on the London–New York route in 1995. Furthermore, the schemes could only have a marginal impact on the competition between travel agents since "truly loyal" agents (defined as those who booked more than 80 per cent of their UK–US ticket sales with BA) represented less than 5 per cent of the total UK—US sales. The court also held that "rewarding customer loyalty promotes competition on the merits". Similarly, as regards section 2 of the Sherman Act, the court held that Virgin had provided no proof of BA's attempted monopolisation of the market.

In contrast, following a more form-based approach, the Commission focused on the incentive structures offered by BA. Of particular concern was the retroactive nature of the discounts, which *might* induce travel agents who were close to the sale's target to promote BA rather than rival airlines at the margin. In condemning these schemes, the Commission stated that

30. For a description of the "principles" of the Chicago School, see Niels and Ten Kate, "Antitrust law in the US and the EU—converging or diverging paths?", *Antitrust Bulletin*, Spring-Summer 2004, 9–10.

31. Niels and Ten Kate, *op cit*, n 30 above, 3–7.

32. In the US, see *Virgin Atlantic Ltd v. British Airways plc*, 257 F3d 256 (2nd Cir 2001); and in Europe see *Virgin/British Airways*, OJ L 3021. On appeal, the European Court of First Instance later upheld the Commission decision (Case T-219/99, *British Airways plc v. Commission*.

"Such commission schemes carried out by a firm enjoying a dominant position as a purchaser of services from travel agents are illegal, regardless of any possibility for the travel agents or competing airlines to minimise or avoid their effects."[33]

This reflects the principle established in EU law by which a dominant firm is only allowed to offer discounts that relate to efficiencies (eg cost savings for large orders), not to encourage loyalty. This ignores the potential reductions in the prices of the tickets offered to final consumers or improvements in the quality of the service offered by sales agents.

In contrast with the US decision, the commercial success of rivals was not given much importance in the Commission's decision. Although the Commission recognised that rival airlines had been gaining market share in the UK, it stated that "it can only be assumed that competitors would have had more success in the absence of these abusive schemes".[34] Finally, to further determine that there had been an abuse of dominance, the Commission used a principle of EU law that establishes that a dominant firm has an obligation not to discriminate; BA's loyalty schemes clearly discriminated between travel agencies.

Similarly, to assess whether cases of margin squeeze, predation and bundling are genuinely affecting competition, it may be necessary to investigate not only whether such practices harm competitors, but also whether they actually harm consumers.

2.4. CONCLUSION

At its core, competition law makes judgements about markets. Economics brings a rich theoretical and empirical body of work that enables analysis to be conducted to support sound judgements.

In the cases of market definition and agreements (both horizontal and vertical), guidelines on the application of competition law are soundly based on economic principles. The current area of debate on whether more economic thinking could benefit legal decision-making is focusing on Article 82 (abuse of dominance). Many economists recommend more use of tests that examine the economic effects of an allegedly anti-competitive action rather than focusing on *per se* abuses, particularly where the alleged abuse results in lower prices for consumers. Thus the interaction between economics and competition law is set to continue.

By using concepts of efficiency, rationality, incentives and rivalry, economists have developed predictive models of behaviour in industries. These can facilitate the understanding of the effects of alleged anti-competitive practices.

33. *Virgin/British Airways*, OJ L 30/1, para 102.
34. *Ibid*, para 107.

2.4. **Economics at the Heart of Competition Policy**

While this approach is, by definition, conducted at a level of abstraction, it remains a central, if not essential, tool for rigorous analysis of any competition law problem.

CHAPTER 3

ARTICLE 81: PROHIBITION AND EXCEPTION

*Vanessa Turner and Marc Reysen, Freshfields Bruckhaus Deringer**

3.1 INTRODUCTION

Article 81 of the EC Treaty is concerned with restrictions of competition arising from multilateral conduct. It is one of the key rules on competition, giving effect to the objective stated in Article 3(g): to ensure that competition in the internal market is not distorted.

While its name has changed over the years,[1] the text of Article 81 has remained unaltered since 1957. The scope of application of the provision has been developed and refined through increasingly determined decision-making of the Commission, as confirmed or corrected by the Community courts as well as through judgments of national courts, often on the basis of preliminary rulings of the Community courts. This has provided, if not yet a comprehensive guidebook on the application of Article 81, at least clarity on some key elements.

The manner in which Article 81 has been enforced has likewise known a period of relative stability. This, however, has recently changed. Regulation 1/2003[2] replaced Regulation 17/62 as the main implementing regulation for Article 81 on 1 May 2004.[3] This represents no minor revolution in the field of Community competition law. The main change of this so-called "modernisation" is that the Commission has given up its monopoly over the implementation of Article 81(3). Since 1 May 2004, Member States' competition authorities and national courts can enforce Article 81 in its entirety.

While the changes brought about by modernisation are primarily of a procedural nature, they have been accompanied by a number of notices on the substantive application of Article 81. In many respects, these depart from the

* The authors thank Jane Carter for her invaluable assistance in the drafting of this Chapter.

1. It was formerly Article 85.

2. 2003 OJ L 1/1.

3. With the exception of Article 8(3), Regulation 17/62 has been completely repealed by Regulation 1/2003 (Article 43, Regulation 1/2003). Mario Monti described the competition reforms as a "smooth revolution", prepared for over a five-year period. "The EU gets new competition powers for the 21st Century", *Competition Policy Newsletter Special Edition 2004*, page 1, available at: http://www.europa.eu.int/comm/competition/publications/special/special_toc.html.

traditional approach in that they rely on a more dynamic analysis than previous practice and require more assessment than previously of the economic effects of agreements under Article 81(1) as well as under Article 81(3).

Against this background, this Chapter will first examine the framework of the prohibition on restrictions of competition in Article 81(1) in section 3.2 below, before considering, in section 3.3, the exception to this prohibition contained in Article 81(3), together with the application of Article 81(3) since May 2004. Section 3.4 briefly describes the consequences of infringement of Article 81(1) as laid down primarily in the Treaty (Article 81(2)—ie voidness) and secondary legislation (Regulation 1/2003—ie potential fines), together with the potentially growing area of private enforcement, for example, through civil damages claims before national courts.

3.2 ARTICLE 81(1): THE PROHIBITION

Article 81(1) prohibits agreements between undertakings, decisions by associations of undertakings and concerted practices which may affect trade between Member States and which have as their object or effect the prevention, restriction or distortion of competition within the common market.

3.2.1 Scope of application: multilateral conduct only

The defining feature of Article 81 is that it is aimed at multilateral conduct only. Purely unilateral conduct falls outside its scope and will only be found to infringe Community competition rules if it results from the abuse of a dominant position under Article 82 (see Chapter 5).

Despite this distinction, the Commission has nevertheless managed to apply Article 81 to conduct that might appear to be unilateral, through a generous interpretation of the notion of "agreement". This has been the case particularly in the context of distribution networks. For example, in the case of *Ford,* the court upheld a Commission decision refusing to exempt Ford's main dealership agreement,[4] confirming that the circular sent by Ford to its German dealers informing them that it would not supply them with right-hand-drive cars, to avoid their being imported parallelly into the UK, did not constitute a unilateral act but formed part of the main dealership agreement. The court found that there was implied acceptance of Ford's policy by dealers—and, thus, an agreement between undertakings—when they were admitted to the network.[5]

This liberal approach to the interpretation of what constitutes an agreement has more recently been curbed by the Community courts in their annulment

4. Case IV/30.696, *Ford-Werke AG*, 1983 OJ L 327/31.
5. Case 25–26/84, *Ford II*, [1985] ECR 2725.

of the Commission's decision in *Bayer AG v. Commission.*[6] In that case, Bayer France and Bayer Spain had reduced the quantity of the blood-pressure drug Adalat made available to wholesalers in France and Spain in order to discourage parallel exports to the UK, where prices were substantially higher. Notwithstanding that the Bayer Group (through Bayer France and Bayer Spain) sought to establish the scheme unilaterally, the Commission found that there was a tacit agreement between Bayer and its wholesalers not to export. The Commission relied on the fact that wholesalers had in fact ceased to supply the UK. The Commission took no account of the fact that it was not in the wholesalers' interests to comply and that they had tried to obtain extra supplies for export.

The Court of First Instance (CFI) annulled the Commission's decision, holding that there was no agreement. It reasserted the basic principle that Article 81 concerns conduct that is coordinated bilaterally or multilaterally.[7] The CFI's judgment was upheld on appeal to the European Court of Justice (ECJ)[8] which distinguished between "cases in which an undertaking has adopted a genuinely unilateral measure, and thus without the express or implied participation of another undertaking, and those in which the unilateral character of the measure is merely apparent".[9] It held that:

> "for an agreement within the meaning of Article [81(1)] . . . to be capable of being regarded as having been concluded by tacit acceptance, it is necessary that the manifestation of the wish of one of the contracting parties to achieve an anti-competitive goal constitute an invitation to the other party, whether express or implied, to fulfil that goal jointly, and that applies all the more where . . . such an agreement is not at first sight in the interests of the other party . . . ."[10]

This judgment is significant as it reasserts that consensus is a central pillar of Article 81(1). It is therefore likely to limit the Commission's previous attempts to extend the boundaries of Article 81 to cover what was essentially unilateral conduct.

3.2.2 The single market integration objective

A study of the type of issues that come to be scrutinised by the Commission reveals that they often concern a very distinct type of case—in particular in

6. Case T-41/96, *Bayer v. Commission,* [2000] ECR II 3383; this was subsequently confirmed in T-208/01, *Volkswagen v. Commission,* para 36, where it was held that proof was required that the distributor had explicitly or implicitly consented to the offending act. See also T-368/00, *General Motors v. Commission* [2003] ECR II 4491, para 88. Both available at http://www.curia.eu.int/en/content/juris/index_form.htm.

7. Bayer, n 6 above, para 64.

8. Joined cases C-2/01 P and C-3/01 P, *Bayer AG v. Commission of the European Communities* [2004] ECR 23.

9. *Bayer, ibid,* para 71.

10. *Bayer,* n 8 above, para 102.

relation to "vertical agreements" (ie agreements between companies at different levels in the economic chain). One of the main reasons for this is that competition cases are often considered with single market integration objectives in mind.[11] This is particularly apparent, for example, in the large number of cases dealing with distribution agreements. Practices that tend to divide the Community along Member State boundaries will receive particularly close attention. A notably severe example of this is the case of *Nintendo,* on which the Commission imposed a fine of €149 million for agreeing with its distributors to prevent the export of Nintendo products to high-price countries from low-price countries within the EU.[12]

3.2.3 Elements of the Article 81(1) prohibition

3.2.3.1 What is an "undertaking"?

Article 81 applies to agreements between "undertakings". The term "undertaking" is not defined in the EC Treaty. What is understood by this term has been developed gradually through the decision-making practice of the Commission and the case law of the Community courts. A working definition was laid down by the ECJ in the case of *Höfner and Elser v. Macroton GmbH*[13] as follows: "The concept of an undertaking encompasses every entity engaged in an economic activity regardless of the legal status of the entity and the way in which it is financed." This broad and open definition encompasses all manner of entities, irrespective of their legal status, whether they are for profit, public or private. In practice, it is necessary to take a functional approach in each case. It could be that an undertaking may fulfil the requirements of the *Höfner and Elser v. Macroton* definition for some purposes, but not for others. Take the example of a public undertaking: when carrying out some of its functions, such as commercial activities, it may act as an undertaking, but when carrying out others, such as when acting under public law powers, Article 81(1) would not normally apply.[14]

Some agreements between undertakings escape the application of Article 81(1). The main exception is where the undertakings represent a single economic entity.[15] According to the ECJ in *Bodson v. Pompes Funèbres,* Article 81(1) would not apply if the undertakings "form an economic unit within which the subsidiary has no real freedom to determine its course of action on the market, and if the agreements or practices are concerned merely with the

11. See Chapter 1.

12. COMP 35.587 PO *Video Games,* COMP 35.706 PO *Nintendo Distribution* and COMP 36.321 *Omega-Nintendo,* 2003 OJ L 255/33.

13. Case C-41/90, [1991] ECR I 1979.

14. See, eg, the most recent (preliminary) judgment concerning the status of public health funds by ECJ Cases C-264/01, C-306/01, C-354/01 and C-355/01, *AOK Bundesverband et al v. Ichthyol-Gesellschaft Cordes, Hermani & Co et al* (not yet published in the ECR); accessible from http://www.curia.eu.int.

15. Case C-73/95 P, *Viho Europe v. Commission* [1996] ECR I 5457.

internal allocation of tasks as between the undertakings".[16] Consequently, agreements between companies within the same group will usually not fall within Article 81(1). To establish that two undertakings are a part of the same group, it is, however, not sufficient that the share capital of two separate undertakings is held by the same person.[17] Similarly, Article 81(1) may apply where companies are part of a corporate group but where they individually enjoy a sufficient level of freedom to define their own market behaviour.

The anti-competitive conduct of one company, eg participation in a cartel, may also be attributed to another company where the first company has not decided independently upon its own conduct on the market, but carried out, or can be implied to have carried out, the instructions given to it by the other company (eg the parent company).[18]

As a general rule, agreements between principal and agent will fall outside Article 81(1). This is discussed in more detail at Chapter 4 below.

3.2.3.2 Agreements between undertakings, decisions of associations of undertakings, and concerted practices . . .

Article 81(1) lists three kinds of conduct that are prohibited, namely agreements between undertakings, decisions of associations of undertakings, and concerted practices. Although these are distinct concepts, there is in practice considerable overlap. Indeed, the Commission is not required to categorise conduct strictly, but can declare conduct to be, for example, an agreement and/or a concerted practice.[19] This approach has been upheld by the CFI[20] and the ECJ, which have stated: "The list in Article [81(1)] of the Treaty is intended to apply to all collusion between undertakings, whatever form it takes. . . . The only essential thing is the distinction between independent conduct, which is allowed, and collusion, which is not, regardless of any distinction between the types of collusion."[21] In the same way, the Commission may treat a particular set of facts to constitute either a decision by an association of undertakings or an agreement between undertakings.[22]

Despite this flexibility of approach, the Commission has nevertheless maintained that the three concepts are distinct.

16. Case 30/87, *Corinne Bodson v. Pompes Funebres des Regions Libérées SA* [1988] ECR 2479.

17. Case C-196/99 P, *Siderurgica Aristrain Madrid SL v. Commission*, 2003 OJ C 275/3.

18. Case C-294/98 P, *Metsä-Serla et al v. Commission* [2000] ECR I 10065, para 27.

19. *PVC*, 1989 OJ L 74/1.

20. Cases T-305/94 etc, *NV Limburgse Vinyl Maatschappij and Others v. Commission* [1999] ECR II 931.

21. Case C-49/92 P, *Commission v. Anic* [1999] ECR I 4125, para 108.

22. This approach has been relied on, for example, in relation to the rules governing the Visa payment card system, namely its by-laws and the international and EU operating regulations; see Case COMP 29.373, *Visa International*, 2001 OJ L 293/24, para 53. In its subsequent Visa decision in 2002, the Commission referred to and relied on this previous double classification: Case COMP 29.373, *Visa International—Multilateral Interchange Fee*, 2002 OJ L 318/17, para 55.

3.2.3.2.1 Agreements

The notion of an agreement in Article 81(1) has been developed and refined through a large volume of case law of the Community courts. The result is a very broad concept. In *Limburgse Vinyl Maatschappij v. Commission ("PVC II")*, the CFI stated that "it is sufficient for the undertakings to have expressed their joint intention to behave on the market in a certain way".[23] More recently, in the *Vitamins* case, the Commission stated that, "an agreement can be said to exist when the parties adhere to a common plan which limits or is likely to limit their individual commercial conduct by determining the lines of their mutual action or abstention from action in the market".[24]

The question of what constitutes an agreement within the meaning of Article 81(1) has been so often debated in the Community courts that one could compile quite a comprehensive checklist of what is not needed, as well as what is. It is not necessary that the agreement is express. Nor need it be intended to be legally binding or in writing; a gentlemen's agreement suffices.[25] Nor is it required that the agreement be adhered to.[26] An agreement can even be found to exist if a participant is an unwilling participant, ie does not intend to comply with it.[27] Finally, it is not necessary that the parties agree upon all the details in advance. Article 81(1) will also apply to agreements under negotiation that will lead to a final agreement.

In terms of the responsibility of the individual undertakings for an agreement contrary to Article 81, the court has recognised that agreements necessarily result from collaboration by several undertakings and the mere fact that each undertaking takes part in ways particular to it does not suffice to exclude its responsibility for the entire infringing agreement. In the case of *Anic*,[28] the ECJ held that infringement of Article 81(1) may result not only from an isolated act, but also from a series of acts or from continuous conduct.

3.2.3.2.2 Concerted practices

The inclusion of concerted practices in Article 81(1) can, in simple terms, be regarded as a catch-all safety measure, to ensure that looser forms of anti-competitive collusion that fall short of an actual "agreement" do not escape prohibition. A concerted practice has been defined by the ECJ as " . . . a form of coordination between undertakings which, without having reached a stage

23. *Limburgse Vinyl Maatschappij NV and Others v. Commission*, n 20 above, para 715.

24. Case COMP E I/37.512, *Vitamins*, 2003 OJ L 6/1, para 554.

25. Case 41/69, *ACF Chemiefarma v. Commission* [1970] ECR 661, paras 106–114.

26. See for example Case 86/82, *Hasselblad*, [1984] ECR 883, para 96.

27. *Fedetab*, [1980] ECR 3125, paras 90–91: eg where representatives of the party are present at but not actively participating in joint meetings where market conduct related information is exchanged.

28. Case C-49/92P, *Commission v. Anic* [1999] ECR I 4125.

where an agreement properly so-called has been concluded, knowingly substitutes practical cooperation between them for the risks of competition".[29] This definition was elaborated upon in *Suiker Unie v. Commission*, where the ECJ held that the notion of concerted practice "must be understood in the light of the concept inherent in the provisions of the Treaty relating to competition that each economic operator must determine independently the policy which he intends to adopt on the common market".[30] The court went on to hold that Article 81 precluded "any direct or indirect contact between such operators, the object or effect whereof is either to influence the conduct on the market of an actual or potential competitor or to disclose to such a competitor the course of conduct which they themselves have decided to adopt or contemplate adopting on the market".[31] This formula has been relied upon in many cases since then.[32]

The question whether, for the Commission to prove that there exists a concerted practice, it is necessary for it to demonstrate that there are anti-competitive effects on the market was dealt with by the ECJ in the case of *Hüls*.[33] There, the ECJ acknowledged that the concept of concerted practice within Article 81(1) implies, besides the undertakings acting in concert with each other, subsequent conduct on the market and a relationship of cause and effect between the two; but that where the participants in the concerted action remain active on the market, it could be presumed that they will take account of the information exchanged with their competitors for the purposes of determining their conduct on the market. This, according to the ECJ, would be all the more true where the undertakings concert on a regular basis over a long period. The parties can rebut this presumption by adducing proof to the contrary. However, this may prove very difficult, in particular where the market structure encourages parallel behaviour even in the absence of any contact.

3.2.3.2.3 Decisions by associations of undertakings

The notion of "association" in Article 81(1) is widely interpreted. It includes cooperatives, professional regulatory bodies, associations without legal personality, non-profit-making associations, associations of associations and associations outside the Community. "Decisions" are the results of the activities of such associations. Decisions typically include articles of incorporation or by-laws or the rules of trade associations.[34]

29. Case 48/69, *ICI v. Commission (Dyestuffs)* [1972] ECR 619, para 64.
30. Cases 40/73 etc, *Suiker Unie v. Commission*, [1975] ECR 1663, para 173.
31. *Ibid*, para 174.
32. See for example *Vitamins*, n 24 above, para 557.
33. Case C-199/92, *Hüls v. Commission* [1999] ECR I 4287, paras 158–166.
34. See for example *Visa International*, n 22 above.

3.2.3.3 . . . which have as their object or effect the prevention, restriction or distortion of competition

Only those agreements between undertakings, concerted practices or decisions by associations of undertakings that have either as their object or effect the prevention, restriction or distortion of competition will fall within Article 81(1).

As a preliminary point, it is important to recall the distinction between a restriction of commercial freedom on the one hand and a restriction of competition on the other. Not every restriction of commercial freedom constitutes a restriction of competition falling within Article 81(1).[35] The courts have held that a restriction does not fall within Article 81(1) where it is necessary to enable the parties to an agreement to achieve a legitimate commercial purpose.[36] In *Wouters*,[37] which concerned a rule adopted by the Dutch Bar Council prohibiting lawyers in the Netherlands from entering into partnership with non-lawyers, the ECJ held that when applying Article 81(1) account first had to be taken of the overall context in which the action was taken or produced its effects, and in particular its objectives. Second, account should be taken of whether the consequential effects restrictive of competition were inherent in pursuing those objectives. Where the restriction could "reasonably be considered to be necessary" in order to ensure the achievement of the—neutral with regard to competition—objectives, then Article 81(1) would not be infringed.

Similarly, the Commission has identified a number of instances where agreements restrictive of the parties' freedom of action will not, as a rule, lead to a restriction of competition. These include cooperation between non-competitors, between competing undertakings that could not independently carry out the activity covered by the cooperation, or concerning an activity that does not influence the relevant parameters of competition.[38]

3.2.3.3.1 Object

The Commission will first consider whether the agreement etc in question has as its object the restriction of competition. Agreements that are restrictive by object involve restrictions that, in the light of the objectives of Community competition rules, are presumed to have negative effects on competition and in respect of which it is therefore unnecessary, for the purposes of applying Article 81(1), to demonstrate any actual effects on the market.[39] According to the Guidelines on the application of Article 81(3) of the Treaty, the factors to

35. Also, not every restriction of competition is contrary to Article 81(1); see further 3.2.3.4.

36. See further Whish, *Competition Law* (5th edn 2003) p 121.

37. Case C-309/99, [2002] ECR I 1577.

38. See Guidelines on the applicability of Article 81 of the Treaty to horizontal cooperation agreements, 2001 OJ C 3/2, para 24.

39. Guidelines on the application of Article 81(3) of the Treaty, 2004 OJ C 101/97 paras 20, 21.

be considered include the content of the agreement, the objective aims pursued by it and the context in which it is (to be) applied, and the actual conduct and behaviour of the parties on the market.[40]

Examples of horizontal agreements found to constitute restrictions by object include price-fixing, output limitations and sharing of markets or customers.[41] Examples of vertical agreements considered to be restrictions by object include minimum resale price maintenance and absolute territorial protection by prohibiting even passive sales into other territories.[42] However, not all agreements that may ultimately have an effect on prices are necessarily restrictions by object. In the *Visa* decision, the Commission specified that it did not consider the multilateral determination by banks within Visa of the "default interchange fee" (a fee paid between banks for every payment card transaction) to be a restriction of competition by object.[43]

3.2.3.3.2 Effect

If no anti-competitive object is established, an agreement, decision or concerted practice may nevertheless infringe Article 81(1) if it has an anti-competitive effect. This will be the case where the agreement affects actual or potential competition to such an extent that negative effects on the market can be expected with a reasonable degree of probability. Negative effects are said to be likely when the parties, either individually or jointly, have market power. It is, however, not always clear how much market power will be required to trigger the application of Article 81(1). Normally, it will be less than that required for a finding of dominance under Article 82. No relevant effects are likely to exist where the market shares of the parties remain below the thresholds of the *de minimis* notice.[44] If these thresholds, or the "safe harbour" thresholds contained in block exemption regulations, are exceeded, there is however no automatic presumption that the agreement concerned has anti-competitive effects.[45]

Under the Commission's Guidelines, the assessment of the effect of an agreement necessitates an extensive economic analysis of its market context.

40. *Ibid*, para 22.

41. Guidelines on the applicability of Article 81 to horizontal cooperation agreements, n 38, para 25. See also 4.3 below. All so-called "hardcore" restrictions that feature in notices and black clauses in block exemption regulations are restrictions by object.

42. See Article 4 of Regulation 2790/1999 on the application of Article 81(3) of the Treaty to categories of vertical agreements and concerted practices. See also 4.1 below.

43. The Commission's objection was based on the fact that the interchange fee had as its effect, in view, to distort the behaviour of acquiring banks *vis-à-vis* their customers because it represented a large cost element in the fee charged by the acquiring banks to their customers. *Visa International—Multilateral Interchange Fee*, n 22 above, paras 68–69.

44. Commission Notice on agreements of minor importance which do not appreciably restrict competition under Article 81(1) of the Treaty establishing the European Community (*de minimis*), 2001 OJ C 368/13.

45. Guidelines on the application of Article 81(3), n 39 above, para 24.

This will invariably require the definition of the relevant market.[46] The Commission's notices reflect recent judgments of the CFI. For example, in *European Night Services* the CFI ruled: "It must be borne in mind that in assessing an agreement under Article [81(1)] of the Treaty, account should be taken of the actual conditions in which it functions, in particular the economic context in which the undertakings operate, the products or services covered by the agreement and the actual structure of the market concerned".[47]

3.2.3.3.3 Ancillary restraints

As explained above, an agreement that, as a whole, is not found to have either as its object or as its effect the restriction of competition will fall outside the scope of Article 81. It may be, however, that such an agreement nevertheless contains restrictions of competition. Provided that these restrictions are directly related to, necessary for and proportionate to the implementation of the main agreement—for example, a non-compete clause in the context of the sale of a business[48]—they will also be considered as falling outside Article 81 according to the doctrine of ancillary restraints.[49]

3.2.3.4 Appreciability: the *de minimis* principles

Agreements that restrict competition are only caught by Article 81(1) if their effect on competition is appreciable. According to the Guidelines, such appreciable effects are likely, as a general rule, to result if one of the parties has, obtains or consolidates some degree of market power.[50]

This principle was first established by the ECJ in a preliminary reference ruling in *Völk v. Vervaecke* in the 1960s.[51] Today, the principle is enshrined in a Commission Notice on agreements of minor importance,[52] which provides that where specified market-share thresholds are not exceeded, agreements are unlikely to appreciably restrict competition within the meaning of Article 81(1).[53] Where the parties are actual or potential competitors, the relevant market share threshold is 10 per cent of the relevant market. In the case of non-competitors, the market share threshold is 15 per cent and for mixed

46. *Ibid*, para 27.
47. Cases T–374/94 etc *European Night Services* [1998] ECR II 3141, para 136.
48. Case 42/84, *Remia v. Commission*, [1985] ECR 2545, paras 17 *et seq*; but today see also "Commission Notice on restrictions directly related and necessary to concentrations", 2001 OJ C 188/5.
49. Or "ancillary restrictions" in the terminology of the court: see Case T-112/99, *Métropole Télévision (M6) et al v. Commission* [2001] ECR II 2459, paras 104 *et seq*.
50. Guidelines on the application of Article 81(3), n 39 above, para 25.
51. Case 5/69, *Franz Völk v. SPRL Ets Vervaecke* [1969] ECR 295, para 7.
52. See n [47].
53. It should be noted, however, that agreements where the parties to the agreement exceed these thresholds do not automatically have an appreciable effect on competition; in such cases, an individual assessment is still necessary. See Guidelines on the application of Article 81(3), n 39 above, para 24.

agreements the market share threshold is 10 per cent.[54] In addition, the Notice specifically recognises the cumulative effects of agreements containing similar restrictions. In such cases of cumulative effects, the Notice sets down a lower market share threshold. Finally, it should be noted that the *de minimis* principle does not apply in the case of specified so-called "hardcore" infringements.[55]

3.2.3.5 Effect on trade between Member States

There is a second appreciability requirement for Article 81 to apply: that is, an appreciable effect on trade between Member States. This requirement serves to define "in the context of the law governing competition, the boundary between the areas respectively covered by Community law and the law of the Member States".[56] The criterion has been of particular relevance since Regulation 1/2003 became effective. Article 3(1) of Regulation 1/2003 requires that where a national competition authority applies national competition law to agreements within the meaning of Article 81(1) that may affect trade between Member States, it must also apply Article 81. Article 3(2) of the Regulation provides furthermore that in such cases, the outcome under national competition law cannot lead to the prohibition of conduct that either does not restrict competition within the meaning of Article 81(1) or falls within the ambit of the exception in Article 81(3) or of a block exemption regulation.

Historically, the concept of effect on trade between Member States has tended to be widely interpreted, probably to compensate for the absence of competition law regimes in some Member States. In *Société Technique Minière v. Maschinenbau Ulm* the ECJ held that "it must be possible to foresee with a sufficient degree of probability on the basis of a set of objective factors of law or of fact that the agreement in question may have an influence, direct or indirect, actual or potential, on the pattern of trade between Member States".[57] These days, however, all Member States have introduced competition laws modelled closely on the Community rules, and more recently there has been evidence of a retreat to a less expansive interpretation of the concept of effect on trade between Member States.[58]

54. Notice on agreements of minor importance, n 47 above, para 7.

55. *Ibid*, para 11. These include, *inter alia*, in the case of agreements between competitors: price-fixing, limitation of output or sales and the allocation of customers. In the case of agreements between non-competitors, these include minimum resale price maintenance, the restriction of cross-supplies between distributors in a selective distribution system and the restriction of passive sales to end users by members of a selective distribution system operating at the retail level of trade.

56. Case 22/78, *Hugin Kassaregister AB v. Commission*, [1979] ECR 1869, para 17.

57. Case 56/65, [1966] ECR 235, 249.

58. See, for example, Case 215/96 etc, *Bagnasco v. BPN* [1999] ECR I-135, paras 50–53. See also *Dutch Banks*, 1989 OJ L 253/1.

3.2.3 Article 81: Prohibition and Exception

As a part of the so-called "modernisation package" to accompany Regulation 1/2003,[59] the Commission adopted a new Notice on the concept of effect on trade between Member States.[60] According to this Notice, three elements must be addressed: the concept of trade between Member States, the notion of "may affect", and the concept of appreciability. These are considered in turn below.

3.2.3.5.1 The notion of "trade between Member States"

For the purposes of Article 81(1), "trade" encompasses a wider variety of activity than would ordinarily be understood by the term. It covers all cross-border economic activity and also includes activities affecting the competitive structure of the relevant market. According to the Notice, the requirement that there must be an effect on trade between Member States "implies that there must be an impact on cross-border economic activity involving at least two Member States".[61] It seems, therefore, that in future, where the territory of only one Member State is affected, Community competition law will normally not apply.[62]

3.2.3.5.2 The notion of "may affect"

The important thing to appreciate here is that this is an objective concept: ie the subjective intent of the parties is not relevant and it is sufficient that the agreement or practice is *capable* of having such an effect. The nature of the agreement and practice, as well as the nature of the products and the market

59. This "package" included a total of one Regulation and six Notices; Commission Regulation (EC) No 773/2004 of 7 April 2004 relating to the conduct of proceedings by the Commission pursuant to Articles 81 and 82 of the EC Treaty, OJ L 123, 27 April 2004, pp 18–24; Commission Notice on cooperation within the Network of Competition Authorities, OJ C 101, 27 April 2004, pp 43–53; Commission Notice on the co-operation between the Commission and the courts of the EU Member States in the application of Articles 81 and 82 EC, OJ C 101, 27 April 2004, pp 54–64; Commission Notice on the handling of complaints by the Commission under Articles 81 and 82 of the EC Treaty, OJ C 101, 27 April 2004, pp 65–77; Commission Notice on informal guidance relating to novel questions concerning Articles 81 and 82 of the EC Treaty that arise in individual cases (guidance letters), OJ C 101, 27 April 2004, pages 78–80; Commission Notice-—Guidelines on the effect on trade concept contained in Articles 81 and 82 of the Treaty, OJ C 101, 27 April 2004, pp 81–96; Communication from the Commission—Notice—Guidelines on the application of Article 81(3) of the Treaty, OJ C 101, 27 April 2004, pp 97–118.

60. Guidelines on the effect on trade concept contained in Articles 81 and 82 of the Treaty 2004 OJ C 101/81.

61. *Ibid*, para 21.

62. This statement contradicts, however, the court's view, for example in *Cementhandelaren*, that "an agreement extending over the whole territory of a Member State by its very nature has the effect of reinforcing the compartmentalisation of markets on a national basis, thereby holding up the economic interpenetration which the Treaty is designed to bring about an protecting domestic production", [1972] ECR 977. To reconcile the two statements, it would thus be sufficient for an agreement to affect trade between Member States if, although involving only two parties in one Member State, it nevertheless created barriers to trade between Member States (eg by exclusively binding one major distributor of the relevant products).

position of the parties, may be relevant factors as well as the factual and legal background.

In considering whether intra-Community trade is affected, there is no need to establish a link between the alleged restriction and the capacity of the agreement to affect trade between Member States. It is the effect of the agreement as a whole that is assessed and not the individual terms of the agreement, provided that the restriction in question forms an integral part of the agreement. This means that even an agreement that on the face of it promotes cross-border trade (eg a distribution agreement between a producer in one Member State and a distributor in another) will "affect trade between Member States".

3.2.3.5.3 Appreciability

The Commission Notice on the effect on trade between Member States provides for a new "*de minimis* rule". According to the Notice, in principle, agreements are not capable of appreciably affecting trade between Member States when the following cumulative conditions are met:

(a) the aggregate market share of the parties on any relevant market within the Community affected by the agreement does not exceed 5 per cent; and
(b) the aggregate annual Community turnover of the undertaking(s) concerned in the products covered by the agreement does not exceed €40 million.

The Notice also states that, in the case of an agreement that is capable of affecting trade by its very nature, eg because it concerns imports and exports or covers several Member States, there will be a rebuttable positive presumption of an appreciable effect on trade when the aggregate turnover of the parties in the products covered by the agreement exceeds €40 million.[63] It is important to note that neither threshold refers to the market shares or turnover affected by the agreement. Thus, the effect of an agreement on trade between Member States may be presumed appreciable for reasons unconnected with the agreement (ie because one of the parties has other activities concerning the same products).

3.2.3.6 Agreements concerning third countries

Finally, the possibility that an agreement that appears to affect only one Member State and a third country, or indeed only third countries, may indirectly affect trade between Member States should not be overlooked. For

63. Notice on the effect of trade concept, n 60 above, para 53.

example, an agreement limiting imports into the Community may affect trade between Member States and so be caught by Article 81.[64] In each case it is necessary to consider—by reference, for example, to the nature of the product and whether any price differential would be eroded by the costs of importation—whether imports into the Community would have been likely. In *Micro Leader Business*, the CFI implicitly accepted that a prohibition on imports into France of a French-language Microsoft product from Canada was capable of affecting trade between Member States.[65] Even agreements concerning solely trade outside the Community must be scrutinised, to see whether they can have an effect on competition within the Community.[66] Whether this is so must be considered with regard to the facts in each individual case.

A similar analysis is applied to restrictions on exports from the Community to third countries. The Commission will look closely in each case at the factors that would influence the likelihood of re-importation. For example, in the case of *Junghans* in the 1970s, the Commission found that a ban on exports to third countries did not affect trade between Member States as there was no incentive for dealers or customers to buy goods that had been exported to a third country owing to the double duty borne by goods crossing the frontiers of the European Community.[67]

3.3 ARTICLE 81(3): THE EXCEPTION

Article 81(3) provides a defence for certain agreements from the strict prohibition contained in Article 81(1). It should be emphasised that Article 81(3) only becomes relevant if an agreement falls within the scope of Article 81(1). Therefore, when assessing whether an agreement, concerted practice or decision by an association of undertakings infringes Article 81, the first step is to check whether the requirements of Article 81(1) are met. If not, then there is no need to consider whether the agreement meets the four cumulative conditions of Article 81(3) described below.

64. See for example *Aluminium Products*, 1985 OJ L 92/1.

65. Case T-198/98, [1999] ECR II 3989.

66. See for example *Suiker Unie v. Commission*, n 30 above, paras 558 *et seq*. See also the case of *Tretorn*, 1994 OJ L 378/45, where the Commission found that the prevention of parallel imports from the US and into Switzerland had an appreciable effect on trade between Member States since the price structure in Europe and in the US made re-exportation into the Community highly probable (para 66). See also Case C306/96 *Javico* ECR [1998] I-1983, a preliminary ruling that concerned an obligation to export to a third country and a prohibition to re-export to the Community.

67. Case IV/5715 *Junghans*, 1977 OJ L 30/10, paras 10 and 24. See also Cases IV/171, IV/172, IV/117, IV/28.173—*Campari*, 1968 OJ L 70/13, para 4.c. The Commission did, however, note that this situation may change in the future in relation to those countries with which the Community had a free trade agreement.

3.3.1 The four conditions for the applicability of Article 81(3)

3.3.1.1 First condition: contribution to improving the production or distribution of goods or to promoting technical or economic progress

In the run-up to May 2004, when Article 81(3) became directly applicable, it was queried whether in the future this condition would be narrowly interpreted—ie as only an efficiency standard—or more broadly, allowing other factors, eg employment, the environment, etc., to be taken into account.[68] It would appear, from the Commission's Guidelines on the Application of Article 81(3) of the Treaty[69] that the Commission has opted for the former, more restrictive view. The Guidelines state that the purpose of this first condition is "to define the types of efficiency gains that can be taken into account and be subject to the further tests of the second, third and fourth conditions of Article 81(3)".

When assessing whether an agreement fulfils the first condition, it should be borne in mind that only objective benefits are relevant. The benefits must be of objective value to the Community as a whole and not merely of private benefit to the parties.

The Guidelines identify four factors that are to be verified and which will therefore require substantiation by the parties: the nature of the claimed efficiencies; the link between the agreement and the efficiencies; the likelihood and magnitude of each claimed efficiency; and how and when each claimed efficiency would be achieved.

As regards the different types of efficiencies, the Guidelines recognise that the categories of efficiencies in Article 81(3) overlap, and state that there is no need for specific categorisation of the efficiency. The Commission identifies two main types of efficiencies: cost efficiencies, for example resulting from a "technological leap" or an integration of assets; and efficiencies of a qualitative nature, whereby value is created in the form of new or improved products.

The Commission recognises that there may be efficiencies other than these two categories; in the Guidelines, the Commission states that cost efficiencies and qualitative efficiencies are "only examples and are not intended to be exhaustive".[70] It would appear, however, that the Commission does not foresee any benefits to be relevant other than those that enhance competition. It is interesting to note that whereas a previous draft of the Guidelines recalled the need to take into account the "fundamental market integration objective of the Community", this objective was not specifically mentioned in the final text of the Guidelines. Perhaps this cautious approach may be attributed to an intention to limit the scope for divergent decisions and rulings at national

68. See Whish *op cit*, n 36 above, pp 151 *et seq*. See also Case IV.F.1/36.718 *CECED*, 2000 OJ L 187/47, where the Commission took environmental benefits into account. See also 4.3.5.7 below.

69. Guidelines on the application of Article 81(3), n 39 above, section 3.2, paras 48 *et seq*.

70. *Ibid*, para 63.

level. In any event, it should be recalled that Commission Notices are not binding and are subject to the Community courts' jurisdiction. Furthermore, it might be argued that the wording of the EC Treaty is not as limited as the Guidelines would lead one to believe.

3.3.1.2 Second condition: allowing consumers a fair share of the resulting benefit

According to the Commission "the concept of '*consumers*' encompasses all direct or indirect users of the products covered by the agreement".[71] The test is therefore not a general public interest test, nor limited to individuals who purchase for personal use, but can include other undertakings.

There is no definition of "fair share" in the Treaty. This is determined on a case-by-case basis and the Commission has wide discretion. The Guidelines explain that this notion implies that the benefits passed on to consumers must at least compensate them for any actual or likely negative impact caused by the restriction of competition. The time taken for the efficiencies to be passed on will be taken into account. The Guidelines also explain that whether the benefits to be passed on are sufficient will depend in turn on the severity of the restriction on competition. Thus, "the greater the restriction of competition found under Article 81(1) the greater must be the efficiencies and the pass-on to consumers".[72]

The Guidelines set out an analytical framework for the assessment of consumer pass-on of efficiency gains. For the assessment of the extent to which cost efficiencies are likely to be passed on to consumers, it is proposed that the following four factors be taken into account:

- the characteristics and structure of the market;
- the nature and magnitude of the efficiency gains;
- the elasticity of demand; and
- the magnitude of the restriction of competition.

As regards the assessment of the pass-on and balancing of other efficiencies, such as new and improved products, the Guidelines state that this will require a value judgement, but note that provided any increase in value stemming from such improvements exceeds any price increase resulting from the agreement, then consumers will be better off than without the agreement.[73]

3.3.1.3 Third condition: indispensability of the restrictions

The requirement that the restrictions must be indispensable to the attainment of the benefits identified under the first condition is a strict test. What is

71. *Ibid*, para 84.
72. *Ibid*, para 90.
73. *Ibid*, para 104.

required is more than a mere causal link.[74] Thus, the question is not whether, in the absence of the restriction, the agreement would not have been concluded. What matters is whether the restrictions go beyond what is necessary to achieve the benefits identified. This is the case if two conditions are met: both the restrictive agreement as such, and the individual restrictions flowing from the agreement, must be necessary to achieve the efficiencies.[75]

As regards the first leg of the test, the Guidelines state that it is particularly relevant to consider whether, having regard to the circumstances of the particular case, the parties could have achieved the efficiencies by means of another, less restrictive, type of agreement and over what time frame. As regards the assessment of the second leg of the test, the Guidelines explain that a restriction will be regarded as indispensable if its absence would eliminate or significantly reduce the efficiencies that follow from the agreement or make it significantly less likely that they will materialise. This assessment necessarily requires considering the effects of alternative solutions on competition and must take into account the actual and potential improvement in the field of competition by the elimination of a particular restriction or the application of a less restrictive alternative.[76]

3.3.1.4 Fourth condition: no elimination of competition

This last condition recognises the importance of preserving the competitive environment, sometimes referred to as "working competition" or "effective competition".

The Commission's Guidelines explain that the application of this condition requires "a realistic analysis of the various sources of competition in the market, the level of competitive constraint that they impose on the parties to the agreement and the impact of the agreement on this competitive constraint".[77] The Guidelines also note that both actual and potential competition should be considered.

Often, little attention is paid to this condition, either because the agreement has already failed on another hurdle, or because, on the contrary, it has sufficient merit for this condition not to be called into question. If it does become significant, then it will be necessary to define the relevant market, as the application of this condition will usually depend on the market share of the undertakings concerned. Regard should also be had to the existence of similar agreements on the market, as the parallel effect may eliminate competition.

It is worth recalling that even where this condition is fulfilled and an agreement is exempted, this cannot prevent the application of Article 82.[78] However, it is suggested that the parties are only exceptionally going to clear

74. Bellamy and Child, European Community Law of Competition (5th edn 2001), para 3–055.

75. Guidelines on the application of Article 81(3), n 39 above, para 73.

76. *Ibid*, para 79.

77. *Ibid*, para 108.

78. Case T-51/89, *Tetra Pak v. Commission* ("*Tetra Pak I*"), [1990] ECR II 309, para 22.

this hurdle if the agreement directly leads to the creation or strengthening of a market-dominating position.

3.3.2 The application of Article 81(3)

Since 1 May 2004, Article 81(3) has become directly applicable. As a result, undertakings no longer have to notify their agreements to the Commission in order to possibly benefit from individual exemptions under Article 81(3). Indeed, it is (subject to some minor exceptions) no longer possible to formally notify agreements at all to get the Commission's view on them. There is, therefore, also no immunity from fines. National courts and national authorities can apply Article 81 in its entirety and Article 81(3) can be relied upon as a defence without a previous administrative act applying the exemption being required. Undertakings will have to conduct their own self-assessment on the applicability of Article 81(3) and thus take the risk of infringing Article 81. This will need to be done on a continuous basis, as market conditions as well as the economic framework within which the agreement operates are subject to change.

This change in the application of Article 81(3) raises a number of new issues.

3.3.2.1 Uniformity of application of European competition law

The Commission's monopoly on the application of Article 81(3) ensured a single, easily accessible[79] body of law, subject only to review by the Community courts. Following decentralisation, and the expansion of the Community to 25 Member States, the number of institutions applying Article 81(3) has exploded. This multiple parallel application of Article 81 represents a challenge. In the new climate of self-assessment, it is important that the rules are not only uniformly applied, but also are seen to be uniformly applied.

Regulation 1/2003 itself foresees this need. Article 11 of the Regulation provides for close cooperation between national competition authorities and the Commission. Article 16 of the Regulation provides that where a matter is already the subject of a Commission decision, national competition authorities and national courts cannot take decisions that would run counter to the decision adopted by the Commission.[80] Furthermore, Article 15 of the Regulation provides for both the national authority of the Member State in

79. That is, in the form of published decisions in the OJ in all official languages.

80. National courts are also required to avoid taking decisions that conflict with a decision contemplated by the Commission in a proceeding that it has initiated, a situation in which national authorities have lost their competence. See 9.2 and 10.4.3.

question and the Commission to submit written observations to the national courts and also for oral observations, with the permission of the court.[81]

As regards the issue of accessibility, Article 15(2) requires that a copy of any judgment applying Article 81 is to be provided to the Commission. The non-confidential versions of these judgments are listed in a database ("Database of National Court Judgments on Antitrust Cases (Articles 81 & 82 of the EC Treaty)[82]").

While these various safeguards may prevent or control diverging decisions to a certain extent, there is still the question of how the results of the many judgments will be communicated effectively to the rest of the Community, so that the current status of the law at any given time is sufficiently certain for undertakings.

3.3.2.2 Practical application of Article 81(3)

In practical terms, the reform of the enforcement of Article 81(3) may not require any significant change in approach by undertakings seeking to assess whether their agreements are compatible with Article 81. As before, most agreements will first be assessed against one of the various "block exemption regulations".[83] Where the proposed agreement does not fall neatly within their terms, the parties will, however, have to rely more heavily on basic principles. The Commission's Guidelines on the application of Article 81(3), which "establish an analytical framework for the application of Article 81(3)",[84] as well as agreement-specific guidelines and notices, will have an important part to play in this exercise.

81. Whether this task can effectively be taken care of by the various competition authorities remains to be seen. It will certainly provide a considerable challenge in terms of resource allocation if used extensively by national courts. See also 10.7.1 below.

82. See http://europa.eu.int/comm/competition/antitrust/national_courts/index_en.html. Judgments are provided in the original language received by the Commission and are classified according to the Member State of origin.

83. See: Council Regulation (EEC) No 19/65 EEC of 2 March 1965 on the application of Article 81(3) of the Treaty to certain categories of agreements and concerted practices, 1965 OJ L 36/533; Council Regulation (EC) No 1215/1999 amending Regulation No 19/65 EEC on the application of Article 81(3) of the Treaty to certain categories of agreements and concerted practices, 1999 OJ L 148/1; Commission Regulation (EC) No. 2790/1999 of 22 December 1999 on the application of Article 81(3) of the Treaty to categories of vertical agreements and concerted practices, 1999 OJ L 336/21; Commission Regulation (EC) No 1400/2002 of 31 July 2002 on the application of Article 81(3) to the motor vehicle sector, 2002 OJ L 203/30; Commission Regulation (EC) No. 2658/2000 of 29 November 2000 on the application of Article 81(3) of the Treaty to categories of specialisation agreement, 2000 OJ L 304/3; Commission Regulation (EC) No 2659/2000 of 29 November 2000 on the application of Article 81(3) of the Treaty to categories of research and development agreements, 2000 OJ L 304/7; Commission Guidelines on the applicability of Article 81 of the EC Treaty to horizontal cooperation agreements, 2001 OJ C 3/2; Commission Regulation (EC) No 772/2004 of 27 April 2004 on the application of Article 85(3) of the Treaty to categories of technology transfer agreements, 2004 OJ L 123/11.

84. Guidelines on the application of Article 81(3), n 42 above, para 5.

3.3.2 Article 81: Prohibition and Exception

The Commission will continue to issue both formal decisions under Article 9 (commitment decisions) or under Article 10 (positive decisions) and informal guidance letters[85] and will post them on its website. Given that these will only be taken where the importance of the case justifies the expenditure of resources, they will provide valuable insight into the Commission's competition policy, but will do so only rarely.[86]

The extent to which the previous decision-making practice of the Commission will be relevant is open to question, as it is not clear whether the methodology for analysis in the future will be the same as it has been in the past. Even a brief examination of recent exemption decisions of the Commission shows that the approach outlined above is one to which the Commission has in the past not adhered, or not closely adhered.[87] Furthermore, statements in the introduction to the Guidelines on the application of Article 81(3) suggest that the Guidelines are not intended merely to be a consolidation of the Commission's existing practice, but go further and put this practice into the context of a modernised world. The Commission states that the Guidelines "outline the current state of the case law of the Court of Justice", but acknowledge that the Commission also intends to explain its policy with regard to issues that have not yet been dealt with in the case law, or that are subject to interpretation.[88] The Commission does, however, claim that the methodology of the Guidelines is based on the economic approach already introduced and developed in the Guidelines on vertical restraints, horizontal cooperation agreements and technology transfer agreements.[89] What is clear is that the methodology of analysis described in the Guidelines is much more sophisticated than that which has been applied in past cases.

Even if past decisions of the Commission cannot be relied upon heavily, the Guidelines are without prejudice to the case law of the Community courts. Existing case law must therefore still be relevant and decisions of the Commission in applying the Guidelines will be subject to the Community courts' jurisdiction. In the meantime, however, it remains ultimately for the parties themselves to bear the risk of assessing compliance with Article 81. The task of self-assessment will be particularly difficult in the case of sensitive agreements relating to new products and services. In such cases, it is often difficult

85. See para 38, preamble, Regulation 1/2003 and Commission Notice on informal guidance relating to novel questions concerning Articles 81 and 82 of the EC Treaty that arise in individual cases (guidance letters), n 59 above.

86. Extensive work by the Commission in this area would run counter to the expressed claim to re-focus its resources on other activities, such as the pursuit of hardcore cartels.

87. See for example, Case COMP/C2 37.398—*joint selling of the commercial rights of the Uefa Champions League*, 2003 OJ L 291/25, where, for example, there is no "pass-on" or balancing analysis along the lines set out in section 3.4 of the Guidelines under the second condition (fair share of benefit to consumers), and no discussion of whether the duration of the contracts (three years) was an indispensable restriction, although the tournament occurs on a yearly basis.

88. Guidelines on the application of Article 81(3), n 39 above, para 7.

89. *Ibid*, para 5.

to define the relevant market, or to calculate the market shares that are frequently used as benchmarks for the application of Article 81.[90]

3.4 THE CONSEQUENCES OF INFRINGEMENT OF ARTICLE 81

3.4.1 Nullity

Infringement of Article 81 carries a number of consequences. The first of these is provided for in Article 81(2), which provides: "Any agreements or decisions prohibited pursuant to this Article shall be automatically void." In practice this means that an agreement which infringes Article 81 will be unenforceable.[91]

In some cases, it may be possible to sever the offending provisions, leaving the remainder of the agreement intact. Generally speaking, national contract law determines whether this is possible. However, sometimes Community law provides specific rules: eg the block exemption regulation on vertical restraints makes a distinction between restrictions that take the whole agreement outside its scope (eg minimum resale price maintenance or the restriction of passive sales[92]) and other restrictions that do not, but which themselves cannot be exempted (eg non-compete obligations of over five years' duration[93]).

Whether a particular agreement falls within Article 81(1) may depend on factors that can change over the life of the agreement (eg market shares). What does this mean for the status of such "variable" agreements under Article 81(2)? In the UK case *Passmore v. Morland*, the Court of Appeal decided that since the prohibition itself is transient, so too is the voidness.[94] Thus an agreement can float in and out of voidness. This result clearly leaves a lot to be desired for undertakings, who must have at least some degree of certainty for the agreements that form the basis of their commercial dealings. The only safe approach for undertakings is thus to opt always for the "least restrictive alternative". While this may be the preferable solution from a competition law enforcer's point of view, it effectively prevents undertakings from entering into, perhaps more restrictive but more efficient, agreements for fear of the possibility that these agreements may, in the future, prove to be illegal. Whatever initial approach is adopted, it is certain that undertakings must keep

90. See for example the recent block exemption Regulation relating to technology transfer agreements, *supra* note 83.

91. See 10.5 below.

92. Articles 4(a) and 4(b) of Regulation 2790/1999 on the application of Article 81(3) of the Treaty to categories of vertical agreements and concerted practices.

93. *Ibid*, Article 5(a).

94. See *Passmore v. Morland plc, Inntrepreneur Pub Company (CPC) Ltd, Inntrepreneur Beer Supply Company Ltd* [1998] EWHC Ch 312, para 25.

their agreements under constant review, keeping a weather eye open to fluctuations in their market share and other market conditions, or changes to the overall structure of competition.

3.4.2 Fines

The second consequence of infringement of Article 81 is provided for by Article 23 of Regulation 1/2003 which gives the Commission the power to impose on each undertaking a fine of up to 10 per cent of its turnover in the preceding business year for intentional or negligent breach of Article 81.[95]

3.4.3 National law

Parties to an agreement falling foul of Article 81 may also face consequences under national law, including fines and, in some Member States, criminal sanctions against individuals.[96] Where Member States enforce Article 81, sanctions must be determined in accordance with national law.

3.4.4 Civil damages claims

Finally, there is also the risk that civil damages claims may be brought in national courts, either by a party to the agreement, or for example by the "victims" of a cartel.[97]

95. See 9.10.4 below.
96. See for example the UK Enterprise Act 2002 and the Irish Competition Act 2002.
97. See 10.6.4 below.

CHAPTER 4

APPLICATION OF ARTICLE 81

Pat Treacy, Laura Anderson, Sophie Lawrance, Bristows, and Peter Willis, Taylor Wessing

4.1 ARTICLE 81 AND VERTICAL AGREEMENTS

4.1.1 What are "vertical" agreements?

For the purposes of competition law, agreements between companies may be described as either "horizontal" or "vertical". The difference is whether or not the parties operate at the same level of the supply and distribution chain. "Horizontal" agreements are those between parties at the same level of supply. An example would be an agreement between two distributors. A "vertical" arrangement is between parties at different levels of supply, for instance between a manufacturer and a distributor, or between a distributor and a retailer. Vertical agreements are often referred to simply as "distribution agreements", although this does not reflect their diversity, which may include purchasing, supply, agency and franchise arrangements.

It is also possible to describe parties as being "upstream" or "downstream" of each other. A manufacturer will buy raw materials from a vendor that is "upstream" of its business, whereas it will sell on finished products to a distributor that is "downstream".

4.1.2 Why are they subject to Article 81?

4.1.2.1 Agreements

Unless a company is fully "vertically integrated", so as to cover all levels of the supply chain from production to retail, it will need to enter into agreements with other companies to enable it do certain things.

As explained above, Article 81 of the EC Treaty does not apply to agreements within the same corporate group structure, so agreements between a company and its subsidiaries (for example acting as distributors) will not be subject to Article 81.[1] Similarly, genuine agency agreements are treated by

1. Case 22/71, *Béguelin Import v. GL Import Export* [1971] ECR 949. The test is whether or not the subsidiary has economic independence.

competition law as being outside Article 81, as the agent is negotiating on behalf of the principal.[2] Otherwise, vertical agreements have the potential to fall within Article 81.

4.1.2.2 Effect on competition

It is often asked whether competition law should be concerned with vertical agreements at all, and whether such agreements are likely to have an appreciable effect on competition. Horizontal agreements give rise to the most high-profile infringements of competition law: cartel-type activity is generally the result of agreements between parties operating at the same level of the supply chain.[3] Vertical agreements between purchasers and suppliers are far less likely to produce serious anti-competitive effects. They may well be pro-competitive, for example, by aiming to bring goods to the customer efficiently.

Reflecting this, vertical agreements are usually treated more leniently than horizontal agreements under the European competition regime. Nevertheless, vertical agreements can have an effect on competition. For example, a supplier may oblige its distributors not to carry competing goods; this could make it difficult for another supplier of similar goods to arrange distribution. A supplier might also agree to appoint only one distributor in a particular territory; that could reduce competition at the distribution level, potentially affecting the terms or prices offered to consumers. Negative effects are likely to be more serious if the agreement is of long duration.

4.1.2.3 Effect on parallel trade

Vertical agreements that isolate particular territories (eg exclusive distribution arrangements limited to a particular country and prohibiting supply outside that territory) may prevent exports. Because of the EU's market integration objectives (see 1.2.2 above), the potential for vertical agreements to impede parallel trade has led to a closer scrutiny of vertical agreements in Europe than elsewhere. Agreements that tend to reinforce national boundaries are regarded with suspicion by the European Commission.

4.1.2.4 The application of the law

Arguments that Article 81 was not intended to apply to vertical agreements were firmly rejected by the ECJ in an early case.[4] The European Commission has stated that for markets to function effectively where vertical agreements exist:

2. Section II of the Commission's Guidelines on vertical restraints ("Guidelines"), 2000 OJ C 291/1.

3. A case before the UK Competition Appeal Tribunal in 2004 demonstrated that a supplier may be instrumental in implementing a cartel between retailers: *JJB Sports plc/Allsports Ltd v. Office of Fair Trading* [2004] CAT 17.

4. Cases 56 & 58/64, *Consten & Grundig v. Commission* [1966] ECR 299.

— there must be competition in the goods that are the subject of the agreement (intra-brand competition);
— there must be competition between those goods and the goods of competing manufacturers (inter-brand competition);
— such competition must exist across the common market (agreements which tend to divide the market along territorial lines are particularly likely to offend); and
— markets must be open to new, as well as existing, participants, so vertical arrangements must not have the effect of raising barriers to entry.[5]

Vertical agreements that appear not to comply with these requirements will be open to review under Article 81(1) and, if not exempted, will be prohibited.

4.1.3 When do agreements not infringe?

4.1.3.1 Agreements of minor importance/no effect on trade between Member States

Some vertical agreements may be outside the scope of EU competition law if they have no appreciable impact on competition[6] or no effect on trade between Member States.[7]

4.1.3.2 The Vertical Agreements Block Exemption[8]

The Commission has passed a Regulation granting a block exemption to vertical agreements that comply with particular requirements. Because of the effect of the *de minimis* Notice, this exemption will only be relevant for agreements where the contracting companies each have a market share exceeding 15 per cent. Regulation 2790/99 creates a presumption of legality for vertical agreements that fulfil the market share thresholds. However, there is no presumption of illegality for agreements falling outside the scope of the block exemption.[9]

The exemption contained in the Regulation applies only to vertical agreements. Vertical agreements are defined in Article 2(1) as:

"agreements or concerted practices entered into between two or more undertakings each of which operates, for the purposes of the agreement, at a different level of the production or distribution chain, and relating to the conditions under which the parties may purchase, sell or resell certain goods or services."

5. See Guidelines, para 107.
6. See 3.2.3.4 below.
7. Commission Notice: Guidelines on the effect on trade concept contained in Articles 81 and 82 of the Treaty; 2004 OJ C 101/87.
8. Regulation 2790/99.
9. Guidelines, para 62.

4.1.3 Application of Article 81

The exemption is available to agreements with more than two parties, but every party must operate at a different level of the supply chain.[10] Article 2(4) provides that it will not be open to direct competitors to disguise an agreement between them as being vertical in nature.[11] The exemption applies only to agreements between undertakings, so a contract with a final consumer would not be covered.

If a vertical agreement is not covered by the block exemption, then restrictions on competition in that agreement (and possibly the agreement as a whole) will be void and unenforceable unless the agreement satisfies the criteria for the application of the exception in Article 81(3) of the EC Treaty. These criteria can be difficult to satisfy and carrying out an analysis can be time-consuming and may not result in certainty.[12] For those reasons, companies often wish to be able to rely on the automatic protection of the block exemption.

4.1.3.2.1 Market share restrictions on the availability of the block exemption

The exemption only applies to agreements where the supplier's market share does not exceed 30 per cent of the relevant product market.[13] In the case of exclusive supply agreements, the relevant market share is that of the buyer, which again must be lower than 30 per cent.[14] Where there is a network of vertical agreements containing similar restraints covering more than 50 per cent of a particular market, the exemption may be declared to be inapplicable.[15]

The block exemption is not available to agreements dealing primarily with intellectual property rights.[16] However, where intellectual property rights are to be assigned to or used by the buyer and are merely ancillary, but directly related, to the main subject of the agreement, an agreement affecting them will not be excluded from the protection of the block exemption.[17]

10. Guidelines, para 93.

11. A non-reciprocal agreement between competing undertakings may be permissible if one of the conditions in Article 2(4) of the Regulation is met. "Competing suppliers" is defined in Article 1(a). See Guidelines, paras 26–27.

12. See Commission Notice: Guidelines on the application of Article 81(3) of the Treaty; 2004 OJ C 101/97.

13. Regulation 2790/99, Article 3(1); market share is "calculated on the basis of the market sales value of the contract goods or services and other goods or services sold by the supplier, which are regarded as interchangeable or substitutable by the buyer, by reason of the products' characteristics, their prices and their intended use" (Article 9). The threshold has some flexibility within the first two years in which it is exceeded (Article 9(2)).

14. *Ibid*, Article 3(2). Exclusive supply agreements are those where there is an obligation on the seller to sell to only one buyer in the EU (Article 1(c)).

15. *Ibid*, Recital 15.

16. *Ibid*, Article 2(3). The Technology Transfer Block Exemption (Regulation 772/2004) may apply instead.

17. See further Guidelines, paras 30–44.

4.1.3.2.2 Agreements with "hardcore" restrictions are not exempt

Article 4 of Regulation 2790/99 lists "hardcore" restrictions. An agreement including any hardcore provision cannot rely on the block exemption. Agreements containing such restrictions are generally unable to benefit from the exception under Article 81(3) of the EC Treaty. The hardcore restrictions are as follows:

(a) *Resale price maintenance ("RPM")*: this is the implementation of a fixed or minimum resale price (the fixing of a maximum price is permissible) and includes RPM by indirect means. Examples include agreements fixing distribution margins; making the award of rebates subject to observance of a particular price level; and threats of contract termination.[18] Such measures will be particularly likely to amount to hardcore restrictions if the supplier also reserves the right to monitor distributors for price-cutting behaviour.

(b) *Territorial restrictions on resale*: territorial restrictions may be achieved directly or indirectly, for example by measures aimed at inducing the distributor not to sell to customers in certain territories, including the withdrawal of bonuses or discounts, refusals to supply, reduction of supplied volumes, or threats of contract termination.[19] Systems monitoring the final destination of goods will mean that such measures are particularly likely to be viewed as restrictions. There are four exceptions to the general rule that territorial restrictions on resale will be hardcore:
   - restrictions on active sales (where the seller approaches the buyer)[20] into an exclusive territory, so long as the restriction does not also limit sales by the buyer's customers;
   - restrictions on any sales (whether active or passive) to end users by a buyer at the wholesale level of trade;
   - restrictions of sales (active or passive) to unauthorised distributors by members of a selective distribution system; and
   - restrictions preventing buyers of components that were supplied for the purpose of incorporation from reselling to customers who would use them to manufacture the same type of goods as those produced by the supplier.

   The same criteria apply to restrictions on sales to particular groups of customers.

(c) *Restrictions on resale by members of selective distribution systems*:[21] This applies to active or passive resales to end users and to cross-supplies between distributors. As a restriction on cross-supplies is hardcore,

18. Guidelines, para 47.
19. Guidelines, para 49.
20. Active sales are to be distinguished with passive sales where the buyer approaches the seller; see Guidelines, para 50.
21. "Selective distribution system" is defined in Article 1(d) of the Regulation 2790/99.

selective distribution cannot be combined with exclusive purchasing, although it may be combined with exclusive distribution.[22] Members of a selective distribution network must remain free to sell to and buy from each other, as well as to buy from the principal supplier. It is permissible to impose restrictions on where dealers in a selective distribution system may locate their premises.[23]

(d) *Limitations on the sale of components as spare parts*: This applies to sales to end users, repairers or service providers. Indirect restrictions may arise when the supplier of spare parts is prevented from supplying technical information and/or special equipment required for the use of spare parts.[24]

If any of the unacceptable restrictions listed in Article 4 is included in an agreement, the whole agreement will be taken outside the scope of the block exemption. This has the result that the whole agreement may be void unless the offending provision can be severed under national law, or unless, following analysis, it is possible to conclude that the exception in Article 81(3) applies even though the block exemption does not.[25]

4.1.3.2.3 Severable restrictions

Article 5 of the Regulation lists further restrictions which, although unacceptable, will merely be severed from the agreement as unenforceable. The agreement's other terms remain within the scope of the block exemption and therefore remain enforceable.[26] The Article 5 restrictions are as follows:

(a) *Non-compete obligations exceeding five years*: non-compete obligations ("NCOs") are defined in Article 1(b) of the block exemption Regulation as any direct or indirect obligation that requires the buyer to purchase from the supplier more than 80 per cent of the buyer's total purchases of the contract goods/services and competing products. The restriction will also apply if the NCO is indefinite in duration or tacitly renewable beyond five years. An exception applies in relation to businesses in tied premises such as pubs or garages.

(b) *Post-termination obligations*: this includes any direct or indirect post-termination obligation on the buyer not to manufacture, purchase, sell or resell goods after termination of the agreement. However, the provision will be acceptable if such restrictions lapse up to one year after the termination of the agreement and are limited:

— to goods which compete with the contract goods; and

22. Guidelines, para 55.
23. Guidelines, para 54.
24. Guidelines, para 56.
25. Article 81(2) of the EC Treaty. In the UK, severance is possible provided it can be achieved simply by striking out the offending sections without rewriting the agreement (the "blue pencil" test).
26. Guidelines, para 67.

— to the premises from which the buyer operated during the contract period; and
— so as to provide indispensable protection to know-how[27] transferred by the supplier to the buyer (know-how that has not yet entered the public domain can be protected indefinitely under the general law of confidentiality).

(c) *Sales of competing goods in a selective distribution system*: any direct or indirect obligation on members of a selective distribution system not to sell the brands of particular competing suppliers will not be permissible. However, a selective distribution system can be combined with a general non-compete provision.[28]

4.1.4 How to analyse vertical agreements: the Guidelines

4.1.4.1 Overview

The provisions of the block exemption are to be interpreted in the light of Guidelines issued by the Commission.[29] The Guidelines do not apply solely to agreements covered by the block exemption, but are of wider application. The Guidelines should assist companies in "mak[ing] their own assessment of vertical agreements under the EC competition rules",[30] as now required following the "modernisation" of competition law from 1 May 2004.[31] Since that date, it is no longer possible for parties to obtain an individual exemption or "comfort letter" from the Commission. Parties must now rely either on a block exemption or on their own assessment of whether an agreement will benefit from an exemption under Article 81(3) of the Treaty.

The Guidelines are critical to any assessment of a vertical arrangement. As well as explaining the matters that will govern the application and withdrawal of the block exemption, topics covered include:

— whether agreements are within the scope of Article 81 at all;
— guidance on definition of relevant markets and on calculating market share;
— how particular types of vertical restraint falling outside the scope of the block exemption will be dealt with by the Commission.

In considering the application of competition law to any vertical agreement, there are a number of stages to be considered:

27. Know-how must be "secret", "substantial" and "identified": Article 1(f) of the Regulation 2790/99.
28. Guidelines, para 61.
29. 2000 OJ C 291/1, [2000] 5 CMLR 1074.
30. Guidelines, para 3.
31. Regulation 1/2003, in force from 1 May 2004, replacing Regulation 17/62, 2003 OJ L 1/1; see also Commission Notice: Guidelines on the application of Article 81(3) of the Treaty, 2004 OJ C 101/97.

— consider the level of the market share:
  — if less than 15 per cent, consider the *de minimis* Notice;
  — if more than 15 per cent but less than 30 per cent, consider the application of the block exemption;
  — if more than 30 per cent, consider whether Article 81(3) of the Treaty applies.[32]
— if the agreement seems likely to fall within Article 81(1), consider how to analyse it and whether it is likely to satisfy Article 81(3).

4.1.4.2 Market definition and market share

4.1.4.2.1 Methodology and sources

It is necessary to consider the parties' market shares in order to assess the impact of many of the competition rules. In this context, the figure of 30 per cent (the level at which the block exemption ceases to be applicable) is probably the most significant.

To be able to establish the level of the parties' market shares, it is essential to have some idea of how markets are defined. A key source of guidance on this is the Commission's Notice on the definition of the relevant market for the purposes of community competition law.[33] The Notice should be read in tandem with section V of the Commission Guidelines discussing market definition and market share calculation issues in the context of vertical restraints.

4.1.4.2.2 Whose market share?

Article 3 of the Regulation provides explicitly that, in applying the block exemption thresholds, the relevant market share is that of the supplier, except in the case of exclusive supply agreements, where the 30 per cent threshold applies to the buyer. In a tripartite agreement, with all parties at different levels of the supply and distribution chain, the market shares of both the upstream parties taken together must not exceed 30 per cent if the agreement is to benefit from the block exemption.[34] For example, in an exclusive supply agreement between a supplier, a wholesaler and a retailer, the aggregate of the supplier and the wholesaler's share must be less than 30 per cent of the relevant product market.

When the agreement does not fall under the block exemption, similar principles will apply (generally the market share of the supplier will be key).[35]

32. The Guidelines provide assistance in relation to all of these issues. In assessing market share, the Guidelines must be read in conjunction with the Commission's other publications on this subject.
33. 1997 OJ C 372/5.
34. Guidelines, para 93.
35. Guidelines, para 96.

4.1.4.2.3 Market definition

For the purposes of calculating market share, Article 9(1) of the block exemption refers to goods or services "regarded by the buyer as interchangeable . . . " This is the standard approach to market definition, and can be tested by applying the SSNIP test: see 2.3.1 above.

4.1.4.3 Does Article 81(1) apply?

In addition to the general Article 81(1) considerations outlined in Chapter 3 above, paragraph 121 of the Guidelines sets out eight factors to be considered in establishing whether a vertical agreement brings about an appreciable restriction of competition under Article 81(1). They must be considered in combination.

(a) *Market position of the supplier*: the consequence of a high market share may be greater market power (although low entry barriers may alter this). Other advantages over competitors should be borne in mind, such as holding essential patents or occupying the best site.
(b) *Market position of competitors*: the consequence of stronger competition in greater numbers is to weaken the position of the supplier, and to make foreclosure of the market or a reduction in inter-brand competition less likely.
(c) *Market position of the buyer*: buying power (a buyer's strong market position) may increase the likelihood of anti-competitive effects, particularly in limited distribution arrangements (eg exclusive or selective distribution); in other circumstances, its effect may be different.
(d) *Barriers to entry*: entry barriers are measured by the extent to which companies already present in the market can increase their prices above the competitive level without new entrants being attracted to the market (becoming evident within one to two years). Entry barriers may result from many factors, including intellectual property rights, economies of scale, government intervention in the market (eg state aid, regulation), the existence of essential facilities, brand loyalty and "first-mover" advantage. However, while these factors are important, the Commission will give less weight to the exclusion of potential competition than to the effect upon actual competition.
(e) *Maturity of the market*: negative effects in vertical agreements are more likely in long-established markets than in young or dynamic markets.
(f) *Level of trade*: negative effects are less likely at an intermediate level of trade than at the level of the consumer.
(g) *Nature of the product*: considerations include the relative expense of the product, whether it is a one-off or repeat purchase, and whether products on the market are more or less heterogeneous. In general, when the product is more heterogeneous, less expensive and more

likely to be a one-off purchase, vertical restraints are more likely to have negative effects.[36]

(h) *Other factors*: these include whether there is a cumulative effect produced by a number of similar agreements, the duration of the agreements, the one-sidedness of obligations, whether the agreement takes place in a regulatory environment, pre-announced price changes, price discrimination and past collusive behaviour.

4.1.4.4 Policy framework: Part VI of the Guidelines

The final section of the Guidelines (comprising around half their total length) deals in detail with the most common types and combinations of vertical agreements in the context of particular types of agreement. As explained above, this section is most useful where an agreement contains restrictions of competition which bring it within Article 81(1) of the Treaty, but, because of the parties' market shares or the types of restriction contained in the agreement, will not be covered by the block exemption. The ability to identify whether or not agreements are likely to fulfil the requirements of Article 81(3) is important now that parties need to "self-assess" their agreements in order to identify the competition law issues outside the scope of a block exemption.

Rather than dealing with each of the cumulative criteria of Article 81(3),[37] the Guidelines provide an overview of the likely positive and negative effects of vertical agreements, give some general rules which apply to their evaluation, and then go on to deal in more detail with some specific types of agreement. An outline of each of these sections is provided below.

4.1.4.4.1 Positive and negative effects of vertical agreements

Article 81(3) is concerned above all with ensuring that the positive effects of vertical agreements outweigh the negative. The Guidelines outline four key negative effects on the market that may result from vertical agreements, and which EU competition law aims to prevent (and, therefore, which are likely to preclude an agreement from fulfilling the requirements of Article 81(3)):

- — foreclosure of other suppliers or buyers by raising barriers to entry;
- — reduction of inter-brand competition by making collusion easier between suppliers or buyers (resulting in conscious parallel behaviour);
- — reduction of intra-brand competition between distributors of the same brand; and
- — creation of obstacles to market integration, including in particular limitations on consumers' freedom to buy goods or services in any Member State they may choose.[38]

36. Guidelines, para 132.

37. The approach taken in the Commission Guidelines on the application of Article 81(3); 2004 OJ C 101/97. See 3.3 above.

38. Guidelines, para 103.

By contrast, vertical agreements may also have a number of positive effects. Typical examples include the following:

— promotion of non-price competition and improved quality of service, both of which may assist entry to a new market, or make an existing market more efficient;[39]
— achieving economies of scale;[40]
— solving the problem of "free-riding", whereby a distributor/supplier seeks to benefit from the promotional efforts of another distributor/supplier;[41]
— achieving quality standardisation.[42]

4.1.4.4.2 General rules for evaluation of agreements

These may usefully be summarised as set of questions that should be applied to the agreement under assessment:[43]

— Is there insufficient inter-brand competition on the market? This is likely if the supplier has a degree of market power.
— Do the vertical agreements reduce inter-brand or intra-brand competition? The former are generally more harmful.
— If a limited distribution group (eg exclusive or selective distribution), are the agreements likely to harm or foreclose more efficient or innovative distributors?
— Does the agreement provide for exclusive dealing? Exclusive dealing arrangements are generally worse for competition than non-exclusive.
— Does the agreement concern branded goods? Vertical agreements in relation to branded goods are generally worse for competition than for non-branded goods.
— Do the agreements concern intermediate or end products? Vertical agreements are generally less harmful when they concern intermediate, rather than final, goods or services.
— Is there a combination of vertical agreements? This is generally more harmful than when vertical restraints are used singly.
— Do several suppliers and their buyers organise their trade in a similar way? There may be an aggravating cumulative effect if this is the case.
— Is the vertical agreement linked to the transfer of know-how? The more closely it is so linked, the more justified it is likely to be.
— Is the vertical agreement linked to relationship-specific investments? The closer the link, the more justified the agreement is likely to be.

39. Guidelines, paras 115 and 116(2).
40. Guidelines, para 116(6).
41. Guidelines, para 116(1).
42. Guidelines, para 116(8).
43. Guidelines, para 119.

— Does the agreement concern a new product, or the sale of a product for the first time on a different geographic market? Vertical agreements linked to opening up new product or geographic markets do not generally affect competition.
— What is the term of the agreement? Vertical agreements that have limited duration (provided the agreement does not automatically renew itself without the specific consent of both parties) are much less likely to affect competition than those of longer duration.[44]
— Are there any other less restrictive terms that could be substituted for the vertical restraints in the agreement? The Guidelines note that the same effect can often be achieved in more than one way. For example, economies of scale in distribution can be achieved by using exclusive distribution, selective distribution, "quantity forcing" or exclusive purchasing. Depending on the circumstances, some of these may affect competition less than others.[45]

These general rules demonstrate the broad approach that will be taken by competition authorities if required to examine an agreement containing vertical restraints, and should also be borne in mind when advising on, or considering the contents of, agreements.

4.1.4.4.3 Specific types of restraint

The Guidelines divide vertical restraints into four broad categories:[46]

— *Single branding group*: this is where a buyer is required to purchase a particular product from only one supplier. Non-compete restrictions, tying and obligations requiring the purchaser to acquire a minimum number of products from the supplier ("quantity forcing") are examples of restraints within this group.
— *Limited distribution group*: examples include exclusive or selective distribution. Other terms that fall into this group include quantity forcing on the supplier.
— *Resale price maintenance group*: this is where the buyer is obliged to resell at a certain price. This includes obligations as to maximum, recommended, fixed or minimum prices.
— *Market partitioning group*: where a buyer is restricted as to where it sources or resells. Exclusive purchasing contracts also fall within this group.

Each of these in turn may entail a number of different types of restraint. Many agreements will have elements from more than one of the groups, so it is not generally necessary to determine which group each restraint falls under.

44. Guidelines, para 117.
45. Guidelines, para 118.
46. Guidelines, paras 104–114.

Indeed, the terminology in this part of the Guidelines does not have any legal force. However, the section provides useful information as to the sorts of restraints that may affect competition, and the ways in which they do this; and the terminology will often be encountered in discussions of the issues.

The Guidelines conclude with a more detailed analysis of certain specific types of agreement. The types of agreement dealt with are: single branding,[47] exclusive distribution,[48] exclusive customer allocation,[49] selective distribution,[50] franchising,[51] exclusive supply,[52] tying[53] and recommended/maximum resale prices.[54] The Guidelines state that other vertical restraints and combinations will be treated according to the same principles, and "with the same emphasis on the effect on the market".[55]

4.1.5 Particular issues

There are a few situations in this area that raise particular difficulties or problems, and which are worth considering in more detail.

4.1.5.1 Agency or distribution?

Competition law draws a distinction between agency and distribution agreements. Whereas an agent and its principal are treated as forming a single economic entity, a distributor and its supplier are independent contracting parties. This distinction is crucial, since it affects whether or not Article 81 applies to the arrangement in question. Given the nature of agency, it will almost inevitably entail the principal setting the prices that the agent will charge to customers. If Article 81(1) is found to apply, this will be a hardcore restriction which would not be capable of exemption under the block exemption or otherwise.[56] The price-setting provision would then be severed, or, if found to be fundamental to the agreement, the whole agreement would become void and unenforceable.

The Guidelines define an agency agreement as covering:

> "the situation in which a legal or physical person (the agent) is vested with the power to negotiate and/or conclude contracts on behalf of another person (the principal), either in the agent's own name or in the name of the principal, for (i) the purchase of

47. Guidelines, paras 138–160.
48. Guidelines, paras 161–177.
49. Guidelines, paras 178–183.
50. Guidelines, paras 184–198.
51. Guidelines, paras 199–201.
52. Guidelines, paras 202–214.
53. Guidelines, paras 215–224.
54. Guidelines, paras 225–228.
55. Guidelines, para 229.
56. Guidelines, para 48: "where an agency agreement falls within Article 81(1) . . . , an obligation preventing or restricting the agent from sharing his commission . . . with the customer would be a hardcore restriction under Article 4(a) of the Block Exemption Regulation."

goods or services by the principal, or (ii) the sale of goods or services supplied by the principal."[57]

The Guidelines distinguish between "genuine" and "non-genuine" agency agreements.[58] Genuine agency agreements generally fall outside the scope of Article 81(1), whereas non-genuine agency agreements may be caught by the legislation relating to anti-competitive agreements. The key characteristic of a genuine agency agreement is that the agent does not bear the financial or commercial risk in relation to the contracts negotiated on behalf of the principal. Such "financial or commercial risk" can be one of two types:[59]

- — risks related to the contracts concluded on behalf of the principal (eg financing of stocks);
- — risks related to market-specific investments, which are those specifically required for the type of activity for which the agent has been appointed.

However, risk must be assessed on a case-by-case basis and the relationship will be analysed on the basis of its substance, rather than its form. A number of further characteristics of genuine agency agreements are set out in the Guidelines:[60]

- — the contract goods do not vest in the agent;
- — the agent does not contribute to costs of the supply/purchase of the contract goods (including cost of transporting the goods);
- — the agent is not required to invest in sales promotion (directly or indirectly);
- — the agent does not maintain stocks of contract goods at his own cost and risk, and must be able to return unsold goods to the principal without charge (unless the agent is at fault);
- — the agent is not obliged to create or operate an after-sales, repair or warranty service (unless fully reimbursed);
- — the agent does not incur liability towards third parties for defective products or take responsibility for customers' non-performance (unless the agent is at fault), although a loss of commission clause can be imposed.

The list given in the Guidelines is not exhaustive. Where the agent incurs one of the listed risks or costs (or an equivalent exposure), Article 81(1) may apply, as with any other vertical agreement.[61] If Article 81(1) does apply, the agreement may nevertheless be able to benefit from the block exemption, provided it does not contain any hardcore restrictions. However, a typical agency

57. Guidelines, para 12.
58. Guidelines, para 13.
59. Guidelines, para 14.
60. Guidelines, para 16.
61. Guidelines, para 17.

agreement contains pricing provisions that would be prohibited under Article 81(1).

It appears that the Commission believes that even genuine agency agreements may, in certain circumstances, infringe Article 81(1). Paragraph 19 of the Guidelines states that non-compete provisions may have an effect on inter-brand competition, and could infringe Article 81(1) if they lead to foreclosure of the relevant market.[62] Conversely, exclusive agency agreements generally affect only intra-brand competition, so are unlikely to lead to anti-competitive effects.

Paragraph 20 of the Guidelines contains the proviso that an agency agreement may fall within the scope of Article 81(1), even if the principal bears all the risks, where the agreement "facilitates collusion". Two examples are given:

- where a number of principals using the same agents collaborate to exclude other principals from using those agents; or
- where a number of principals use the same agents to collude on marketing strategy or to exchange sensitive market information.

Such collusion would give these principals an advantage over other existing or future participants on the market, and could affect inter-brand competition. These issues are aspects of horizontal collaboration, where the agent is used as a conduit.

4.1.5.2 Internet sales: active or passive?

The distinction made in the block exemption between "active" and "passive" selling raises the question as to how sales made using the internet are treated.

In general, "active" sales are defined as those made through the seller's approaches to particular customers or customer groups, whereas "passive" sales are made in response to unsolicited requests.[63] The Guidelines state that the internet is not generally to be considered a means of active selling.[64] Thus, an agreement imposing restrictions on a party selling goods via a website, for example by a supplier who wishes to prevent its distributor from selling into another distributor's exclusive territory, will amount to a ban on passive sales, and will be incompatible with the requirements of the block exemption. This approach applies regardless of the language used on the website (so, for example, a Spanish distributor who sets up an English-language website is still not deemed to be engaging in active selling in the UK).

However, the existence of a website may in fact amount to active selling "if it is used to target customers primarily inside the territory of another exclusive

62. See also Guidelines, paras 138–160.
63. Guidelines, para 50.
64. Guidelines, para 51.

distributor, for instance with the use of banners or links in pages of providers specifically available to these exclusively allocated customers". This raises the question of whether a website written in a particular language could in fact constitute a method of targeting specific customers in another exclusive distributor's territory. If, for example, the Spanish distributor referred to above had set up his internet site not in English but in Greek, and the distribution network included an exclusive Greek supplier, could this be said to be a form of active selling?

This in turn raises the further question of whether a supplier could seek to prevent such activities in its distribution agreements without infringing Article 81(1). The Guidelines in fact state that an outright ban on internet (or catalogue) selling is possible, provided there is objective justification. This seems to refer primarily to qualitative grounds, but it is arguable that it could be construed more widely. An example is the case of B&W Loudspeakers which notified its distribution agreements across Europe to the Commission in 2000. The agreements were refused an individual exemption as they contained a number of hardcore restrictions, including an outright prohibition on distance sales, including those made over the internet. In June 2002, the Commission issued a comfort letter confirming that B&W's agreements could benefit from the block exemption, having deleted the most serious hardcore violations. With regard to the internet sales, the Commission was satisfied by B&W's amended terms, B&W could refuse to permit distance/internet sales by way of written notice and on criteria concerning the need to maintain the image and reputation of the B&W brand. The criteria had to be applied in a non-discriminatory manner, and had to be comparable to similar restrictions on sales from retail outlets.

4.1.5.3 Relationship with Article 82

Where an undertaking has a dominant position in a market, its conduct in that market must not amount to an abuse. Many of the adverse effects of anti-competitive agreements are also possible to achieve through unilateral action by a dominant company (or, more rarely, through joint dominance of two or more undertakings).

For example, it would be contrary to Article 81(1) for a supplier to agree with its wholesaler customers that they will not resell the contract goods outside a particular territory. It might similarly be contrary to Article 82 if a supplier adopted a unilateral policy discriminating against those customers who engaged in reselling outside that territory, for example by refusing to continue to supply. Article 82, rather than Article 81, could also become relevant if a highly vertically integrated organisation undertook all its distribution via its own subsidiaries. Any agreement between the parent company and its subsidiaries would fall outside the scope of Article 81, as it would not be an "agreement between undertakings", but could well be subject to Article 82.

4.1.6 The treatment of vertical agreements in the UK

UK competition law is designed to mirror Articles 81 and 82. The Competition Act 1998 incorporates equivalent provisions into UK law, with the proviso that there must be an effect on trade within the UK.

In the past, vertical agreements have been treated more leniently in the UK than at a European level, since they have benefited from a blanket exclusion order regardless of the market share of the parties. However, this exclusion ceased to apply on 1 May 2005, with the effect that vertical agreements are now fully subject to competition law at a domestic, as well as European, level. The UK Office of Fair Trading ("OFT") has published guidance on the treatment of vertical agreements under the Competition Act, which is available online.[65]

4.2. COMPETITION LAW AND INTELLECTUAL PROPERTY RIGHTS—LICENCE AND SETTLEMENT AGREEMENTS AND THE APPLICATION OF ARTICLE 81

4.2.1 Introduction

Competition law and intellectual property ("IP") law are closely linked. While intellectual property law grants a limited monopoly—for example to inventors, enabling them to control the production and supply of goods incorporating their technology—competition law seeks to ensure free competition and a minimum of restraint on commercial activity. Though both competition law and intellectual property law have similar policy objectives of encouraging technical development and consumer welfare, they approach this goal in different ways.

There is thus an inherent tension between intellectual property law and competition law: one seeks to control, while the other seeks to ensure, free competition. This means that developments in competition law will be of interest to all of those advising on the acquisition, protection and disposal (whether through licensing or assignment) of intellectual property rights.

4.2.2 Licensing of IP (Article 81)

4.2.2.1 What is IP?

Intellectual property consists of a series of legal rights. IP rights range from patents, which may protect the active ingredient of a particular drug, to copyright, which may protect a software program or a piece of music.

65. http://www.oft.gov.uk/Business/Legal-Powers/Modernisation/publications.htm.

4.2.2 Application of Article 81

IP rights are essentially negative in nature. They give their owner a right to prevent others from doing certain things. Some IP rights, such as patents and trade marks, are registrable, requiring compliance with some form of registration procedure, whereas others come into existence automatically when a piece of work is produced, and require no formal procedure for their creation. Both copyright and design rights are non-registrable.

Certain IP rights, such as patents, give their owner "monopoly" rights that can be infringed and subsequently enforced without the need for the owner to show that any copying has occurred. On the other hand, copyright infringement can occur only where there is evidence of actual copying of the copyright owner's work.

States provide protection for IP rights in order to encourage technological development and artistic creation. Without monopoly rights and the protection afforded by IP rights, companies would not be willing to invest time and money in research, development or creation, as the fruits of their endeavours would simply be replicated by third parties free of charge. All IP rights are territorial. This means that a right in the UK does not affect activities that take place wholly outside of the UK. Parallel IP rights in different territories may be acquired by, or transferred to and owned by, different parties.

4.2.2.2 How is IP exploited?

Intellectual "property" is intangible, but, in common with any other item of property, it can be exploited in a variety of different ways. Clearly, the owner of IP rights may choose to exploit those rights itself, manufacturing and selling products protected by the relevant rights and enforcing its rights where necessary. In these circumstances, Article 81(1) will not be relevant: the mere exercise of IP rights does not infringe Article 81(1) and there is no agreement between undertakings relevant to the exploitation to which Article 81(1) could apply.

However, owners of IP rights will often involve third parties in connection with exploitation, whether by way of the outright disposal of the IP rights, such as by way of an assignment in return for a payment, or by way of the owner permitting others to exploit the rights under a licence.

An outright assignment of IP rights will generally not be caught by Article 81(1) as it amounts to the substitution of one rights-owner for another. However, if the assignment is more than a straightforward transfer and involves ongoing contractual obligations placed on the parties, it can fall within Article 81(1), and the principles that have been developed in connection with licences of IP rights will apply.

Most agreements relating to the exploitation of IP include licences of one sort or another, although they can occur in a variety of contexts—including, for example, research and development collaboration, mergers and joint ventures, settlement agreements and "simple" technology transfer arrangements. The principles that apply to technology transfer (or licence) arrangements will generally apply to other IP agreements, so it is on such arrangements that this paper now focuses.

4.2.2.3 Restrictive clauses in licence agreements

The ECJ and the Commission have adopted a favourable approach to "pure" licences, where a licensee is granted the right to exploit the licensor's intellectual property in return for a royalty payment but without being subject to any controls or restrictions. Any such licence should clearly increase competition by introducing additional entrants to the market and increasing intra-brand competition. However, licensors will not normally grant a "pure" licence, but will want to place some contractual restraints on the licensee's rights of exploitation.

Many clauses commonly found in licence agreements have been held by the ECJ and/or the Commission to be likely to breach Article 81(1). These include:

— the grant of territorial exclusivity;
— export bans;
— tying and bundling of products or licences, where the licensor makes the grant of a licence to use one particular IP right conditional upon the licensee also paying for a licence to use a separate IP right;
— restrictions on prices or customers; and
— non-compete clauses.

4.2.2.3.1 Exclusivity

Exclusivity is, of course, a common feature of many licences. It is the EU competition authorities' view that exclusive arrangements lead to the partitioning of the internal market and may restrict competition, particularly where a number of exclusive licences are granted to different licensees in different Member States. The grant of an exclusive licence by a licensor inevitably prevents that licensor from licensing a third party in the territory or from exploiting the technology itself in that territory. On the other hand, licensees are often unwilling to accept a licence on anything other than an exclusive basis.

The ECJ has seemed more willing than the Commission to accept that, in certain circumstances, the grant of an exclusive licence does not breach Article 81(1). In the Maize Seeds case,[66] a case dealing with plant breeders' rights, the ECJ found that the contractual relationship between a licensor and a licensee was not anti-competitive (in the particular circumstances of the case) where the only restriction accepted by the parties was the licensor's undertaking not to grant other licences in respect of the same territory and not itself to compete with the licensee in that territory. The Commission has indicated

66. Case 258/78, *Nungesser v. Commission* [1982] ECR 2015.

that, in its view, the judgment in the Maize Seeds case is confined to exclusive patent or know-how licences that are:

"concerned with the introduction and protection of a new technology in the licensed territory, by reason of the scale of the research which has been undertaken, of the increase in the level of competition, in particular inter-brand competition, and of the competitiveness of the undertakings concerned resulting from the dissemination of innovation within the Community."[67]

The ECJ has also held that certain exclusive licences of copyright do not infringe Article 81(1). In *Coditel v. Ciné Vog Films*[68] the ECJ held that the grant of an exclusive right to broadcast a film did not in itself infringe Article 81(1). It held that, as a film is capable of infinite repetition, and as royalties are paid to the licensor by reference to the number of performances of the film, the exclusivity was required to protect the licensee.

The Commission has not, however, sought to extend the ECJ's analysis and has adopted the position that exclusive licences almost certainly restrict competition, and infringe Article 81(1). Advisers to companies entering into such licences therefore need to exercise caution.

4.2.2.3.2 Export bans

Often, exclusive licensees will seek additional contractual protection in relation to their exclusive territory, and the licensor may seek to impose restrictions on licensees from supplying licensed products outside their territory. An exclusive licensee will be investing considerable sums of money and will want its market to be protected from sales by licensees based outside its territory.

The approach of the Commission and the European courts has been to distinguish between direct sales bans that prevent active sales by one licensee into the territory of another, and provisions that restrict passive sales, ie the meeting of unsolicited orders received by a licensee from customers based outside of that licensee's territory.

In the context of exclusive licences, bans on active sales are seen as permissible. If exclusive licensees are able to sell directly into each other's territories, the very nature of the exclusive sales licence would be undermined. However, bans on "passive sales" are seen as being more restrictive of competition and are, therefore, not generally acceptable.[69]

Export bans are less common in non-exclusive licences, as licensees already face domestic competition and, therefore, will be less inclined to seek territorial protection from the licensor. For this reason, in the context of a non-

67. Recital 10, Technology Transfer Regulation, 240/96. Regulation 240/96 was repealed with effect from 1 May 2004 and replaced by the new Technology Transfer Block Exemption Regulation, 772/2004 2004 OJ L 123, p 11. Although this Regulation 240/96 is no longer in force, the statement remains relevant. See 4.2.3 below.

68. Case 262/81, [1982] ECR 3381.

69. The Commission's Guidelines that accompany the Vertical Agreements Block Exemption consider the distinction between active and passive sales. The distinction is dealt with in the same way in the context of technology licences. See Guidelines, paras 50–51.

exclusive licence the competition authorities tend to view any form of export ban as being unnecessarily restrictive and capable of leading to artificial partitioning of the market.

4.2.2.3.3 Tying and bundling

A licensor may seek to oblige a licensee to acquire unprotected products or materials from the licensor or an appointed supplier for use in connection with the exploitation of the licensed IP rights. These so-called "tie-in" clauses can give rise to competition concerns where the effect is to close rival suppliers out of the market. However, where obligations are imposed to ensure a technically satisfactory exploitation of a licensed invention, or to maintain the consistent reputation and goodwill of a trade mark owner, they will not infringe Article 81(1).

4.2.2.3.4 Restrictions on prices or customers

So-called "downstream" restrictions may also fall within Article 81(1). These are provisions which restrict a licensee in connection with the onward sale of licensed products. Downstream pricing restrictions may amount to resale price maintenance, which the Commission and ECJ regard as being in breach of Article 81(1). Restrictions as to the customers to which a licensee can sell may also infringe Article 81(1), particularly where the licensor and licensee are competitors.

Obligations on a licensee to exploit the licensed IP rights in only certain fields of use or product markets are commonly included in licence agreements and will not usually infringe Article 81(1). An example could be a technology licence granted to enable the licensee to manufacture drugs to treat a particular condition. However, it is important to distinguish field-of-use restrictions from customer restrictions, which are not generally permissible. The field of use must be defined objectively by reference to meaningful technical characteristics of the licensed product.

4.2.2.3.5 Non-compete obligations

It is not uncommon for a licensor to seek to prevent competition between itself and its licensees, or between individual licensees themselves. The control of competition will often be addressed by the grant of exclusivity and export bans, as described above. However, in addition, a licensor may seek to impose a contractual ban on competition on its licensees. Such a blanket restriction will infringe Article 81(1), although the withdrawal of certain benefits in the event that a licensee starts to compete (in particular, exclusivity) will be permissible.

4.2.2.4 Application of Article 81 to different types of IP licence

Many licences of IP rights will contain similar provisions and restrictions even though they relate to different types of intellectual property. As a result, much of the analysis of the European courts and Commission in relation to certain IP rights can be applied to others.

The authorities have tended to treat licences of patents and licences of know-how in a very similar manner, viewing these as licences of technology. Originally covered by two separate block exemptions, patent and know-how licences are now both covered by the Technology Transfer Block Exemption (see 4.2.3 below).

Trade marks perform a fundamentally different role from other types of IP right in that they are an indication of origin and can continue in force indefinitely, provided the trade mark registration is renewed by its owner. There is no block exemption relating to trade mark licensing (although arrangements that include ancillary trade mark licences, such as distribution or franchise agreements, may be covered by the Vertical Agreements Block Exemption). However, when applying Article 81(1), in general, similar principles can be applied for trade marks as for other IP rights.

There are fewer authorities relating to the application of Article 81(1) to copyright and design right licences as compared to those relating to patents or trade marks. Licences of software copyright and designs are now covered by the Technology Transfer Block Exemption. However, there is no block exemption relating to licences of other types of copyright. Similar principles can be applied for non-software copyright as have been established for other types of IP rights.

The lack of block exemptions for trade marks and certain copyrights has meant that, when drafting licences relating to these rights, parties need to be particularly careful not to fall within Article 81 and will often look to the Technology Transfer Block Exemption to assist in analysing which contractual provisions may prove to be problematic.

4.2.3 The Technology Transfer Block Exemption

The parties to any licence of intellectual property rights likely to apply in the EU should consider whether the licence contains any clauses that may restrict competition and infringe Article 81(1). As indicated above, many licences will contain such clauses. Subject only to the question of whether or not the agreement is likely to result in an "appreciable" effect on competition, such agreements will require exemption if they are not to be prohibited by Article 81(1) and be enforceable in their entirety. For most would-be licensees and licensors, the first port of call is to consider whether a block exemption may be applicable.

Block exemptions have been adopted to remove certain categories of standard commercial agreement from the scope of the prohibition in Article 81(1) where these agreements are, on balance, pro-competitive. An agreement that falls within the scope of a block exemption is not prohibited by Article 81(1). The block exemption that is most likely to apply to an IP licence is the Technology Transfer Block Exemption. In relation to agreements permitting the sale of products subject to IP rights, the Vertical Agreements Block Exemption may also be relevant.

A detailed overview of the Technology Transfer Block Exemption (Regulation 772/2004)[70] and the application of the Vertical Agreements Block Exemption (Regulation 2790/99)[71], to IP provisions is set out below. Note also that there are other block exemption Regulations that may be relevant to intellectual property: these include the Specialisation Block Exemption (Regulation 2658/2000)[72] and the Research and Development Block Exemption (Regulation 2659/2000) (see 4.3.5.2.5 and 4.3.5.1.4 below, respectively).[73]

4.2.3.1 Overview of the Technology Transfer Block Exemption

The Technology Transfer Block Exemption Regulation applies to certain categories of intellectual property licence. This regulation came into effect on 1 May 2004 and replaced the Technology Transfer Regulation (240/96).

The Technology Transfer Block Exemption covers many intellectual property licences. If an intellectual property licence contains anti-competitive restrictions, the parties should ascertain whether the Technology Transfer Block Exemption applies. If it does, the parties may proceed with their agreement. If the licence falls outside the scope of the block exemption, the parties must either assess the terms of the licence under Article 81(3) themselves to determine if it can benefit from the exemption, or attempt to redraft the licence, either to bring it within the scope of an exemption or to remove the restrictions.

The Regulation applies to:

- The licensing of own patents, including designs and utility models (pure patent licensing agreements);
- The licensing of non-patented technical information (pure know-how licensing agreements);
- The licensing of software copyright;
- Combined patent, know-how and/or software copyright licensing (mixed agreements).

The Technology Transfer Block Exemption applies only to bipartite agreements and to the effect these agreements will have within the EU. Where licensing agreements contain obligations relating to both non-Member States and territories within the EU, the presence of the former does not prevent the Regulation applying to territories within the EU. When undertakings in non-member countries have licensing agreements that have effects within the EU, such agreements will still be covered by the Regulation.

70. 2004 OJ L 123/11.
71. 1999 OJ L 336/21.
72. 1985 OJ L 153/1.
73. 1985 OJ L 153/5.

4.2.3 Application of Article 81

The Regulation will apply only where the licensee itself manufactures the licensed products or has them manufactured for its account. Where the licensed product is a service, the licensee must provide the service itself or have the service provided for its account. In all cases the licence agreement must permit "the production of contract products".[74] Agreements solely for the purpose of sale are not covered by the Regulation.

If the block exemption applies, then the agreement will be exempt for as long as the underlying IP rights remain in force, provided that the qualifying criteria for the applicability of the block exemption remain satisfied. If the IP in question is know-how, the exemption endures while the know-how remains secret.

The provisions of the Technology Transfer Block Exemption are also useful in assessing which clauses the Commission will permit in licence agreements to which the block exemption does not apply, for example pure non-software copyright or trade mark licences, as well as licences that fall outside the market share thresholds of the block exemption.

The Commission has also published Guidelines on the application of the new Technology Transfer Block Exemption and on the general approach to licences under the EU competition regime.[75] These contain detailed (if sometimes complex) discussion of the new provisions and examples of their application.

Understanding the Regulation requires the application of several key concepts:

- *Different treatments for licence agreements concluded between competitors and those between non-competitors.*[76] The general view of the Commission is that agreements between competitors are more likely to have serious anti-competitive effects that those between non-competitors, and there is therefore a stricter regime governing the exemption of agreements between competing undertakings.
- *Market share threshold levels* have been introduced. The block exemption will cover agreements between competitors provided that their combined market shares do not exceed 20 per cent, and those between non-competitors provided that neither party's market share exceeds 30 per cent. If these threshold levels are exceeded, the agreement in question is not automatically illegal, but must be assessed by the parties to determine if it may benefit from the Article 81(3) exception.
- *Agreements containing hardcore restrictions will not be exempted* by the Technology Transfer Block Exemption. There are two lists of hardcore restrictions, with a stricter regime in place for agreements

74. Regulation 772/2004, Article 2.

75. Guidelines on the application of Article 81 of the EC Treaty to technology transfer agreements, 2004 OJ C 101/2 ("Guidelines").

76. The Guidelines provide assistance in assessing whether entities are actual or potential competitors by reference to their activities in the relevant product and technology markets.

between competitors and a shorter list of hardcore terms for agreements between non-competitors.

— The Regulation also identifies a number of "*excluded restrictions*". These are terms that are not granted automatic exemption from the Article 81(1) prohibition, but are not presumed to be illegal either. Importantly, they do not prevent the rest of the agreement in which they are found from remaining within the safe harbour afforded by the Technology Transfer Block Exemption. They include provisions commonly found in technology transfer agreements that may have positive market effects, such as back-licensing or assignment of improvements, no-challenge clauses and (for agreements between non-competitors) non-compete obligations.

4.2.3.2 The terms of the Technology Transfer Block Exemption

Details of the Technology Transfer Block Exemption are set out below.

4.2.3.2.1 Article 2: the block exemption

This is the operative provision of the block exemption. It provides that any bipartite technology transfer agreement permitting the production of contract products that is subject to Article 81(1) of the EC Treaty is exempt, provided the criteria relating to market share are satisfied and the agreement contains no hardcore terms. Therefore, provided these criteria are satisfied, the terms of the agreement need not be considered further from a competition law perspective—the agreement is deemed to benefit from the exception in Article 81(3).

4.2.3.2.2 Article 3: the market share thresholds

There are different standards for those agreements between competitors and those between non-competitors. For agreements between competitors, the parties' combined market shares must not exceed 20 per cent. For non-competitor agreements, neither party may have a market share over 30 per cent.

In assessing whether the parties are competitors or non-competitors, it is necessary to ask whether, in the absence of the agreement, the parties would have been actual or potential competitors in any relevant market affected by the agreement.[77] If this is the case, the parties are considered competitors; otherwise they are non-competitors.

Competitors are defined as undertakings that compete on the relevant technology market (ie they license competing technologies) and/or the relevant product market and geographic market where the contract products are sold. They are considered actual competitors where, without infringing each

77. See Article 1(j) and Guidelines, paras 26–33.

other's IP rights, they are active on either the same technology or product market.

They are potential competitors where, again without infringing each other's IP rights, it is possible for one of the parties to enter the relevant market within a short period, usually between one and two years. For example, if the parties are presently active on different geographical/product markets, they will be considered potential competitors. In assessing potential competition, the Guidelines state that it is only necessary to look at the product market and not the technology market for the purposes of applying the block exemption.[78]

The Guidelines provide two examples of situations in which the parties will be considered non-competitors.[79] The first deals with IP "blocking positions" —most likely to arise because of patent rights—and states that the parties are considered to be non-competitors if their technologies are in a one-way or two-way blocking position.[80] A "one-way" blocking position exists where a technology cannot be exploited without infringing another technology. A "two-way" or "mutual" blocking position exists where neither of the parties can exploit its technology without a licence or waiver from the other party. The second example concerns so-called "drastic innovations". The Guidelines state that the parties will not be considered competitors where the technology being licensed represents such a drastic innovation over the existing technology of one of the parties that it will be sufficient to render that technology obsolete or uncompetitive.[81]

The definition of the product market that must be considered when assessing an agreement is considered to include products that are regarded by purchasers as interchangeable with, or substitutable for, the contract products that incorporate the technology that underlies the agreement. Factors to be considered when identifying substitutable products include the products' characteristics, prices and intended uses.

The technology market is defined to include the licensed technology and technologies that are regarded by licensees as substitutable for the licensed technology. Factors to be considered include the technologies' characteristics, royalties and intended uses. The approach to definition is the same in both product and technology markets: first, the other products/technologies to which the purchasers/licensees could switch in response to a small increase in the price of the licensed product/technology. Alternatively, the technology

78. Guidelines, paras 30 and 66.

79. Guidelines, paras 32–33.

80. The Commission states that it will rely on "objective factors" to determine whether a blocking position exists. Where the parties have a common interest in claiming the existence of a blocking position—ie because this will allow them to be considered as non-competitors—the Commission states that it will require "particularly convincing evidence" such as court decisions, including injunctions, and opinions of independent experts to show the existence of such a position. Guidelines, para 32.

81. The Guidelines mention CD technology replacing the LP as an example of a "drastic innovation." Presumably DVDs replacing VHS video tapes and digital imaging replacing celluloid film photographs are other potential examples.

market may be assessed by reference to the market for products incorporating the licensed technology.[82]

Market shares are calculated on the basis of market sales value data for the preceding calendar year.[83] This means that a new technology that has not generated any sales will initially be assigned a zero market share. Where market share information is not available, estimates can be based on other reliable market information, including sales volumes.[84]

4.2.3.2.3 Article 4: the hardcore restrictions

The so-called "hardcore" restrictions are divided into two lists. One relates to agreements between competitors and one to agreements between non-competitors.[85] The inclusion of any of these restrictions, with certain limited exceptions, prevents the entire agreement from benefiting from the Technology Transfer Block Exemption.

For agreements between competitors, there are four classes of hardcore restriction:

(a) *Price fixing*: this includes the fixing of maximum or recommended, as well as minimum, retail prices.

(b) *Output restriction*: there are two exceptions to this hardcore restriction. If the competing parties license non-competing technology, it is permissible to impose an output restriction on the licensee. Even where the agreement concerns competing technology, it is permissible to restrict output, but only if there are at least two licensees and only one of them is being restricted in its output.[86]

(c) *Allocation of markets/customers*: certain types of restriction that could constitute market-sharing are specifically excepted from the list of hardcore restrictions. These include field-of-use restrictions, sales restrictions, captive use restrictions and alternative source of supply situations.

Field-of-use restrictions are commonly included in technology licences because technology can often be used to make different products or can sometimes be incorporated into products belonging to different product markets.[87] Such restrictions usually limit the exploitation of the licensed technology by the licensee to one or more

82. See Guidelines, paras 19–25.

83. See Article 8(1)(a)–(b) and Guidelines, para 72.

84. *Ibid.*

85. See, respectively, Articles 4(1) and 4(2).

86. Article 4(1)(b). These exceptions to the rule against restricting output follow the distinction between "reciprocal" and "non-reciprocal" agreements. Reciprocal agreements are cross-licensing arrangements between competitors in which the licensed technologies are competing or can be used to generate competing products. Non-reciprocal agreements are either those in which only one party licenses its technology, or where there is a cross-licence but the cross-licensed technologies are non-competing. See Articles 1(c) and (d) and Guidelines, para 74.

87. The Guidelines use as an example a new moulding technology which can be used to make plastic bottles and plastic glasses. See para 179.

particular fields of use without limiting the licensor's ability to exploit the licensed technology. The parties can also be restricted from exploiting the licensed technology within specific product markets or exclusive territories. Such restrictions are usually acceptable, provided they do not in fact amount to market-sharing or customer allocation.

It is permissible for a technology transfer agreement to be a sole licence, with the licensor prevented from licensing any other licensees within a particular territory. As both parties are free to exploit the technology, both reciprocal and non-reciprocal sole licences are block exempted.[88]

Sales restrictions are commonly imposed to protect a licensee's investment in the exploitation of licensed technology and to prevent free-riding from other parties, including other licensees. Such restrictions either concern active or passive selling.[89] It is necessary to consider both sales restrictions between the licensor and the licensee as well as restrictions imposed in licences which protect any given licensee from other licensees.

The Technology Transfer Block Exemption and Guidelines confirm that restrictions on active and passive sales in a reciprocal agreement between competitors are hardcore. This is also the case where the licensor licenses several licensees and wishes to include restrictions on passive sales that prevent any one licensee selling into the territory or to a customer group allocated to another licensee. However, the Technology Transfer Block Exemption contains some flexibility and permits competitors to impose certain restrictions. Provided the agreement is non-reciprocal, it is possible to gain exemption if the parties include restrictions both on active and passive sales.[90] Where the licensor licenses several licensees, the Technology Transfer Block Exemption also exempts restrictions on any one licensee actively selling into the territory or customer group allocated to another licensee, provided the agreement is non-reciprocal.[91]

Obligations on the licensee restricting it to production of component contract products for use in its own products (so-called "captive use" restrictions) are within the block exemption, provided that the licensee is not restricted from making active sales of the components as spare parts for its own products.

88. See note 86 above.

89. Active sales are sales made by actively promoting the product (eg by soliciting orders and advertising). Passive sales are sales made in response to a purchaser independently approaching the licensee.

90. See Article 4(1)(c)(iv) and Guidelines, para 87. These restrictions will be block exempted up to the 20 per cent market share threshold.

91. See Article 4(1)(c)(v) and Guidelines, para 89.

In non-reciprocal agreements, it is possible to restrict the licensee to production of contract products for sale to only one customer, provided that the purpose of the technology transfer agreement is to generate an alternative source of supply for that customer.

(d) *Non-compete restrictions*: a restriction preventing the licensee from using its own technology or restricting either party from carrying out research and development is also hardcore, unless that obligation is indispensable to prevent the disclosure of licensed know-how to third parties. It is therefore possible for an agreement preventing the licensee from carrying out research and development with third parties to benefit from the block exemption.[92]

For agreements between non-competitors, the list of hardcore restrictions is shorter, covering only the following:

(a) *Price-fixing*: In this case, only minimum resale price fixing is caught.

(b) *Passive sales restrictions on the licensee*: In principle, restrictions on passive sales by the licensee are hardcore. However, there are a number of exceptions to this rule, by virtue of which certain limitations on the licensee's ability to respond to passive sales requests are permissible under the block exemption.[93]

The restriction of passive selling into an exclusive territory or to an exclusive customer group reserved for the licensor is permitted.[94] Where there are several licensees, the Technology Transfer Block Exemption also exempts for two years any restriction on passive selling between licensees.[95]

In agreements between non-competitors it is also possible to restrict the licensee to the production of component contract products for its own use, provided it can still sell the components as spare parts.

Terms obliging the licensee to produce only for a particular customer are also exempt, provided the licence was granted to generate an alternative source of supply for that customer.

It is also permissible to prevent the licensee from selling contract products to end users, restricting sales only to wholesale-level customers. Such agreements enabling the licensor to assign the wholesale function to the licensee are normally considered to fall outside Article 81(1).[96]

92. See Article 4(1)(d) and Guidelines, paras 94–95.
93. See Article 4(2) and Guidelines, paras 96–106.
94. See Article 4(2)(b)(i) and Guidelines, para 100.
95. See Article 4(2)(b)(ii) and Guidelines, para 101. The two-year period starts from the date on which the licensee benefiting from the restrictions first puts the product incorporating the licensed technology on the market inside his exclusive territory.
96. See Guidelines, para 104.

A licensor is permitted to require that the licensee becomes part of a selective distribution system, thereby preventing sales to unauthorised distributors.

(c) *Retail-level licensees*: It is a hardcore restriction for a licensor to limit either active or passive sales to end users by a licensee who is a member of a selective distribution system. The licensor retains the ability to prevent the licensee from operating from unauthorised premises, and can also require the licensee to operate only at the wholesale level.

If undertakings are non-competitors when the technology transfer agreement is entered into, but later become competitors, the Technology Transfer Block Exemption provides that the hardcore restrictions applicable to non-competitors will apply for the life of the agreement "unless the agreement is subsequently amended in any material respect". Therefore, if the agreement remains unaltered, there is no need to reassess the agreement from the standpoint that the parties are now competing.[97]

4.2.3.2.4 Article 5: the excluded restrictions

There are four types of restriction that may offend Article 81(1) but are not block exempted. These "excluded restrictions" require individual assessment to determine whether their pro-competitive effects are sufficient to enable them to benefit from the exception under Article 81(3). If these clauses do fall within Article 81(1), then they do not render the entire agreement void under Article 81(2), but if they do not satisfy Article 81(3) they are (subject to national laws) capable of severance from the remainder of the agreement.

The excluded restrictions are terms that cover the exclusive grant-back or assignment of improvements made by the licensee to the underlying technology, or oblige the licensee not to challenge the licensed IP right.

Article 5 also removes from the protection of the block exemption obligations between non-competitors that restrict the licensee's ability to exploit its own technology or restricts either party from carrying out research and development, unless that obligation is indispensable to prevent the disclosure of licensed know-how to third parties.

4.2.3.2.5 Article 6: withdrawal of the benefit of the block exemption

The Commission has retained the right to withdraw the applicability of the Technology Transfer Block Exemption in individual cases where, notwithstanding the fact that the requirements of the block exemption are satisfied, the agreement does not have the benefits anticipated by Article 81(3). Such circumstances include those in which third parties are unable to bring their technologies to the market as a result of a network of restrictive agreements

97. See Article 4(3).

preventing licensees from exploiting third-party technology, or if the parties to the agreement without any objective justification refuse to exploit the licensed technology.

4.2.3.2.6 Article 10: transitional provisions

The Technology Transfer Block Exemption came into force on 1 May 2004, and simultaneously repealed the previous Regulation 240/96. Agreements that were concluded before 30 April 2004 that do not satisfy the conditions of the block exemption are granted immunity from Article 81(1) until 31 March 2006, provided that they satisfied the requirements for block exemption under Regulation 240/96.

4.2.4 Comments on the Technology Transfer Block Exemption

4.2.4.1 Distinction between competitors and non-competitors

The application of the block exemption is based on whether parties are competitors or non-competitors.[98] In practice, and particularly for the dynamic industries that are increasingly likely to seek to rely on the revised Technology Transfer Block Exemption, it is often difficult to assign one or the other label to a party when circumstances may change quickly.

The more liberal approach for agreements between non-competitors, in comparison with that for agreements between competitors, has generally been welcomed. However, there is a concern that too much weight may be placed on the distinction between competitors and non-competitors when this distinction is often difficult to apply in practice. There can be significant difficulty in identifying the correct market product and technology markets for assessment.

For agreements between non-competitors, there may nevertheless be serious anti-competitive concerns in particular circumstances—for instance where one party's capacity to innovate under a licence agreement is affected or where a licensee is obliged to accept non-compete obligations.

4.2.4.2 Use of market share thresholds

The introduction of market share thresholds into the Technology Transfer Block Exemption has been criticised. The general difficulty in defining relevant markets is exacerbated when it comes to innovation markets and research and development.

The block exemption requires that market shares be calculated by reference to the previous year's sales data. This can be problematic in the case of new technologies where no final product exists at the time at which the agreement is put in place. This is often the case where innovative patented technology is

98. This is an issue in the context of horizontal and vertical agreements as well.

licensed with a view to development of a potential product. The potential product could be entirely new (eg treatment for a previously untreatable form of cancer) and may never even make it to market. It may thus be impossible to ascertain precisely the boundaries of the relevant market and calculate market share in the normal manner. This is likely to be the case with all innovative technologies where the problem in ascertaining market share is essentially one of timing. The Guidelines are of some assistance in this regard, as they state that new technologies that have not yet generated any sales will have a zero market share assigned to them.[99]

There are also considerable difficulties in relation to dynamic industries where market shares—even assuming they can be reliably ascertained in the first place—[100] can change very quickly. When this reality is combined with the difficulty in ascertaining whether the parties are competitors or non-competitors, it can make the application of the Technology Transfer Block Exemption difficult in a commercial context. Future developments must be considered too, as the parties' market shares are likely to change during the term of the agreement. If the technology is exploited successfully, then market shares may increase and exceed the applicable thresholds, and thereby take the agreement outside the scope of the block exemption. If this situation persists for longer than two years,[101] the parties will have to consider whether the agreement satisfies the Article 81(3) criteria.

Under the modernised regime, those drafting and negotiating licences should have regard to the following potentially applicable market share thresholds:

- 10 per cent horizontal *de minimis.*
- 15 per cent vertical *de minimis.*
- 20 per cent/25 per cent specialisation/R&D/joint venture licences.
- 20 per cent licences between competitors (joint market shares).
- 30 per cent licences between non-competitors (either party).

This complex matrix of potentially applicable thresholds, with varying legal consequences as to what may or may not be permissible, may give rise to uncertainty for commercial undertakings wishing to negotiate and grant (or accept) licences. In this regard at least, the scope of the modernised block exemption is less certain than was the case under the previous regime.

4.2.4.3 Treatment of dominant companies

Concern has also been expressed about the inability of dominant companies to rely on the Technology Transfer Block Exemption, on the grounds that a

99. Guidelines, para 70.

100. In relation to some of the problems of defining relevant markets and assessing market shares in industries where innovation is a key competitive driver, see the Economic Discussion Paper on Competition and Innovation published by the UK's Office of Fair Trading in March 2002, particularly pp 54–57.

101. See Article 8(2).

dominant entity will almost certainly exceed the relevant market share threshold. It is not necessarily the case that such companies cannot meet the requirements set out under Article 81(3).

It is generally accepted that dominant companies are free to engage in normal commercial conduct and practices. Denying dominant companies the ability to benefit from the block exemption restricts such companies (which are often very innovative) in their ability to enter into licences on normal terms. Instead, they must assess individual agreements to determine whether or not, on balance, they can benefit from the Article 81(3) exemption. This unquestionably places an extra burden on dominant companies, and raises the level of risk that they undertake when entering into technology licensing agreements. How this increased risk will affect the behaviour of such companies has yet to be seen.

4.2.4.4 Multi-party licences, cross-licensing and bilateral pools

Multi-party licence programmes, multilateral pools and licence packages are excluded from the Technology Transfer Block Exemption, which is restricted to bipartite agreements. Multi-party arrangements of this kind are likely to be pro-competitive when between non-competing undertakings, especially when they cover only essential IP rights.

Competitors in today's dynamic industries (eg information technology) often need to cooperate and some form of cooperation has increasingly become the norm (eg patent pools for CDs and DVDs). The development and commercialisation of new technology is often reliant on multiple third-party rights. Accordingly, the Commission's traditional approach of viewing any form of contact between competing companies with suspicion may be misplaced.

4.2.5 Vertical Agreements Block Exemption

It is common for vertical agreements relating to the sale and purchase of goods or services to include incidental provisions relating to IP rights—for example the right for a distributor to produce marketing literature containing a product's trade mark, or the right for a franchisee to use a franchiser's trade mark, copyright works and know-how in operating its franchise.

These types of arrangement focus principally on supply and, as a result, the Vertical Agreements Block Exemption is likely to be relevant. See 4.1.3.2 above.

Article 2(3) of the Vertical Agreements Block Exemption clarifies that the exemption provided under Article 2(1) shall apply to vertical agreements containing provisions relating to the assignment or licensing of IP rights, provided the following conditions are met:

- — the IP provisions must be part of a vertical agreement, ie an agreement with conditions under which the parties may purchase, sell or resell certain goods or services;
- — the IP right must be assigned to, or for use by, the buyer;
- — the IP provisions must not constitute the primary object of the agreement;
- — the IP provisions must be directly related to the use, sale or resale of goods or services by the buyer or his customers;
- — the IP provisions, in relation to the contract goods or services, must not contain restrictions of competition having the same object or effect as vertical restraints that are not exempted under the block exemption Regulation.
- — The Vertical Agreements Block Exemption will only apply if all five conditions are met. The Commission block exemptions are mutually exclusive, so if a licence is covered by the Technology Transfer Block Exemption, the Vertical Agreements Block Exemption cannot apply.

The introduction of the Vertical Agreements Block Exemption cleared up uncertainty in relation to certain types of copyright licences. The Commission's Guidelines on Vertical Restraints specifically state[102] that supplies of software for resale under shrink-wrap licences are to be treated as the supply of goods for the purposes of the Vertical Agreements Block Exemption, rather than a licence of copyright.

4.2.6 Settlement agreements

Disputes relating to IP rights are often settled by way of licensing, enabling both parties to achieve a commercially satisfactory outcome to the dispute without the risk and expense of a trial. The rights-holder receives royalties on the licensee's product sales, whereas the alleged infringer is able to continue with its operations. In the case of complex disputes, in which both parties are asserting IP right against each other, settlement may proceed by way of a cross-licence.

Measures such as these are not generally restrictive of competition, as both parties are able to exploit their technologies after the settlement. The individual terms of such agreements may, however, fall within the ambit of the competition rules.

4.2.6.1 No-challenge clauses

One such issue that is frequently raised in the context of settlement negotiations is the insertion of a no-challenge provision.

The inclusion in a settlement agreement of an obligation not to challenge the validity of the IP rights in question (or, often, not only those rights but also

102. Commission Notice 2000/C 291/01, para 40.

surrounding rights) is capable of falling within the scope of the prohibition in Article 81(1) of the EC Treaty on the basis that:

(a) public policy requires that everyone ought to be able to bring proceedings challenging the validity of monopoly rights that have been wrongly granted or are being wrongly maintained; and
(b) an obligation not to challenge the validity of a right may restrict competition within the meaning of Article 81(1) by leaving intact a right that might inhibit companies wishing to enter or compete on a particular market (ie the continuing existence of rights that should be declared invalid may amount to a significant barrier to entry).

Until relatively recently, the general position was that no-challenge clauses in respect of any IP right were regarded by the Commission and the ECJ as within the scope of the prohibition in Article 81(1) and not capable of exemption. In *Windsurfing*,[103] the ECJ held that a clause requiring a licensee to acknowledge the validity of a trade mark clearly infringed Article 81(1). In addition, no-challenge clauses were "blacklisted" in the know-how and patent licensing block exemptions.

The attitude of the authorities towards no-challenge clauses has since softened. In the case of *Bayer v. Süllhöfer*,[104] the ECJ held that in certain circumstances a no-challenge clause in a settlement agreement relating to patent litigation did not automatically fall within the scope of Article 81(1). No-challenge clauses are not hardcore restrictions under the Technology Transfer Block Exemption, but fall with the Article 5 list of excluded restrictions. The clause must therefore be assessed individually to determine whether it can benefit from exemption under Article 81(3).

The Commission's Guidelines[105] state that, for settlement and non-assertion agreements, no-challenge clauses are generally considered to fall outside Article 81(1), as the purpose of the agreement is to avoid dispute and give both parties the freedom to continue to exploit the licensed technology. However, the Guidelines appear to go further in scope than the ECJ's *Bayer v. Süllhöfer* judgment, as the ECJ was somewhat critical of the Commission's then point of view that Article 81(1) did not apply to settlement agreements. Whether or not the ECJ will have another opportunity to clarify this area is uncertain.

In any settlement agreement, it is therefore essential to consider carefully the scope of any proposed no-challenge clause and its possible effect on competition. The scope of no-challenge clauses should be limited to what is necessary to ensure that the settlement agreement is effective and should have regard to the principles set out in the Technology Transfer Block Exemption and accompanying Guidelines.

103. Case 193/83, *Windsurfing International v. Commission* [1986] ECR 611.
104. Case No: *Bayer v. Süllhöfer* [1988] ECR 5249.
105. See Guidelines, paras 204–209.

4.2.6.2 Trade mark delimitation agreements

Another common source of friction between IP and competition law arises from circumstances where companies that own similar or identical trade marks enter into an agreement about the way in which they will use those marks. These agreements may also come about as part of a settlement arrangement in the context of a trade mark dispute.

Such an agreement may be prohibited by Article 81(1) if its object or effect is to share markets or to partition the EU. If, for example, the agreement permits each company to use its version of the mark only in some EU Member States, this is likely to be regarded as within the scope of the prohibition in Article 81(1).[106] However, delimitation agreements that do not inhibit the free movement of goods may be outside the scope of Article 81(1), for example, if the companies agree to use different get-up or trade dress.[107] Even in such agreements, however, companies should be cautious about including further restrictions such as a no-challenge clause.

4.3. APPLICATION OF ARTICLE 81 TO HORIZONTAL AGREEMENTS

Peter Willis, Taylor Wessing

4.3.1 Introduction

Horizontal agreements are agreements between undertakings operating at the same level of the supply chain. They are therefore much more likely than vertical agreements to involve cooperation between competitors. For that reason, the competition authorities generally scrutinise them rather more carefully than vertical agreements. Horizontal agreements range from hardcore cartels—generally perceived as being the most serious infringements of the competition rules—to agreements involving perfectly legitimate cooperation on issues such as research and development.

The Commission's approach to horizontal agreements has become more polarised in recent years: it has taken increasingly vigorous enforcement action against hardcore cartels, imposing ever-heavier fines and introducing its cartel leniency policy in order to improve detection rates; whereas its approach to horizontal agreements that are capable of producing economic benefits has become much more flexible and focused on economic reality.

This section first briefly examines the content and treatment of hardcore cartel agreements, then describes the assessment of horizontal cooperation agreements.

106. *Sirdar/Phildar,* 1975 OJ L 125/27; *Toltecs/Dorset* [1983] 1 CMLR 412.
107. *Persil Washing Powder,* [1978] OJ L 60/19.

4.3.2 *Hardcore cartels*

4.3.2.1 Definition of a cartel

A widely accepted and useful definition of a cartel is that formulated by the Organisation for Economic Co-operation and Development (OECD):[108]

> "an anti-competitive agreement, anti-competitive concerted practice or anti-competitive arrangement by competitors to fix prices, make rigged bids (collusive tenders) establish bilateral restrictions or quotas, or share and divide markets by allocating customers, suppliers, territories or lines of commerce"

Hardcore cartels are a good illustration of the basic Article 81 principle that an agreement infringes if its object or effect is to restrict competition. The Commission does not need to demonstrate that a cartel has had an actual restrictive effect on competition, because that is a cartel's object.[109]

4.3.2.2 Types of cartels

4.3.2.2.1 Price-fixing

The most obvious form of cartel consists of an agreement between competitors to fix prices. This general description covers a wide range of agreements relating to prices or components of prices, including:

- agreements to set a minimum price;
- agreements to recommend a specific price;
- agreements to coordinate price increases;
- agreements on particular components of prices, such as discounts or rebates; and
- agreements to pass on all or part of specific cost increases to customers.

Article 81(1) of the EC Treaty assimilates to price-fixing agreements those that fix other trading conditions, such as terms of guarantee, terms of delivery and terms of payment.

Price-fixing cartels often take the form of concerted practices rather than express agreements. They very often consist of disclosure of future pricing intentions that facilitate or lead to the participants charging the same prices.

4.3.2.2.2 Bid-rigging

Bid-rigging involves members of the cartel agreeing between themselves the manner in which they will bid (or not) in a competitive tender situation. It may

108. Recommendation of the Council concerning effective action against hardcore cartels, http://www.oecd.org/dataoecd/39/4/2350130.pdf.

109. Cases T-25/95 etc, *Cimenteries CBR v. Commission*, [2000] ECR II-491(the Cement case).

include agreeing whether or not to bid and which cartel member should win the bid—generally achieved by ensuring that that member submits the lowest bid and that the other bidding members submit higher "cover bids" designed to give the semblance of a competitive tender. This is a clear infringement of Article 81(1): it is for each bidder to determine independently whether or not it will submit a bid, and, if so, at what price.

4.3.2.2.3 Output limitation

Limiting output has an effect similar to that of fixing prices.

4.3.2.2.4 Market-sharing

Market-sharing involves the allocation, as between the participants and the cartel, of customers or territories.

4.3.2.3 Treatment of cartels

The Commission has consistently declared that cartels are among the most serious forms of infringement of Article 81. This is reflected in the fact that:

- the Commission's leniency policy is directed at cartels as opposed to other types of infringement;[110]
- cartels are likely to be the most frequent target of the Commission's power to carry out on-site investigations;[111]
- cartels are considered to have the object of restricting competition, so that it is not necessary to demonstrate they have an anti-competitive effect;
- cartels have been the subject of some of the heaviest fines imposed by the Commission;
- in some Member States, participation in a cartel is a criminal offence.

4.3.3 Horizontal cooperation agreements before the Commission's 2001 Guidelines

This section briefly addresses the treatment of horizontal cooperation agreement before the publication of the Commission's Guidelines in 2001. It covers two issues: the treatment of certain structural forms of cooperation under the EC Merger Regulation (which remained unchanged after 2001), and the approach adopted by the Commission in horizontal cooperation cases under Article 81, which is still relevant because it underlies some of the analysis set out in the Guidelines.

110. See 9.10.4.2 below.
111. See 9.5.4 below.

4.3.3.1 Application of the ECMR to full-function joint ventures

Horizontal agreements take a range of legal forms. They may consist of agreements that bring about a structural change in the participants, by creating some form of joint-venture vehicle in order to carry out the cooperative activity, or they may consist of simple cooperation agreements, strategic alliances or partnering arrangements. Joint ventures that amount to concentrations fall within the EC Merger Regulation and require notification to the Commission.[112] In order to be a concentration, a joint venture must satisfy the relevant turnover thresholds, and must involve:

— The parents acquiring joint control of the joint venture; and
— The joint venture performing on a lasting basis all the functions of an autonomous economic entity.[113]

Article 81 and the EC Merger Regulation apply different substantive tests: whereas a cooperation agreement constituting a full-function joint venture is assessed according to whether it significantly impedes effective competition, a partial-function joint venture—or a cooperation agreement that does not involve joint control—is assessed according to whether it has as its object or effect the appreciable prevention, restriction or distortion of competition. Having said that, the assessment of a full-function joint venture also involves, in addition to an assessment of whether it gives rise to a significant impediment to effective competition, a further assessment under Article 2(4) of the EC Merger Regulation of the coordination of the competitive behaviour of undertakings that remain independent.

In Article 2(4) cases, cooperation is assessed under Article 81. The Commission will consider whether the parties to the joint venture retain significant activities, in the same market as the joint venture, in a market which is directly upstream or downstream from that of the joint venture or in a neighbouring market.[114] It will essentially assess any spillover of the joint venture onto relations between the parents, and in particular will assess whether:

— The coordination of behaviour between the parents is likely to result in the elimination of competition in respect of a substantial part of the products or services in question; and
— the coordination is a direct consequence of the creation of the joint venture, rather than of any other pre-existing sectors.[115]

4.3.3.2 The Commission's economic approach

In cases other than full-function joint ventures,[116] the Commission originally applied a strict test, according to which the majority of joint ventures notified

112. See Chapter 8 below.
113. Regulation 139/2004, Article 1 and 3(4): 2004 OJ L 24, p 1.
114. Regulation 139/2004, Article 2(5), first indent.
115. Regulation 139/2004, Article 2(5), second indent.
116. The distinction was previously between cooperative and concentrative joint ventures.

to it were held to infringe Article 81(1) and therefore to require exemption under Article 81(3).[117] However, its approach softened throughout the 1990s, as exemplified *in Elopak/Metal Box—Odin.*[118] This relaxation was particularly noticeable in the analysis of whether the parties to a cooperation agreement were potential competitors. The Commission was further encouraged in this by the judgment in *European Night Services*[119] in 1998. In that case, the Court of First Instance ("CFI") annulled a decision in which the Commission concluded that the joint venture for the operation of night passenger transport services through the Channel Tunnel infringed Article 81(1), but granted an exemption, subject to conditions, under Article 81(3). The CFI emphasised the need to carry out a more economics-based assessment.

In its pre-1999 analysis, the Commission considered the following types of possible restrictive effect of joint ventures and other horizontal cooperation agreements:

— *Spillover*: the possibility that the links between the parents through the joint venture will allow them to coordinate their behaviour, either on the same market as the market on which the joint venture is active, or on a related market. Relevant factors here include the parties' market share, the duration of the joint venture and the extent of the parties' overall activities on the relevant market accounted for by the joint venture. The more significant the joint venture, the higher the likelihood of cooperation.

— *Foreclosure*: the possibility that the agreement might exclude third parties from the relevant market. This may arise from an exclusive or preferential supply or licensing agreement between the parties, or between a joint venture and its parents.

— *Network effects*: the possibility that whereas the effect of a single cooperation agreement between the parties might not restrict competition, the overall effect of a series of agreements between the parties, and with third parties, might be to restrict competition.

It will be seen that these concerns still underlie a number of the issues highlighted in the Guidelines.

4.3.4 Horizontal cooperation agreements under the Commission's 2001 Guidelines

The Commission published its horizontal cooperation Guidelines in 2001,[120] which set out a much more flexible approach to such agreements. They

117. See for example *GEC/Weir,* 1977 OJ L 327, p 26.

118. *Elopak/Metal Box—Odin,* 1990 OJ L 209, p 15.

119. Cases T-374/94 etc, *ENS v. Commission* [1998] ECR II 3141.

120. Guidelines on the applicability of Article 81 of the EC Treaty to horizontal cooperation agreements, 2001 OJ C 3, p 2.

accompanied two block exemptions for research and development[121] and specialisation agreements[122] and followed the more economics—based approach pioneered in the Commission's guidelines on the application of Article 81 to vertical agreements.[123]

The Guidelines first set out some general principles, and draw the distinction between agreements that fall outside Article 81(1), those that almost always fall within Article 81(1), and those that may fall within Article 81(1). The Guidelines then go on to examine a number of specific types of horizontal agreement.

4.3.4.1 Agreements falling outside Article 81(1)

According to the Commission's Guidelines, certain types of horizontal agreement normally fall outside Article 81(1) because they do not involve coordination of the parties' competitive behaviour. The only exception is where one or more of the parties have significant market power and the agreement is likely to cause foreclosure of third parties.

4.3.4.1.1 Parties are non-competitors

If the parties to a horizontal agreement are not competitors, an agreement between them cannot (subject to the proviso mentioned above) restrict competition. In this context, it is important to consider not only whether the parties are actual competitors, but also whether they are potential competitors. The approach to this issue under the guidelines reflects the more realistic post-*Metal Box* approach.[124] It is described in more detail in relation to research and development agreements at 4.3.5.1 below.

4.3.4.1.2 Parties cannot carry out the activity independently

Even where the parties are competitors, in that they operate on the same market, an agreement between them will not restrict competition if they would be unable to perform independently the activity envisaged in the agreement. An example of this is the *Upjohn/Pharmacia* agreement outlined below.[125]

4.3.4.1.3 Cooperation that does not affect competition

Cooperation relating, for example, to sharing canteen facilities, or exchanging information on security threats to the parties' premises, falls outside Article 81(1) because it does not cover an activity in relation to which the parties are in competition with each other.

121. Regulation 2659/2000, 2000 OJ L 304, p 7.
122. Regulation 2658/2000, 2000 OJ L 304, p 3.
123. See Chapter 3.
124. See note 118.
125. Case IV/M.631.

4.3.4.1.4 Minor agreements

Although not expressly mentioned in the Guidelines, horizontal agreements of minor importance, where the parties have a combined market share of less than 15 per cent, are also unlikely to have an appreciable restrictive effect on competition, and therefore to fall outside Article 81(1).

4.3.4.2 Agreements that almost always fall within Article 81(1)

This category of agreements is dealt with fairly briefly: effectively it covers agreements involving hardcore cartel activity.

4.3.4.3 Agreements that may fall within Article 81: general principles

4.3.4.3.1 Factors relevant to the assessment

The starting point in determining the impact of a horizontal agreement is to define the relevant market or markets affected by the agreement. The method is set out in the Commission's Notice on market definition. The Guidelines provide additional guidance on particular types of markets relevant to horizontal agreements, such as future markets in research and development agreements.

The parties' absolute combined market share is only one factor: the uplift in market share resulting from the agreement is also important. A very small addition to even a large market share may have little restrictive effect on competition.

Market concentration is also relevant, as are the stability of market shares, barriers to entry and countervailing buyer power.

4.3.4.3.2 Application of Article 81(3)

Where a horizontal cooperation agreement restricts competition for the purposes of Article 81(1), it is then necessary to consider whether it satisfies the conditions for exemption under Article 81(3). These have been considered in Chapter 3 and are not addressed further here.

4.3.5 Specific horizontal agreements

4.3.5.1 Research and development agreements

3.5.1.1 Introduction

Research and development agreements are an obvious example of agreements that generally either do not restrict competition, or even have pro-competitive benefits, by promoting technical progress. This section examines the treatment of research and development agreements under the guidelines and, briefly, under the Research and Development Block Exemption.

4.3.5.1.2 Relevant markets

As in all analyses of agreements under the competition rules, the first step is to define the relevant market. Research and development agreements may be intended to result in a product or technology that competes with existing products or technologies—in which case the relevant market will be the market for those existing products or technologies. Alternatively, they may be designed to result in the development of an entirely new product, which creates a new market, in which case the relevant market to consider in examining the impact of the cooperation in research and development will be the market for that particular innovation. This distinction is worth exploring in further detail. It will be seen that a number of cases referred to are merger decisions, rather than decisions under Article 81: the approach to market definition is very similar.

EXISTING PRODUCTS

Where R&D concerns substitutes for existing products, the relevant market will be the market for those existing products. This is the approach followed in the Commission's block exemption for R&D agreements, discussed below at 4.3.5.1.4, where Article 4(2) imposes a market share cap, by reference to the "relevant market for the products capable of being improved or replaced by the [products arising out of the joint R&D]".

The first question will therefore be to determine whether the product under development is merely a substitute for existing products, in which case competition can be assessed by reference to those existing products. For example, in Case IV/M.555 *Glaxo/Wellcome* OJ (1995) C065/3, the Commission examined the possible overlap in anti-migraine drugs, concluding that a Wellcome drug in the pipeline, 311C, had a similar profile to that of Glaxo's existing product Imigran and therefore took into account Glaxo's existing market position (as well as the future market, as outlined below). Where the product under development represents a significant development, so that existing products are not substitutes for the new ones, the long-term impact on the future market may require analysis. This is examined below.

TECHNOLOGY MARKETS

In addition to markets for products, it may be necessary to consider markets for technology, for example where IP rights are marketed separately from the products based on them. The same principles of market definition apply as in the case of product markets: the relevant market consists of the technology and its substitutes. For example, in Case IV/M.269, *Shell/Montecatini* [1996] OJ L294/10, the Commission identified a worldwide market for the technology to produce polypropylene from propylene, concluding that the joint venture in question would give rise to a dominant position on the polypropylene technology market and would require divestiture of the polypropylene technology business, including R&D activities, to a separate company.

4.3.5 Application of Article 81

MARKETS FOR INNOVATION OR "FUTURE MARKETS"

Where products under development are not substitutes for existing products, either because they present significant advantages over existing products or because they are being developed for a new intended use, it may be necessary to consider a future market.

The Commission explained the issues in its decision in Case COMP/M.1878, *Pfizer/Warner-Lambert* OJ C104 12.4.2005 p 5, as follows:

"In the pharmaceuticals industry, a full assessment of the competitive situation requires examination of the products which are not yet on the market but which are at an advanced stage of development. As noted in the *Ciba-Geigy/Sandoz* decision, R&D projects undergo three different phases of clinical testing: Phase I marks the start of clinical testing on humans, currently some eight to 10 years before a product is marketed. Statistically, projects in Phase I generally have no more than a 10 per cent chance of being successful. Phase II, some four to five years before the product is marketed, involves working out the proper dose for the patient and defining the areas of application. The success of Phase II is generally acknowledged to be approximately 30 per cent. Phase III, starting three years before the product is marketed, involves establishing the product's effectiveness on larger groups of patients. The risk of failure in Phase III is reported to be over 50 per cent.

The potential for these products to enter into competition with other products which are either at the development stage or already on the market can be assessed by reference to their characteristics and intended therapeutic use. The Commission has to look at R&D potential in terms of its importance for existing markets, but also for future market situations.

Insofar as research and development must be assessed in terms of its importance for future markets, the relevant product market can, in the nature of things, be defined in a less clear-cut manner than in the case of existing markets. Market definition can be based either on the existing ATC classes or it can be guided primarily by the characteristics of future products as well as by the indications to which they are to be applied."

4.3.5.1.3 Assessment under Article 81

AGREEMENTS UNLIKELY TO FALL WITHIN ARTICLE 81(1)

In its guidelines, the Commission identifies a number of types of agreement that are unlikely to fall within the Article 81(1) prohibition:

- agreements relating to R&D at a theoretical stage, far removed from the commercial exploitation of the results;
- agreements relating to the outsourcing of previously captive R&D to specialist research bureaux that are not involved in the commercialisation of the results;
- agreements between non-competitors.

This last, which is an expression of the general principle outlined at 4.3.4.1.1 above, is probably the most important in practice. It is explored below.

At this stage, it is important to consider not only whether the parties are actual competitors, but also whether they are potential competitors. Again, this is a general principle for horizontal agreements, but is particularly important in the case of R&D agreements, because the parties may well be cooperating in relation to a future product market in which neither of them is currently active, and in which they may therefore be only potential competitors.

For example, in the Commission's 1990 decision in *Elopak/Metal Box —Odin*,[126] the Commission considered a joint venture to carry out R&D for a container with a carton base and separate closure that could be filled by an aseptic process with UHT-processed foods.

Each parent had activities in separate fields outside the field of the joint venture. The Commission concluded that neither party could in the short term enter the market alone, because entry would require a knowledge of the other party's technology, which could not be developed without significant and time-consuming investment. Both parties' experience and resources would be necessary to develop the new product. The technical risks for each party involved in carrying out research in what would be a new area of technology for each of them would realistically preclude each party from attempting to carry out R&D on its own. The joint venture would not have any impact on any existing competitive relationship between the parties, because they were not actual or potential competitors in fields outside the field of the joint venture. The creation of the joint venture would not lead to foreclosure of similar possibilities to other potential competitors, because there were a number of other manufacturers in the respective field of each of the parents.

In contrast, in its 1994 decision in *Asahi/Saint Gobain*,[127] the Commission rejected the parties' arguments that they were not competitors. The joint venture involved cooperation in the joint research and development of bi-layer products and technology. These are products resulting from laminating glass with plastic film, for use in motor-vehicle glazing and the construction industry. The parties argued that neither could independently enter the market. However, the Commission took the view that the parties were already competitors in the existing market for automotive safety glass, for which the bi-layer products were a substitute, and the parties could carry out the project individually: both had set up their own pilot plants and had provided non-commercial samples to their respective potential customers.

In the Commission's decision in Case IV/M.631, *Upjohn/Pharmacia*, the Commission took the view (at paragraph 25) that the parties were medium-sized pharmaceutical companies for which the costs of R&D were becoming very heavy to bear and that their merger would give them sufficient critical mass to be a competitive player on the worldwide R&D market. This suggests that the Commission will take the view that even medium-sized pharmaceutical companies will not necessarily be in a position to carry out major R&D

126. 1990 OJ L 209, p 15.
127. 1994 OJ L 354, p 87, at para 16.

independently and that therefore they will not necessarily be potential competitors for the purposes of assessing a restriction of competition.

In *Pasteur Mérieux/Merck*,[128] the Commission expressed the opinion that:

> "as regards future products in an advanced state of clinical trial [post Phase II] ('pipeline products'), it is realistic to assume that the parties, in view of their past performance, financial strength and existing vaccine knowledge, can be considered as potential competitors for those new [vaccines] for which their actual R&D portfolio shows an overlap."

However, there was less likelihood of the parties being potential competitors in relation to R&D further removed from the market. The Commission pointed out that:

> "an assessment of the restriction of competition between the parties for other new [vaccines] in earlier stages or R&D ('future pipeline products') is far more difficult, in view of the extremely broad range of such future research and the lack of precise indications as to the chances of bringing successful products to the markets."

In other words, the more removed from the market the particular R&D project is, the greater the uncertainty as to whether the parties would be in a position to carry out the R&D independently. This ties in with the Commission's observation, at paragraph 55 of its guidelines on horizontal agreements, that "most R&D agreements do not fall under Article 81(1) . . . . , this can be said for agreements relating to cooperation in R&D at a rather theoretical stage, far removed from the exploitation of possible results".

AGREEMENTS THAT ALMOST ALWAYS FALL UNDER ARTICLE 81(1)
Not surprisingly, R&D agreements that are no more than disguised cartels will fall within Article 81(1).

AGREEMENTS THAT MAY FALL WITHIN ARTICLE 81(1)
Where the parties to R&D agreement are competitors in existing product markets, their cooperation may lead to coordination in relation to the existing product markets, or a reduction in the level of innovation. However, this is likely to be possible only where the parties together have significant market power. It may occur where the parties agree not to carry out separate R&D in the same field, or where the effect of the joint R&D is that they forego independent R&D. Article 81 may similarly apply where the parties accept restrictions on their ability to exploit the R&D independently.

Similarly, cooperation in R&D may restrict competition in a downstream product market if the product undergoing R&D will be a key input into that downstream product.

In relation to R&D where there are no existing products for which the new products will be a substitute, a rather different analysis is conducted, albeit with the same objective in mind. In such cases, the assessment focuses on

128. 1994 OJ L 309, p 1.

"poles of research". As the Commission explains in its Guidelines on horizontal agreements, at paragraph 51:

"In the pharmaceutical industry, the process of innovation is structured in such a way that it is possible at any early stage to identify R&D poles. R&D poles are R&D efforts directed towards a certain new product or technology and the substitutes for that R&D, ie R&D aimed at developing substitutable products or technology for those developed by the cooperation, and having comparable access to resources as well as a similar timing. In this case, it can be analysed if after the agreement there will be a sufficient number of R&D poles left. The starting point of the analysis is the R&D of the parties. The credible competing R&D poles have to be identified. In order to assess the credibility of competing poles, the following aspects have to be taken into account: the nature, scope and size of possible other R&D efforts, their access to financial and human resources, know-how/patents or other specialised assets, as well as their timing and their capability to exploit possible results. An R&D pole is not a credible competitor if it cannot be regarded as a close substitute for the parties' R&D effort from the viewpoint of, for instance, access to resources or timing."

This is seen rather better in some of the Commission's decisions under the merger Regulation than in its Article 81 decisions. So, for example, in case COMP/M.1878, *Pfizer/Warner-Lambert*, the Commission examined the overlap in the parties' R&D activities in the field of oncology. The Commission concluded that although the parties had no overlap in relation to existing cancer drugs (Pfizer had no sales and Warner-Lambert had minimal sales), it was necessary to consider the parties' overlap in their pipeline products. One of the factors taken into account by the Commission was the fact that there were numerous other pipeline products in Phase II or III of development.

Probably the most interesting analysis of future competition in relation to pipeline products was set out in Case IV/M.555, *Glaxo/Wellcome*. In that case, the Commission examined the merging parties' activities in anti-migraine drugs. Glaxo had a leading anti-migraine drug, Imigran. Wellcome had one anti-migraine drug on the market, which had been off-patent for over 20 years and was supplied in generic and branded form by a number of other companies. The Commission concluded that the combination of these two products did not give rise to serious competition concerns. Both parties also had anti-migraine drugs in clinical trials. Wellcome's product, 311C, was in Phase III clinical trials and its mode of action and pharmacological profile were very similar to those of Imigran. Glaxo had undertaken to grant an exclusive licence to a third party to develop and market either Wellcome's 311C or Glaxo's future anti-migraine drug. Glaxo would choose which of the two to license.

The Commission then went on to examine whether there were other compounds in a similar situation to that of Wellcome's 311C. It found that there were a number of compounds with the same mode of action and pharmacological profile as Imigran under R&D by large multinational pharmaceutical groups. At least two of them were at Phase III. The Commission stated that although "uncertainties always remain about the materialisation of potential competition in two successfully competing products, even for compounds in Phase III of clinical trials, the identified potential competitors are in a very similar situation to that of Wellcome, and the effect of the removal of Wellcome as a possible competitor of Glaxo's Imigran is therefore limited". A senior Commission official at the time, writing unofficially, commented that:

"The Commission did not wish to express a view on which new product was likely to succeed, and treated them all equally. This led it to say implicitly that if Wellcome was not successful, the disappearance of Wellcome's future product as a competitor to Glaxo was not important, but that if they were all successful Glaxo would have competition. The risk that the Commission was taking (that the competitors' products would not appear, and that Wellcome's product would be valuable) could only be dealt with by the exclusive licence which Glaxo promised".[129]

The Commission has never said expressly how many of these competing poles of research it will need to find before it is satisfied that the future market will be competitive.[130] In *Glaxo/Wellcome*, the Commission seems to have considered that two other credible poles would be sufficient. Subsequently, in Case COMP/M.1846, *Glaxo Wellcome/SmithKline Beecham*, the Commission examined the parties' pipeline products for the treatment of chronic obstructive pulmonary disease ("COPD") and asthma. SmithKline Beecham ("SB") had no existing respiratory products on the market, but Glaxo Wellcome ("GW") had a number of market-leading products. In relation to asthma, there were a large number of competitors with pipeline products in Phase II and, as at least one competitor's product was likely to be launched before SB's product reached the market, the Commission concluded that competition concerns were unlikely to arise. In the field of second-line therapy (ie products used in combination with other therapies) for COPD, GW had a strong market position. Both GW and SB had products in Phase III of development for COPD: GW's existing asthma product Seretide and SB's new compound Ariflo. The Commission considered that, as COPD was an attractive market for future R&D, as GW and SB were pursuing different lines of research, and as there were a large number of current pipeline products and large players active on the market, this would not lead to a reduction of the overall R&D. However, the Commission was concerned at the risk that the use of SB's Ariflo for second-line treatment, where GW was already particularly strong, would reduce competition. The Commission noted that four competing compounds were in Phase III development—including products under development by AstraZeneca and Byk Gulden, both of which had sufficient resources to launch their product. However, because of GW's existing strength on the market, the Commission was concerned that the addition of Ariflo would

129. "European Community Antitrust Law—Innovation Markets and High Technology Industries", John Temple Lang, Fordham Corporate Law Institute, 17 October 1996.

130. Note that, in the TTBE Guidelines (note 74 above), at para 131, the Commission indicates that four or more further independently controlled technologies may suffice to eliminate any prospect of a restriction of competition (other than in the case of hardcore restrictions).

reinforce this position, particularly if the other Phase III products were to fail. The Commission noted that compounds at Phase III have a success rate of about 50 per cent and therefore accepted the parties' undertaking to out-license Ariflo if the other competing Phase III pipeline compounds for second-line therapy of COPD failed.

FORECLOSURE

The next issue to consider in the context of R&D agreements is possible foreclosure of the market. This may occur in the context of R&D agreements between non-competitors, where the agreement relates to the exclusive exploitation of the results of the R&D and if one of the parties has significant market power with respect to key technology, whether or not the parties are competitors.

The Commission considered the issue in its decision in *Pasteur Mérieux/ Merck.*[131] The Commission considered that the exclusivity granted to this joint venture might foreclose the market. It noted that, in view of the exclusivity arrangements, other producers would:

> "be limited in their possibilities to collaborate either with the parent companies or with the joint venture as a source for them to get access to [potentially important technology]. Given the position of the parties on the relevant markets, this will result, as regards existing and imminent vaccine technology, in an appreciable restriction of competition towards third parties. However, in relation to future products, the number of potential competitors for the products and technology meant that the joint venture was unlikely to lead to foreclosure of the market."

4.3.5.1.4 The R&D Block Exemption

An R&D agreement that falls within Article 81(1) will be exempted if it satisfies the conditions in Article 81(3).

This may happen automatically, if the agreement falls within the requirements of the R&D Block Exemption.[132]

SCOPE

The R&D Block Exemption, which follows the supposedly more flexible and less prescriptive economics-focused model first adopted in the Vertical Agreements Block Exemption, applies to agreements between two or more undertakings relating to:

- Joint R&D of products or processes and joint exploitation of the results.
- Joint exploitation of the results of R&D of products or processes jointly carried out pursuant to a prior agreement.
- Joint R&D without joint exploitation of the results.[133]

131. See note 128 above.
132. Regulation 2659/2000, 2000 OJ L 304, p 7.
133. *Ibid*, Article 1(a)–(c).

For these purposes, exploitation of the results of R&D means the production or distribution of products, the application of processes or the assignment or licensing of IP rights resulting from the R&D.[134] R&D or exploitation of the results of R&D occurs jointly where the work is carried out by a joint team, organisation or undertaking, is jointly entrusted to a third party, or allocated between the parties by way of specialisation in research, development, production or distribution.[135] This means that parties to an R&D agreement can divide between them the various elements of the R&D project, and can then agree between them that one of the parties will be responsible for manufacturing and distributing the resulting product.

CONDITIONS

The R&D block exemption is subject to a number of conditions:[136]

— All parties must have access to the results of the R&D, except that research bureaux that provide commercial R&D services without normally exploiting the results may agree to limit their use of the results to carrying out further research.

— Where the agreement does not provide for joint exploitation, each party must be free to exploit the results independently, although non-competitors may agree to limit their exploitation to specific technical fields of application.

— Any joint exploitation must relate to results protected by IP rights or constitute know-how, that substantially contributes to technical or economic progress and the results must be decisive for the manufacture of the products or the application of the processes.

— Except where the agreement provides for joint distribution of the products, any undertakings (parties or third parties) responsible for manufacture must be required to fulfil orders for supplies from all parties.

MARKET SHARE

Where the parties are not competing undertakings, the exemption lasts for the duration of the R&D and thereafter, where the results are jointly exploited, for seven years from the time that the products are first placed on the market within the European Economic Area ("EEA"), or until the parties' combined market share reaches 25 per cent.[137]

Where the parties are competing undertakings, the exemption lasts for the duration of the R&D only if, at the time that they enter into the agreement, the parties' combined share of the market for the products that are capable of being improved or replaced by the products resulting from the R&D does not exceed 25 per cent. As in the case of agreements between non-competitors, it

134. *Ibid*, Article 2(8).
135. *Ibid*, Article 2(11).
136. *Ibid*, Article 3.
137. *Ibid*, Article 4(1) and (3).

then lasts for seven years from the time that the products are first placed on the market within the EEA, or until the parties' combined market share reaches 25 per cent.[138]

Essentially, there is a grace period of up to a total of two years, essentially where an initial combined market share of not more than 25 per cent rises above that level during the term of the agreement. The questions of whether the parties are competitors, and of their combined market shares, while leading to a more realistic assessment of the impact on competition, can also introduce a significant element of uncertainty. In many cases it will be unrealistic to carry out a detailed assessment, given timing or budgetary constraints.[139]

Blacklisted restrictions

The block exemption does not apply[140] to agreements that:

- restrict the freedom of the parties to carry on R&D, independently or with third parties, in a field unconnected with the field of the joint R&D or, after the completion of the joint R&D, in the field of the joint R&D or a related or connected field;
- prohibit the parties from challenging relevant IP rights (however, it is permissible to provide for termination of the agreement in the event of a challenge);
- limit output;
- fix prices when selling the products to third parties;
- restrict the customers that the parties may serve after a period of seven years from the date on which the products are first placed on the market;
- prohibit one party from making passive sales into territories reserved for the other;
- prohibit the parties from making active sales into each other's territories after a period of seven years from the time when the products are first placed on the market within the EEA (in other words, each party has a seven-year window of protection against active sales from other territories);
- prohibit a party from licensing third parties to manufacture the products or apply the processes where neither party exploits the results of the joint R&D;
- prohibit the parties from meeting demand for the products from customers in their respective territories who would parallel-export the products into other territories within the EEA;
- include a requirement to make it difficult for users or resellers to obtain the products from the parties, in particular by using IP rights to partition the EEA.

138. *Ibid*, Article 4(2) and (3).
139. *Ibid*, Article 6.
140. *Ibid*, Article 5.

4.3.5 Application of Article 81

WITHDRAWAL OF THE BLOCK EXEMPTION

The Commission (or, since the entry into force of Regulation 1/2003, a national competition authority)[141] may withdraw the benefit of the block exemption where an agreement has effects incompatible with Article 81(3). Examples are set out in the R&D Block Exemption.[142]

R&D AGREEMENTS OUTSIDE THE BLOCK EXEMPTION

The guidelines set out a number of factors specific to R&D agreements that will be relevant to an assessment of whether an agreement that falls outside the block exemption (in particular because the parties' combined market share is more than 25 per cent) satisfies the conditions for exemption on an individual basis.

4.3.5.2 Production agreements

4.3.5.2.1 Introduction

The Commission's guidelines similarly address the treatment of joint production agreements. These include joint production agreements themselves, where the parties agree to produce certain products jointly; specialisation agreements, where the parties allocate between themselves the production of certain products and then enter into supply agreements with each other; and subcontracting agreements. The latter are covered by the Guidelines only where they involve subcontracting between competitors.

The main source of competition problems in production agreements is the coordination of the parties' competitive behaviour as suppliers. This is likely to occur where the parties are competitors on the market directly affected by the cooperation, or on an upstream, downstream or closely related market. However, cooperation is likely to lead to coordination only where it relates to an activity that accounts for a significant proportion of the parties' costs. In *Philips/Osram*,[143] the jointly produced glass accounted for only 2 or 3 per cent of the parties' downstream lamp production and the Commission concluded that there was no restriction of competition on the lamp market. In contrast, joint production of a major component of a downstream product is more likely to lead to a coordination of the parties' prices on the downstream market.

Other possible issues include foreclosure as a result of one of the parties having a strong market position, for example in an upstream market, that allows the parties to raise their rivals' costs.

4.3.5.2.2 Agreements that fall outside Article 81(1)

Production agreements between non-competitors are therefore unlikely to be caught by Article 81(1), in the absence of foreclosure issues.

141. By virtue of Article 29(2) of Regulation 1/2003, where an agreement has effects incompatible with Article 81(3) in the territory of a Member State.

142. In Article 7.

143. 1994 OJ L 378, p 37.

Production agreements between competitors are also unlikely to fall within Article 81(1) where the cooperation is the only possible commercially justifiable way of entering a new market, launching a new product or carrying a specific project. Coordination is also unlikely where the parties only have a small proportion of their total costs in common.

4.3.5.2.3 Agreements that almost always fall within Article 81(1)

As usual, production agreements that fix prices, limit output, or share customers or markets, almost always fall within Article 81(1).

4.3.5.2.4 Agreements that may fall within Article 81(1)

Production agreements between competitors that create a significant degree of commonality of costs, but do not involve hardcore restrictions, will require individual analysis. Relevant factors will be market share (the Guidelines note that below 20 per cent market share, and provided that other relevant conditions are satisfied, the agreement will fall within the Specialisation Agreements Block Exemption and there is therefore no need to conduct an in-depth analysis), concentration and number of players on the market.

4.3.5.2.5 The Specialisation Agreements Block Exemption

The Specialisation Agreements Block Exemption[144] adopts an approach similar to that of the R&D Block Exemption.

SCOPE

The block exemption applies to the following types of agreements between two or more undertakings:[145]

- *Unilateral specialisation agreements*, under which one party agrees to cease production, or not to commence production, of certain products and to purchase the products from a competing undertaking, and the other party agrees to produce and supply those products.
- *Reciprocal specialisation agreements*, under which two or more parties agree to cease production, or not to commence production, of certain different products and to purchase those products from the other parties, who agree to produce and supply those products.
- *Joint production agreements*, under which two or more parties agree to produce certain products jointly.

The exemption also applies where the parties accept an exclusive purchase and/or supply obligation in the context of one of these three types of agreement, or where the parties do not sell the products independently, but provide

144. Regulation 2658/2000, 2000 OJ L 304, p 3.
145. *Ibid*, Article 1(1).

for joint distribution or, in the context of a joint production agreement, appoint a non-competing third party as distributor.

MARKET SHARE

The block exemption applies on condition that the parties' combined market share does not exceed 20 per cent.[146] As in the case of the R&D Block Exemption, there is a grace period of up to a total of two years where the market share level is exceeded.[147]

BLACKLISTED RESTRICTIONS

With a couple of limited exceptions, the exemption does not apply to agreements that fix prices when selling the products to third parties, limit output or sales, or allocate markets or customers.[148]

WITHDRAWAL OF THE BLOCK EXEMPTION

As in the case of the R&D Block Exemption, the Commission or a national competition authority may withdraw the benefit of the block exemption where the conditions of Article 81(3) are not being met.[149]

4.3.5.3 Purchasing agreements

Purchasing agreements are agreements under which two or more parties join together in order to carry out purchasing activities. They are often entered into in order to secure better terms and conditions than would be available to individual purchasers.

There may be two relevant markets to consider in this type of arrangement: the market in which the purchasing takes place and, where the participants in the joint purchasing agreement compete as sellers on a downstream market, that market as well.

Concerns arising in relation to the purchasing market may arise where the parties to the joint purchasing agreement have a high combined share of the purchasing market and compete on the downstream selling market. Lower prices paid by the parties on the purchasing market may not be passed on to customers on the downstream selling market. The higher the parties' combined share of the selling market, the more likely it is that they will coordinate their behaviour on that market. In addition, competitors on the selling market who are not parties to the purchasing agreement may find their access to efficient suppliers limited, and may find prices increased to them to compensate for lower prices secured by the purchasing group.

The Commission considers that such problems are unlikely to occur where the parties have a combined share of less than 15 per cent of the purchasing market and less than 15 per cent of the selling market. Above that share, there

146. *Ibid*, Article 4.
147. *Ibid*, Article 6.
148. *Ibid*, Article 5.
149. *Ibid*, Article 7.

is no automatic presumption of competition problems, but a closer examination will be required.

A particular subset of joint purchasing agreements is business-to-business ("B2B"). These are electronic marketplaces putting purchasers and sellers in contact with each other with a view to increasing choice and reducing transaction costs. Their analysis requires consideration of purchasing and selling markets. They give rise to two main competition concerns: collusion and foreclosure of third parties.

The risk of collusion results from the transparency that is a feature of B2B exchanges—it may be possible for businesses to have access to each other's price information. For example, in the context of an exchange in the form of an online auction, it may be possible for bidders to see each other's offers, and similarly sellers may have access to each other's sale prices.

In the *Volbroker* case,[150] involving the creation of a joint venture to provide an electronic brokerage service for trading in foreign currency options, the Commission first elaborated guidelines to create safeguards against collusion. These *Volbroker* guidelines, which have been applied in subsequent cases, are as follows:

- none of the staff or management of the exchange should have any contractual or other obligation towards any of the parents of the joint venture;
- the staff and management of the exchange must be in a location geographically distinct from that of the parents;
- the representatives of the parents on the board of the exchange joint venture must not have access to commercially sensitive information relating to each other or to third parties;
- the parents must not have access to the information technology and communication systems of the exchange joint venture;
- the parents must ensure that the staff and management of all the parents and of the joint venture itself understand and appreciate the importance of maintaining the confidentiality of sensitive commercial information and that sanctions for breach are spelt out.

The other main risk is foreclosure—the possibility that non-members of an exchange, or certain classes of member, will be disadvantaged. In *Covisint*,[151] relating to an internet marketplace joint venture of that name established by Ford, DaimlerChrysler, General Motors, Renault and Nissan (and subsequently PSA Peugeot and Citroën), the Commission pointed out that B2B marketplaces were in general expected to have pro-competitive effects. They should create more transparency and might also create market efficiencies by reducing search and information costs and improving inventory management.

150. "Commission approves the Volbroker.com electronic brokerage joint venture between six major banks" IP/00/896, 31 July 2000.

151. "Commission clears the creation of the Covisint Automotive Internet Marketplace" IP/01/1155, 31 July 2001.

However, the Commission pointed out that such exchanges might have negative effects on competition that could outweigh these market efficiencies. This would in particular be the case where there was discrimination against certain classes of users leading to foreclosure. The Commission noted that Covisint was open to all firms in the industry on a non-discriminatory basis. This appears to be recognition that Covisint (which would be used by many major component suppliers as well as motor manufacturers) would, because of its size, lead to network effects. Similarly, in *Volbroker*, the Commission recognised that the liquidity of the exchange was such that it was likely to find the market tipping in its favour, and therefore sought remedies to address possible exclusionary effects.

4.3.5.4 Commercialisation agreements

Commercialisation agreements include agreements for joint selling, promotion, distribution, after-sales service and advertising. Of these, distribution agreements are covered by the Vertical Agreements Block Exemption.

Because these types of agreement have effects closer to the market than, for example, R&D agreements, they present a greater risk of hardcore restrictions of competition such as price-fixing and market-sharing. Joint selling agreements between competitors are particularly likely to infringe Article 81(1). The Guidelines set out the factors to be taken into account in both the Article 81(1) and Article 81(3) analyses.

4.3.5.5 Information exchanges

Information exchanges are not specifically mentioned in the horizontal agreements Guidelines. However, they are relatively common, particularly in the context of trade associations. At one end of the spectrum, they provide a means by which undertakings can align themselves with best industry practice. At the other end, they may involve exchanges of price information that allow competitors to anticipate or respond to each other's behaviour. In this way, exchanges of information may form the basis of a concerted practice relating to price rises. Disclosure of information prior to a price movement will therefore invariably be treated as a serious infringement.

Disclosure of information after a price movement will not automatically be treated as a serious infringement. However, the regular and systematic exchange of specific information on prices between competitors will infringe Article 81(1) where it covers, or allows competitors to work out, confidential information relating to individual undertakings.

The smaller the number of undertakings operating in the market, the more frequent the exchange, and the more sensitive and confidential the nature of the information that is exchanged, the more likely an infringement is.

While exchanges of non-price information are not so clearly anti-competitive as exchanges of price information, they may nevertheless infringe the competition rules if they permit competitors to adjust their behaviour on the basis of what they learn.

The exchange of information on matters other than price may have an appreciable effect on competition depending on the type of information exchanged and the market to which it relates. The exchange of statistical data, market research and general industry studies, for example, are unlikely to have an effect on competition provided that the information exchanged relates to what the Commission has called "opinion and experience" and does not enable confidential or sensitive business information to be shared.

In general, the exchange of information on output and sales should not affect competition provided that it is sufficiently historical and cannot influence future competitive market behaviour. There may, however, be an appreciable effect on competition if it is possible to disaggregate the information and identify the participants. This may also be the case if the exchange relates to recent, current or future information.

The Commission set out useful guidance in this area in its decision on the exchange of non-price information in the agricultural tractor sector.[152] In those cases, the Commission found that an exchange of very recent data, derived from vehicle registration documents, allowed manufacturers to compare market share and sales figures and was likely to eliminate competition and to increase entry barriers by identifying new market entrants and allowing existing players to respond quickly. In particular, the Commission highlighted, as one of the important reasons for the adverse impact on competition of the scheme, the oligopolistic nature of the market. Four undertakings accounted for 80 per cent of total sales on the UK market. The CFI and the ECJ upheld the Commission's decision. The Commission subsequently issued "comfort letters" in relation to the tractor information exchange system, setting out the following principles:

- individual data may not be exchanged until 12 months after the event to which the information relates; and
- aggregate market data that may be less than 12 months old may be exchanged if the data are supplied on behalf of at least three independent dealers. If there are fewer than three dealers, data may be exchanged only if they relate to more than 10 tractor units. The concern in this case is obviously to ensure that data cannot be disaggregated to give the figures for individual dealers.

Again, the Commission pointed to the high degree of concentration in the market.

In the press release accompanying the comfort letters, the Commission stated that the principles set out in the comfort letters "set out clear guidelines

152. *UK Agricultural Tractor Registration Exchange*, 1992 OJ L 68, p 19; Case C-7/95, *John Deere v. Commission* [1998] ECR I 3111; Commission Press Release IP(99)690.

for any exchanges of information in other economic sectors as highly concentrated as the market for tractors and agricultural machinery".

4.3.5.6 Standardisation agreements

The guidelines also address standardisation agreements, under which parties define technical or quality requirements with which products or services may comply. An agreement on technical or design standards may lead to an improvement in production by reducing costs or raising quality, or it may promote technical or economic progress by reducing waste and consumers' search costs. The agreement may, however, have an appreciable effect on competition if it includes restrictions on what the parties may produce or is, in effect, a means of limiting competition from other sources, for example by raising entry barriers.

Where participation in standard-setting is voluntary and there is no obligation to comply with the standard, there is unlikely to be any restrictive effect. In contrast, agreements that impose standards as a means of excluding certain competitors are likely to infringe Article 81(1). Generally, the restrictive effect of a standardisation agreement depends on the extent to which the parties remain free to develop alternative standards or products that do not comply with the agreed standard. High market shares of the parties to the agreement are of concern only where the standard forecloses the market.

4.3.5.7 Environmental agreements

Agreements to achieve specific environmental objectives are generally treated positively under Article 81. Agreements whereby a large proportion of production on a particular product market is phased out in favour of products with a lower environmental impact are likely to fall within Article 81(1). The environmental benefits of such agreements must be weighed against their restrictive effect and their compliance costs. Where there is a net benefit to individual consumers, there is no need to consider the aggregate environmental benefit. Otherwise it may be necessary to consider net benefits for consumers in general. As always, the agreement will not fall within Article 81(3) if the restrictions are not indispensable or if the agreement results in the elimination of competition in respect of a significant part of the market.

For example, in *CECED*,[153] manufacturers representing approximately 90 per cent of EEA washing-machine supply agreed to phase out less energy-efficient models. The agreement clearly restricted competition. The Commission then considered the application of Article 81(3), assessing both benefits to individual consumers and the overall benefit of the agreement, noting that on reasonable assumptions the benefits to society resulting from reduced carbon dioxide, sulphur dioxide and nitrous oxide emissions was more than

153. 2000 OJ L 187, p 47.

seven times the increased purchase costs of more energy-efficient washing machines.[154]

4.3.6 A methodology for analysis

It will be clear from the preceding sections that horizontal agreements are very diverse and raise a wide range of possible competition concerns. It can be difficult to know where to start in an analysis, particularly where an agreement includes more than one of the elements examined above. One possible approach is as follows:

- Does the agreement create a full-function joint venture that constitutes a concentration with a Community dimension for the purposes of the EC Merger Regulation? If so, it requires notification to the Commission. Coordination of the parents' competitive behaviour on the market affected by the joint venture, or a related market, requires analysis under Article 2(4) ECMR, applying Article 81(1) and (3) of the Treaty.
- Does the agreement contain hardcore restrictions? If so, consider whether it is a cartel in disguise, requiring immediate termination and possible leniency application.
- What is or are the relevant market or markets? Consider the market for the products or services directly affected by the cooperation, and upstream and downstream markets.
- Are the parties actual or potential competitors in any of those markets? In considering whether they are potential competitors, consider whether they would realistically enter the market independently or perform the activity that is the subject of the agreement.
- If they are not competitors, competition problems are unlikely in the absence of significant market power in one market leading to foreclosure in a related market.
- If they are competitors, what is their combined market share? If it is less than, say, 15 per cent, competition problems are unlikely. A shortcut at this stage is to take the view that if the "centre of gravity" of the agreement is R&D and the parties' combined market share is less than 25 per cent, or if it is joint production or specialisation and the parties' combined market share is less than 20 per cent (in both cases subject to grace periods), it is unnecessary to analyse any possible restriction of competition in detail, because the agreement will be

154. But note that environmental benefits are not expressly mentioned in the Commission's guidelines on the application of Article 81(3); see 3.3.1 above. Given that it is unlikely that an agreement conferring environmental benefits would be held not to satisfy Article 81(3), it seems likely that environmental benefits would be subsumed under technical or economic progress generally.

exempted under the relevant block exemption if it does not contain blacklisted restrictions.

— If it is not possible to take the view that a block exemption applies, what is the centre of gravity of the agreement—joint R&D, specialisation, purchasing, commercialisation etc? Assess the agreement in the light of the Guidelines applicable to that type of agreement. Does the agreement appreciably restrict competition, either by giving rise to coordination in the market affected by the product or a related market, or by foreclosing third parties?

— If the agreement gives rise to an appreciable restriction of competition, does it satisfy the conditions for exemption, either automatically under one of the two block exemptions, or individually?

CHAPTER 5

ARTICLE 82: PRINCIPLES AND APPLICATION

Martin Baker, Taylor Wessing and Pat Treacy, Bristows

5.1 INTRODUCTION

Article 82 of the EC Treaty applies only to firms that have dominant market power, and seeks to prevent the abuse of such power for anti-competitive ends. It prohibits the abuse of dominant market power either by the unilateral conduct of a single dominant firm or by the independent action of several oligopolists. It is the abuse of a dominant position that is prohibited, rather than the dominant position itself.

Article 82 provides:

"Any abuse by one or more undertakings[1] of a dominant position within the common market or in a substantial part of it shall be prohibited as incompatible with the common market insofar as it may affect trade between Member States."

In interpreting Article 82, competition authorities may, with an appropriate degree of caution, draw on cases from other areas such as Article 81 and merger decisions, which may share common elements such as dominance in neighbouring markets,[2] portfolio power[3] and bundling.[4]

Recent cases focusing on elements of dominance such as the trilogy of merger cases starting with *Airtours*[5] show that the Commission can be challenged in its assessment of dominance (both in its legal, and particularly its factual, elements). Since 1 May 2004, both the Commission and national competition authorities ("NCAs") will have to be more transparent in the reasoning for their decisions and far more thorough in proving each of the elements of abuse of dominance that are analysed below.[6]

1. An undertaking is any entity engaged in an economic activity regardless of its legal status and the way in which it is financed (Case C67/96, *Albany International BV* [2000] 4 CMLR 446).

2. *Walters Kluwer/Reed Elsevier*, Report on Competition Policy 1998, p 53.

3. Case M.833, *Coca-Cola/Carlsberg*, 1998 OJ L 145, p 41; Case M.938, *Guinness/Grand Metropolitan*, 1998 OJ L 288, p 24.

4. Case M.2220, *GE/Honeywell*, IP/01/939.

5. Case T-342/99, *Airtours v. Commission* [2002] ECR II 2585; Case T-310/01, *Schneider Electric v. Commission* [2002] ECR II 04071; Case T-5/02, *Tetra Laval v. Commission* [2002] ECR II 4381.

6. By virtue of Regulation 1/2003, 2003 OJ L 1, p 1.

The new competition regime in place means that NCAs must apply Article 82 as well as the equivalent national rules where abusive conduct may affect trade between EU Member States, although stricter national rules may be applied.

5.2 RELEVANT MARKET

Market definitions are key to determining whether a dominant position exists. The narrower the market, the greater the likelihood of an undertaking holding a position of market power.

5.2.1 Product market[7]

The product market is the market for all the products and/or services in question that are regarded as interchangeable, or substitutable, by the consumer by reason of their use, price and characteristics.[8]

Product markets tend to be defined narrowly. In one case, the Commission defined a relevant product market as the market for brass band instruments for British-style brass bands (rather than the market for brass instruments as a whole).[9] Several new product market areas are developing, such as secondary markets and technology markets.

5.2.2 Geographic market

The geographic market is the area in which the undertakings concerned are involved in the supply and demand of products or services, in which the conditions of competition are sufficiently homogeneous, and which can be distinguished from neighbouring areas because the conditions of competition are appreciably different in those areas.[10]

5.3 DOMINANT POSITION

The test for establishing dominance has been set out clearly by the European Court of Justice ("ECJ") as:

"a position of economic strength enjoyed by an undertaking which enables it to prevent effective competition being maintained on the relevant market by giving it the power to

7. Other Chapters in this book analyse the concept of relevant product markets in greater detail.
8. Commission Notice on the definition of the relevant market, 1997 OJ C/372/03, para 7.
9. *BBI/Boosey & Hawkes* [1988] 4 CMLR 67.
10. Commission Notice on the definition of the relevant market, n 8 above, p 3.

behave to an *appreciable extent* independently of its competitors, customers and ultimately of its consumers".[11] (Emphasis added.)

It has been suggested that the dominant position must enable the undertaking to influence the market at will.[12]

5.3.1 Assessment of dominance

Once the relevant product and geographic markets are ascertained, it is then necessary to decide whether the undertaking is dominant in those markets. Dominant companies are not necessarily monopolists, although monopolists will generally have a dominant position.

Dominance is assessed on a case-by-case basis depending on a number of factors, no one of which is conclusive,[13] for example:

- — high, stable market shares, especially in relation to competitors;
- — access to raw materials and capital;
- — technical knowledge and expertise;
- — barriers to entry; and
- — existence of any abusive behaviour.[14]

5.3.2 Market share

An important factor, though not always conclusive, is the existence of a large market share.

11. Case C-322/81, *Michelin NV v. Commission* [1985] 1 CMLR 380.
12. Advocate-General's Opinion, Case C-34/01, *Enirisorse SpA v. Ministero delle Finanze*, 7 November 2002 (opinion not published).
13. Commission Guidelines on market analysis and the calculation of significant market power, 2002 OJ C 165, p 6.
14. Case 27/76, *United Brands v. Commission* [1978] 1 CMLR 429; Case T-203/01, *Michelin II v. Commission* [2004] 4 CMLR 923.

5.3.2 Article 82: Principles and Application

Table 1: Market share and dominance

Market share	Observation
85–90%	Usually conclusive of dominance.[15]
75%	Indicative of dominance.[16]
more than 50%	Strong evidence of dominance, where held for three years, except in exceptional circumstances.[17]
40% or more	Evidence of dominance.[18] Considered with other factors.
25–40%	Single dominance unlikely unless there is a fragmented market and significant other factors.[19]
20%	Possibility of dominance left open. Considered with other factors.[20]
10%	Too small.[21]

The lowest market share where the Commission has established dominance is 39.7 per cent.[22]

5.3.3 Relative size of market share

Another relevant consideration is the relative size of the market shares of the firm's nearest rivals. In *Vitamins*,[23] a market share of 47 per cent in the market for vitamin A was sufficient where the competitors only had market shares of 22 per cent, 18 per cent and 1 per cent. The weaker and smaller the competitors, the less capable they are of exerting real competitive pressure on the dominant undertaking.[24]

15. Case C-85/76, *Hoffmann-La Roche* [1979] 3 CMLR 211. But see merger cases such as Case M.068, *Tetra Pak v. Alfa-Laval*, 1991 OJ L 290, p 35, where even a market share of 90 per cent did not confer dominance. In such cases countervailing buying power is often a relevant factor: see Case M.1225, *Enso/Stora* [1998] Reports on Compensation Cases 54 and Case M.1684, *Carrefour/Promodes*, European Commission website.

16. Case C-85/76, *Hoffmann-La Roche* [1979] 3 CMLR 211.

17. Case C-62/86, *Akzo v. Commission* [1991] ECR I 3359. But note that other factors were also regarded as relevant. (Referred to in Case T-395/94, *Atlantic Container Line v. Commission* [2002] ECR II 595 and Case 322/81, *Michelin v. Commission* [1985] 1 CMLR 380.)

18. Case C-85/76, *Hoffmann-La Roche* [1979] 3 CMLR 211.

19. *Grundig*, 1985 OJ L 233, p 1; [1988] CMLR 865.

20. *Metaleurop*, 1989 OJ C 100, p 2; [1989] 4 CMLR 745.

21. Case 75/84, *SABA II Metro SB v. Commission (No 2)* [1987] 1 CMLR 118.

22. Case T-219/99, *British Airways plc v. Commission* [2004] 4 CMLR 19 (subject to appeal in Case C-94/04).

23. Case 85/76, *Hoffmann-La Roche v. Commission* [1979] ECR 461.

24. Case T-395/94, *Atlantic Container Line v. Commission* [2002] ECR II 595, para 341.

5.3.4 Stability of market share

The undertaking must have the ability to maintain its market shares in the longer term through the exercise of its market power.[25] The period of time required will depend on the facts of the case. In *Vitamins*, a market share of between 29 and 51 per cent over a three-year period was not sufficient to confer dominance in the vitamin B3 market. Fluctuating market shares tend to suggest an absence of dominance. It is for this reason that high market shares in a new market are not a sufficient indication of dominance.[26]

5.3.5 Leveraged market power

Where an undertaking has dominance on a specific market, it may also be deemed to have dominance on a closely related market, if the links between the two markets are such that market power on one market can be leveraged into the other.

Where an undertaking is able to exercise leveraged market power over a market other than the dominated market, it may infringe Article 82 by abusing its position on that other market. In *Tetra Pak II*,[27] the court held that special circumstances existed since Tetra Pak was not only in a quasi-monopoly position on the market but also held a strong market position on the associated market. Customers on one market were potential customers on the other, so Tetra Pak was in a position comparable to that of a company holding a dominant position on the markets in question as a whole.

5.3.6 Potential competition

Where potential competitors are able to enter the market and provide a significant competitive deterrent, then dominance is unlikely to arise. Bidding markets, where businesses compete *for* the market, rather than *in* the market, provide a good illustration of where an analysis of market share alone is inadequate. The key issue is whether there are a sufficient number of credible bidders left in the market to take part in future bids.[28]

5.3.7 Entry barriers

Entry barriers play a key role in assessing dominance. The higher the barriers, the less the likelihood of market entry and the greater the likelihood of market power being maintained.[29] Entry barriers include:

25. Case T-65/98, *Van den Bergh v. Commission* [2004] 4 CMLR 1.
26. Case IV/M.469, *MSG Media Services*, 1994 OJ L 364, p 1.
27. Case C-333/94P *Tetra Pak International SA v. Commission* ("Tetra Pak II") [1994] ECR II 755.
28. See for example Case M.950, *Hoffmann-La Roche/Boehringer Mannheim*, 1998 OJ L 234, p 14; Case M.225, *France Telecom/Equant*, IP/01/426, 22 March 2001.
29. Costs of doing business need to be distinguished from sunk costs.

— regulatory factors;
— intellectual property ("IP") rights;
— brand strength and customer loyalty;[30]
— standards,[31] official or unofficial; and
— portfolio power.

Barriers to entry will depend on the sector. In the telecoms sector, for example, they are often high, due to existing legislative and regulatory requirements that can limit the number of available licences.[32]

5.3.8 Intellectual property

The mere ownership of one or more intellectual property ("IP") rights does not of itself create a dominant position.[33] But in many cases, the ownership of IP rights, where taken in conjunction with other factors such as a high market share, may result in a finding of an absence of effective competition and hence dominance.[34]

5.3.9 Portfolio power

"Portfolio power" is a controversial concept. It is the market power accruing to a business as a result of the addition of a number or range of leading brands that exceeds the sum of the component parts. It is a particular example of purchasing complementarities and range effects.

As the Commission explained in *Guinness/Grand Metropolitan*:[35]

"The holder of a portfolio of leading . . . brands may enjoy a number of advantages. In particular, his position in relation to his customers is stronger since he is able to provide a range of products and will account for a greater proportion of their business, he will have greater flexibility to structure his prices, promotions and discounts, he will have greater potential for tying, and he will be able to realise economies of scale and scope in his sales and marketing activities. Finally the implicit (or explicit) threat of a refusal to supply is more potent."

The concept has been applied in a number of cases by the Commission.[36] In the Commission's decision to block the GE/Honeywell merger, it considered it a significant factor that there would be an increased incentive for the merged

30. Case T-65/98, *Van den Bergh v. Commission* [2004] 4 CMLR 1.
31. *NDC Health/IMS Health*, 2002 OJ L 059, p 18.
32. Commission Guidelines on market analysis and the calculation of significant market power, n 13 above, p 6.
33. Case C-241/91P, *RTE v. Commission* [1995] 4 CMLR 718.
34. Case C-53/92P, *Hilti AG v. Commission* [1994] 4 CMLR 614.
35. Case M.938, *Guinness/Grand Metropolitan*, 1998 OJ L 288, p 24.
36. Case M.950, *Hoffmann-La Roche/Boehringer Mannheim* 1998 OJ L 234, p 14; See also Case M.877, *Boeing/McDonnell Douglas*, 1997 OJ L 336, p 16, and Case M.2220, *GE/Honeywell*, 2004 OJ L 48, p 1.

entity to engage in bundling of products, given the massive product portfolio it would have.[37] The concept of portfolio power has also been adopted by the UK competition authorities.[38]

However, a portfolio of products on different markets can also be an effective *deterrent* to anti-competitive behaviour. In *Babyliss v. Commission*,[39] a merger case, the European Court of First Instance ("CFI") considered the "product range effect". The Commission argued that if the total turnover on the relevant markets where the merged entity would have a dominant position only represented a small amount of the parties' total turnover, retailers would be able to punish any attempt at anti-competitive behaviour by the entity on other markets. The CFI accepted the possibility of such an effect, but on the facts it found that the Commission had not considered the entirety of the dominated markets and that it had not taken into consideration the total turnover for those markets in order to verify the possibility of a product range effect.

5.3.10 Integration

An increased level of vertical integration, whether upstream or downstream, can in fact be pro-competitive, as it can increase efficiency and limit interdependence[40] if undertakings promote their own distribution channels over those of other undertakings. However, it may also prevent market entry and permit other types of abusive behaviour.[41]

5.3.11 Abusive behaviour

The fact that acts amounting to abusive behaviour may be considered as evidence of dominance was asserted in *United Brands*.[42] It was followed by the Commission in *Michelin II*[43] in finding that Michelin's practice of granting a wide range of loyalty rebates was an indication of its dominant position.

5.3.12 Collective dominance

Collective dominance, which is prohibited, tends to occur where there are a smaller number of businesses in a market who take strategic decisions by taking into account the prospective conduct of their rivals. The practical

37. Commission Decision in Case M.2220, *GE/Honeywell*, 2004 OJ L 48, p 1, para 361.
38. *Interbrew/Bass Brewers*, Cmnd 5014, January 2001.
39. Case T-114/02, *Babyliss v. Commission* [2003] ECR II 01279.
40. Case T-342/99, *Airtours v. Commission* [2002] ECR II 2585, para 106.
41. See *Deutsche Telekom*, 2003 OJ L 263, p 9; Case T-228/97, *Irish Sugar v. Commission* [1999] 5 CMLR 1300.
42. Case 27/76, *United Brands v. Commission* [1978] ECR 207, paras 67–68.
43. Case T-203/01, *Michelin II v. Commission* ("Michelin II") [2004] 4 CMLR 923.

difficulty is that businesses are entitled to adapt their own market strategy to the existing or anticipated conduct of their competitors.[44]

The court set out in *Compagnie Maritime Belge* the principle that "a dominant position may be held by two or more economic entities legally independent of each other, provided that from an economic point of view they present themselves or act together on a particular market as a collective entity".[45] In *Airtours*[46] the court interpreted the concept of collective dominance to mean, in effect, a situation of tacit collusion.

To establish a position of collective dominance, one has to assess any economic links between competitors, particularly structural links,[47] on a case-by-case basis to ascertain whether the operation would change the competitive relations between them, thereby making anti-competitive parallel behaviour more likely. Important points to bear in mind are that:

- — no agreement is required;[48]
- — other connecting factors, such as market structure, are relevant;[49]
- — vertical links do not preclude collective dominance.

Unlike single-company dominance, a high market share coupled with other general indicators of dominance will not be sufficient to establish collective dominance: something more is necessary.

The concept of collective dominance came under particular scrutiny in the *Airtours* case,[50] in which the CFI overturned the Commission's decision to block a bid by Airtours (now MyTravel) for First Choice in a highly critical judgment. The court concluded that the Commission had comprehensively failed to show that a collectively dominant position or oligopoly would be created that would impede effective competition in the market. It confirmed the principle of collective dominance, but set out clear guidelines for conditions which must be met to make such a finding:

- — each member of the oligopoly must know how the others are behaving so that it can follow the same policy on issues such as pricing and supply;
- — members must be deterred from changing their policy through fear of retaliation;
- — the oligopoly must be so powerful that it can withstand challenge from other competitors, potential new market entrants and customers.

44. Case C-7/95P, *John Deere v. Commission* [1993] ECR I 1375.

45. Case C-395/96P, *Compagnie Maritime Belge v. Commission* [2000] 4 CMLR 971.

46. Case T-342/99, *Airtours v. Commission* [2002] ECR II 2585—the principles are applicable even though this was a merger case.

47. Case T-342/99, *Airtours v. Commission* [2002] ECR II 2585; and see Case 209/99, Case C-309/99, *Wouters* [2002] ECR I 1577.

48. Case C-395/96P, *Compagnie Maritime Belge v. Commission* [2000] 4 CMLR 971. The Commission cannot recycle Article 81 factors to establish a sufficient linkage although these factors *may* be sufficient if they are sustainable.

49. Case C-395/96P, *Compagnie Maritime Belge v. Commission* [2000] 4 CMLR 971, para 45.

50. Case T-342/99, *Airtours v. Commission* [2002] ECR II 2585.

5.4 THE COMMON MARKET, OR A SUBSTANTIAL PART OF IT

This is decided from an economic,[51] and generally not a geographic, perspective.

Even geographically small areas may be a substantial part of the common market if they are of particular economic importance. Although a single Member State, or even a part of a Member State, has been recognised as a substantial part of the common market, this will not always be the case. If competitive conditions throughout a national market are constant, so that the national market must be regarded as the relevant market for the purposes of establishing a dominant position, a strong position on a regional market will not suffice to bring the holder's conduct within Article 82.

Examples of "substantial parts of the common market" include:

- — The London airports;[52]
- — The ports of Genoa and Holyhead;[53]
- — The UK-France electricity interconnector;[54]
- — The German region of Rheinlandpfalz.[55]

5.5 ABUSE OF A DOMINANT POSITION

5.5.1 What is an abuse?

An abuse is any conduct on the part of a dominant undertaking which has the effect of hindering the maintenance of the degree of competition still existing in the market or the growth of that competition.

Article 82 provides that such abuse may, in particular, consist in the following (although this is not an exhaustive list):

(a) directly or indirectly imposing unfair purchase or selling prices or other unfair trading conditions;
(b) limiting production, markets or technical development to the prejudice of consumers;
(c) applying dissimilar conditions to equivalent transactions with other trading parties, thereby placing them at a competitive disadvantage; and
(d) making the conclusion of contracts subject to acceptance by the other parties of supplementary obligations which, by their nature or

51. Case 40/73, *Suiker Unie v. Commission* [1976] 1 CMLR 295.
52. Case IV/33.544, *British Midland v. Aer Lingus* [1993] 4 CMLR 596.
53. Case IV/34.174, *Sealink/B&I* [1992] 5 CMLR 255.
54. IP/01/341, 12 March 2001.
55. Advocate-General's Opinion, Case C-475/99, *Ambulanz Glockner v. Landkreis Südwestpfalz* [2001] ECR I 8089.

according to commercial usage, have no connection with the subject of such contracts.

5.5.2 Aspects of abuse

The mere strengthening of a dominant position is, at least in theory, not an abuse in itself.[56] However, if the undertaking in a dominant position strengthens that position so that the degree of dominance then reached substantially fetters competition, this will be an abuse. This is so regardless of the means or the procedure by which it is achieved, and is irrespective of any fault.[57] Abuse occurs where:

- Acts or omissions go beyond normal competitive behaviour (eg competing on price, quality, innovation and service) and the dominant enterprise reaps benefits which it would not have obtained had there been normal competition.
- The undertaking behaves in a way that influences the structure of a market where, as a result of the presence of the dominant undertaking, the degree of competition is weakened, through the use of methods different to those that condition normal competition, and that behaviour hinders the maintenance of the degree of competition still existing in the market or the growth of that competition.[58]
- An existing dominant position is strengthened. (Creation of a dominant position is not prohibited.)

In some circumstances businesses that have a dominant position may be precluded from taking action that is not of itself an abuse and which would be permissible if undertaken by a non-dominant business.[59] A recent example is *Van den Bergh Foods*, where an exclusive agreement was found to be an abuse despite the fact that exclusive agreements between non-dominant companies are generally pro-competitive.[60]

5.5.3 Where the effects of abuse are felt

The effects of the abuse need not be felt on the market in which the enterprise is dominant in order to fall within Article 82. They may occur on a related

56. Case C-250/92, *Gottrup-Klim* [1994] ECR I–641 [1996] 4 CMLR 191.

57. Case 6/72, *Europemballage and Continental Can v. Commission* [1973] ECR 215, para 26, confirmed by Case C-395/96P, *Compagnie Maritime Belge v. Commission* [2000] ECR I–1365, 4 CMLR 1076, para 114; Case T-128/98, *Aéroports de Paris v. Commission* [2000] ECR II 3929, para 170, upheld on appeal by ECJ in Case C-82/01, [2002] ECR I 9297; Case T-65/98, *Van den Bergh Foods v. Commission* [2004] 4 CMLR 1.

58. Case C-85/76, *Hoffmann-La Roche v. Commission* [1979] 3 CMLR 211; Case C-322/81, *Michelin v. Commission* [1985] 1 CMLR 380; and as affirmed in Case T-228/97, *Irish Sugar v. Commission* [1999] 5 CMLR 1300.

59. Case T-111/96, *ITT Promedia v. Commission* [1998] ECR II 2937 at 2987; Case T-65/98, *Van den Bergh Foods Ltd v. Commission* [2004] 4 CMLR 1.

60. Case T-65/98, *Van den Bergh Foods v. Commission* [2004] 4 CMLR 1.

market; however,[61] the related market must be sufficiently connected with the market where the enterprise is dominant.[62] The abuse need not occur in the EU.

The Decision in *Aéroports de Paris*[63] illustrates that it is irrelevant if the effects are felt in another market if the abuse takes place in a market where the dominant position exists. In this case, the dominated market was the market for management services in the Paris airports but the effects were felt on the market for ground handling.

Another example is *De Post/La Poste*, where the Belgian postal operator used the financial resources of its monopoly in general mail to leverage its dominant position into a separate and distinct market for business-to-business services with a view to eliminating Hays, the document exchange company.[64]

5.5.4 Abuse or legitimate competition?

5.5.4.1 The special responsibility

Dominant enterprises have a special responsibility not to allow their conduct to impair competition.[65]

Business practices generally considered to be normal may constitute an abuse within Article 82 of the Treaty if they are carried out by an undertaking that holds a dominant position. Any differences must be objectively justified.[66] This, however, does not prevent dominant enterprises from competing, even vigorously, and even with small competitors or new entrants,[67] in order to protect their own position,[68] provided that they do not go beyond the legitimate and proportionate protection of their legitimate interests.

The actual scope of the dominant firm's special responsibility will depend on the degree of dominance it holds and the special characteristics of the market that may affect the competitive situation.[69]

5.5.4.2 Objective justification

Case law indicates that certain objectively justified behaviour is not abusive. While accepting the principle of objective justification, the Commission and

61. Case C-311/84, *Centre Belge d'Étude de Marché-Telemarketing v. CLT and IPB* [1986] 2 CMLR 558, and Case C-333/94P, *Tetra Pak International SA v. Commission* ("Tetra Pak II") [1994] ECR II 755.

62. Case T-219/99, *British Airways plc v. Commission* [2004] 4 CMLR 19, subject to appeal in Case C-95/04.

63. Case T-128/98, *Aéroports de Paris v. Commission* [2000] ECR II 3929, upheld on appeal by ECJ in Case C-82/01 [2002] ECR I 9297.

64. *De Post/LaPoste*, 2002 OJ L 61/32 and 21 Reports on Competition Cases, para 113.

65. Case 322/81, *Michelin v. Commission* [1985] 1 CMLR 380.

66. *Aeropuertos Españoles y Navegacion Aerea ("AENA")*, 2000 OJ L 208, p 36.

67. *Akzo*, 1985 OJ L 374, p 1; [1986] 3 CMLR 273.

68. Case C-395/96P, *Compagnie Maritime Belge v. Commission* [2000] ECR I–1365, 4 CMLR 1076.

69. *Deutsche Post II*, 2001 OJ L 331, p 40, at para 103, following Case T-83/91, *Tetra Pak II* [1994] ECR II 755.

the courts have been reluctant, in practice, to apply it. Some examples of objective justified behaviour are:

- — A legitimate public interest objective, such as the protection of health.
- — Efficiency gains that outweigh any alleged anti-competitive effects. The authorities are unlikely to accept short-term efficiency gains outweighed by long-term harm to the competitive process.[70]

It will be legitimate for an undertaking to use profits that it derives from activities for which it enjoys a legal monopoly in order to finance the acquisition of control in a company that is active on a neighbouring market open to competition, provided that those profits are not derived from abusive practices themselves.[71]

Some illustrations of what a dominant company can and cannot do are as follows:

A dominant business	
Can	**Cannot**
— Take reasonable steps to protect its position	— Act to strengthen a dominant position by excluding competition
— Meet prices to match offers to existing customers	— Act disproportionately
— Compete vigorously and defend its legitimate interests proportionately	— Act in a way that foreseeably limits competition more than necessary
— Use profits from a reserved area to move into a non-reserved market	— Use profits of abuse to do so
— Make reasonable use of an exclusive right	— Go beyond the purpose of that right or use it to prevent the entrance of a new product or exclude competition on another market

5.5.5 Superdominant companies

Whether a practice amounts to an abuse depends, at least in part, on the degree of dominance.[72]

When an entity enjoys a position on a market of such overwhelming dominance as to constitute a monopoly or quasi-monopoly (a position of "superdominance"), it will have sufficient market power to restrict competition

70. For an analogy, see ECMR Horizontal Guidelines 2004 OJ C 31/5.
71. Case T-175/99, *UPS v. Commission* [2002] ECR II 1915.
72. Case T-203/01, *Michelin II v. Commission* ("Michelin II") [2004] 4 CMLR 923.

through behaviour which, in entities with a lower level of dominance, will not have the same effect.[73]

Superdominant companies have a particularly onerous special responsibility.[74] In circumstances of superdominance, behaviour which in other dominant companies would not be regarded as anti-competitive may in fact still allow the undertaking to eliminate competition. In *Compagnie Maritime Belge,*[75] the Advocate-General stated that, where such an undertaking applies selective price-cutting, particularly where it can do so with relative autonomy from costs, this can constitute abuse even if it continues to sell above cost, which would not otherwise generally be abusive.

5.5.6 Categories of abuse

Examples of abuse include:

- — deliberately changing product specification to deter market entry;[76]
- — in exceptional circumstances, the enforcement of IP rights by the holder[77] and abuse of a trade mark;[78]
- — failure to negotiate promptly and in good faith;[79]
- — entering into agreements which would otherwise benefit from a block exemption (eg an exclusive distribution agreement);[80]
- — de-listing suppliers who buy from competitors;[81]
- — excessively high pricing,[82] predatory pricing,[83] discriminatory discounts[84] or selective discounts,[85] price squeezing,[86] loyalty discounts;[87]

73. Opinion of Advocate-General Fennelly, Case C-395/96, *Compagnie Maritime Belge v. Commission* [2000] 4 CMLR 1076.

74. Case C-395/96, *Compagnie Maritime Belge v. Commission* [2000] 4 CMLR 1076.

75. Opinion of Advocate-General Fennelly, Case C-395/96, *Compagnie Maritime Belge v. Commission* [2000] 4 CMLR 1076.

76. Case C-333/94P, *Tetra Pak II* [1997] 4 CMLR 662.

77. Cases C-241/91P and C-242/91P, *RTE and ITP v. Commission (Magill)* [1995] ECR I 743, paras 49–50; Case T-504/93, *Tiercé Ladbroke v. Commission* [1997] 5 CMLR 309, as reinforced by Case T-198/98, *MicroLeader Business v. Commission* [2000] 4 CMLR 886.

78. *Duales System Deutschland AG (Green Dot)*, 2001 OJ L 166, p 1, IP/01/584.

79. Case C-53/92P, *Hilti AG v. Commission* [1994] 4 CMLR 614.

80. Case C-333/94P, *Tetra Pak II* [1997] 4 CMLR 662.

81. Case C-27/76, *United Brands v. Commission* [1978] 1 CMLR 429.

82. Case 26/75, *General Motors v. Commission* [1975] ECR 1367.

83. Case C-62/86, *Akzo v. Commission* [1986] 3 CMLR 273.

84. Case 85/76, *Hoffmann-La Roche v. Commission* [1979] 3 CMLR 211; Case T-128/98, *Aéroports de Paris v. Commission* [2002] ECR II 3929, upheld on appeal by ECJ in Case C-82/01, [2002] ECR I 9297.

85. Case T-228/97, *Irish Sugar* [1999] 5 CMLR 1300.

86. Case T-5/97, *Industrie des Poudres Sphériques v. Commission* [2000] ECR II 3755; also *Deutsche Telekom*, IP/03/717.

87. Case 85/76, *Hoffmann-La Roche v. Commission* [1979] 3 CMLR 211; Case T-203/01, *Michelin v. Commission* [2004] 4 CMLR 923.

— attempting to remove allegedly dangerous and inferior products on safety grounds;[88]
— unilateral prohibition of exports;[89]
— refusal to supply or licence;[90]
— refusal of access to an essential facility.[91]

5.5.6.1 Pricing

Article 82's function is not to act as a price control. However, often pricing will be the means by which market abuse is practised, and Article 82 will then step in.

Unfortunately, the Commission and the courts adopt a rigid, form-based, approach to pricing abuses. As a result, certain pricing practices are condemned as almost *per se* violations of Article 82. In practice, there tends to be little economic analysis as to whether any emasculation or elimination of competition has occurred.

5.5.6.1.1 Unfair and excessive pricing

The imposition by a dominant undertaking of selling prices that are unfair or disproportionate to the economic value of the service provided can constitute an exploitative abuse.[92] Under the *United Brands* test, there may be an abuse where the dominant undertaking has made use of the opportunities arising out of its position in such a way as to reap trading benefits that it would not have reaped had there been normal and sufficiently effective competition.[93]

In *United Brands*, the ECJ considered that charging a price that was excessive because it had no reasonable relationship to the economic value of the product supplied would be an abuse.[94] Since *United Brands*, the case law has shown that considering price in relation to costs and prices of competing products alone is not sufficient. The test should be one of proportionality as other factors may have an impact on the true economic value of a product. Where products are covered by IP rights, the mere fact of a higher price for a protected product as compared with that of a non-protected product does not necessarily constitute an abuse.[95]

88. Case C-53/92P, *Hilti AG v. Commission* [1994] 4 CMLR 614.
89. Case T-198/98, *Micro Leader v. Commission* [2000] 4 CMLR 886.
90. Cases 6/73 and 7/73, *Commercial Solvents v. Commission* [1974] ECR 223, [1974] 1 CMLR 309; Cases C-241/91P and 242/92P, *RTE and ITP v. Commission (Magill)* [1995] ECR I 143.
91. *SWIFT*, 1997 OJ L 335, p 73; *Irish Continental Group v. CCI Morlaix* [1995] 5 CMLR 177; *FAG Flughafen Frankfurt/Main*, 1998 OJ L 72, p 30.
92. Case C-340/99, *TNT Traco SpA v. Poste Italiane SpA* [2001] ECR I 4109; Case C-322/93, *Centre d'Insémination de la Crespelle* [1994] ECR I 5077.
93. Case C-27/76, *United Brands v. Commission* [1978] 1 CMLR 429.
94. For cases where excessive pricing was established see Case 26/75, *General Motors v. Commission* [1976] 1 CMLR 95; Case 226/84, *British Leyland v. Commission* [1987] 1 CMLR 184.
95. Case 53/87, *CICRA v. Renault* [1988] ECR 6039, [1990] 4 CMLR 265.

5.5.6.1.2 Margin squeezing

A dominant company may use its market power to create an anti-competitive effect in a downstream market by imposing a margin squeeze or price squeeze. This occurs where a dominant company in an upstream market supplies an essential input in a downstream market, in which the dominant company is also active, at a price that does not enable its competitors in the downstream market to remain competitive.[96]

Deutsche Telekom's vertical integration as the dominant provider of both wholesale and retail access to the local telecommunications loop in Germany provided it with an opportunity to indulge in a margin squeeze between the wholesale and retail tariffs by charging its competitors higher rates for local loop access than it charged end users, thereby leaving new market entrants to the wholesale market no margin to compete for retail subscribers.[97]

5.5.6.1.3 Predatory pricing

Predatory pricing refers to the situation where a dominant company sells below cost in order to eliminate competitors or deter entry, enabling it to further increase its market power.

In *Akzo*,[98] it was decided that where prices are below average variable cost, predatory behaviour is to be presumed.[99] When prices are above average variable costs but below average total costs, predatory pricing exists if there is the intention of eliminating a competitor. There can be little or no justification for selling at such a low price except as part of a strategy to exclude a competitor from the market in the long term and so allowing the dominant enterprise to consolidate its position and increase its prices.

Predatory pricing is a notoriously difficult area.[100] Not only is extensive cost and other data required, there is generally also the need to establish at least some degree of intent to exclude a competitor from the market or limit its growth.

Selling at less than average variable cost is not the only type of predatory abuse. Deep, selective, price cuts in order to meet the prices of a competitor have also been regarded as a predatory abuse.[101]

96. Case T-5/97, *Industrie des Poudres Sphériques v. Commission* [2000] ECR II 3755.

97. *Deutsche Telekom*, 2003 OJ L 263, p 9.

98. Case C-62/86, *Akzo v. Commission* [1991] ECR I 3359.

99. Case C-62/86, *Akzo v. Commission* [1991] ECR I 3359 and Case C-395/96P, *Compagnie Maritime Belge* [2000] 4 CMLR 1076, paras 89–121. In *Akzo*, the ECJ declined to adopt the test of predatory price-cutting suggested by economists Areeda and Turner. According to this test, pricing above average variable cost should be presumed lawful.

100. The UK's Office of Fair Trading has been more willing to take predatory pricing cases under the equivalent provisions of the Competition Act 1998 than the European Commission has under Article 82.

101. Case T-24/93, *Compagnie Maritime Belge v. Commission* [1997] 4 CMLR 273.

5.5.6.1.4 Cross-subsidisation

Predatory pricing may include cross-subsidisation.

It may be an abuse for an undertaking with a monopoly position in one market to exploit its leverage potential by using funds from that restricted market to subsidise its entry into a new commercial market.

In *Deutsche Post I*,[102] the Commission made it clear that where a service in a commercial market is provided by the beneficiary of a monopoly in another market, then the price charged must at least cover the costs attributable to, or incremental to, branching out into the competitive sector.[103] Any cost coverage below this level is to be considered as predatory pricing.

5.5.6.1.5 Discriminatory pricing

Discriminatory treatment of customers may infringe Article 82.

Discriminatory pricing—charging different prices to customers in the same circumstances without justification, or charging uniform prices to customers whose circumstances are different—is recognised as one of the most frequently cited direct measurements of market power, especially where the absence of cost differences is readily discernible.[104] The following points should be borne in mind:

- Prices do not have to be identical, but any differences must be justified by objective and non-discriminatory considerations.
- Any fee must not be arbitrary.
- In the event of a disparity, it is for the defendant to justify the reasons for, and the correctness of, the differences in rates.[105]
- It is irrelevant if the discriminatory treatment has effects on another market if the discrimination takes place in a market where the dominant position exists.
- It is sufficient that the service offered by the supplier is necessary for the exercise of the recipient's own activity.[106]

Discounts that are not related to cost savings to the supplier may be abusive. Discounts intended to secure loyalty on the part of customers, such as retrospective discounts, may infringe Article 82. This will be irrespective of whether they are originally proposed by the dominant supplier or the non-dominant customer.

102. Case COMP/35.141, *Deutsche Post I*, 2001 OJ L 125, p 27; 21 Reports on Commission Cases, para 108.

103. Deutsche Post was not fined for predatory pricing (although it was fined in relation to fidelity rebates) since the Commission considered that the cost concepts used to establish predatory pricing of this type were not sufficiently developed when the infringement occurred.

104. Commission Decision in *Trans-Atlantic Conference Agreement* 1999 OJ L 95, p 1.

105. Case C-82/01, *Aéroports de Paris v. Commission* [2002] ECR I 9297, para 77.

106. *Ibid*, para 91.

Discrimination in the level of charges or prices between Member States, or based on geographical location, is also an abuse.[107] This may also take the form of a supplier charging a company in the same Member State a different amount, which cannot be objectively justified.[108]

Whether discounts are unlawful depends on the circumstances. Discounts targeted at increasing the chance of winning sales from competitors are viewed more critically than those directed at growing the market.

5.5.6.1.6 Loyalty-inducing pricing

Loyalty or fidelity discounts are regarded as close to a *per se* abuse of Article 82. This is largely because rewarding past loyalty tends to induce future loyalty and to make it harder for existing players or new entrants to enter the market and expand. At the very least, loyalty discounts are seen as a means of reinforcing the dominant companies' existing market position. Loyalty-inducing discounts have been described as equivalent to a tie, as they prevent customers from accepting the most advantageous offer at any time.[109] A particularly clear example of a loyalty rebate was Deutsche Post's rebate under which the customer received a rebate even if volumes decreased, so long as Deutsche Post's percentage share of the customer's total requirements did not reduce.[110]

Recent examples of the CFI's hardline attitude to fidelity rewards and other pricing practices by dominant companies are the judgments in *British Airways*[111] ("BA") and *Michelin II*.[112] In both cases, the CFI emphasised that it was not necessary for anti-competitive effects to be established; it was sufficient that anti-competitive effects were likely to occur. Both cases emphasised that discounts or rebates that apply to all sales, and not merely those above a threshold, have loyalty-inducing effects and fall within Article 82. Thus BA's performance reward scheme was discriminatory since the level was based on attainment of a sales growth target based on a prior reference period, and attainment of the target led to an increase in the rate of commission on all products sold during the reference period.

5.5.6.1.7 Pricing practices

Pricing structures are one of the most difficult issues that face dominant companies. In the words of the Commission:

107. Compare *Tetra Pak II* [1994] ECR II 755.
108. *Clearstream*, IP/04/705.
109. Case T-203/01, *Michelin v. Commission* [2004] 4 CMLR 923.
110. *Deutsche Post I*, 2002 OJ L 125, p 27. Deutsche Post was fined €24 million.
111. Case T-219/99, *British Airways plc v. Commission* [2004] 4 CMLR 19, subject to appeal in Case C-95/04.
112. Case T-203/01, *Michelin v. Commission* [2004] 4 CMLR 923.

5.5.6.1.7 Article 82: Principles and Application

"Dominant companies must be careful not to engage in practices that exclude other players from the market. Rebates and bonuses are normal commercial practices but . . . some types are illegal when they are granted by a company in a dominant position and have an exclusionary effect."[113]

Discriminatory prices between different customers or different classes of customers for similar products are prohibited.[114] *Bona fide* quantity discounts are allowed, although these should be capable of being justified either by the provision of extra services or by cost savings on a per order basis.[115]

Dominant companies must:

- Ensure volume-related discounts reflect actual cost savings or the provision of extra services.[116]
- Ensure discounts or rebates are clear, transparent and applied uniformly.[117] Subjective elements must be avoided.
- Avoid loyalty discounts[118] or rebates and group commitment discounts.[119] This includes retrospective discounts based on a long reference period,[120] as these will have loyalty inducing effects. Periods in excess of three months will be increasingly risky. This will be irrespective of whether the discount is originally proposed by the dominant supplier or the non-dominant customer.[121]
- Avoid obligations on the part of customers to obtain all or most of their requirements exclusively from the dominant enterprise,[122] or the granting of rebates for exclusivity.[123] However, in some situations such as bidding markets, where the customer can, without penalty, switch

113. Commissioner Monti, on 20 June 2001, fining Michelin €19.76 million for operating a complex system of quantitative rebates, bonuses and commercial agreements that constituted a loyalty-inducing and unfair system *vis-à-vis* dealers, 2002 OJ L 143, p 1; IP/01/873. The Commission's Decision was upheld by the CFI (Case T-203/01, *Michelin v. Commission* [2004] 4 CMLR 923).

114. See 5.5.11 above.

115. Case C-163/99, *Portugal v. Commission* [2002] 4 CMLR 1319. See also the Commission Decision in *Trans Atlantic Conference Agreement*, 1999 OJ L 95, p 1, where currency adjustment factors were found not to be economically justified and hence abusive.

116. Case T-228/97, *Irish Sugar*, 1997 OJ L 258, p 16, [1999] 5 CMLR 1300.

117. Case COMP/E 2/36.041/PO—*Michelin*, 2002 OJ L 143, p 1; but note that the CFI found that "a loyalty-inducing rebate system is contrary to Article 82, whether it is transparent or not" (Case T-203/01, *Michelin v. Commission* [2004] 4 CMLR 923.)

118. Case COMP/35.141, *Deutsche Post*, 2001 OJ L 125, p 27; Case T-203/01, *Michelin v. Commission* [2004] 4 CMLR 923; Case 85/76, *Hoffmann-La Roche* [1979] 3 CMLR 211.

119. Case C-395/96P, *Compagnie Maritime Belge v. Commission* [2000] 4 CMLR 1076.

120. Case T-203/01, *Michelin v. Commission* [2004] 4 CMLR 923; the CFI commented that although it had not been expressly stated in *Michelin I* that a reference period could not exceed three months, as suggested by the Commission in *Michelin II*, the loyalty-inducing effect increases in proportion to the length of the reference period.

121. Case C-393/92, *Almero v. Energiebedrif Ijsselmij NV* [1994] ECR I 1477.

122. Case T-65/98, *Van den Bergh Foods v. Commission* [2004] 4 CMLR 1; Case T-203/01, *Michelin v. Commission* [2004] 4 CMLR 923.

123. Case 85/76, *Hoffmann-La Roche* [1979] 3 CMLR 211.

from one supplier to another, an exclusive supply contract may make competitive bidding more intense and drive down prices.[124]

— Avoid rebate policies aimed at tying customers and thereby foreclosing market entry.
— Not apply discriminatory or selective discounts where there is no connection between differences in price and the services offered where the services are identical.[125]
— Only provide supplementary incentives where these reflect extra services provided or efficiencies realised.
— Avoid margin squeezing, which may result in exclusion of new entrants to the market.[126]
— Not use so-called "English clauses" that require the other party to provide the exact price offered by a third party and enable the dominant supplier to decide whether to accept that opportunity.

5.5.6.2 Limiting production, markets or technical development

A firm whose dominant position in a market allows it to control access to that or another market abuses its position if it unreasonably denies other firms access to the market. In *Nordion*,[127] exclusive and long-term contracts were entered into by Nordion with its principal worldwide customers for Molybdenum 99, a base product for radiopharmaceuticals used in nuclear medicine. This was considered to prevent the only European competitor from developing competitive products, with the consequential risk of eliminating it from the market and making the entry of new competitors impossible.

The court observed in *Van den Bergh Foods*[128] that market foreclosure does not have to be complete but must be significant.

5.5.6.3 Tying and bundling

5.5.6.3.1 Tying

Tying is making a contract subject to supplementary obligations that by their nature or commercial usage have no connection with the subject-matter of the

124. *IRI/Nielsen*, 26 Reports on Competition Cases p 144; also *Digital Undertaking*, IP/97/868; 27 RCC para 69.

125. *AENA*, 2000 OJ L 208, p 36. Case C-179/90 and Case C-266/96, *Corsica Ferries v. Gruppo Antichi Ormeggiatori del Porto di Genova Coop* [1998] ECR I 3949.

126. *Deutsche Telekom*, 2003 OJ L 263, p 9. The Commission has said that vertically integrated operators like Deutsche Telekom must fix their retail prices at a level sufficiently above the wholesale prices to allow new entrants to compete.

127. Commission Press Release 98/647; 28 Reports on Competition Cases paras 74 and 321.

128. Case T-65/98, *Van den Bergh v. Commission* [2004] 4 CMLR 1.

contract. It is a way of extending dominance into another market. For an abuse to take place:

— there must be an element of compulsion; and
— there must be no objective justification for the tying of the two products.

Efficiencies in production and distribution can provide a justification for tying, as may safety considerations, and the need to ensure the quality of all elements of a system.

An important recent decision on tying is the Commission's decision in *Microsoft*,[129] in which the Commission decided that Microsoft had illegally tied its Windows Media Player ("WMP") into its Windows operating system, thus weakening competition on the merits for other versions of media-player software, and consequently stifling innovation and ultimately reducing consumer choice.

The Commission set out four conditions that must be satisfied for tying:[130]

— the tying and tied goods must be two separate products;
— the undertaking concerned is dominant in the tying product market;
— the undertaking concerned does not give customers a choice to obtain the tying product without the tied product; and
— the tying forecloses competition.

Tying WMP with the dominant Windows operating system made WMP the platform of choice for complementary content and applications, which in turn risked foreclosing competition in the market for media players. This had spill-over effects on competition in related products, all of which created a serious risk of foreclosing competition and stifling innovation.

It is important to note that the Commission did not find that the tying had in fact foreclosed the market—merely that it was liable to have the effect of putting at risk an effective competitive structure.[131]

5.5.6.3.2 Bundling

Bundling differs from tying in that it is not compulsory. The circumstances in which bundling is anti-competitive is an issue upon which there is little

129. *Microsoft*, appealed to the CFI. For an analysis of Microsoft's arguments against the Commission's Decision, see the Order of the President of the CFI, available on the CFI website but not yet reported.

130. Para 794 of the Decision.

131. Sections 838–842 of the Decision. See also sections 395–399 of the Order of the CFI dated 22 December 2004 identifying the novel aspects of this analysis and that Microsoft's arguments were not *prima facie* unfounded.

agreement at present, even between anti-trust authorities.[132] Bundling typically involves the sale of complementary products through package deals at a lower price than when sold separately. It can take a number of forms:

— *mixed bundling*: complementary products are sold together at a price which, owing to the discounts across the range, is lower than the price charged when sold separately;
— *pure bundling*: only the bundle is sold and the individual components are not sold on a stand-alone basis (this is equivalent to a tie);
— *technical bundling*: where the individual components only function effectively as part of a bundled system and cannot be used alongside components of other suppliers.

Bundling is only a problem under Article 82 when it results in foreclosure effects.

In the *Tetra Laval/Sidel* Decision, the risk was of bundling carton packaging and PET plastic packaging equipment. The CFI decided that although bundling of such products could potentially strengthen an undertaking's position sufficiently to weaken competition, the Commission had not shown that on the evidence it would in fact significantly weaken competition.[133]

5.5.6.4 Refusal to deal

5.5.6.4.1 Generally

There is no general duty, even on a dominant company, to contract. Where a unilateral refusal to supply is coupled with a lack of objective justification, then Article 82 may apply.

A refusal to supply by a dominant company will, unless objectively justified, generally constitute an abuse where it substantially weakens competition. Refusal to supply for *bona fide* commercial reasons, such as creditworthiness, shortage of stock, or where the business would be unprofitable, cannot be criticised provided that the criteria are applied on a non-discriminatory and proportionate basis. Article 82 does not attack normal commercial behaviour. Refusal to deal on its own is not sufficient to constitute an abuse; there must be anti-competitive effects.

A refusal to supply will be assessed differently depending on the background of the case. Factors to take into account include whether the refusal occurs in an existing commercial relationship or to a new customer; whether the customers are competitors or potential competitors; and whether the refusal is retaliation to pro-competitive behaviour by the other party. A sudden and immediate termination is more likely to be regarded as an abuse than termination by an appropriate period of notice.

132. See, for example, the debate generated by the Commission's decision in Case M.2220, *GE/Honeywell.*

133. Case T-5/02, *Tetra Laval v. Commission* [2002] ECR II 4381. Some care is required in interpreting this decision as it was a merger control case.

5.5.6.4.2 The Commercial Solvents *doctrine*

In *Commercial Solvents*,[134] a company dominant in the production of raw materials for use in certain tuberculosis drugs decided to manufacture the derivative drugs itself and, in order to facilitate its own access to this market, suddenly ceased supplying the raw materials to a long-term customer who was dependent on these supplies. The ECJ said that the dominant undertaking could not eliminate its competitors by denying them access to the raw materials. In this case it was the raw materials that constituted the relevant product market rather than the subsequent market of the finished product.

Commercial Solvents established that it is an infringement of Article 82 for a dominant undertaking to refuse to supply a competitor in a downstream market if this would result in the elimination of all competition in that market.

5.5.6.4.3 Neighbouring markets

Refusals to supply may infringe Article 82 even where they do not relate to the dominated market.

In *Tetra Pak II*,[135] a firm holding a dominant position in the production of aseptic milk cartons and carton-filling machinery and technology took over a competitor and acquired an exclusive licence for a new filling process. Following a complaint by a smaller competitor, the Commission concluded that the concentration of technology in the hands of a dominant firm without objective justification, and without the licensor of one of the processes being entitled to grant further licences, constituted an infringement of Article 86 (now Article 82). Here Article 82 was applied in relation to a separate, distinct market from the dominated market. Special circumstances existed, since Tetra Pak was not only in a quasi-monopoly position in the market but also held a strong market position in the associated market. Customers in one market were potential customers in the other, so placing Tetra Pak in a position comparable to that of a company holding a dominant position on the markets in question as a whole.

5.5.6.4.4 Refusal to supply in order to prevent parallel imports

A case involving Microsoft and a parallel importer, *Micro Leader*, introduced a new dimension to parallel imports.[136] Micro Leader imported from Quebec, where Microsoft products were cheaper, into France. Microsoft took action against the parallel imports by banning the importation of its French-language products from Canada into France.

134. Cases 6/73 and 7/73, *Commercial Solvents v. Commission* [1974] ECR 223, [1974] 1 CMLR 309.

135. Case T-83/91, *Tetra Pak International v. Commission* [1994] ECR II 755.

136. Case T-198/98, *Micro Leader Business v. Commission* [2000] 4 CMLR 886.

The CFI, when it reviewed the Commission's decision not to launch an investigation, decided that while reliance on copyright by Microsoft would not generally amount to abusive conduct, it could do so in exceptional circumstances. Although the CFI did not state what circumstances would be regarded as exceptional, it appears that the CFI considered that an undertaking adopting differential pricing within the EEA and outside the EEA is capable of amounting to such exceptional circumstances.

In *SYFAIT v. Glaxo Greece*,[137] the ECJ was asked whether:

- a refusal to supply by a dominant company is a *per se* abuse where that refusal is to prevent parallel trade;
- a refusal to supply additional quantities or partial quantities destined for export is an abuse;
- it was discriminatory for Glaxo Greece to refuse to supply a particular product while continuing to supply others; and
- it was necessary for the wholesaler's continued survival as a business to be threatened.

In a potentially far-reaching opinion, the Advocate-General answered the first question in the negative. He then went on to say that because of the particular legislative and regulatory features of the pharmaceutical market, a refusal to supply in order to restrict parallel trade, at least where large quantities were being parallel traded, was not an abuse. Even if he was wrong on this point, he considered that the refusal was in the circumstances objectively justified, with the result that it did not infringe Article 82.[138]

5.5.6.5 Essential facilities

5.5.6.5.1 Introduction

Under the "essential facilities" doctrine a refusal by a dominant firm to grant access to an essential facility that it controls amounts to an abuse of a dominant position if such restriction has significant effects on competition. An "essential facility" includes an infrastructure such as a port, airport, pipeline or railway line, access to which is essential for the competitor to compete in a downstream market.

The doctrine of "essential facilities" presupposes that in order for there to be effective competition, competitors must have access to resources to enable them to compete.

137. Case C-53/03, order for reference 2003 OJ C 101, p 32, Opinion of Advocate-General Jacobs delivered on 28 October 2004, not yet reported.

138. On 31 May 2005, the ECJ concluded that the reference was inadmissable, because the Greek competition authority that made the reference was not a court or tribunal. This leaves the substantive questions unanswered.

Facilities arc only "essential" where they are necessary or essential for market entry.[139] There must be no viable alternatives available to potential competitors.[140] "Essential" means "essential", not merely "desirable".

5.5.6.5.2 *Sealink/B&I–Holyhead*

In *Sealink/B&I–Holyhead,*[141] Sealink operated a port at Holyhead in North Wales from which it operated a ferry service to Ireland. A rival company, B&I, complained to the European Commission that Sealink deliberately organised its sailing schedules so as to cause maximum disruption to B&I's services and inconvenience to its passengers. The Commission held that this was a *prima facie* case of abuse and ordered interim measures requiring Sealink to change its schedules. It stated that:

> "A dominant undertaking which both owns or controls and itself uses an essential facility . . . and which refuses its competitors access to that facility or grants access to competitors only on terms less favourable than those which it gives its own services, thereby placing the competitors at a competitive disadvantage, infringes Article 82, if the other conditions of that Article are met."

5.5.6.5.3 *Oscar Bronner v. Mediaprint*

The case of *Oscar Bronner v. Mediaprint*[142] set out the main features of the doctrine of essential facilities. It involved an action by Oscar Bronner, an Austrian newspaper publisher, against a company called Mediaprint alleging that Mediaprint had abused its dominant position on the market by refusing Bronner access to its newspaper home delivery service, which Bronner claimed was an "essential facility" since it was the only economically viable home delivery scheme existing in Austria on a national scale.

The ECJ distinguished the judgment in *RTE and ITP v. Commission and Magill TV Guide Ltd* relating to refusals to license (see 5.6.3.1 below) and said that even if *Magill* was applicable it would be necessary to show that:

— the refusal would be likely to eliminate all competition in the daily newspaper market and was incapable[143] of being objectively justified; and

— the service was indispensable to carrying on the business, inasmuch as there was no actual or potential substitute.

In *Bronner* there were no technical, legal or even economic obstacles making it impossible, or even unreasonably difficult, for any publisher to establish its

139. Case C-7/97, *Oscar Bronner v. Mediaprint* [1999] 4 CMLR 112.

140. Cases T-374/94, T-375/94, T-384/94 and T-388/94, *European Night Services Ltd and Others v. Commission* [1998] ECR II 3141.

141. *Sealink/B&I–Holyhead*, 1989 OJ L 43/27.

142. Case C-7/97, *Oscar Bronner v. Mediaprint* [1999] 4 CMLR 112. This case has been cited as authority for refusals to license despite the fact that *Magill* was distinguished.

143. Interpreted by the English courts as "clearly unjustified": *Get Mapping v. Ordnance Survey* [2002] EWHC 1089 (Ch).

own scheme of home delivery. This therefore excluded the possibility of Mediaprint's service being "indispensable" and for its refusal to allow access to constitute an abuse within the meaning of Article 82.

The decision upheld Mediaprint's assertions to the effect that "the fact that it holds a dominant position does not oblige it to subsidise competition by assisting competing companies". In short: "essential" means "essential".

5.5.6.5.4 Airports

In 1998 the Commission found that the operator of Frankfurt airport, Flughafen Frankfurt AG ("FAG"), had abused its dominant position by not giving access to other companies wishing to provide ground handling services.[144] The Commission concluded that there were two separate markets involved: the market for the provision of airport facilities for the landing and take-off of aircraft; and the neighbouring market for the provision of ramp handling services such as baggage handling, cleaning and push-back services.

FAG held a dominant position in the first market and had abused that position in order to reserve the ramp handling services market to itself. FAG's ramp handling system, including its automatic luggage conveyor system, was an efficient tool for optimal use of the infrastructure and it was unlikely that alternative suppliers would be able to offer an efficient alternative. Therefore, the monopoly on the system itself was not challenged. However, access to the system for other handlers was necessary. By refusing access, FAG had abused its position as exclusive provider of the facility to deny airlines the right to self-handle and thereby obliged the users of the airport facilities to purchase from it the ramp handling services that they needed.

Since FAG could not objectively justify such a position, the Commission found its behaviour to be in breach of Article 82 and FAG was required to submit a plan for opening up the ramp handling services market to independent third-party handlers and self-handling airlines.

A key point about *FAG* is that it extends the essential facilities doctrine from providing access to infrastructure to include potential operators who, although not users of the infrastructure, are willing to render services to meet a demand originating within the facility.

5.5.6.5.5 Conclusion on essential facilities

For a refusal to grant access to a facility to be abusive, the following conditions must be satisfied:

- the facility owner is dominant in at least a "substantial part" of the EU market;
- there is an insurmountable barrier to entry for competitors of the dominant enterprise and/or competitors without access would be subject to a serious competitive handicap;

144. Case IV/34.801, *Flughafen Frankfurt/Main AG*, 1998 OJ L 72, p 30.

- refusal to grant access has significant effects on competition, including in a downstream or neighbouring market;
- "essential" means "essential" and not merely "desirable";
- the refusal must not be objectively justifiable;
- provision of access is dependent on the existence of spare capacity in an essential facility.

Note that the infrastructure owner may charge a premium for use of the essential facility, provided it does not charge its own operations a lower price than it charges its competitors.

Although in the short term it may appear to be pro-competitive to open up new markets, it can also be anti-competitive in the long run if this leads to a discouragement of innovation and investment.

5.6 INTELLECTUAL PROPERTY RIGHTS AND ARTICLE 82[145]

5.6.1 Introduction

In its evaluation report on the recently revised Technology Transfer Block Exemption, the European Commission recognises the potential conflict between IP rights and competition law, but concludes that, at the highest level of analysis, IP rights and competition law are actually complementary since they both aim to promote consumer welfare.[146]

The Commission makes several general points:

- competition policy expertise is useful in helping to shape IP law, eg on issues such as scope and duration;
- competition policy has to play its normal role where IP rights are used to produce an anti-competitive effect beyond the exploitation of the IP rights;
- there is a lack of agreement on how far competition policy should interfere with the exploitation of IP rights in individual cases.

The final point identifies the area of most practical concern when considering the application of Article 82 to the exploitation of IP rights.

The general application of Article 82 is considered above. This section focuses on the treatment of IP rights under Article 82, including the subject of compulsory licensing. Finally, there is a brief overview of the use of so-called "Euro-defences" based on Article 82 in IP litigation in the UK.

145. By Pat Treacy, Bristows.

146. The report is available at: http://www.europa.eu.int/comm/competition/antitrust/technology_transfer/.

5.6.2 The application of Article 82 to the exercise of IP rights

Article 82 of the EC Treaty prohibits companies with substantial market power from abusing that power. Article 82 applies only to companies in a "dominant position". The ownership of intellectual property does not automatically confer a dominant position within the meaning of Article 82. However, the ECJ has held that, in some cases, existence of IP rights may result in or bolster a dominant position. The question then arises whether the exercise or exploitation of such IP rights may amount to an abuse within the meaning of Article 82.

Generally, the view has been that the mere enforcement of IP rights could not amount to an abuse. However, case law indicates that, in certain limited circumstances, the way in which a dominant company enforces and exploits its IP rights may amount to an abuse under Article 82. Some of these areas are discussed below.

5.6.3 The application of Article 82: refusals to license

For a number of years after the entry into effect of the European competition rules, it was unclear whether there were circumstances in which the exploitation of IP rights, and particularly refusal to license IP rights, might be prohibited by Article 82. This issue came before the ECJ for the first time in *Volvo v. Veng*.[147] This case concerned body panels for Volvo cars, over which Volvo had IP rights. Veng imported and marketed Volvo body panels in the UK manufactured without Volvo's consent. Volvo sued for infringement. The issue before the ECJ was whether, in refusing to license Veng to deal in the body panels, Volvo had infringed the competition rules. The court's judgment is critical to all subsequent European law on this issue. In two important passages, the ECJ held:

"It must . . . be emphasised that the right of the proprietor of a protected design to prevent third parties from manufacturing and selling or importing, without its consent, products incorporating the design constitutes the very subject-matter of his exclusive right. It follows that an obligation imposed upon the proprietor of a protected design to grant to third parties, even in return for a reasonable royalty, a licence for the supply of products incorporating the design would lead to the proprietor thereof being deprived of the substance of his exclusive right, and that a refusal to grant such a licence cannot in itself constitute an abuse of a dominant position.

It must however be noted that the exercise of an exclusive right by the proprietor of a registered design in respect of car body panels may be prohibited by Article [82] if it involves, on the part of an undertaking holding a dominant position, certain abusive conduct such as the arbitrary refusal to supply spare parts to independent repairers, the fixing of prices for spare parts at an unfair level or a decision no longer to produce spare

147. [1988] ECR 6211; see also *CICRA v. Renault* [1988] ECR 6039.

parts for a particular model even though many cars of that model are still in circulation, provided that such conduct is liable to affect trade between Member States."[148]

The court concluded:

"The refusal by the proprietor of a registered design in respect of body panels to grant to third parties, even in return for reasonable royalties, a licence for the supply of parts incorporating the design cannot in itself be regarded as an abuse of a dominant position within the meaning of Article [82]".[149]

In *Volvo*, the ECJ took the view that mere refusals to license could rarely be prohibited under Article 82. Nevertheless, the ECJ expressly stated that in some circumstances an abuse could arise. The efforts of lawyers and their clients to identify more precisely what circumstances might give rise to a finding of abuse has led to a limited number of further cases dealing with this issue.

5.6.3.1 RTE and ITP v. Commission and Magill TV Guide Ltd[150]

Magill is a key case in the subsequent development of the law. *Magill* concerned the extent to which a refusal to license information protected by IP rights (in that case copyright) may be contrary to Article 82 and established that there are circumstances in which a refusal to license may be abusive.

Magill had sought access to RTE's copyrighted lists of television programmes in order to publish his own comprehensive weekly television listings guide. When RTE refused, Magill complained to the European Commission that the broadcasters were breaching Article 82 by refusing to grant licences of their IP rights.

In *Magill*, the ECJ expressly confirmed its view, first, that mere ownership of an IP right does not automatically confer a dominant position; but second, that if a dominant position did exist, a refusal to grant a licence could be abusive in "exceptional circumstances". The ECJ also explicitly rejected the argument that the exercise and exploitation of IP rights were, to some extent, immune from the full rigour of the competition rules, holding:

"[The appellants] wrongly presuppose that where the conduct of an undertaking in a dominant position consists of the exercise of a right classified by national law as 'copyright', such conduct can never be reviewed in relation to Article [82] of the Treaty.

Admittedly, in the absence of Community standardisation or harmonisation of laws, determination of the conditions and procedures for granting protection of an intellectual property right is a matter for national rules. Further, the exclusive right of reproduction forms part of the author's rights, so that refusal to grant a licence, even if it is the act of an undertaking holding a dominant position, cannot in itself constitute abuse of a dominant position . . . .

148. [1988] ECR 6211, at p 6235.
149. [1988] ECR 6211, at p 6236.
150. [1995] ECR I 743.

However, it is also clear . . . that the exercise of an exclusive right by the proprietor may, in exceptional circumstances, involve abusive conduct."[151]

It has been suggested that *Magill* is an application of the essential facilities doctrine to copyright.[152] A combination of the essential facilities doctrine with the ECJ's holding in *Magill* that the Commission has the right to order compulsory licences of IP rights in cases where that is the only effective remedy might be of concern to all rights owners. It could easily be argued that, where an IP right is "necessary" to allow access to a certain market, the IP owner is then at risk of compulsory licensing. This question is far from settled: the case law shows that the European courts have struggled, and continue to struggle, to balance the interests of IP owners and the interests of would-be competitors. These efforts come against a policy background of intense discussion of the roles that IP rights and competition law play in enhancing consumer welfare over both the short and long term.

Shortly after *Magill*, the Commission commented on the difficulties to be expected in this area:

"At the current stage of EC competition law, it is highly doubtful whether one could impose an obligation upon a dominant firm . . . as a remedy to ensure the maintenance of effective competition . . . to share its intellectual property rights with third parties, to allow them to develop, produce and market the same products which the dominant firm is seeking to develop, produce and market."[153]

In fact, the *Magill* judgment has only rarely been relied upon with any measure of success. The checks and balances that the ECJ was mindful to insert in both *Volvo* and *Magill* appear to have prevented the "free-for-all" that some had feared. Nevertheless, the scope and interpretation of the *Volvo* and *Magill* judgments remains unclear and the law continues to develop.

5.6.3.2 Tiercé Ladbroke SA v. Commission[154]

Tiercé Ladbroke SA alleged that the Sociétés des Courses had abused a dominant position by refusing to license rights to the TV pictures and sound commentaries of French horse races to enable Ladbroke to televise French horse races at its betting outlets in Belgium.

The CFI rejected Ladbroke's argument, explaining *Magill* as follows:

151. *Magill*, ECJ judgment, paras 48–50.

152. The doctrine of "essential facilities" (see 5.5.6.5 above) has become fashionable in EU competition law over recent years. It has been imported from the US, and its principal thrust is that a company that "owns or manages and uses itself an essential facility, ie a facility or infrastructure without which its competitors are unable to offer their services to customers, and refuses to grant them access to such a facility is abusing its dominant position": *Port of Rødby*, OJ L 55/52. There have been suggestions that the doctrine may apply to IP as well as to physical infrastructure. There is a detailed discussion of the scope and application of the essential facilities doctrine by the Advocate-General in the *Bronner* case; see 5.5.6.5.3 above.

153. Report on Competition Policy 1994, p 410.

154. [1997] ECR II 923.

"the decisive factor in the *Magill* case was that the abusive conduct of the television channels concerned consisted in preventing the marketing of a new product to the detriment of consumers' interests, whereas in this case the relaying of sound and pictures for horse races did not constitute a *service which genuinely differed from that already provided* to bettors, namely the taking of bets."[155] (Emphasis added.)

This passage suggests that *Magill* requires the marketing of a new product, or at least something that provided consumers with additional and different choices. However, later in the judgment, the CFI appeared to suggest that this element was not essential to the application of Article 82:

"the refusal to supply the applicant could not fall within the prohibition laid down by Article [82] unless it concerned a product or service which was *either* essential for the exercise of the activity in question, in that there was no real or potential substitute, *or* was a new product whose introduction might be prevented, despite specific, constant and regular potential demand on the part of consumers."[156] (Emphasis added.)

The precise meaning of this passage has subsequently become the subject of intense debate.

5.6.3.3 Summary

Following the court's judgments in these leading cases, together with a number of Commission Decisions (eg those with an "essential facilities" element or those where control of a right or "facility" enables a dominant company to control a separate but neighbouring, or downstream, market) and other court judgments[157] it is at least clear that:

- the exercise of IP rights does not fall outside the scope of Article 82;
- even the basic right of an IP right holder—to refuse to license others to use his right—can be undermined;
- however, such an interference with the prerogatives of the IP owner would only be appropriate in unusual, and carefully examined, circumstances where the impact on competition was extremely serious.

The precise scope of the possible obligation to license has come under close scrutiny in the *IMS Health* case, which is discussed further below.

5.6.4 Recent development: NDC Health/IMS Health[158]

The most significant recent case involving IP rights and Article 82 has been the Commission's interim measures decision in *IMS Health* and the subsequent appeals, together with a separate but related Article 234 reference to

155. [1997] ECR II 923, para 22.
156. [1997] ECR II 923, para 131.
157. Eg *British Midland/Aer Lingus*, 1992 OJ L 96/365; *B&I/Sealink Holyhead* [1992] 5 CMLR 255; *London European/Sabena* [1989] 4 CMLR 84; *Telemarketing* [1985] ECR 3261.
158. 2002 OJ L 55/18.

the ECJ. Both cases arose from the same facts (although the procedural routes were separate) and the procedural complexities of the cases mean that they are worth discussing at some length.[159]

5.6.4.1 Background

The *IMS Health* case arose from a dispute between National Data Corporation ("NDC") and IMS. One limb of the dispute resulted in a complaint by NDC to the Commission that IMS had refused to license NDC to use a pharmaceuticals sales data structure known as the "1,860 brick" structure. The other limb of the dispute arose from IMS's decision to sue NDC in Germany for alleged breach of its IP rights in the brick structure.

The data structure consists of a map of Germany divided up into 1,860 territorial segments or "bricks" based on postal codes and geographic boundaries containing at least four or five pharmacies. The structure is used to compile regional data reports concerning sales of pharmaceutical products by wholesalers to pharmacies. These reports are used by pharmaceutical manufacturers.

5.6.4.2 The Commission Interim Measures Decision

The Commission concluded that IMS had a dominant position in the market for German regional sales data services (the relevant market) and that it had abused its position by refusing to license its 1,860 brick structure to its competitors. According to the Commission Press Release:[160]

> "the Commission has considered that IMS's refusal to grant a licence for use of the structure, which has become a national standard in the German pharmaceutical industry, constitutes a *prima facie* abuse of a dominant position."

The Commission required IMS to grant a licence of its brick structure by way of interim measures, basing its decision on *Magill*, *Ladbroke* and *Bronner*:[161]

> "The Commission considers that there are exceptional circumstances in this case within the meaning of the phrase used by the ECJ in *Magill* (paragraph 50) read in conjunction with the *Ladbroke* and *Bronner* cases. IMS has created, in collaboration with the pharmaceutical industry . . . a brick structure which has become the *de facto* industry standard for the presentation of regional data services and which the Frankfurt court has found is its intellectual property right. IMS is now excluding all competition from the market for regional data services by refusing, without objective justification, to licence this structure to competitors."[162]

The Commission imposed the licensing remedy despite the fact that:

159. Christopher Stothers's article, "IMS Health and its implications for compulsory licensing in Europe", 10 EIPR 2004, provides a helpful examination of the background to the various *IMS Health* cases.

160. IP/01/941.

161. See 5.6.3.1, 5.6.3.2 and 5.5.13.4.3 above, respectively.

162. 2002 OJ L 55/18, para 180.

— it would benefit *competitors* of IMS active on the *same* market as IMS; and
— these competitors were not seeking to introduce a new product.

The Commission attempted to dispel concerns about an undue encroachment on IP rights, commenting:

"The Commission fully recognises the essential role played by intellectual property rights in promoting innovation and competition. Nevertheless, as IMS admits and as the court established in the *Magill* judgment . . . Community law can apply to the exercise of that right in exceptional circumstances. Such exceptional circumstances exist in this case. A dominant company has negotiated over a long period with its customer industry, who are now dependent on it, so as to produce a structure which it subsequently claims is its intellectual property, and refuses to license this structure to competitors so that no competing products based on this structure can be produced. These circumstances, which give rise to an abuse of Article 82, are extremely specific."[163]

The Decision required IMS to license its 1,860 brick structure to its competitors on a non-discriminatory basis for a reasonable royalty to be agreed, or, failing agreement, by an independent expert. This Decision was suspended by order of the CFI.

5.6.4.3 The Order of the CFI

In suspending the Commission's interim measures Decision until judgment in the main action, the CFI said that the Commission's interpretation of Article 82 appeared to be relatively novel, not least because the Commission's Decision amounted to a finding that IMS had used its copyright as an instrument of abuse to prevent its competitors from remaining on the market and from competing with it successfully.[164]

The CFI noted that there were a number of potentially important differences between the circumstances of *Magill* and those in *IMS Health*, notably that, in *IMS Health*, the Commission had taken a "non-cumulative interpretation" of the conditions regarded as constituting "exceptional circumstances" in *Magill*".[165] The CFI stated:

"In the present proceedings, instead of seeking to exclude the emergence of a new service on a separate market, the applicant's refusal to grant a copyright licence to NDC . . . appears . . . to be designed to prevent the latter from furnishing regional sales-data services based on freely available data, provided *on the same market and to the same potential clients* . . . . In essence, the Commission's analysis would appear to be that the prevention, by means of a refusal to license an intellectual property right, of the emergence of new competitors willing to offer, at most, new variations of the same services and on the same market as the dominant undertaking, may amount to an

163. *IMS Health*, Commission Decision, para 211.
164. [2001] ECR I 03193, para 89.
165. *IMS Health* (CFI), para 100.

abuse where those competitors cannot otherwise access the market in question because the protected work constitutes a *de facto* industry standard."[166] (Emphasis added.)

The CFI also expressed doubts about the Commission's interpretation of the case law, saying:

"The Commission's provisional conclusion that the prevention of the emergence of a new product or service for which there is potential consumer demand is not an indispensable part of the notion of 'exceptional circumstances' developed by the Court of Justice in *Magill* constitutes, at first sight, an extensive interpretation of that notion."[167]

One of the CFI's main concerns was that IP rights should not be reduced, by the obligation to license, to a mere right to receive royalties:

"The fundamental rationale of copyright is that it affords the creator of inventive and original works the exclusive right to exploit such works . . . , thereby ensuring that there is a 'reward for the creative effort' . . . . To reduce it to a purely economic right to receive royalties dilutes the essence of the right and is, in principle, likely to cause potentially serious and irreparable harm to the rightholder."[168]

The CFI concluded that there was a risk that the Commission's decision could cause serious and irreparable harm to IMS. Accordingly, the Decision was suspended.[169]

5.6.4.4 The parallel reference to the ECJ

In parallel national proceedings, the German court held that IMS's copyright was infringed, but that IMS could not refuse to grant a licence to NDC if such a refusal would infringe Article 82. The court asked the ECJ about the circumstances when a refusal to grant a licence could be abuse of a dominant position. The ECJ held that refusal by a dominant undertaking to grant a licence to a would-be competitor could amount to an Article 82 infringement if three conditions were satisfied:

- the party wishing to receive the licence must intend to offer new products/services not offered by the right holder, and for which there is a potential consumer demand;
- the right holder must be unable to justify its refusal to license on objective grounds; and
- the refusal to grant a licence must reserve the relevant market sector to the right holder, eliminating all competition in that market.

The German national court now has to decide the case on the facts, taking into account the ECJ's responses to its questions. The ECJ's ruling is ambiguous in part, as it has stated that Article 82 will only be infringed if the

166. *IMS Health* (CFI), para 101.
167. *IMS Health* (CFI), para 102.
168. *IMS Health* (CFI), para 125.
169. This order was subsequently upheld by the ECJ: [2002] 5 CMLR 1.

potential licensee is to offer "new products", but it has not explained what constitutes a new product. The only guidance given is that the potential licensee must avoid "essentially duplicating" the goods or services already offered.

5.6.5 Recent development: the Commission's Microsoft *Decision*

In March 2004, the Commission found that Microsoft had infringed Article 82, fining it over €400 million. Microsoft was found to have abused its dominant position as follows:

— by refusing to supply interoperability information and allowing it to be used to develop and distribute server operating system products; and
— by tying the Windows operating system to Windows Media Player.

The Commission also ordered Microsoft to:

— make the relevant interoperability information available to any undertaking interested in developing server operating system products;
— establish an evaluation mechanism by which interested third parties could determine the scope and terms of use of the interoperability information; and
— offer a full-function version of the Windows operating system that does not incorporate Windows Media Player (though a bundled version of Windows may still be offered).

In relation to the remedy requiring Microsoft to make interoperability information available, the Commission's Decision comments:

"to the extent that this Decision might require Microsoft to refrain from fully enforcing any of its intellectually property rights, this would be justified by the need to put an end to the abuse."[170]

Microsoft's appeal against the substance of the Decision is still outstanding. However, the CFI has ruled on Microsoft's application to stay the remedies imposed by the Commission. In a judgment of December 2004, the CFI refused to impose a stay, holding that Microsoft had failed to show that suspension of the interim remedies was a matter of urgency.[171] This does not reflect adversely on Microsoft's prospects of success on the substantive issues: the legal test for obtaining a stay on interim measures imposed by the Commission is very difficult to meet.

170. Commission Decision of 24 March 2004, Case COMP/C 3/37.792, para 1004.
171. Case T–201/04, available on http://www.curia.eu.int.

5.6.6 The application of Article 82: other abuses

There are a number of other circumstances in which the conduct of an IP owner may be prohibited by Article 82. In some instances, this may arise from the way the IP rights are exercised. In others, it is the fact of dominance, possibly bolstered by the existence of the IP rights, that may impose a special obligation. Some of the cases and Decisions referred to below are quite old, and in some instances unique. Philip Lowe, the Director-General for Competition, has said that the general relationship between IP rights and Article 82 will form part of the Commission's current review of the application of Article 82. Nevertheless, it would be foolish to disregard the flexibility of Article 82. If, in particular circumstances, a given course of conduct involving the exercise of IP rights had a sufficiently serious effect on competition, the authorities could intervene. Companies must always have regard not only to the form of their conduct, but also to its real effect.

5.6.6.1 "Unfair" licences

There have been a limited number of instances in which the Commission has reviewed particular provisions in licences and held them to be "unfair".

In *Eurofima*,[172] the buyer of standard European railway passenger carriages on behalf of six national railway administrations was found to have abused its dominant position when, in its calls for tenders from railway carriage manufacturers and equipment engineers, it insisted on "unfair" terms in licence agreements.

Particularly objectionable was a provision requiring unrestricted rights for the purchaser to use the designs, documents, patents and other proprietary rights arising from the planning and execution of the contract. The Commission said:

> "The claim to give licences for the future patent rights and for third parties without consulting or giving additional compensation to the contractor is materially improper. This condition of tender represents abuse within the meaning of Article [82]."

In an early investigation into the terms of IP licences granted by Microsoft, the Commission found that certain licensing practices foreclosed the European market for operating software. Particular issues of concern were:

- an obligation on licensees to pay a minimum royalty to Microsoft, irrespective of use (minimum commitments);
- an obligation to pay royalties to Microsoft on every PC produced whether or not they actually had Microsoft software installed ("per system/per processor" licences); and
- the duration of the licences under review.[173]

172. [1973] CMLR D 217.
173. See Report on Competition Policy 1994.

5.6.6 Article 82: Principles and Application

In *Re YKK's Complaint*,[174] the Commission held that certain provisions in a patent licence infringed Article 81(1):

- provisions restricting a licensee's freedom to fix sales prices;
- provisions requiring extensive future licences of all future patents or know-how developed by one of the parties, extending beyond the originally licensed technology; and
- provisions where a patent owner agreed not to exploit his rights in a Member State where the other party, a competitor, was active in the same field.

In addition, the Commission considered it to be an abuse under Article 82 for a dominant company to have started several actions for patent infringement, where it subsequently agreed to suspend those actions only on condition that the defendant entered into a restrictive agreement.

5.6.6.2 Excessive royalties

Article 82(a) provides it may be an abuse to "directly or indirectly impos[e] unfair purchase or selling prices or other unfair trading conditions". However, it seems that the charging of excessive royalties will only rarely be found to constitute abusive conduct.

The meaning of Article 82(a) was considered generally (though not in relation to IP rights) in *United Brands v. Commission*.[175] In *Parke, Davis & Co v. Probel*, the ECJ suggested that royalties might in some circumstances be excessive:

> "A higher sales price for the patented product as compared with that of the unpatented product . . . does not *necessarily* constitute an abuse."[176] (Emphasis added.)

In *Hilti*, the CFI criticised Hilti for seeking high royalties with a view to delaying entry.[177] Hilti's patents were subject to the licence of right provisions under English law. As Hilti would only offer to license third parties at unacceptable royalties, the grant of licences of right was delayed, as the Comptroller of Patents had to settle the royalty.

5.6.6.3 Exclusive licences

In *Tetra Pak v. Commission*,[178] the ECJ held that a company may abuse its dominant position in a market by acquiring an exclusive licence to use new technology, where in doing so it strengthens its own dominant position and prevents or delays others from entering the market.

174. [1978] 3 CMLR 44, paras 6–7.
175. [1978] ECR 207, para 266.
176. [1968] ECR 55, p 74. See also *Deutsche Grammophon v. Metro* [1971] ECR 487.
177. [1991] ECR II 1439, para 49.
178. [1990] ECR II 309.

The Commission also considered whether a policy by a dominant firm of extending its patent coverage by repeatedly registering patents for small alterations might be an abuse. The Commission concluded that such a policy was not itself abusive, even if the aim of the policy was to eliminate competition. However, the Commission said that such a strategy might infringe Article 82 if it formed part of an overall course of conduct with other policies and practices restricting competition.

5.6.6.4 Limiting technical development

Article 82(b) of the Treaty provides that it may be an abuse for a dominant company to limit production, markets or technical development to the prejudice of consumers. The application of Article 82(b) to cases involving IP was considered in *Decca Navigator System*.[179] Racal Decca was held to have infringed Article 82 by granting restrictive licences to certain alleged proprietary rights in the Decca Navigator System. The licences eliminated all innovative competition in the products by obliging the licensees to supply only downgraded features and by restricting use of the licensed technology to a narrow field of use. This partitioning of the market was an abuse of Racal Decca's dominant position, which limited users' freedom of choice in that market.

Racal Decca had argued that, as this was a licence agreement, it was entitled to impose restrictions on the use of its rights. The Commission dismissed this argument:

> "The substance of the copyright alleged does not justify an agreement containing such far-reaching restrictions of competition. In any event, the object of these agreements is to allocate the markets . . . . The Community system of competition does not allow an improper use of rights under national copyright laws which frustrates Community competition law."[180]

5.6.6.5 Other recent developments

5.6.6.5.1 The Commission's AstraZeneca investigation

The Commission announced an investigation into AstraZeneca in July 2003.[181] It alleges that AstraZeneca has made misrepresentations in its applications for Supplementary Protection Certificates—the certificates allowing patent protection for pharmaceutical products to be extended for up to five years—and has misused regulatory procedures in the withdrawal of marketing authorisations for medicinal products.

The Commission argues that this infringes the competition rules because both generic manufacturers and parallel importers have unlawfully been prevented from competing and providing EU consumers with cheaper products

179. 1989 OJ L 243.
180. 1989 OJ L 243, para 104.
181. Commission Press Release IP/03/1136 of 31 July 2003.

and alternatives. The Commission claims to be following the approach of the US Federal Trade Commission ("FTC") and the US courts in recently challenging research and development-based pharmaceutical companies seeking to maintain market exclusivity for their blockbuster drugs through misrepresentation or other unlawful means.

5.6.6.5.2 The OFT's British Horseracing Board ("BHB") investigation

In 2001, the High Court upheld the BHB's database right.[182] The Office of Fair Trading ("OFT") then announced that it was investigating whether the assertion of the database right was an abuse of a dominant position under Chapter II of the Competition Act 1998.[183] The OFT was concerned that the exercise of the database rights could lead to:

- — uncompetitively high prices;
- — unfair distribution of money received from data sales to race tracks, depriving them of incentive to improve; and
- — a restriction on the outflow of data, to the detriment of consumers in the betting markets.

The BHB has agreed measures to address the competition concerns. These proposed measures include the creation of a separate body with responsibility for the commercial exploitation of the BHB's racing database. The BHB will also ensure that data is licensed on a non-discriminatory basis and provide for independent arbitration of price disputes. This demonstrates the potentially extensive reach of competition law over many IP rights, and the breadth of measures that may result from a competition investigation.

5.6.7 Competition law in IP litigation: "Euro-defences"

The term "Euro-defence" has traditionally been used in the UK to describe a defence in civil litigation invoking rights under the EC Treaty to defend against an alleged breach of a claimant's IP rights. The recent history of "Euro-defences" in IP litigation is considered briefly below.

The term "Euro-defence" appears to have acquired something of a pejorative meaning in the English courts, implying a last-ditch (and usually doomed) attempt to invoke competition law as a defence to breaches of "national law".[184] Defences based on Articles 81 and 82 of the Treaty in IP litigation in

182. *British Horseracing Board Ltd v. William Hill Organisation Ltd (No 1)* [2001] 2 CMLR 12.

183. OFT Press Releases of 12 June and 22 October 2001.

184. Lawrence Collins J stated that the expression "Euro-defence" must not be treated as a pejorative term in *Heathrow Airport Ltd v. Forte (UK) Ltd* [1998] Eu LR 98, p 105.

England have even been referred to as the "infringer's defence".[185] Now that provisions mirroring Articles 81 and 82 have been made part of UK law in the Competition Act 1998, and as the European courts have made it increasingly apparent that the rights arising under the competition rules of the Treaty are mandatory rights which must be enforced,[186] it remains to be seen whether this view can be sustained. Of course, for the reasons discussed above, it will be rare for the competition rules to have any relevance to the enforcement of an IP right in litigation.

The following provides an overview of recent cases in which "Euro-defences" were pleaded, with a focus on cases dealing with claims of refusals to license.[187] *Magill* has been relied upon in most of these cases, but so far with limited success. Many pleadings are "struck out" at an early stage as unsustainable.

5.6.7.1 Philips Electronics v. Ingman[188]

This was an action for patent infringement. The defendants raised a defence based on Article 82, namely that the plaintiff, which owned patents in the field of CD technology, had abused a dominant position by refusing to license those patents on fair and reasonable terms.

In considering an application to strike out the Article 82 defence, Laddie J reviewed a number of arguments based on ECJ cases, including cases explicitly based on "essential facilities".[189] Among other matters, he reviewed the reasonableness of the terms and whether offering such terms might be argued to be an abuse:

> "Even if the royalties sought by the plaintiff are objectively unreasonable and have the effect of destroying the competitiveness of the defendant, it is not an abuse of a dominant position defined by reference to the existence of the intellectual property right. Indeed the proprietor may offer terms which no reasonable competitor could accept. It is difficult to see how that can be worse, or commercially different, to offering no terms at all—ie to refusing a licence—a course the rights owner is entitled to take."[190]

185. "Community Intellectual Property Law in English Courts", in Jacobs and Andenas (eds), *European Community Law in the English Courts*, 1998, p 210. Jacob J states that "I think it remains the case that even today, save in relation to goods put in free circulation in the Common Market by the IP right holder, no defence of Community law has ever succeeded in the English courts. I do not find this particularly surprising since in most cases if there is no defence to an infringement claim apart from the Treaty, it is not self-evident that the Treaty should somehow come to the rescue."

186. Eg *Aéroports de Paris v. Commission* [2000] ECR II 3929, para 241.

187. For a discussion of early IP cases in which competition defences where considered, see eg Jacob J, in Jacobs and Andenas, *op cit*, n 189 above.

188. [1998] 2 CMLR 839. (Note that this case was decided before the Advocate-General's opinion in *Bronner*.)

189. Eg *Port of Rødby* [1994] 5 CMLR 457.

190. [1998] 2 CMLR 839, para 54.

Laddie J came to the conclusion that the plea of abuse of a dominant position in the "licence market" was without substance. He emphasised that *Magill* was exceptional and said that:

"If a party is to rely on *Magill* to resist the enforcement of an intellectual property right, it is incumbent on him to plead explicitly what are the exceptional features which take the case outside *Volvo v. Veng*. Mere assertion will not do."[191]

5.6.7.2 Sandvik v. KR Pfiffner and Others[192]

In response to Sandvik's claim of patent infringement, the defendants alleged that contractual restrictions imposed by Sandvik amounted to a disguised customer restriction or an unlawful territorial restriction and constituted an abuse of a dominant position.

Neuberger J emphasised that to resist an application to strike out an Article 82 claim, the defendant must:

- have pleaded an arguable case that Sandvik enjoyed a dominant position;
- have pleaded an arguable case that Sandvik was abusing its dominant position;
- show that such abuse would materially affect trade between Member States; and
- show that these elements, if satisfied, would give the defendants an arguable defence, and that a clear link must exist between the alleged abuse and the remedy sought.[193]

Neuberger J held that the defendants' Article 82 arguments were insufficiently pleaded, but allowed amendments to be made in the interests of justice.

5.6.7.3 HMSO and Ordnance Survey v. Automobile Association[194]

The claimants claimed that the Automobile Association ("AA") had infringed the copyright contained in Ordnance Survey maps. The AA responded by pleading that the claimants were abusing a dominant position in the way they exploited these rights. Laddie J considered whether an abuse might consist in offering a licence only upon unreasonable and discriminatory terms.

In striking out the Article 82 defence, Laddie J emphasised the limits of *Magill*:

"They do not mind taking a licence, as long as the royalty rate is zero. The royalty rate of zero means effectively that the intellectual property right might just as well not exist. There is no authority that I know of which would suggest that even in the most

191. [1998] 2 CMLR 839, para 63.
192. [2000] FSR 17.
193. [2000] FSR 17, p 71.
194. [2001] ECC 34.

favourable climate *Magill* could be stretched to any such length. It would amount to Article 82 being used to destroy intellectual property rights."[195]

5.6.7.4 Jobserve v. Network Multimedia Television[196]

This case did not involve compulsory licensing, but is important to those pleading Article 82 claims, or those based on the equivalent provision in the Competition Act 1998 (s 18). Mummery LJ emphasised that abuse of a dominant position is a complex question of mixed fact and law, which should generally be determined at trial on the basis of full evidence rather than on a summary basis.[197]

Mummery LJ also reiterated the ECJ's point in *Bronner*[198] that the question of elimination of competition has to be considered from the perspective of the party pleading exceptional circumstances:

"On its facts *Bronner* can be treated as an 'essential facilities' case ie one in which an undertaking is seeking to gain access to an essential facility owned and controlled by a competitor . . . . In order to establish an abuse in such a case it has to be demonstrated that, without that access, the claimant could not provide a competing service."[199] (Emphasis added.)

This interpretation has arguably been confirmed by the ECJ's judgment in *IMS Health*, as discussed at 5.6.4.4 above.

5.6.7.5 Intel v. VIA Technologies[200]

A patent infringement action was brought by Intel. As well as disputing validity and infringement, VIA raised defences under competition law, alleging that Intel's refusal to license its patents on reasonable terms was an abuse of a dominant position. The competition defences were struck out at first instance. Lawrence Collins J considered that VIA had not shown the existence of "exceptional circumstances" within the meaning of *Magill*. He held that *Magill* required *all* competition to be eliminated and, on that basis, VIA's defence did not have a real prospect of success.

VIA appealed and had the defences reinstated.[201] The Court of Appeal considered that it was too restrictive to limit "exceptional circumstances" to those in *Magill*. Morritt VC gave the leading judgment:

"It does not follow that other circumstances in other cases will not be regarded as exceptional. In particular it is at least arguable, as the [CFI] recognised in *IMS*, that the Court of Justice will assimilate its jurisprudence under Article 82 more closely with that of the essential facilities doctrine applied in the United States. In that event there

195. [2001] ECC 34, para 50.
196. [2001] EWCA Civ 2021.
197. [2001] EWCA Civ 2021, para 12.
198. [1998] ECR I 7791, Advocate-General's Opinion, para 43.
199. [2001] EWCA Civ 2021, para 12.
200. [2002] EWHC 1159 (Ch).
201. [2002] EWCA Civ 1905 (CA).

could be a breach of Article 82 without the exclusion of a wholly new product or all competition."

The Vice-Chancellor recognised that the width of Article 82 itself suggested that it would be premature to assume that only the circumstances envisaged in *Magill* could give rise to an abuse. The judgment also makes clear the Court of Appeal's view that the *Magill* line of cases applies to patent rights as well as other forms of IP.

5.6.8 Conclusion

This Chapter contains only an overview of a complex and developing area. Over the years, some of the answers to the questions that are still open at the time of writing may emerge. The ever-increasing importance of IP rights (reflected, for example, in the number of patents filed[202]) means that this area of law will remain relevant in the future. Competition law and competition-law makers have a genuine respect for the benefits of IP and it is only with reluctance, and in rare cases, that they will intervene in the prerogative of IP owners to exercise their rights. Where "exceptional circumstances" exist (whatever that phrase may mean) competition law is available to remedy serious market problems.

5.7 THE FUTURE OF ARTICLE 82

The Commission is reviewing the application of Article 82 and has indicated that it intends to issue guidelines. What can be expected?

The review will be wide-ranging, covering the relevant market, the question of dominance and also abuses. Any enhanced role for economic analysis is likely to feature significantly, although there has not yet been any comment from the new Chief Competition Economist on Article 82.

On substantive abuses, the following will hopefully feature:

— Exploitative abuses: unfair or excessive prices are not easy to determine and the Commission should develop a methodology for determining this through a comparison of prices charged by the dominant undertaking against those of competitors and against those it charges in other markets.

— An assessment of the issue of predatory pricing and in particular the extent to which recoupment should be taken into account.

— A more realistic approach to loyalty rebates, taking into account their benefits for consumers, their potential efficiency gains and the reasons why customers request them.

202. A list of patent owners is at http://www.ipo.org. In 2003, for example, IBM was awarded 3,415 patents in the US, thereby attaining the number one spot. In total, IBM currently holds around 37,000 patents worldwide.

— The effects of a refusal—especially the question why there should be different criteria for existing and new customers.
— Tying and bundling: however, the Commission is not going to do anything that might impact on its *Microsoft* decision.

CHAPTER 6

ARTICLE 86

Chris Bright and John Schmidt, Shearman & Sterling LLP

6.1 INTRODUCTION

Preceding Chapters have considered the rules applicable to undertakings (Articles 81 and 82). This Chapter considers the state's obligations in relation to undertakings. This interface between public and private law has three main pillars:

(i) Article 86, which sets out the rules in relation to state enterprises, ie companies granted special or exclusive rights by the state and those having the character of a revenue-producing monopoly. This is addressed in this Chapter.

(ii) Article 87, which contains the law relating to state aid, that is, financial assistance provided by the state to certain companies. The rules on state aid are addressed in the following Chapter.

(iii) The "loyal cooperation" requirement of Article 10, which requires Member States to take appropriate measures to ensure that the Treaty obligations and requirements for actions issued by Community institutions are fulfilled, and to abstain from measures jeopardising the Treaty objectives. It is usually applied in the context of Article 81, where a law or state measure facilitates an agreement that has as its object or effect the restriction of competition, and that affects trade between Member States. It is relied upon against the state in enforcement proceedings. Good examples of Article 10 predicaments include:

— ministerial quotas that extend pre-agreed quotas to an entire industry;

— laws that prevent commissions from being passed back to the consumer; and

(iii) government approval of a previously fixed air tariff.

Article 10 is not addressed further here.

6.2 ARTICLE 86

Article 86 contains three basic elements. The first paragraph forbids a Member State from protecting public undertakings and those enjoying special rights. Article 86(2) provides a limited derogation for services of general economic interest, and the third paragraph gives the Commission power to legislate to ensure the proper application of Article 86.

While Article 86 has to be read in conjunction with other Treaty articles, its use is not in any way limited to competition law infringements, although it is frequently used in conjunction with Article 82 (abuse of a dominant position), and rather less frequently with Article 81 (anti-competitive agreements). Aside from the competition law provisions of the Treaty (Articles 81–89), Article 86 may also be used in conjunction with Article 12 (discrimination on grounds of nationality), Article 28 (free movement of goods), Article 39 (free movement of workers), Article 43 (freedom of establishment) and Article 49 (free movement of services). Its application is thus quite far-reaching and applies in all sectors in which state enterprises are commercially active, eg telecommunications, utilities, postal services and transport.

6.2.1 Article 86, paragraph 1

Article 86(1) ensures that no special protection is afforded to businesses in which the state is involved:

"In the case of public undertakings and undertakings to which the Member States grant special or exclusive rights, Member States shall neither enact nor maintain in force any measure contrary to the rules contained in this Treaty, in particular to those provided for in Article 12 and Articles 81–89."

The provision refers to two types of enterprises: public companies, or companies over which the state has dominant influence, and private companies entrusted with exclusive or special rights. This latter definition has been held to include, among others, agricultural marketing boards; monopolies over recruitment; the right to organise dock work for third parties; waste management partnerships between the state, the local authority and private companies; and the right to operate a mobile phone network. Hence the type of measures to which Article 86 is applicable is very wide, but it is also important to note that such measures need not be legally binding. Interestingly, Article 86 is useful not only against the state enterprises themselves, but also against the state itself for imposing the measures in question.

One notable feature of the relationship between Articles 82 and 86 is that Article 82, in its regulation of abusive conduct by dominant companies, may also cover cases where dominance is a consequence of the rights conferred by the state, and abuse arises in the exercise of those rights. Some cases that have treated this area of overlap between the two articles include:

- *Höfner & Elser v. Macrotron*,[1] where a German public employment agency was granted exclusive rights but displayed a systematic inability to meet demand;

1. Case C-41/90, ECR I-1979, 1991 OJ C 132, p 7.

- *Ert v. Dimotiki*,[2] where a Greek TV and radio monopoly was compromised by a conflict of interest; and
- *RTT v. GN-INNO-BM*,[3] where a Belgian telephone monopoly also selling telephony equipment extended its monopoly into a neighbouring market.

6.2.2 Article 86, paragraph 2

The second paragraph of Article 86 reads as follows:

"Undertakings entrusted with operation of services of general economic interest or having the character of a revenue-producing monopoly shall be subject to the rules contained in this Treaty, in particular the rules on competition, *insofar as the application of such rules does not obstruct the performance, in law or in fact, of the particular tasks assigned to them*. The development of trade must not be affected to such an extent as would be contrary to the interests of the Community." (Emphasis added.)

Article 86(2) applies to "services of general economic interest", a concept that is not further defined but which has been taken to cover postal and certain transport services. A "revenue-producing monopoly" could include a state concession to a private company, and the use of the term "entrusted" requires a specific act of public authority and not just an approval of the undertaking's existence. Interestingly, the adverse effect on the development of trade specified in Article 86 is therefore narrower than the "effect on trade" required by Article 81, and the situation calls for the evaluation of "particular tasks".

Derogations under Article 86(2) must be construed narrowly. There is no overall exemption for an undertaking itself, but only for anything necessary for it to carry out its tasks. For the derogation to apply, the application of Treaty provisions (eg Article 82) must obstruct the performance of these tasks. Furthermore, any restriction of competition must satisfy the principle of proportionality, in that the state measure or behaviour must be indispensable to achieve the objectives and any restrictions must be outweighed by benefits for the general interest. There have been several cases in which Article 86(2) has operated to provide a derogation from Article 82, for example:

- *Corsica Ferries*,[4] where a company with a monopoly in the market for universal mooring services was found compatible with Article 86(2) because national safety regulations required these to be provided to all vessels using a port;
- *Albany*,[5] where supplementary pension services to young healthy people were deemed compatible because they enabled the provider to also offer such services to individuals who were bad insurance risks; and

2. Case C-260/89, *Ert v. Dimotiki* [1991] ECR I–2925.
3. Case C-18/88, *RTT v. GN-INNO-BM* [1991] ECR I–5981.
4. Case C-18/93, *Corsica Ferries* [1994] ECR I 1783.
5. Case C-67/96, *Albany* [1999] ECR I–5751.

— *Ambulanz Glöckner v. Landkreis Südwestpfalz*,[6] where emergency ambulance services were deemed compatible with Article 86(2) because the operator needed to achieve economically viable conditions in order to continue with business.

Article 86(1) and (2) have direct effect, which means that they may be used in actions against Member States in national courts and third parties may be able to sue for damages (Article 86(1)). However, it should be noted that the final sentence of Article 86(2) seems not to have direct effect since it is only the Commission that is responsible for the assessment of Community interests.

6.2.3 Article 86, paragraph 3

The third and last paragraph of Article 86 reads as follows:

"The Commission shall ensure the application of the provisions of this Article and shall, where necessary, address appropriate Directives or Decisions to Member States."

This text was dormant until 1980 and is now used primarily in regulated industries. It allows direct action through Directives and Decisions by the Commission without the need for recourse to the courts.

Directives often act as instruments to prevent future infringements of Article 86(1). For example, the Transparency Directive[7] obliges Member States to introduce laws that require companies that are owned by the state to have transparent accounts. However, some also play a part in achieving liberalisation; for example, the Terminal Equipment Directive[8] required Member States to abolish exclusive rights over telecommunications terminal equipment. Furthermore, the Telecommunications Services Directive[9] implemented the same measure in the services sector, and the Full Competition Directive[10] extended this abolition to voice telephony.

Secondly, Decisions of the Commission are used in this context as "instruments of repression", insofar as they declare that an infringement is taking place and order the Member State to act in order to remedy it. Recent examples of Decisions include those in the postal sector concerning national legislation hampering competition between postal companies and mail preparation firms; in the airports sector concerning legislation that established discriminatory landing fees favouring locally established airlines; and in the shipping sector concerning legislation establishing discriminatory discounts on pilotage fees in some of Europe's most important ports. Crucially, however, there is no power to fine an infringing Member State under Article 86. The

6. Case C-475/99, [2001] ECR I–8089.
7. Directive 80/723 1980 OJ L 195/35.
8. Directive 88/301, 1988 OJ L 131/73.
9. Directive 90/388, 1990 OJ L 192/10.
10. Directive 96/19, 1996 OJ L 74/13.

next step following a Member State's failure to comply with a Decision would be to initiate infringement proceedings under Article 226.

Generally, there are two main types of abuse that are common to state enterprises: foreclosure and leveraging. Foreclosure refers to the maintenance of monopolies after a market has been liberalised; leveraging refers to the use of power in one market to gain a foothold in another.

Foreclosure may comprise any of the following:

- Long-term agreements with customers.
- In network industries, refusal to grant access, including margin squeezing. (The latter may be defined as when a dominant vertically integrated company wholesales a product to distributors at a price that is insufficient to allow them to make a profit even if they are as efficient as the vertically integrated company's own downstream business.)
- Discriminatory access terms.

In relation to leveraging, which may comprise bundling or cross-subsidies, it may be useful to look at an example. In the *Deutsche Post*[11] case, the Commission received a complaint that Deutsche Post was using revenues from its letter-mail monopoly to maintain below-cost prices in the liberalised mail-order parcel services market. The Commission applied Article 86 to the case in conjunction with Article 82, and held that Deutsche Post was dominant in the relevant product market, and that the abuse necessary for Article 82 to apply was found in the predatory pricing policy that it was using in relation to the liberalised market. The Commission found that predatory pricing was made possible by cross-subsidisation by using profits from another market in which Deutsche Post was dominant. It further held that prices in a liberalised market must cover at least the incremental costs related to this activity, and ordered a series of remedies, including a separation of Deutsche Post's entity providing mail-order services from the rest of the company, full financial transparency between its entities, and any further "input" from other Deutsche Post entities to be provided at arm's length.

Another interesting case is *Deutsche Telekom*,[12] which concerned a 1998 obligation imposed on the former telecommunications state monopolies to provide access to local loops. Deutsche Telekom was a gatekeeper for German local telecommunications loops, and furthermore the only operator with nationwide coverage in Germany. Following liberalisation of the market, the company emerged with a market share of close to 95 per cent. The Commission ruled that access fees for wholesalers were set above Deutsche Telekom's retail price, which meant that potential market entrants were *de facto* excluded, regardless of their level of efficiency. Deutsche Telekom was fined €12.6

11. Case C-147/97, [2000] ECR I-825.
12. Commission Press Release, IP/03/717, 21 May 2003.

million and the decision is still considered an important precedent and warning for other industries where the incumbent has shut off access to a market in this way.

6.3 CONCLUSION

Looking ahead, it is becoming increasingly difficult for state enterprises to engage in anti-competitive behaviour, and for anti-competitive state measures to be ignored. The categories of abuse for either offence are well developed. The Commission has become well disposed towards complainants, although complainants must be prepared to be patient for a case to reach its outcome, as proceedings often take years to complete. Liberalisation of markets within the EU is a Commission enforcement priority, and there is an ongoing alignment between competition laws and sector-specific rules. It should be noted that the Commission favours the financial and legal separation of entities belonging to the same company, so that a greater level of transparency and distance is created between a single company's presence on several markets in proximity.

CHAPTER 7

STATE AID

Chris Bright and John Schmidt, Shearman and Sterling LLP

7.1 INTRODUCTION

A further example of the interface between public and private law (see Chapter 6) is the state aid regime contained in Article 87 of the EC Treaty. The rules concern any financial support provided by governments to companies. State aid needs to be regulated because it distorts competition if given in too high a dose, and provides a crutch to companies that cannot stand up to competition. Unsubsidised firms who must compete with those receiving public support may ultimately run into economic difficulties, causing loss of competitiveness in the market. Furthermore, state aid exports unemployment and inhibits the creation of the single market and the efficiency of resource allocation within the EU. Nevertheless, it would be wrong to assume that the Commission sees all aid as contrary to Community law. In fact, several forms of state aid are looked upon favourably; most of those have a social character, as will be seen below.

According to the Commission, Member States must continue their efforts to reduce the level of aid granted, in terms of percentage of gross domestic product, while at the same time redirecting aid towards horizontal objectives of Community interest, such as employment, environmental protection, research and development, the development of small and medium sized enterprises, as well as the strengthening of economic and social cohesion.[1] There have been several recent high-profile state aid cases, such as:

- *France/Telecom*,[2] where a tax break worth approximately €800 million to €1.1 billion was found to be illegal; and
- *France/Alstom*,[3] where rights issues worth over €1 billion were cleared, as well as an extensive debt-for-equity swap, while the Commission imposed significant conditions such as the opening up of the national rail procurement business, the divestment of assets worth over €1.6 million, and an obligation to find industrial partners for Alstom's main operations.

1. 32nd Report on Competition Policy 2002, p 93.
2. Cases C–13a/2003 and C–13b/2003.
3. Case C–58/2003.

7.2 ARTICLE 87 AND THE LEGISLATIVE STRUCTURE OF STATE AID

The legislative structure of EU state aid is manifested in Articles 87 to 89 of the Treaty. Article 87 lays down the general prohibition but also sets out situations in which aid benefits from an automatic exemption or where an exemption could be possible. Articles 88 and 89 then provide practical procedures, as well as the power of the Council to adopt implementing and exempting Regulations. Article 87 provides a four stage test, prohibiting (a) any aid, (b) granted by a Member State or through state resources in any form whatsoever, (c) which distorts or threatens to distort competition by favouring certain companies or the production of certain goods, and (d) that affects trade between Member States. Situations in which state aid is granted either directly or indirectly are therefore almost endless, and the aid itself can take a variety of forms, such as state grants, interest relief, tax relief, state loan guarantee or holding, and provision by the state of goods and services on preferential terms (eg renting land on preferential terms, preferential rate for power supply or supply of raw materials, and state participation in the capital on unusually favourable terms).

Parallel to the general provisions in the Treaty, the Commission has adopted a range of Guidelines and framework Directives to clarify its state aid policy in a number of areas where more detailed rules and procedures have been warranted. These include underdeveloped areas (ie regional aid), protection of the environment, rescue and restructuring of firms in difficulty, and specific industries such as agriculture, coal, electricity, fisheries and transport. Regulations have also been created in order to enable block exemptions, rules on procedure, implementing Regulations and various Commission communications.[4]

The concept of "aid" is defined very widely. What is important is the overall effect of the measure, insofar as whether it confers a benefit or advantage which the recipient would not have received in a normal market. The main legislative issue is the Member State's financial participation in the company receiving aid. Is it acting as a lender or a shareholder? Are there any burdens on public finances? For example, in *France/Alstom*[5] there was a clear financial burden on the central government. It is also sufficient to shown a strain on the regional or local authorities. But, as other cases show, the financial problems must not directly affect the central government or its regional offices and in *Caisse National de Crédit Agricole*[6] it was publicly funded bodies that were affected. Another factor to take into account is whether the aid is selective insofar as it is granted to a single company or the industry as a whole; in other

4. See http://europa.eu.int/comm/competition/state_aid/legislation/ for a full list of all Guidelines, block exemptions and Regulations in force.
5. *France/Alstom.*
6. Case 290/83, [1985] ECR 439.

words, whether the aid would provide the recipient (either a company or a whole industry) with a competitive advantage over another.

A third factor when assessing the concept of "aid", which was initially developed to judge state participation in company equity/debts but is now being used more broadly in relation to other state aid issues, is the so-called "market economy investor principle". It is a private investor test, which examines the conditions under which the state funding was made available to a company, and then compares it with the conditions that would have been acceptable to a comparable private investor operating under market conditions at the same time and in comparable circumstances. The question is whether a private investor would have taken the same decision and the same financial risk. It is now being used to measure all public funding (eg the *Belgium/Ryanair* case[7]).

The third stage in Article 87 considers whether the aid, as given by a Member State or through state resources, distorts or threatens to distort competition by favouring certain companies or the production of certain goods, and the fourth considers whether the aid affects trade between Member States. These criteria are quite easily fulfilled and it is merely a question of whether one firm's position is strengthened in comparison with other firms in the market. There is no *de minimis* rule, but, as we will see below, exemptions may apply. The effect-on-trade criterion should be assessed in the same manner as under Articles 81 and 82 and consequently it is sufficient to show that the aid could potentially affect trade between Member States. As a general rule, purely local companies would therefore escape the scrutiny of Article 87 and the EU rules on state aid.

7.3 EXEMPTIONS

7.3.1 Automatic exemptions

As indicated above, the Commission acknowledges that certain aid schemes may have an overall beneficial impact on the Union, and consequently Article 87(2) allows for automatic exemptions to the general rules of prohibition in certain cases without the need for specific authorisation. It should be noted that these cases are interpreted narrowly:

- Aid having a social character, granted to individual consumers without discrimination. The ultimate beneficiary of the aid must be an individual consumer, and not an undertaking or a whole region.
- Aid to make good the damage caused by natural disasters and exceptional circumstances, such as floods, droughts, tornadoes, forest fires and earthquakes, but not frost, ice and hail unless damage suffered represents at least 30 per cent of normal production. Neither does it

7. Case C–76/2002.

include pure financial loss due to commercial decisions of economic operators, whatever the motive, nor costs associated with normal entrepreneurial risk or eg a factory fire.

7.3.2 Individual exemptions

Where a scheme does not fall within the criteria for automatic exemption under Article 87(2), as outlined above, Member States may seek individual authorisation under Article 87(3) for the following categories of aid:

- Aid designed to promote the economic development of underdeveloped areas. The assessment must be made by reference to the average Community level and not the average national level in that Member State. Furthermore, the aid must provide a lasting increase in income or reduction in unemployment.
- Aid to promote the execution of an important project of common European interest, or to remedy a serious disturbance in the economy of a Member State. Any project receiving aid under this exception must form part of a transnational European programme involving several Member States.
- Aid to facilitate the development of certain activities or areas. This involves aid to regional areas, where the benchmark is the national average.
- Aid designed to promote culture and heritage conservation.

A third alternative is for the Council to authorise categories of aid following a Commission proposal under Article 87(3)(e). For such circumstances, a qualified majority is needed. It is also possible to achieve a specific Council derogation under Article 88(2) if justified by exceptional circumstances, but here the vote needs to be unanimous.

7.3.3 Commission Guidelines for individual exemptions

To accompany the individual exemptions and to further explain the underlying principles, the Commission has issued Guidelines for individual exemptions.[8] In general terms, the support must target a Community interest and not a national one and there must not be any other means by which the Member State can ensure the success of the project. In other words, the state aid must be necessary. Furthermore, important factors will always be the intensity, duration and the effect that the aid will have on the Community. Guidelines have also been adopted for specific sectors such as textiles, motor vehicles, shipbuilding, coal and steel, agriculture and fisheries, as well as

8. See http://europa.eu.int/comm/competition/state_aid/legislation/ for a full list of all Guidelines, block exemptions and Regulations in force.

transport.[9] Regional aid, which accounts for a significant proportion of all aid reported to the Commission, must be focused on areas where the GDP is less than 75 per cent of the EU average. Through its case law, the Commission has allowed a varying level of intensity.

Guidelines have also been issued for horizontal aid given across an industry without any regional or sectoral focus, such as research and development, environmental protection, small and medium sized enterprises, employment, training aid and deprived urban areas. Another set of Guidelines, which have received a lot of attention in recent cases (such as aid to *British Energy*[10] in the UK, *Alstom* in France, and in general to companies in the aviation industry), are the Guidelines for rescue and restructuring aid.[11] It may be useful to examine this type of aid somewhat more closely, given its economic impact on competition and the controversy it can cause amongst competitors.

Rescue and restructuring aid always go hand in hand. After an initial injection of immediate cash, the rescue aid must be followed by a more detailed restructuring plan within 6 months, where the parties involved aim to restore the target company's long-term viability. Aid for restructuring raises particular competition concerns, as it may shift the burden of structural adjustment and economic problems onto the other competitors in the market, who manage their business without any need of government intervention. According to the rescue and restructuring Guidelines, measures must be taken to mitigate as far as possible any adverse effects of the aid on competitors. This condition usually involves a commitment to reduce the market presence of the company subject to the aid after the end of the restructuring period. The Commission sees this as a compensatory factor in favour of the company's competitors and states that it must be proportionate in relation to the distorting effects that the aid may have on the relevant market. The reduction must, furthermore, be stipulated in the restructuring plan. However, it should be noted that the Commission may derogate from this principle should a reduction result in a manifest deterioration in the structure of the market, such as having an indirect effect of creating a monopoly or oligopoly market situation.

Although compensatory measures may take different forms, the Guidelines mention two main approaches. If there is a EU-wide or EEA-wide structural excess of production capacity in the relevant market, the company's production capacity, alongside its market presence, must be irreversibly reduced. For example, the German aluminium producer *Rackwitz Aluminium GmbH*[12] received €35 million in aid from a Norwegian state-owned company but received the Commission's approval since the parties agreed to reduce the company's capacity by 55 per cent. Interestingly, the Commission does not

9. See eg http://europa.eu.int/comm/competition/state_aid/legislation/aid3.html#G.

10. Case NN 101/2002.

11. Community Guidelines on state aid for rescuing and restructuring firms in difficulty, 2004 OJ C 244/2.

12. Case NN 76/98.

normally count the sale of capacity to competitors as a means to meeting such a condition. Secondly, if the relevant market does not suffer from such excess, the Commission may nevertheless demand limitations of market presence and subject the approval to a divestment criterion with regard to assets or subsidiaries. The key purpose of any compensatory measures imposed is to force the beneficiary of the aid to make significant contributions to the rescuing plan from its own resources and to reduce the recipient company's market presence. As a final remark in relation to rescuing and restructuring aid, it seems that any reductions in capacity only involve the target and its subsidiaries, and not just any companies under the control of the Member State.

Finally, the Commission has also introduced several block exemptions, such as those for training aid, small and medium sized enterprises and employment aid, and a *de minimis* exemption where, if the aid is less than €100,000 and given over a period of three years, it is deemed to be compatible with EU state aid law. However, the latter does not apply to the agriculture, fishing and transport sectors, nor to export aid and aid that discriminates against imported products.

Recent activities within the Commission suggest that this threshold may be increased to €1 million. That would further fall in line with the overall modernisation across all fields in which the Commission is active in order to reduce the enormous workload it faces in several main categories, including state aid.

7.4 PROCEDURES

Each aid package to a company, whether it is new or amends an existing one, requires the scrutiny of the Commission, unless exemptions apply (see 7.3.1 above). Notably, it is the Member State concerned that must notify the planned measures, and not the company receiving the aid.

To facilitate such procedures, the Commission has issued several standard notification forms for most types of aid. According to the procedural Regulation implementing detailed rules for the Treaty articles on state aid,[13] the Commission must conduct a preliminary examination of the aid within two months of the day following the receipt of a complete notification. Should the Commission find that a formal investigation into the aid is warranted, it may issue a decision summarising the relevant issues of fact and law, as well as include a preliminary assessment of the doubts as to the compatibility of the aid with the common market. Interestingly, the regulation applies a non-binding deadline so that the Commission must "endeavour" to reach a final decision within 18 months from the opening of the formal investigation. This may then be extended by a further two months should the Commission not

13. Commission Regulation 794/2004, implementing Council Regulation 659/1999 laying down detailed rules for the application of Article 93 of the EC Treaty, 2004 OJ L 140/1.

have reached a decision at the end of the 18-month period and should the Member State request a decision. Hence, an investigation into a state aid could theoretically continue more or less indefinitely. Should the Member State during those two months not receive any official communication from the Commission, it may send a notice of implementation of the aid, which will trigger a 15-day period in which the Commission must adopt a decision, otherwise the aid scheme is deemed cleared.

During its investigation, the Commission holds powers similar to those it enjoys under the "dawn raid" rules for combating cartel activities.[14] In essence, this means that the officials have, for example, the right to enter premises, ask for oral explanations on the spot, and examine records. However, when making a more detailed comparison between Articles 81 and 82 and the rules on state aid, the similarities are as striking as the differences. Both sets of rules have seen efforts by the Commission to shift the enforcement burden to national courts,[15] and the Commission has started to concentrate much more on substantial infringements and less on those with minimal competitive effect. The main differences are that under the state aid rules there is no real depth of economic analysis, and third-party rights are still fairly limited. For example, it is notable that the Commission does not publish any facts regarding notifications that have been made. Consequently, third parties will be totally ignorant of the filing until a detailed investigation has commenced, at which point the Commission invites comments on the notified aid scheme.

Aid that is notifiable under these procedures may not be put into effect until the Commission has reached a final decision by either clearing the aid, requesting modifications or blocking the aid. Where a Member State fails to notify aid, the aid becomes automatically unlawful and the Commission can initiate proceedings itself, order interim suspension of the aid, and request information to be submitted so that a decision can be taken.

In cases of unlawful aid and where the Commission takes a negative decision, it must also order the Member State to initiate all necessary measures to recover the aid. The procedure will be each state's national law. It should be noted that the Commission must initiate a recovery procedure within 10 years of the date on which the unlawful aid was awarded. Any decisions taken by the Commission are subject to review by the European Court of Justice. Recent years have seen a sharp increase in the number of cases where the Commission has ordered repayment of unlawful aid.

The role of the national courts in state aid proceedings is mixed. The EU state aid rules have a direct effect, insofar as enforcement by third parties may be possible in order to challenge aid schemes that have not been properly notified or schemes that have been granted before an investigation has been

14. See 9.5.4. below.
15. See Chapter 10 below.

completed. It is, furthermore, the national courts that must order the repayment of non-notified aid, and any rights to damages should also be decided under national law. However, given the practical difficulties that exist for third parties in gathering information about defendants and the aid scheme under investigation, the actual use of national courts may be less useful than intended by the Commission. The largest number of state aid cases in national courts seems to concern alleged discriminatory tax regimes.

7.5 RYANAIR/CHARLEROI AIRPORT

A recent case that signifies many of the points made above, and will therefore act as a good example of how the state aid rules apply in practice, is the *Ryanair/Charleroi Airport* case.[16] Several incentives were offered to Ryanair so that it would stay at the Charleroi airport in Belgium. Brussels South Charleroi Airport ("BSCA") itself offered a €250,000 subsidy for accommodation costs, €160,000 subsidy for each new route Ryanair would open from the airport to other destinations and €768,000 subsidy towards recruitment, as well as office space and fixed and discounted charges for ground handling services (€1 per passenger). Furthermore, the Walloon region also offered certain incentives, such as a 50 per cent reduction in landing charges and a guarantee for compensation towards losses incurred as a result of increased airport taxes and changes in airport operational hours.

In essence, the aid was seen as a state measure, as BSCA was a public undertaking over which the Walloon region exercised control and had a dominant influence. Furthermore, the scheme was selective: there was a clear absence of publicly available information for third parties and confidentiality clauses meant that no notification to other airlines was made in regard to the terms of the agreement between Ryanair and the airport. The scheme also failed the "private investor" principle, and the aid was seen to benefit Ryanair not only in Belgium but across its entire network. The Commission finally held that the state aid was partly compatible and partly incompatible with EU state aid rules. Certain new-route subsidies, where offered, as well as subsidies towards office space and accommodation, were acceptable. However, the extensive recruitment and set-up subsidies and the ground handling discounts could not be exempted and consequently were deemed to be infringing Article 87. The Commission ordered a recovery of the aid. An appeal has been lodged with the Court of First Instance.

7.6 CONCLUSION

Recent developments in the state aid sector have seen aid in the pre-enlargement EU decrease from €67 billion in 1997 to €49 billion in 2002. Companies

16. Case C–76/2002.

are making more use of their right to complain and the number of recovery orders has increased, as part of Brussels's increased priority to battle loans and capital injections. Financial institutions are now becoming more aware of the dangers of dealing with state aid recipients. Furthermore, the Commission is focusing its resources on measures that have an indirect but substantial impact on competition, but at the same time it is keen to share the burden of enforcement with national courts and to concentrate on substantial infringements. For other, less important, forms of aid, the block exemptions, as mentioned above, will be used to the greatest extent possible.

The Commission has further discussed the introduction of simple economic tests to identify measures that do not qualify for block exemptions but nevertheless do not have any significant impact on competition and thus should be subject to quick approval procedures.[17] Draft instruments on how these economic formulae are to be constructed are currently being prepared and a consultation process will, hopefully, follow shortly.

17. Speech by Philip Lowe, 1 December 2003, "State Aid: the Commission's plans for reform—the significant impact test".

CHAPTER 8

MERGER CONTROL

Stephen Wisking, Herbert Smith, and Giulio Federico and Diana Jackson, Charles River Associates

8.1 LEGAL STRUCTURE

8.1.1 Introduction and summary

The EC Merger Regulation ("ECMR") was introduced in 1989.[1] Its purpose was and is to ensure that mergers and acquisitions did not damage competition in the EU. It was introduced because it was clear that, while Articles 81 and 82 of the EC Treaty could apply to certain transactions, they were not adequate for preventing mergers and acquisitions that might have significant anti-competitive effects.

The ECMR therefore introduced a system where certain types of transactions that meet the thresholds set out in the ECMR are pre-notified to the Commission. The Commission must review these transactions and determine whether they can proceed, proceed with modifications or not proceed at all.

The ECMR was amended in 1997 and has now been further amended, effective from 1 May 2004, as part of a package of reforms to merger control at the Community level.

This Chapter describes the basic legal structure of EU merger control with, particular reference to:

— the relevant legal instruments;
— the jurisdiction of the Commission under the ECMR;
— the substantive competition test against which mergers are assessed; and
— procedures under the ECMR.

8.1.2 Legal Instruments

It is useful at the outset to briefly describe the various legal instruments relevant to EC merger control.

First, there is the ECMR itself, which, as a result of the most recent amendments, has been recast in a new Council Regulation of 20 January

1. Regulation 4064/89 of 21 December 1989.

2004,[2] which took effect on 1 May 2004. The ECMR sets out the jurisdiction of the Commission, the substantive test applicable to the assessment of mergers and the basic procedural framework.

Second, and also as a consequence of the reforms, there is a new Implementing Regulation.[3] The Implementing Regulation addresses the detailed procedural requirements of merger control, including the relevant forms by which mergers are to be notified.

Third, there are a series of Commission Notices that assist in the interpretation of certain aspects of the ECMR. There are Notices dealing with:

— the concept of a "concentration" under the ECMR, that is, what kinds of mergers and acquisitions are caught by the ECMR;[4]
— what is meant by "undertakings" in the ECMR;[5]
— the calculation of turnover that is relevant to the jurisdiction of the Commission;[6]
— the concept of full-function joint ventures that may also be caught by the ECMR;[7]
— case referrals between the Commission and Member States;[8]
— the simplified procedure for certain transactions;[9]
— the giving of commitments to resolve competition concerns;[10]
— ancillary restrictions;[11] and
— the assessment of horizontal mergers under the ECMR,[12] which sets out in detail how the Commission proposes to assess transactions.

The Commission also proposes to issue guidelines on the assessment of vertical and conglomerate mergers.

Fourth, the Commission has reissued Guidelines on best practice which deal with the procedural aspects of merger control (the "Best Practices Guidelines"). There are also best practice guidelines and model forms for the giving of commitments.

Fifth, although not exclusively relevant to merger control, the Commission's Notice on the definition of a relevant market for the purposes of community competition law[13] will be relevant to the substantive assessment of mergers.

2. 139/2004.
3. 802/2004.
4. 98/C66/02.
5. 98/C66/03.
6. 98/C66/04.
7. 98/C66/01.
8. 2005/C56/02.
9. 2005/C56/04.
10. 2001/C68/03.
11. 2005/C56/03.
12. 2004/C31/03.
13. 97/C372/03.

Sixth, there is a body of past Commission decisions on factual questions such as market definition, which, although not binding in future cases,[14] nevertheless serves as a useful insight into the likely Commission approach to market definition. Such decisions also establish the Commission's approach to legal questions that might arise (for example, on matters of procedure or jurisdiction). Finally there is also a small number of European Court Decisions which arise from appeals against Commission merger Decisions.

8.1.3 Jurisdiction

8.1.3.1 Introduction

The ECMR, for reasons of legal certainty, seeks to lay down in as objective a fashion as possible the circumstances in which transactions will be subject to the ECMR. Once a transaction falls within the ECMR then (subject to the possibility of referrals to Member States, see 8.1.3.4 below) the parties benefit from a "one-stop shop"; that is, review by the Commission excludes similar merger control processes in the Member States. Where the ECMR does not apply, transactions may be subject to merger control in one or more Member States.

The ECMR applies to all concentrations with a Community dimension,[15] irrespective of whether the merger gives rise to competition issues.

8.1.3.2 Concentration

A concentration arises where there is a change of control in a commercial entity on a lasting basis. This could occur where two previously independent businesses merge or one business acquires control of another through the acquisition of shares or assets.[16] A concentration may also arise through the creation of a joint venture performing on a lasting basis all the functions of an autonomous economic entity.[17] To fall within this latter definition of a concentration, a joint venture would need to have the following elements:

- First, the parents must jointly control the joint venture; that is, each parent must have a veto over key strategic decisions (for example, the approval of annual budgets and business plans and the appointment of senior management).
- Second, the joint venture must operate on a market in the same way as other businesses operating on that market, ie it must have sufficient resources to carry out its activities and be sufficiently independent of its parents.

14. See *Coca-Cola Co v. Commission* [2000] 5 CMLR 467.
15. Article 1(1) of the ECMR.
16. Article 3(1).
17. Article 3(4).

— Third, it must be intended that the joint venture operate on a lasting basis (ie that it is not established for a short, finite duration).[18]

8.1.3.3 Community dimension

A concentration has a Community dimension where certain turnover thresholds in the ECMR are met. These are designed to catch transactions that have potential effects on competition in the EU but outside the territory of a single Member State.

It should be noted that the ECMR uses the concept of "undertakings" for the purposes of these thresholds. Broadly speaking, an undertaking refers to the corporate group of the acquirer or the business being acquired, or the corporate groups merging or forming a joint venture.[19]

There are two sets of turnover thresholds in the ECMR. Satisfying either set of thresholds will result in a transaction having a Community dimension. The first set of thresholds is as follows:

— the combined aggregate worldwide turnover of all the undertakings concerned is more than €5 billion;
— the aggregate community-wide turnover of each of at least two of the undertakings concerned is more than €250 million;

unless each of the undertakings concerned achieves more than two-thirds of its aggregate Community-wide turnover within one and the same Member State.

The second set of thresholds is lower in absolute terms but seeks to catch transactions that have the potential to affect a number of Member States. These are as follows:

— the combined aggregate worldwide turnover of all the undertakings concerned is more than €2.5 billion;
— in each of at least three Member States, the combined aggregate turnover of all the undertakings concerned is more than €100 million;
— in each of at least three of the same Member States, the aggregate turnover of each of at least two of the undertakings concerned is more than €25 million; and
— the aggregate Community-wide turnover of each of at least two of the undertakings concerned is more than €100 million;

unless each of the undertakings concerned achieves more than two-thirds of its aggregate community-wide turnover within one and the same Member State.

18. See generally the Notices on the concepts of a concentration and full-function joint ventures.
19. See generally Article 5 of the ECMR and the Notice on undertakings.

The Commission has published a notice on the calculation of turnover with the aim of ensuring that the application of the turnover thresholds is both objective and consistent. Turnover for the purposes of the thresholds is the undertaking's revenue from its ordinary activities from the preceding financial year. Where only part of a business is being sold, only the turnover attributable to that part being sold is taken into account for the purposes of the turnover thresholds. The thresholds also require the geographic allocation of turnover. The basic principle is that turnover should be allocated to the place where the customer is located since this is where the deal was made, the turnover was generated and the competition with alternative suppliers took place. Special rules apply for the calculation of turnover of financial institutions and insurance undertakings.

8.1.3.4 Reallocation of jurisdiction

However, notwithstanding the principles of legal certainty and the one-stop shop that underlie the ECMR, there is some limited ability on the part of the parties to a transaction, as well as Member States, to seek to reallocate jurisdiction, either from the Commission to Member States or from Member States to the Commission.

Under the ECMR, once a transaction has been notified to the Commission, Member States have always had the ability to seek referral of that transaction back to them for review.[20] A Member State has also been able to ask that the Commission examine a transaction over which that Member State has jurisdiction[21] (although this facility has rarely been used).

The reforms to the ECMR have sought to streamline referral requests by Member States, but in addition, and importantly, also introduce the possibility of referrals at the request of the parties *prior* to notification. Each of these referral possibilities are summarised below.

8.1.3.4.1 Pre-notification referral requests

TO THE COMMISSION FROM MEMBER STATES

Under Article 4(5) of the ECMR, the parties to a concentration that does not have a Community dimension, but that is capable of being reviewed by at least three Member States, may request that the Commission examine the concentration.

The process by which this is done is to make a reasoned submission to the Commission. This submission must be made before any national notification has been made. A form (Form RS) for this purpose is set out in the Annex to the Implementing Regulation. In particular, in section six of the Form, the parties are required to specify which Member States have jurisdiction to review the transaction. The Commission transmits the completed Form RS to

20. Article 9 of the ECMR.
21. Article 22 of the ECMR.

the network of competition authorities in all Member States. Member States then have 15 working days from receipt of Form RS to express any disagreement on the request to refer. If all competent Member States (ie those with jurisdiction to review the transaction) have not expressed disagreement within 15 working days, the Commission will have exclusive jurisdiction over the transaction and no national notifications need to be made. However, if even one competent Member State disagrees, the Commission cannot take jurisdiction and national notifications will need to be made.

Obviously, reasons need to be given in Form RS to justify the Commission taking jurisdiction. It needs to be established that the Commission is the most appropriate reviewing authority. This could be the case where:

- a transaction is genuinely cross-border in nature;
- there is a potential impact on competition in markets that are wider in geographic scope than national;
- there are potential competition concerns in a number of national markets, such that the Commission would be best placed to investigate given the importance of consistency, the use of appropriate investigative powers and the need to address any competition concerns through coherent remedies; and
- there would be time and cost savings compared with making a number of national filings.[22]

There have already been a number of cases where this procedure has been used to confer jurisdiction on the Commission.

The procedure has real benefits for the parties in enabling them to avoid the need to notify in a number of different Member States. However, Form RS does require a considerable amount of detail and there is no certainty of referral to the Commission. In these circumstances, it may be easier and quicker to notify straightforward transactions that raise no competition issues in Member States, rather than seeking a referral to the Commission.

There is also a heavy burden in ensuring the accuracy of information submitted as part of Form RS. Inaccurate information could threaten the legal basis of any referral to the Commission and subsequent Commission Decision. This is potentially quite problematic, since a number of Member States use market share or similar jurisdictional thresholds for their own national merger control. In many cases there are a variety of credible market definitions and information relating to shares of the parties in various alternatively defined markets may be difficult to obtain with any reliability. As a consequence, there is a very real risk that information contained in Form RS (including identifying which Member States have jurisdiction), although submitted in good faith by the parties, may be inaccurate. As a result, although the process described is ultimately a jurisdictional one, it forces the parties to do considerable work on the substantive aspects of their case, ie market definition

22. See paras 25–32 of the Notice on case referral.

and market shares. That said, this work has to be undertaken for the notification to the Commission (if it takes jurisdiction) and may be useful for Member State notifications if the Commission does not take jurisdiction.

To Member States from the Commission

Where a concentration has a Community dimension (and the Commission has jurisdiction) but the concentration may significantly affect competition in a market within a Member State that presents all the characteristics of a distinct market, the parties may apply to the Commission to refer all or part of the transaction to that Member State for review under national merger control law.[23]

There are therefore two conditions for such a referral. First, that the concentration *may* significantly affect competition in a market(s). That is, parties must demonstrate the transaction has a potential impact on competition. There is no obligation to conceed an actual effect on competition and submissions made at this stage would be without prejudice to the ultimate outcome of the investigation. The Commission's guidelines suggest that it would be enough if there is an "affected" market[24]—that is, a market where the combined market shares of the parties exceed 15 per cent or where one party to the transaction is active in product markets upstream or downstream of the other and their individual or combined market shares at either level is 25 per cent or more.

Second, the markets in question must be within a Member State and present all the characteristics of a distinct market. That is, the markets in which competition may be affected by the transaction are national or narrower than national in scope.

The process for seeking such a referral is that the parties make a submission to the Commission using Form RS before notification of the transaction. That submission is sent to all the Member States by the Commission. The Member State to which it is proposed that the referral be made has 15 working days of receipt of this submission to express its agreement or disagreement. If it makes no decision within that period, it is deemed to have agreed.

The Commission may then decide to make a referral to the Member State if the Member State has agreed to accept the referral and the Commission finds that the requirements for such a referral exist. The Commission's decision has to be made within 25 working days from the receipt of Form RS by the Commission.

The Commission may refer the whole transaction for review by the Member State, in which case there is no need for a notification at all to the Commission, or only part of the transaction, in which case the parties will still be required to notify the Commission and the Commission will be required to make a decision with respect to that part over which it retains jurisdiction.

23. Article 4(4) of the ECMR.
24. See paras 16 and 17 of the Notice on case referral.

This option is unlikely to be used by parties on a frequent basis. First, it requires at least a concession of a potential effect on competition. Second, there is a real risk that only part of the transaction will be referred to the Member State, thereby requiring the parties to make two notifications and deal with two competition authorities. Moreover, one principle underlying the referral of cases is to ensure the most appropriate authority deals with a case; it is not intended to be a aid to forum shopping.

In practice, this provision is likely to be used where it is anticipated that a Member State might seek a reference back after notification of the transaction by the parties to the Commission pursuant to Article 9 (see 8.1.3.4.2 below). In these circumstances, the parties may wish to resolve this question earlier in the process so that they can avoid the disruption and complexities that might flow from a post-notification referral.

8.1.3.4.2 Post-notification referral requests

FROM THE COMMISSION TO MEMBER STATES

Where the Commission has jurisdiction under the ECMR, a Member State may, either on its own or at the invitation of the Commission, seek a referral of all or part of the transaction to it for review.

Such requests are made after the transaction has been notified to the Commission pursuant to Article 9 of the ECMR. The Commission provides a copy of the formal notification (Form CO) to each of the Member States. A Member State must seek a referral from the Commission within 15 working days of receipt of the notification from the Commission.

The request can be made on either of two bases:

- The transaction threatens to significantly affect competition in a market within that Member State that presents all the characteristics of a distinct market; or
- The concentration threatens to affect competition in a market within that Member State that presents all the characteristics of a distinct market *and* which does not constitute a substantial part of the common market.

Under the first ground, the Commission retains a discretion whether or not to refer the case back to the Member State. Under the second ground, the Commission is obliged to make a reference of the whole or part of the case that relates to the distinct market concerned if it considers that such a distinct market is affected. The Commission has 35 working days from notification as a general rule where the case is in phase one of the two-stage review process (see the discussion of time periods in 8.1.5.4 below), but no more than 65 working days where the case has gone into phase two.

If the Commission does refer all or part of the case back to a Member State, the Member State's competition authority must, within 45 working days of the referral, inform the parties of its preliminary competition assessment and what further action, if any, it proposes to take.

A reference to a Member State clearly has the potential to slow down the notification and clearance process and certainly add to the work of the parties, since it requires them to make a notification after having fully notified the transaction to the Commission. It is for these reasons, as indicated above, that the ability of the parties to force a decision on this question pre-notification is of most value.

TO THE COMMISSION FROM A MEMBER STATE

Member States may also request that the Commission examine a transaction that does not have a Community dimension but that affects trade between Member States and threatens to significantly affect competition within the territory of the Member State making the request.[25]

Such request should be made within 15 working days of notification of the transaction to the Member State (or where no notification is required, such as in the UK, within 15 working days of the transaction becoming known to the Member State). The Commission informs all other Member States of the request and they may decide to join the request within 15 working days of being informed by the Commission. While a decision is being made on the request, national time limits relating to the transaction are suspended. The Commission has a further 10 working days to decide whether to accept jurisdiction. If it does accept jurisdiction, then national merger control will not apply in the Member States referring the transaction and the ECMR procedures will apply to the case.

8.1.3.5 Suspension of concentrations

A transaction that is subject to the ECMR, or in respect of which the Commission has jurisdiction pursuant to Article 4(5), cannot be implemented before it is notified and cleared by the Commission.[26] Such a transaction will be invalid.[27]

There are certain exceptions to this general rule, in particular where control is obtained through a public bid or through conversion into listed securities, provided that the transaction is notified to the Commission as soon as possible and the acquirer does not exercise voting rights attached to the securities in question (save to the extent necessary to protect the full value of their investment).[28]

The Commission may, on request, grant derogations from the suspension obligation. Such derogations have been sought and granted only on very few occasions. This has tended to be where the business being acquired is in severe financial difficulties that would be exacerbated if the transaction could not be implemented as quickly as possible.

25. Article 22 of the ECMR.
26. Article 7(1).
27. Article 7(4).
28. Article 7(2).

8.1.3.6 Anti-avoidance measures

It is not possible to avoid the application of the ECMR by breaking up a transaction into parts so that they do not satisfy the turnover thresholds. Article 5(2) of the ECMR provides that where two or more transactions take place within a two-year period between the same parties, the transaction should be treated as part of the same transaction arising on the date of the last transaction.

Furthermore, the recitals to the ECMR[29] provide that it is appropriate to treat as a single transaction, separate transactions that are closely connected, for example, if they are linked by conditions, or a series of transactions in securities taking place within a reasonably short period of time (eg "creeping takeovers").

8.1.4 The substantive test

The substantive test has been changed as a result of the amendments to the ECMR. The question for the Commission is whether the transaction would "significantly impede effective competition" (the "SIEC test") in the common market or in a substantial part of it, in particular as a result of the creation or strengthening of a dominant position (see, further, 8.2.2.5, below). If it does not, then it should be declared compatible with the common markets and in effect cleared by the Commission.[30]

In making its appraisal, the Commission is obliged to take into account:

— the need to maintain and develop effective competition within the common market having regard to the structure of the markets concerned and the actual or potential competition from undertakings located in or outside of the Community; and

— the market position of the undertakings concerned and their economic and financial power, the alternatives available to suppliers and users, their access to supplies or markets, any legal or other barriers to entry, supply and demand trends for the relevant goods and services, the interests of the intermediate and ultimate consumers, and the development of technical and economic progress (provided that it is to consumers' advantage and does not form an obstacle to competition).[31]

The new SIEC test is a shift from the old test, which was whether the transaction would create or strengthen a dominant position. The Commission says that the change reflects a necessary clarification to ensure that the ECMR

29. See recital 20.

30. See Articles 2(2) and 2(3) of the ECMR. Note that joint ventures with coordination effects are appraised in accordance with the criteria of Article 81(1) and 81(3); see Articles 2(4) and 2(5) of the ECMR.

31. Article 2(1).

can cover all conceivable anti-competitive mergers while at the same time preserving 14 years of Commission case law based on the dominance test. Under the SIEC test, dominance will be the main, but not the only, way in which a significant impediment to competition may result from the merger. This formulation is also intended to ensure that the test applied by the Commission is convergent with other jurisdictions that apply a substantial lessening of competition ("SLC") test.

So in practice, it is understood that the Commission will continue to use dominance as the main analytical tool for assessment of mergers, although SIEC can in theory be proved without the need to show the creation or strengthening of dominance. It is anticipated that the analysis of transactions will be much more economics-based with regard to whether the merger results in anti-competitive effects.

The Commission will also take account of any substantial and likely efficiencies arising from the transaction. Such efficiencies may counteract the adverse effects on competition and potential harm to consumers. As a result, the transaction may not significantly impede effective competition.

The Commission's framework for the analysis of horizontal mergers is set out in the Notice on horizontal mergers (this is discussed more fully in 8.2 below). As indicated above, the Commission also contemplates publishing similar Notices dealing with vertical and conglomerate mergers.

It is important to note that the Commission bears the burden of proof for establishing SIEC.

There have been a number of decisions in European court cases where Commission decisions to block mergers have been overturned. The judgments in those cases have been highly critical of the way in which the Commission had handled those cases.[32] The high burden of proof required by the court, coupled with the more economic approach to assessment of transactions, is likely to result in far more burdensome requests for information from the Commission during the merger review process.

8.1.5 Procedural issues

While decisions under the ECMR are formally made by the Commission as a whole, the review of mergers is effectively undertaken by Directorate-General ("DG") for Competition and in particular a case team of officials from DG Competition.

8.1.5.1 The obligation to notify

Concentrations with a Community dimension *must* be notified to the Commission prior to implementation[33] unless a derogation has been granted (see

32. *Airtours*, Case T-342/99 [2002] All ER (EC) 783; [2002] 5 CMLR 7; *Schneider/Legrand*, Case T-310/01 [2004] All ER (EC) 314; and *Tetra Laval/Sidel*, Case T-5/02 [2003] All ER (EC) 762; [2002] 5 CMLR 28.

33. Article 4(1) of the ECMR.

8.1.3.5 above). The notification obligation falls on the acquiring undertaking, or, in the case of a joint venture or merger, all the parties to the transaction (the "notifying parties"). However, implementing a transaction without clearance means it will be invalid and therefore affects all parties to the transaction.

Previously, the ECMR provided that notification had to be made within seven days of the announcement of a public bid, the acquisition of a controlling interest or the conclusion of an acquisition agreement. This was rarely adhered to, given the need for pre-notification contacts with the Commission (see 8.1.5.4.1 below) and commercial confidentiality constraints in many cases that prevented the parties doing preparatory work for notifications or having pre-notification contacts with the Commission prior to the signing of the agreement or the announcement of a bid.

The changes to the ECMR introduce greater flexibility by removing the seven-day deadline but also allowing notifications to be made earlier on the basis of a good faith intention to conclude an agreement or, in the case of a public bid, the public announcement of an intention to make a bid where the intended agreement or bid would result in a concentration with Community dimension. The parties must satisfy the Commission that their proposed concentration is sufficiently "concrete", for example, that is an agreement in principle, a memorandum of understanding or a letter of intent signed by all the undertakings concerned.

8.1.5.2 The notification

Notification is made by the submission of Form CO to the Commission. The form itself is set out in the Annex to the Implementing Regulation. The form requires the parties to submit considerable detail regarding the transaction and this includes a description of the parties and the transaction, identification of the relevant markets affected by the transaction, the competitive features of these markets and the position of the parties in these markets.

The amended Form CO (effective as of 1 May 2004) increases the amount of information required, as follows:

- With regard to supporting documents that need to be submitted pursuant to section 5.4 (analyses, reports, studies, surveys etc prepared by or for any member of the board of directors which assess the concentration by reference to market shares, competitive conditions, competitors, rationale etc), the parties now must also provide details for each document regarding the date of preparation and the name and title of each individual who prepared the documents.
- Section 6 of the form focuses on the identification of "affected markets". These are markets where the combined market shares of the parties exceed 15 per cent or where one party to the transaction is active in product markets upstream or downstream of the other and their individual or combined market shares at either level is 25 per

cent or more. It now requires considerable information in relation to other "neighbouring" markets (section 6.3).

- The level of information required for "affected markets" has also been increased (section 7). In particular, for each affected product market, considerable information has to be provided for each Member State and EFTA State (ie potentially 28 countries) where the parties to the concentration do business, including calculations of the concentration of these markets (see 8.2.2.4.1 below).

There is a short Form CO for cases where a simplified notification procedure applies. The Commission Notice sets out four situations in which the simplified procedure can apply, namely:

(i) one undertaking acquires sole control over an undertaking over which it already has joint control (eg one joint venture partner buying out the other partner);
(ii) there are no affected markets;
(iii) there are no horizontal or vertical overlaps between the parties' activities; or
(iv) the formation of a joint venture with limited activities in the EEA (where the turnover of the joint venture is less than €100 million in the EEA and the assets contributed to the joint venture are less than €100 million in the EEA).

The Commission may waive the notifying parties' obligations to provide certain information in Form CO and/or require more detailed information on particular issues. This normally arises from pre-notification contacts with the Commission (see 8.1.5.4.1 below). There are no filing fees.

8.1.5.3 Commitments

Where a transaction notified to the Commission may result in a significantly adverse effect on competition, it is open to the parties to offer to modify the transaction to address the adverse effect on competition. For example, the parties could offer to divest an existing business or one being acquired as part of the transaction. If the Commission finds that, following the modification, the transaction does not have the effect of significantly impeding effective competition, then it can clear the transaction, finding that it is compatible with the common market.

The Commission may also attach conditions and obligations to its clearance decision to ensure that the parties comply with the commitments given to modify the transaction.[34] The Commission may revoke its clearance Decision if an obligation attached to that Decision is not fulfilled.[35]

34. Article 6(2) and 8(2) of the ECMR.
35. Article 6(3) and 8(6) of the ECMR.

The Commission has published a notice on the types of remedies that will be acceptable to it and its specific requirements for the submission and form of acceptable commitments.[36] In broad terms, the Commission prefers commitments that are structural (ie a divestment of a business) rather than behavioural (for example, giving an undertaking to behave or refrain from behaving in a certain way in the future). Furthermore, the commitments should in general be capable of implementation in the short term without any ongoing or long-term monitoring required. Where a divestment commitment is given:

- The business being divested will, pending sale, have to be held separate from the merged business and its viability as a competitive force on the market maintained. This obligation is monitored by an independent monitoring trustee that reports directly to the Commission.
- The business will have to be divested within a short period of time, usually six to 12 months.
- In the event that the event that the business is not sold within this short period, an independent divestment trustee is empowered to take over and complete the sale process. The divestment trustee also reports directly to the Commission.

8.1.5.4 Time limits

The Commission's review of transactions is divided into three stages:

- Pre-notification discussions with the Commission. This is an important part of the review process, which developed as a matter of practice and is formalised to some extent in the Best Practices Guidelines.
- Once the transaction is formally notified, there is a short phase one review, which enables the Commission to deal with straightforward transactions. However, where a transaction raises "serious doubts" as to its compatibility with the common market (pursuant to the SIEC test) the Commission may initiate a more detailed phase two review. However, it is open to the parties in phase one to modify the transaction so as to remove such serious doubts and enable the transaction to be cleared in phase one; for example, by offering commitments to divest businesses within a short time period.
- Phase two, which is initiated when the Commission reaches a Decision that the notified transaction raises serious doubts as to its compatibility with the common market.[37] Phase two comprises a longer and more detailed investigation, during the course of which the Commission must produce a detailed Statement of Objections ("SO")

36. Commission Notice on remedies acceptable under the ECMR (2001/C68/03).
37. Article 6(1)(c) of the ECMR.

setting out its case, which the parties have an opportunity to answer, both in writing and at an oral hearing.

8.1.5.4.1 Pre-notification contacts

The ECMR does not address pre-notification discussions with the Commission.[38] Pre-notification discussions serve a number of purposes, including:

- briefing the Commission about the transaction;
- ensuring sufficient and appropriate information is contained in Form CO; and
- clarification of jurisdictional, procedural or other legal issues.

The Best Practice Guidelines states that pre-notification discussions should start about two weeks before the expected date of notification (although a longer period will usually be necessary in complex cases). These discussions are usually launched with the submission of a briefing paper to the Commission. The briefing paper is also an opportunity to raise jurisdictional or procedural questions about the case. The Commission may respond orally or in writing to the paper, and in some cases pre-notification meetings are arranged.

The next step normally involves the preparation of a draft Form CO, which is submitted to the Commission for review and comment. This provides the parties with an opportunity to seek derogations from the formal requirements of Form CO where it may not be appropriate in a particular case. It also gives the Commission an opportunity to assess whether Form CO is complete and whether further information is required on particular aspects of the transaction. The Commission may require five working days to review the draft Form CO although in some cases it can be done more quickly. Following that review, the Commission may ask the parties to submit a further draft Form CO taking account of the Commission's comments.

The Commission will in principle be prepared to confirm formally the adequacy of the draft Form CO at the pre-notification stage; however, this does not preclude the Commission at some later stage declaring the notification incomplete as a result of omissions discovered after notifications. In such circumstances the Commission will allow the parties a short period (maybe one or two days) to rectify the omission unless it immediately hinders the investigation of the transaction. If that is the case, the Commission could declare the notification incomplete. The parties would then have to re-notify the transaction and phase one would not start until it was re-notified.

Although the Commission's fact-finding in relation to the transaction will normally commence after the notification in phase one (see 8.1.5.4.2 below), in some cases it may start, prior to notification if the transaction is in the public domain subject to the parties' views.

38. See paras 5–23 of the Best Practices Guidelines.

8.1.5.4.2 Phase one

The deadline for phase one is 25 working days from notification. However, this time period is automatically extended by a further 10 working days (ie to 35 working days) where:

— the parties have offered to modify the transaction (offer commitments to the Commission (see 8.1.5.3 above)). The purpose of the extension is to enable the Commission to consider commitments offered and to "market test" them; or

— a Member State makes a referral request pursuant to Article 9.

The Commission will, upon receipt of the notification, commence its fact-finding by sending written requests for information regarding the transaction and its effects to customers and competitors of the parties (and in some cases suppliers) in the "affected markets" with a view to obtaining responses within the first two to three weeks of phase one. The Commission may also seek further information from the parties. These requests will be sent as "simple" requests under Article 11 of the ECMR (see 8.1.5.7 below). The Commission will also publish a Notice in the Official Journal inviting comments on the transaction.

Within three weeks (15 working days), the Commission will offer to hold a "state of play" meeting with the parties.[39] The purpose of this meeting is to report the Commission's preliminary views on the notification, which will include the results of consultation with third parties. This will enable the parties to consider whether to offer commitments. Within phase one, the deadline for commitments is 20 working days. For commitments to be acceptable in phase one they must provide a straightforward answer to readily identifiable competition concerns; it must be a "clear-cut solution".

Furthermore, once commitments are offered in phase one, it is only possible to make limited modifications to those commitments because of the short time available to the Commission to assess and market test any changes. Acceptable modifications include clarification, refinements and/or improvements that ensure the commitments are workable and effective. These will generally be made in response to the results of the Commission's market testing of the initial commitments offered.

8.1.5.4.3 Phase two

As the investigation in phase two is more detailed, the deadline for phase two is 90 working days. This can be automatically extended by 15 working days to 105 working days where commitments are proposed. However, there will be no extension if commitments are submitted at an early stage (ie less than 55 working days into phase two[40]).

39. See para 33 of the Best Practice Guidelines.
40. See Article 10(3) of the ECMR.

As noted above, the phase two investigation is initiated by a finding by the Commission that the transaction raises serious doubts as to its compatibility with the common market (a decision under Article 6(1)(c) of the ECMR). The parties will be provided with a copy of the Commission's reasoned Decision. The Commission will normally offer, within two weeks following that "6(1)(c)" Decision, a further state of play meeting during which the parties are able to provide the Commission with comments on the Decision. The purpose of this meeting is to enable the parties to better understand the Commission's concerns and enable the Commission to determine the appropriate framework for its further investigations in phase two. These investigations may include further evidence-gathering from the parties and third parties (which may be onerous) as well as economic analysis.

During phase two, if it proposes to prohibit the transaction, the Commission will prepare a written SO that sets out in a fully reasoned form its concerns about the transaction. Prior to the issue of an SO, the Commission should offer the parties a further state of play meeting in order for them to better understand its preliminary views following its phase two investigations and the type of concerns that may be set out in the SO. In a small number of cases, the Commission, following further investigation in phase two, has not proceeded to an SO and has cleared the transaction.

The parties may request access to the Commission's files once the Commission has issued an SO.[41] This is an important element of the parties' rights of defence. Access to the files enables the parties to consider and respond to the underlying documents on which the SO was based. In addition, the Commission will also try to obtain the views of the parties and third parties on key documents obtained by the Commission. This will tend to be on an *ad hoc* basis.

As a further element of the rights of defence, the parties have the right to reply to the SO both in writing and at an oral hearing.[42] The oral hearing is an opportunity for the parties to put their response orally to the Commission case team. It is available at the parties' option and is presided over by a Commission Hearing Officer, who is not empowered to reach any decision on the substance of the case. Representatives of the competition authorities of the Member States may also be present at the oral hearing, as well as parties with an interest in the transaction, such as complainants, who may also make submissions.

The Commission should offer the parties a state of play meeting following the reply to the SO and the oral hearing. The purpose of this meeting is to enable them to understand the Commission's position after it has considered

41. Article 18(3) of the ECMR and Article 17 of the Implementing Regulation. DG Competition has appointed a consumer liaison officer responsible for contacts with consumer organisations.

42. See Article 18 of the ECMR and Article 13 of the Implementing Regulation.

their reply in writing and at the oral hearing. This may be an opportunity to discuss the scope and timing of possible remedies.

In phase two, there is a greater opportunity to fine-tune commitments. The Commission will have a better understanding of the nature of any competition problems as a result of its more detailed investigations. This enables the parties to offer more precise commitments. There is also more time in phase two to assess and refine the commitments.

In phase two, there is the ability to "stop the clock". The phase two period can be extended by a maximum of 20 working days but only at the request of the parties or by the Commission with the parties' consent. Where the parties want to make such a request it must be made within 15 working days of the start of phase two. The purpose, from the Commission's perspective, is to allow for longer investigation and verification of the facts and arguments.

There is also a provision for the exceptional suspension of time in phase two[43] where the parties have failed to provide information requested by the Commission or refused to submit to an inspection. In these circumstances, the phase two period is suspended from the date on which the information is requested until the information is provided, or from the date on which the inspection has been sought until the inspection is completed.

The Commission may not make a decision in phase two without consulting the Advisory Committee, which comprises representatives of the relevant authorities of each Member State. The Advisory Committee delivers an opinion on the Commission's draft Decision (if necessary by taking a vote). That opinion will be in writing. The Commission is not bound by that opinion but must take utmost account of it.

The Commission will also offer the parties a state of play meeting before the Advisory Committee meets, for discussion on proposed remedies and the results of market testing of remedies. This provides an opportunity to offer improvements to the proposed remedies.

8.1.5.5 Liaison with authorities of the Member States

Even where the Commission retains jurisdiction, it continues to liaise with the relevant authorities of the various Member States. It provides a copy of the notification to the Member States as well as copies of the most important documents prepared by the parties or the Commission in relation to the case.[44]

There is often dialogue between the relevant authorities of Member States and the Commission, particularly where there is an affected market in a Member State. Furthermore, as set out above, Member States are involved in oral hearings and the Advisory Committee.

43. See Article 10(4) of the ECMR and Article 9 of the Implementing Regulation.
44. Article 19(1) of the ECMR.

8.1.5.6 Involvement of third parties

Third parties with a sufficient interest in the merger investigation process include customers, suppliers, competitors, the management of the undertakings involved, and recognised workers' representatives of those undertakings.[45] They are recognised as having an important role in the merger review process.[46] The Commission is also interested in the views of third parties such as consumer organisations.[47]

The role of third parties may involve:

- responding to Commission's requests for information;
- making submissions containing additional relevant information and evidence concerning the likely effects of the transaction;
- where a case moves to phase two, being provided with edited copies of the SO (excluding confidential information) to allow them to make their views known on the content of that document; and
- participation at the oral hearing.

Due to the involvement of third parties the Commission may hold "triangular" meetings involving the parties to the transaction, the case team and third parties to enable the case team to hear the views of the parties and the third parties in the same forum. These meetings are voluntary and are not intended to replace the oral hearing, but are intended to take place where there are opposing views and where such a meeting would facilitate the Commission's investigations.

8.1.5.7 Investigatory powers of the Commission

The normal method by which the Commission seeks information during an investigation, either from the parties or from third parties, is by the issue of requests for information.[48] These are written requests which require a written response within the specified time period. There are two kinds of request: "simple" and "by decision". There is no sanction for failing to respond to a simple request for information, although there are financial penalties for supplying incorrect or misleading information. The Commission may also seek information "by decision", in which case there are, in addition, financial penalties for failing to respond by the specified time.

Under the amendments to the ECMR, the Commission now has the power to conduct interviews.[49] It may do so only with the consent of the interviewee and there is no sanction for refusing to consent. The Commission now also has power to carry out inspections[50] with the assistance of Member States.[51] This

45. See Article 11 of the Implementing Regulation.
46. See Article 18(4) of the ECMR and Article 16 of the Implementing Regulation.
47. See Article 16(3) of the Implementing Regulation.
48. Article 11 of the ECMR.
49. Article 11(7).
50. Article 13.
51. Article 12.

includes the power to enter premises, examine records and take copies of such records. It also includes, significantly, the power to seal premises and all records for a period of time and the power to ask a representative or member of staff of the undertaking for explanations of facts or documents relating to the subject-matter and purpose of the inspection, and record those answers. Such inspections are limited to business premises.

8.1.5.8 Enforcement

Financial penalties[52] may be imposed for:

- failing to respond to information requests or supplying misleading or incorrect information;
- failure to notify a concentration;
- implementing a concentration without a clearance or which the Commission has found to be incompatible with the common market.

Pursuant to Article 8(4) of the ECMR, where:

- a transaction has been implemented without clearance and the Commission has determined that the transaction is incompatible with the common market; or
- the transaction has been implemented in contravention of a condition attached to a decision.

Then the Commission may require the parties to dissolve the transaction completely, which may involve the disposal of all the shares or assets acquired. The purpose is to restore the *status quo.*

8.1.5.9 Ancillary restrictions

Decisions by the Commission declaring the transactions compatible with the common market will automatically cover any restrictions that the parties have accepted which are directly related to and necessary for the implementation of the transaction. These may include non-compete obligations on the part of the vendor to ensure effective transfer of goodwill to the purchaser; similarly they may include non-solicitation obligations on the vendor with respect to employees or the business being sold, or transitional agreements between vendor and a purchaser in respect of the provision of inputs to the business being sold to ensure an effective transfer.[53]

The Commission will therefore not normally deal expressly with ancillary restrictions. However, the parties may request express treatment of such restrictions if there are "novel or unresolved questions giving rise to genuine uncertainty". These will be restrictions that are not addressed by the Commission Notice on ancillary restraints.

52. Article 14.
53. See recital 21, Article 6(1) and Article 8(1) of the ECMR.

8.1.5.10 The end of the review?

Phase one will end (if a phase two procedure is not initiated) by a reasoned written Commission Decision either clearing the transaction or clearing it subject to certain conditions and obligations.[54] At the end of phase two, the Commission will publish a reasoned Decision that either clears the transaction, clears it subject to conditions, or blocks it.[55]

The parties, and third parties with a sufficient interest, can appeal a Commission Decision to the Court of First Instance. If successful, the Commission decision will be annulled either in whole or in part. The Commission will then have to re-examine the transaction in the light of market conditions current at the time of re-examination. The parties may need to submit a supplementary notification. In effect, phase one restarts.

The notifying parties may withdraw their notification prior to a Decision. The Commission will not then have jurisdiction to reach a Decision on the withdrawn notification where it is clear that the parties no longer intend to proceed with the transaction as notified.

8.2 THE ECONOMICS OF HORIZONTAL MERGERS UNDER THE ECMR[56]

8.2.1 Introduction

In February 2004 the European Commission issued new Guidelines for the assessment of horizontal mergers ("the Guidelines").[57] This was a welcome move, following, as it did, a period of significant upheaval in European merger control during which some key Commission merger decisions had been overturned by the Court of First Instance. The Guidelines accompanied a new substantive test in the revised ECMR,[58] and to a large extent took their lead from the well-established US Department of Justice and Federal Trade Commission Guidelines on horizontal mergers.[59]

In this section we look at the Commission's Guidelines in detail from an economic perspective and explain the fundamental mechanisms driving the approach to merger investigations outlined in them. In particular, we focus on the two mechanisms through which mergers can generate price increases (or

54. See Articles 8(1)–(3).

55. See Article 6(1)(b). In some cases the Commission may publish a Decision that the transaction falls outside the scope of an ECMR: Article 6(1)(a).

56. By Giulio Federico and Diana Jackson, Charles River Associates. The authors are grateful to Andrea Coscelli, Alan Overd and Rameet Sangha for helpful comments on this section.

57. Guidelines on the assessment of horizontal mergers under the Council Regulation on the control of concentrations between undertakings, 2004 OJ C 31/5.

58. Council Regulation 139/2004 on the control of concentrations between undertakings, 2004 OJ L 24/1.

59. Federal Trade Commission/Department of Justice, "1992 Horizontal Merger Guidelines (Revised 1997)", April 1997.

other types of competitive harm): unilateral and coordinated effects. We describe the differences between these effects, their economic underpinnings and the types of economic evidence that the Commission will take into consideration in the assessment of each effect. We also briefly discuss the other horizontal merger considerations laid out in the Guidelines, namely entry; buyer power; efficiencies; and the "failing firm" defence.

8.2.2 Unilateral effects

The first type of merger effects considered in the Guidelines are "unilateral" or "non-coordinated" effects. The Guidelines use the second of these terms, but the two are equivalent, and we use the term unilateral effects throughout this paper, as it is the more standard term in the economic and anti-trust literature (partially due to the influence of the US Horizontal Merger Guidelines).

8.2.2.1 The basic principle of unilateral effects: individual pricing incentives

Unilateral effects can be defined as the effects that arise when, due to a merger, market participants find it individually profitable to increase prices as a result of the loss of competition between the merging parties. This mechanism does not rely on any form of coordination between firms remaining in the market post-merger, and is instead based on individual (ie unilateral) profit-maximising behaviour by all the firms in the market in response to the removal of the competitive constraint that the merging parties formerly exercised on each other. The most direct form of unilateral effect is the impact of the concentration on the pricing incentives of the merging parties themselves, as a result of the loss of competition between them. However, this itself is likely to soften the competitive constraints facing other firms post-merger.

The logic of unilateral effects relies on firms having some degree of market power, so that they can influence the market price. A firm with market power faces a trade-off between price and volume when deciding at which price to offer its goods in a market—the higher the price, the less it will be able to sell. This typically induces it to raise prices above the competitive level (where the unit price equals its cost of production of the last unit offered), in order to earn higher profits on the remaining quantity offered in the market. A firm will increase the price until the loss in profit on the production not offered to the market (the "output loss") starts to outweigh the resulting increase in profits on the remaining output that is still sold.

Figure 3 illustrates this mechanism. This illustrates the standard pricing decision of a firm that faces a downwards-sloping demand curve for its product, and a constant cost of production. In this example, the firm faces unilateral incentives to increase prices, since the profit gain on its remaining volume following an increase in price (from the original selling price P_1 to a new selling price, P_2) is greater than the profit loss on the output reduction (from the initial output level Q_1 to a lower level, Q_2). This is illustrated by the relative size of the shaded rectangles in the figure, which represent the profit gain from the price increase on remaining output, and the profit loss on output that is no longer offered to the market.

Note the importance of the level of the remaining sales versus the output loss in determining whether a price increase is profitable: the greater the level of remaining sales and/or the smaller the output loss, the larger the profit from a given increase in price—and therefore the greater the incentives to raise prices.

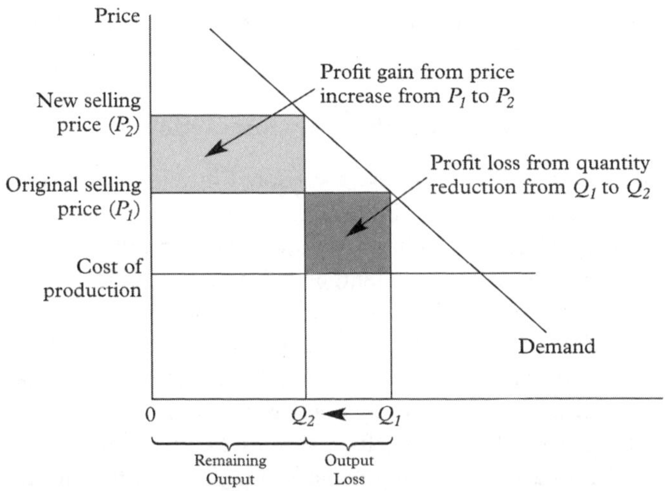

Figure 3: Illustration of pricing decision by a single firm

The basic intuition behind the unilateral effect of a merger is linked to the individual price-optimisation of the firm, as explained above, through two possible mechanisms:

— *The merger reduces the output loss stemming from the higher price.* Unilateral effects arise in this setting because the merger brings together different assets that were previously competing. Post-merger competition between them is internalised, so that those customers who would have switched to one of the merging parties following a price increase by the other merging party are now "captured" by the combined entity. The effective output loss of the firm raising prices is therefore mitigated, giving it greater incentives to raise prices. This mechanism is particularly important in markets with differentiated products when the merging firms are particularly close competitors.

— *The merger increases the volume base over which a given price increase would apply.* The volumes that were previously sold by the acquired firm are now part of the merged firm's output base, and will directly benefit from any price rise implemented by the firm. This therefore adds to the incentive to increase price post-merger. This mechanism applies particularly in markets with homogeneous products (such as certain commodities), where one price applies to all sales in the market.

In the absence of cost efficiencies due to the merger, the direction of change in price associated with unilateral effects is unambiguous: economic theory predicts that prices will increase. However, this effect may not be large: its practical importance will depend on a number of empirical factors, reviewed below.[60]

8.2.2.2 Unilateral effects and oligopoly interaction

The example given in Figure 3, and the related intuition given for unilateral effects from a merger illustrate the pricing incentives for a single firm in the market. However, all firms within an oligopoly will typically face incentives to adjust their pricing decisions post-merger as a result of the loss of competition between the merging parties. This is because in an oligopoly the optimal price-volume decisions made by firms are interdependent: each firm's best course of action depends on what its rivals are doing.[61] Any reaction by non-merging firms to a merger does not, however, imply that players are coordinating their actions post-merger. Players will face incentives to adjust their behaviour unilaterally following a merger, on the basis of their individual profit-maximising decisions. There is no system of "promises" and "threats" over time of the type required to show coordination.[62]

It is therefore not sufficient only to look at the change in the incentives of the merging parties to measure the impact of a merger, even in the context of unilateral effects. In an oligopoly, the unilateral effect of a merger will be the outcome of the combined responses of all market players to the merger. The

60. See also Ivaldi, Jullien, Rey, Seabright and Tirole, "The economics of unilateral effects", *Interim Report for DG Competition, European Commission (preliminary and incomplete)*, March 2003.

61. Economists rely on game theory to study this interdependence, and on the concept of static "Nash equilibrium" to predict the outcome of oligopolistic interaction that is not repeated over time. A Nash equilibrium prevails when each player (in this setting, each firm) is behaving optimally, *given what the other players (firms) are doing*. Unilateral effects are the result of the change in the static Nash equilibrium induced by a merger.

62. In this sense, unilateral effects arise from *static* interaction between firms. However, this does not imply that some dynamic considerations (eg product repositioning and entry) do not play a role in affecting the unilateral effects arising from a merger (see 8.2.2.4.2 below for a discussion of these factors).

term "unilateral" does not therefore imply that the only effect from the merger is due to the change in actions by the merged entity. Instead, this effect arises from the individual and independent responses of *all firms* in a market to the loss of competition between the merging firms. In this sense, the term "non-coordinated" effects used in the EU Guidelines may be clearer than the term unilateral, although the two are equivalent from an economic perspective.

8.2.2.3 Applying the concept of unilateral effects to different market conditions

As we have briefly outlined above, the concept of unilateral effects is applicable to mergers in markets with different characteristics. Markets are broadly divisible into two groups: differentiated and homogeneous goods markets.

8.2.2.3.1 Differentiated product markets

Arguably the better-understood context for unilateral effects is a merger between producers of two brands of differentiated goods. For example, in the market for cereals we can think of the two competing brands as Weetabix and Alpen muesli. Pre-merger, when Weetabix considers an increase in its price, it will lose a proportion of its customers to other competing cereal brands, including Alpen. This will lower its incentive to increase its price. Post-merger (having bought Alpen), part of Weetabix's volume loss due to any price increase will be "captured" by Alpen, and will represent an additional profit from the price rise for the merged entity (rather than a loss, as it would have done pre-merger). This will increase Weetabix's incentives to raise its price. A similar effect will also apply to Alpen's prices, since its customers may switch to Weetabix in the event of an Alpen price rise. Both merging parties will tend to face incentives to increase price post-merger.

As indicated above, the final unilateral effects from the merger will also incorporate the responses of other firms. If the merging parties increase their prices, their rivals will face an increase in demand (as customers switch to them). This will provide them with incentives to raise prices too, contributing to the overall price increase due to the merger, and *magnifying* the initial price impact of the merger.

The key factor determining the extent and size of unilateral effects in a merger with differentiated goods is the relative closeness between the merging parties, and the competitive constraints they were exercising on each other pre-merger. If this is high (ie the two brands are close substitutes), the unilateral effects from the merger can be expected to be significant. In our example, this would be due to the fact a high proportion of customers switching from Weetabix in the event of a price increase would choose Alpen as their next best alternative cereal, therefore mitigating the volume loss from such a price increase post-merger.

8.2.2 Merger Control

In markets with differentiated products, the market shares of the merging parties do not necessarily reflect the substitutability of two products, and provide only a very rough indication of the possible size of unilateral effects. For example, mergers involving relatively small firms may lead to significant unilateral effects if the firms' products are perceived by customers to be close substitutes.[63] The recognition of this feature of unilateral effects in differentiated product markets lay behind much of the debate in EU merger policy on whether the pre-2004 substantive test for merger appraisal was sufficiently wide. The question debated was whether the possibility of significant unilateral effects resulting from mergers of close substitutes, but without creating a single dominant or leading player, was captured by focusing on a market share-based concept of dominance. We expand on this point in 8.2.2.5 below.

8.2.2.3.2 Homogeneous product markets

Markets that trade relatively homogeneous goods (such as the wholesale market for oil) can also be subject to unilateral effects. The intuition for unilateral effects developed in the context of differentiated goods does not fully apply here, since customers do not prefer the good supplied by one firm over another on the basis of brand characteristics, and there is only one market clearing price.

What matters more for the assessment of unilateral effects in this context are the pre-merger volumes, capacities and cost structures of the merging firms. A merger in this type of market brings together different capacities (with different costs), and will increase the volume base over which a given price rise would apply. This can increase the incentives to withhold production from the market.

The magnitude of unilateral effects in these markets will depend on the size of the merging parties, and on their relative cost structures. If both parties own low-cost production capacity relative to the market, then unilateral effects from the merger can be expected to be small (because the loss in profits on withdrawn capacity is large, even post-merger). However, if the merger brings together capacities of different kinds (both high and low cost), or particularly "strategic" (price-setting) capacity, then the size of unilateral effects can be expected to be larger.

The likely response of the non-merging firms in the case of homogeneous goods is to increase their output levels and (partially) fill the volume gap,

63. The market shares of the merging parties will of course depend on the market definition used for the merger assessment: if this is relatively narrow and based on the characteristics of those firms, then firms that are small on a wider definition of the market will have larger market shares.

partly offsetting the initial increase in the overall market price. The magnitude of this response will depend on the availability and cost of unutilised capacity in the market, and also on the concentration of the non-merging firms.[64] If the other firms have relatively large amounts of low-cost capacity and if they are not very concentrated (so that each firm has greater incentives to expand output), then the response of non-merging firms to the initial price increase will be larger.

8.2.2.4 Factors affecting the size of unilateral effects

The discussion above has already revealed a number of factors that affect the size of any unilateral effects resulting from a merger, depending on the market in which the merger is taking place. In this section we briefly present all the key determinants of unilateral effects, starting with a discussion of concentration indicators.

8.2.2.4.1 Market shares and concentration levels

The size of the merged entity within a well-defined anti-trust market, and that of its competitors, is clearly an important determinant of the size of unilateral effects arising from a merger, as it directly affects the volume base that would benefit from any post-merger price increase. However, market shares are imperfect proxies of unilateral effects, in particular in the context of differentiated goods, as they may over- or underestimate the actual closeness between merging products. Competition authorities in particular may be worried about under-estimating the possible impact of mergers between relatively small firms, selling products that are relatively close substitutes.

The Guidelines therefore set concentration thresholds that are relatively low, capturing mergers involving firms with relatively small market shares. These thresholds are summarised in Figure 4. These are expressed in terms of the post-merger "Herfindahl-Hirschman Index" ("HHI"), which equals the sum of the squares of the post-merger market share of each firm in the industry,[65] and the increase in the HHI resulting from the merger (typically referred as the "Delta"). According to the Guidelines, a concentration is more likely to lead to competitive concerns if:

(i) the post-merger HHI is between 1,000 and 2,000, and the increase in the HHI is greater than 250 (this relates to relatively large mergers in relatively unconcentrated markets) or

64. Willig, "Merger Analysis, Industrial Organisation Theory and Merger Guidelines", *Brookings Papers in Microeconomics* (1991).

65. For example, a market with four firms each with a 25 per cent market share after a merger would have an HHI of $4(25)^2 = 2,500$.

(ii) the post-merger HHI is greater than 2,000, and the increase in the HHI is greater than 150 (this applies to smaller mergers in relatively concentrated markets).

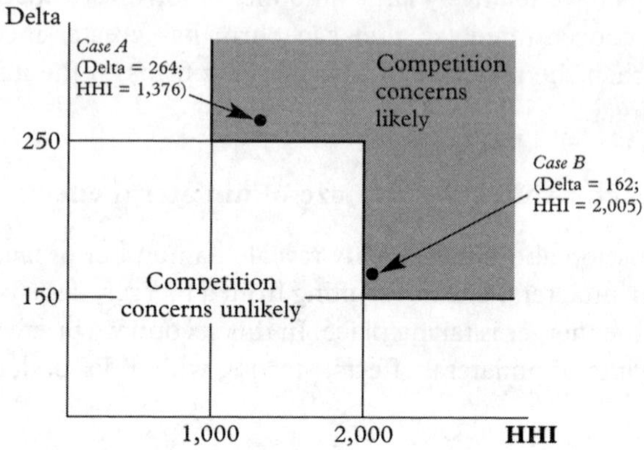

Figure 4: The Guidelines' concentration thresholds

These thresholds can capture what may appear to be relatively innocuous mergers (at least from a unilateral effects perspective). For example, in Figure 4 we illustrate two cases with relatively low market shares that would meet these thresholds: (i) Case A, a merger between two equal-sized firms both with 11.5 per cent of the market, facing seven other rivals, all with 11 per cent of the market;[66] and (ii) Case B, a merger between two equal-sized firms both with 9 per cent of the market, facing four other rivals, each with 20.5 per cent of the market.[67]

8.2.2.4.2 Other factors affecting the size of unilateral effects

We have already seen that the key considerations for a unilateral effects assessment are the incentives of the merged entity to raise price post-merger (which is particularly determined by the closeness of competition between the merging products and the size of the production base over which the merged entity could enjoy that price increase), and the extent to which rival firms will respond to any output restriction or price increase by the merged entity. Other important determinants of the possibility of significant unilateral effects from a merger that need to be carefully considered are:

— *Product repositioning by rival firms.* Non-merging firms may respond to

66. In this case the pre-merger HHI is given by: $7(11)^2 + 2(11.5)^2 = 1{,}112$. The post-merger HHI is given by: $7(11)^2 + (23)^2 = 1{,}376$. The Delta is therefore equal to $1{,}376 - 1{,}112 = 264$.

67. In this case the pre-merger HHI is given by: $4(20.5)^2 + 2(9)^2 = 1{,}843$. The post-merger HHI is given by: $4(20.5)^2 + (18)^2 = 2{,}005$. The Delta is therefore equal to $2{,}005 - 1{,}843 = 162$.

any price increase by the merging parties by repositioning their products, so that they become a stronger competitive constraint on the merging brands. This can reduce the size of unilateral effects. Product repositioning will be a more effective restraint on any price increase if it can be implemented rapidly and at a relatively low cost (which is more likely to be the case in a merger of "low-end" brands).

— *Elasticity of aggregate demand.* An elastic industry demand (ie when demand is very responsive to prices) will tend to mitigate the size of unilateral effects from a merger, since the post-merger firms will face a larger output loss following a price increase.

— *Efficiencies.* Cost reductions arising from a merger will provide the merging parties with greater incentives to expand output (or at least not to reduce it), by increasing the available profit margin on each unit sold. This therefore mitigates the size of the unilateral effects. The treatment of merger efficiencies under the Guidelines is discussed further at 8.2.4.3 below.

— *Entry.* The possibility of entry of new players in the market following a price increase is a very significant determinant of the ultimate size of unilateral effects. This is discussed separately at 8.2.4.2 below.

8.2.2.5 Unilateral effects and dominance

The introduction and description of the concept of unilateral effects in the Guidelines is closely linked to the new ECMR (Article 2(3)). This introduces the concept of Significant Impediment to Effective Competition ("SIEC") as the main test on the effects of a merger, and makes the creation of a dominant position subordinate to SIEC. This reflects recognition that the notion of dominance may be too narrow to incorporate all the possible anti-competitive effects from a merger. In particular, a dominance-based test does not capture the possibility of unilateral effects arising as a result of mergers that do not create a single firm with a dominant position (with the corresponding unilateral incentives to increase prices), nor raise issues of coordination (discussed at 8.2.3 below). As discussed above, a merger of two particularly close substitutes with relatively low market shares may fall into this third category (a potential "gap" in the old ECMR).

The Guidelines explicitly state in paragraph 25 that unilateral effects are part of the revised test. However, the ECMR is also careful to narrow the scope of SIEC, making it clear that it should be seen as "extending, beyond the concept of dominance, only to the anti-competitive effects resulting from the non-coordinated behaviour of undertakings which would not have a dominant position on the market concerned". That is to say, the concept of SIEC adds a general "unilateral effects test" to the appraisal of mergers under the new ECMR.[68]

68. For an economics-based discussion of these issues see Vickers, "Merger Policy in Europe: Prospect and Retrospect", *European Competition Law Review*, 25(7), 455–463 (2004).

8.2.2.6 The empirical measurement of unilateral effects

Unilateral effects do not involve a structural change in the way players interact with each other in the market. Under unilateral effects, both pre- and post-merger firms are assumed to be optimising their behaviour, given what other firms are doing. This makes it possible to predict the likely size of unilateral effects with some degree of confidence using pre-merger data, since these are based on the same kind of market interaction that is expected post-merger.

Most empirical techniques associated with the measurement of unilateral effects focus on the issue of how close the merging products are. As discussed, this is a particularly important driver of unilateral effects in differentiated product markets. A battery of empirical techniques exists to measure the closeness between products. These range from relatively simple to the more technically advanced:[69]

- *correlation and stationarity analysis* is used to determine whether the prices of two brands move together, suggesting a degree of competition between them;
- *bidding ("win-loss") analysis* is used in markets characterised by tendering processes, to establish whether the merging parties are often the first and second choice supplier;[70] and
- *direct econometric estimation* of cross-price elasticities between the products can allow the "closeness of competition" between rival products to be very precisely analysed, but requires large quantities of high-quality data.

All these tools seek to measure the importance of the competitive constraints that would be lost as a result of the merger, and therefore provide an indication of the likely post-merger price increase.

A tool that is becoming increasingly common for the estimation of unilateral effects is direct merger simulation.[71] This relies on simplified models of optimised behaviour by firms in the market that can be used to predict the price impact of a merger, based on assumptions about the key features of the market (such as the nature of competition in the market; the cost structure of market players; the form of market demand; and the substitution patterns between products in the industry that can be estimated econometrically). These simulations can be powerful tools, combining several factors affecting unilateral effects in a unified and coherent framework, capable of making a prediction on the ultimate impact of the merger. However the applicability and

69. For a discussion of these methods, see Lexecon Ltd, *Introduction to Quantitative Techniques in Competition Analysis* (MIMES).

70. This technique was used, for example, in the EU investigations into *GE/Instrumentarium* and *Oracle/PeopleSoft*.

71. A merger simulation was used by the Commission in its 2000 investigation of the Volvo-Scania merger (Case No COMP/M 1672). The recent inquiry by the UK Competition Commission on the acquisition of Dynegy Storage (Rough) by Centrica also relied on a merger simulation (see paragraphs 2.87–2.125 of the CC Report, and the analysis annexed to the CC report at Appendix 5.5).

validity of merger simulations as a tool to estimate unilateral effects crucially depends on the availability of good data on the market that is being studied, and on the possibility of capturing the essence of competition in the industry through a simplified model.

8.2.3 Coordinated effects

8.2.3.1 What are coordinated effects?

The European Commission has for several years applied the concept of "joint" or "collective" dominance to describe a situation where several firms between them coordinate their actions, to take account of a market position which is *jointly* (but not individually) dominant. Economically, this situation is termed "tacit collusion". In the anti-trust community, the concept is known as "coordinated effects" in the US Merger Guidelines, and now also under the EU Guidelines. All these terminologies mean the same thing: that a group of firms use the fact that they compete repeatedly over time in order to act in a coordinated manner, resulting in increased prices and reduced consumer welfare.

Coordinated effects differ from unilateral effects in that they rely on firms in the market competing against one another *over time* for the anti-competitive outcome to be attained and sustained. Coordinated effects arise when a merger makes it likely that firms will tacitly collude with one another after a merger where they could not have done so before. This relies on the dynamic nature of the interactions between firms in the market: having the chance to compete time and time again, each time responding to each other's actions in previous "rounds" of competition. Another key distinction between coordinated effects and unilateral effects is that even the direction of price impact from coordinated effects arising from a merger is ambiguous: a merger could either enhance or undermine the ability of the remaining firms in an industry to coordinate their actions.

Tacit collusion is based on the same underlying mechanism as explicit collusion (cartels), but without the need for any formal communication or meetings between the parties.[72] Rather, the firms involved come to realise that over time it will be in their best interests to produce less or price higher than they would choose to if they were competing strongly with one another. Each firm realises that although, in the short run, it could make more money by setting a more competitive price and winning customers from its rivals (that is, following its unilateral best response), in the longer term its rivals would simply respond to any such behaviour ("punishing" the deviating firm), leading to lower profits for all the firms in the industry. If the long-term profit from maintaining the collusion or coordination is greater than that from "cheating"

72. See 3.2.3.2.2 above.

(and reaping the resulting "punishment"), then firms will choose to coordinate their actions.

8.2.3.2 The economic mechanism underlying coordinated effects concerns

In a merger setting, the key question is whether a merger makes it more likely that firms in an industry will be able to behave in this way—or, if they are already behaving in this way, makes such behaviour more stable and sustainable. Clearly, having one fewer player to coordinate with to some extent simplifies the problem, and therefore may by itself make coordination more likely. However, the loss of an independent player is a universal feature of all mergers and far from sufficient grounds for a coordinated effect to be found.

The necessary conditions for a finding of coordinated effects from a merger (as set out in the 2002 Court of First Instance ruling in the *Airtours* case and now incorporated in the Guidelines) are as follows.[73]

- — Firms in the industry must be able to *reach terms of coordination*: that is, they must be able to identify a single coordinated outcome that would make them all better off over time than following their individual best competitive strategies.
- — Firms must be able to *monitor* each others' behaviour, and detect if a rival firm has deviated from ("cheated on") this coordinated outcome.
- — If firms detect that a rival firm has departed from the coordinated action in this way, it must be possible, and in their interests, to undertake a *retaliation* strategy against this "cheating"—one which has a sufficiently strong detrimental impact on the cheating firm's profits to make such cheating unattractive in the first place.
- — Finally, it must be the case (as for unilateral effects) that there are no serious *external constraints* preventing coordination (eg the ability of new firms to enter if prices increase, or the ability of customers to use countervailing buyer power to avoid price increases).

There is no clear, straightforward relationship between the number of firms in an industry and the likelihood of the above conditions being met. Rather, whether the conditions for tacit coordination are met will depend on many different industry characteristics. The Guidelines clarify that the relevant consideration in a merger investigation is whether the merger makes tacit coordination likely to occur where previously it was not taking place or strengthens pre-existing coordination.

73. For a more detailed discussion of the *Airtours* case, see Alan Overa, "After the Airtours Appeal" European Competition Law Review 23 (2002) p 375.

8.2.3.3 Practical assessment

The key problem, then, is to ascertain under what circumstances these conditions will be met, meaning that coordination is likely to arise as a result of a merger. This has two parts, depending on whether or not the firms in the market already coordinating their actions. If not, will the merger make it easier for them to coordinate? If they do, will it make that coordination more stable, or more effective (leading to higher prices)?

It is clearly not the case that every oligopolistic market (ie market with few players) is subject to tacit collusion. However, assessing which market structures are consistent with coordinated behaviour among firms is a difficult task. Even if it assumed that for any given set of industry characteristics there is some level of concentration at which coordination is likely to arise, estimating the level of concentration at which this would occur is far more complex than a unilateral effects assessment. Rather, economists tend to be forced back into a step-by-step assessment of whether the combination of prevailing industry characteristics is conducive to tacit coordination or not. While far from perfect, as a starting point the characteristics of the industry can at least provide some guidance as to the ability of firms to find terms of coordination, monitor each other's behaviour, and punish any deviations from a coordinated outcome.

8.2.3.3.1 Reaching terms of coordination

Before coordination can occur, there must be some clear common strategy that the firms in the industry know will be acceptable to all of them, and generate higher profits for each of them individually (in the long run) than the non-coordinated outcome.

This will typically be easier in cases where the firms concerned are similar. To give an example, a firm benefiting from more modern production facilities and lower production costs may prefer to see lower prices and higher output than a rival with older plant and higher unit production costs. Such low-cost firms will have a greater incentive to deviate from any agreed coordinated outcome, as they can profitably make sales at lower prices.

Smaller firms may also have a greater incentive to "cheat", as, because their share of the cake is small, they earn less from the coordinated outcome, relative to the potential sales they could gain by deviating from coordination (subject to their own capacity constraints, which are likely to prevent them from quickly expanding to this degree).

Mergers can clearly affect these asymmetries, by reallocating assets (capacity, brands, know-how) between the remaining firms in the market. This reallocation has the potential to either increase or reduce the ability of the remaining firms in the market to coordinate their actions. For example, if efficiencies arising from the merger make the merged entity able to produce at lower cost, then it may have an incentive to compete on its own merits rather than take part in a coordinated outcome. On the other hand, a merger that takes a low-cost, "maverick" firm out of the market may make coordination easier to sustain, without the threat of the maverick firm continuing to undercut the coordinated group.

It can be seen therefore, that it is difficult to draw any strong relationship between a simple measure of industry concentration and the likelihood of coordination. A reduction in the number of firms does not necessarily make coordination more likely. An increase in HHI could be associated with a *reduced* risk of coordination, if it were due to an increased asymmetry in the market shares and cost structures of the remaining firms in the market.

Complex product markets will also make it more difficult to reach terms of coordination. Where products are highly differentiated, with customers selecting their supplier not only on the basis of price but also on the basis of product characteristics (eg quality, design, location, service, fashion, or particular technical features), then terms of coordination will have to deal with all these various product characteristics. It will not be sufficient then to find simply a mutually acceptable price or output level. If these were the only coordinated product characteristics, then firms would simply compete instead on quality, design, or advertising, etc. Therefore, in a complex differentiated product market, there are far more elements that must be coordinated and monitored, and on the basis of which cheating can occur.

Volatile market conditions are also likely to be problematic for reaching terms of coordination—each firm is likely to have a different perception of current conditions, their likely development in the future, and the best response to those conditions. Moreover, firms may have a strong incentive to "cheat" under certain business conditions. For example, if a new technology is developed such that there is the opportunity to win a large number of new customers today, firms may face strong incentives to abandon the coordinated outcome in order to win more of these new customers, in the expectation that future profits will be relatively lower (so that being "punished" tomorrow is a small price to pay for "cheating" today). The same incentives to "cheat" may occur in a bidding market when a particularly large contract comes up for tender: the benefits of winning the contract may be seen to far outweigh the costs of being "punished" on smaller contracts in the future.

8.2.3.3.2 Monitoring rivals' behaviour

It is important to recognise that under any coordinated outcome, each firm will have an incentive to cheat on the agreement. If rivals are producing less, and holding prices above the competitive level, then it will always be profitable for an individual firm to produce more and take advantage of these higher prices. The only reason this may not happen is if the firm realises that its rivals will be able to detect the cheating behaviour, and retaliate against it (by taking action that will harm the cheating firm's long-run profits).

A key issue in collective dominance cases is therefore transparency. Can firms monitor their rivals' behaviour, so that they would know if a rival firm cheated? If so, and if retaliation can then be applied, this clearly undermines the incentive of any firm to cheat. Firms do not have to be able to monitor every element of their rivals' behaviour: for example, it may be sufficient to just monitor prices, or quantities. Alternatively, if firms are engaging in "semi-collusion" (where coordination takes place on capacity, restricting maximum output levels, after which free competition takes place up to those capacity levels) then prices and quantities need not be monitored, but capacity levels at rival operations must be visible.

Several factors will affect whether a market is sufficiently transparent to allow coordination to be maintained. For example, visible list prices, or prices set in a public forum (such as commodities exchanges) clearly can be an aid to coordination—although only if there are no secret (privately negotiated) discounts to these prices. That is, the visible price must be the one actually available to the customer, not simply the advertised price. The presence of secret discounts clearly reduces the transparency of the market. Moreover, discounts may vary across customers, so that it is difficult for firms to establish whether a discount (even if they can observe it) constitutes "cheating" by its rivals or simply reflects the nature (for example, in terms of size or bargaining power) of the customer receiving the discount.

In cases where prices are not visible, it may still be possible to monitor rival output levels. Even if a firm cannot see the price charged by rivals, it might be able to see how many customers its rival is serving, or to infer what volume of sales they are making. One way to implement coordination in these circumstances is to "allocate" customers (so any customer defection from one supplier to another will be interpreted as cheating). The initial allocation need not be the subject of a formal agreement, but could be implicit—for example that firms keep their existing customers, and do not poach customers from rivals, or that firms will not compete in each other's key geographic areas.

Factors such as product differentiation and market volatility will also make effective monitoring more difficult to achieve. For example, in the case of differentiated products, how should I interpret a change in *mix* of my rivals' sales? Or an increase in the quality of their sales, with no commensurate increase in output or prices? Whether or not this constitutes cheating is a difficult issue. Similarly, in a stable market I may be able to infer my rival's behaviour by simply looking at my own sales (if I have lost business, I assume that my rival has cheated). But in a market where such shifts could also have been caused by a change in customer tastes, or in the overall sales of the industry as a whole, then it is not safe to assume that cheating must be the cause of any loss in sales.

8.2.3.3.3 Punishing deviations from coordinated behaviour

If deviation from the coordinated outcome is detected, then it must also be the case that the detecting firm can impose a sufficiently tough punishment on the cheating firm, and will have an incentive to do so. Otherwise a firm can cheat with impunity, even if it knows such cheating will be detected, as there is no long-term pain to offset against the short-term benefits of the cheating behaviour. The punishment must be very clearly interpreted as a punishment (that is, as a direct response to the cheating), which is more likely to be the case if it takes place immediately after the observed violation, and in the same market. Any delay to the implementation of the punishment (for example, if it takes a long time to observe the cheating, or when firms only compete infrequently for large, "lumpy" contracts) will also reduce the cost of the punishment to the cheating firm and therefore increase the attractions of deviation.

The typical form for punishment to take is that of a price war, with the non-cheating firms cutting their prices in order to drive down the profitability of the cheating firm. This strategy relies on the punishing firms having sufficient spare capacity to expand their output to meet the increase in demand that such a price cut would generate. If one firm in an industry has spare capacity, while the others do not, then any such punishment is likely to fail: the firm with spare capacity can use this capacity to cheat, without any fear of the rivals being able to impose a price war, as they are capacity-constrained.

Other types of punishments may also be effective: for example, withdrawing from a joint venture, or some other form of economic link between the rivals. Clearly, however, even if a punishment strategy can be implemented, it has a serious cost for the punishers as well as for the cheater. A key condition for the punishment to occur is therefore that it is in the punishing firms' interests to carry it out—for example by inducing all firms to return to the coordinated outcome and preventing future cheating—without inducing excessive costs in the short run. A trade-off will need to be made between the short-term costs of imposing the punishment, and the long-term benefits of a return to a stable, coordinated outcome.

8.2.3.4 Empirical assessment: risks of the checklist approach

Clearly the descriptive use of industry characteristics, as outlined above, is imperfect, and at its worst can result in the use of a mechanistically applied "checklist" of industry features, divorced from a coherent argument of how the merger would enhance firms' ability to find a mutually agreeable outcome, monitor each other's behaviour, and inflict punishment in the case of deviation. In this context, the Guidelines are of great help in illustrating the economic context of the assessment, and how the different industry characteristics should be viewed together as part of an overall and coherent theory of anti-competitive effects.

However, predicting future coordinated effects as a result of a merger is inherently more difficult than predicting unilateral effects: even the direction of the merger's impact on prices is unclear. In the case of coordinated effects, the question is whether firms will stop following their short-term best response (which, assuming no prior coordination, was generating the previous market outcomes), and instead behave in a different way. Predicting at which point this switch in behaviour would occur based on historical data is an economically difficult problem. Once the dynamic element necessary to understand coordinated effects is added to an economic model, then there will generally be a large number of possible outcomes from a given market structure, which may range from perfect competition to perfect collusion.

Developing useful empirical tests for coordinated effects is an area where a great deal of economic research remains to be done, and several recent papers by Federal Trade Commission economists have focused on this area.[74] However, for the foreseeable future, a step-by-step assessment of whether the conditions of the market are such that tacit coordination can take place, and to what extent any merger affects these market conditions, are likely to remain central to any coordinated effects analysis—as they are in the Commission's Guidelines.

8.2.4 Other elements of merger assessment under the Guidelines

The Guidelines consider a number of additional economic factors that are relevant to the assessment of mergers raising either unilateral or coordinated concerns, and need to be taken into account when assessing the likely impact of concentration.

8.2.4.1 Countervailing buyer power

The Commission will consider whether buyers themselves can counteract any anti-competitive effect of a merger. The Guidelines lay out the circumstances under which this will be a consideration: in particular where customers are sufficiently large that the loss of their business constitutes some realistic threat to the seller (and where there is a credible alternative buyer for them to go to), and, in particular cases, where the buyer can actively assist an entrant or expanding rival in meeting its needs. However, where such an ability exists, it will already have acted as a constraint prior to the merger, and it will generally be the case that the merging parties increase their bargaining power relative to that of the buyer. Therefore, buyer power is more likely to ameliorate rather than remove any competition concerns. Moreover, buyer power is not sufficient if it only benefits the few large buyers who hold it, as concerns will still remain concerning the conditions facing smaller buyers. "Buyer power" arguments are most likely to be successful where market entry is relatively easy, but where one or more large buyers have skills or assets that would assist in the effectiveness of such entry (known as "sponsored entry"), and would have the incentive to provide such assistance. In practice, these are demanding restrictions on the applicability of buyer power arguments.

74. See Coleman, "Empirical Analyses of Potential Coordinated Effects from a Merger", Federal Trade Commission (2003), and Scheffman and Coleman, "Quantitative Analyses of Potential Competitive Effects from A Merger", Federal Trade Commission (2003).

8.2.4.2 Entry

Entry has always played a key role in the competition analysis of mergers. In the absence of significant barriers to entry, unilateral or coordinated effects will clearly be undermined: the higher prices achieved through the merger effect would simply attract new entry to the market, which would undermine the initial price increase effect. Entry can therefore be a considerable mitigating factor on any anti-competitive effects from a merger. However, assessing the prospects for entry is inevitably a forward-looking and partially speculative exercise. The Commission may be therefore reluctant to assign significant weight to entry considerations when assessing a merger unless there is a realistic and imminent prospect of new entry.

The Guidelines include indications of the types of entry barrier that will be taken into account. These include legal barriers (such as those arising from regulation), incumbent advantages, and the timeliness and sufficiency of potential entry.

8.2.4.3 Efficiencies

The role of efficiencies in merger analysis had, prior to the new ECMR and the Guidelines, been a hotly contended area. Several commentators felt that efficiencies tended to work against the likelihood of a merger being cleared, rather than in favour of a merger, as economic theory would suggest they should. The Guidelines make clear that the Commission will not pursue allegations of "efficiency offence" when reviewing a merger—ie the idea that the efficiencies arising from a merger could damage competition by making it impossible to compete with the merged firm.[75]

Economically, this is a welcome confirmation that merger efficiencies should be seen as a benefit to competition, not a detriment. Merger efficiencies can lead to new gains from trade, which could not be achieved without the merger. Indeed, in a textbook setting, all mergers are driven by a combination of two driving forces: the desire to increase market power and achieve higher prices, and/or the wish to achieve efficiencies and therefore be more competitive against rivals, generating greater profits for the firm in question, but also greater welfare for consumers. Therefore, if no efficiencies are claimed for a merger, then the authorities are likely to be suspicious that firms are simply merging in order to enhance their market power.

Moreover, the Guidelines give helpful guidance on the types of efficiencies that will be accepted as beneficial to competition. As well as being "substantial and timely", the benefit of the efficiencies must flow to consumers, rather than shareholders (paragraph 79). Economically, this focus on consumer benefits pushes the focus onto savings in variable or marginal, rather than fixed, costs.

75. For example, in the merger between AT&T and NCR, the Commission stated that: "It is not excluded that potential advantages flowing from synergies may create or strengthen a dominant position." (Paragraph 30.) The transaction was cleared, partly on the basis that these synergies were seen as unlikely to be achieved in practice.

However despite emphasising their importance, the Guidelines do not purely focus on marginal cost savings. For example, the Commission will take into account that a merger may allow an innovation to be pursued that would not have been carried forward by either party acting alone (paragraph 81).

Finally, the Guidelines specify that efficiency benefits must be merger-specific, and unlikely to be achievable through any less anti-competitive means. If applied in an absolute way, this may represent a tough hurdle to jump: it is often the case that efficiencies arising from a merger can in theory be achieved through some contractual arrangement that may be of less concern from a competition perspective. However, the authorities have made clear in the past that an entirely theoretical alternative is not sufficient. Therefore, while an investment that could equally easily have been made by a single firm is unlikely to be seen as merger-specific, investments that make use of the complementary talents and assets of both firms may be taken into account as a merger benefit.

8.2.4.4 "Failing firm" defence

"Failing firm" defences have been explored since the earliest days of the ECMR but rarely with success. These defences are based on a claim that one of the merged firms would in any case have exited the market, and therefore the pre-merger situation is not an appropriate comparison with the merger outcome. However, as with efficiencies, these defences are now given a formal place in European merger control with their inclusion in the Horizontal Merger Guidelines.

The key support for a failing firm defence from an economic viewpoint comes from the principle that mergers should be assessed against a clear "but for the merger . . . " scenario. It is, however, vital that this "but for" scenario is carefully defined, on the basis of the most likely market outcome (and its competitive implications) absent the merger. It is easy to assert that a rival would have become a less effective competitor in the future, but more difficult to demonstrate convincingly that this would be the case. Historically, few mergers have been cleared on this basis, although it is more common for the Commission to recognise that the relevant "but for" comparator is not the pre-merger situation: for example, this was acknowledged in the Andersen accounting mergers.

The Guidelines formalise this "but for" approach: "the basic requirement is that the deterioration of the competitive structure that follows the merger cannot be said to be caused by the merger" (paragraph 89). More specifically, it must be clear that the failing firm would inevitably leave the market, with no less anti-competitive merger available, and the assets of the merging firm inevitably exiting the market. If these assets were not going to exit the market in the event of failure, then the Commission would feel that the risk of leaving the failing firm in the market to stand or fall would be worthwhile, as the worst case outcome of exit would be no worse than the merger outcome.

8.2.4.5 Conclusion

The Commission's Horizontal Merger Guidelines represent a welcome clarification of the European Commission's approach to horizontal merger cases, and provide useful guidance for merging parties and their advisers. The Guidelines are well founded in economic principle, and provide a useful "common ground" for interested parties in a merger to understand the likely approach to be taken by the Commission. Although there remains, as there must, a good deal of discretion for the Commission in its treatment of mergers, the Guidelines do provide a helpful baseline for the economic assessment of horizontal mergers. Proposed future guidelines on vertical and portfolio effects will hopefully prove of equal value.

CHAPTER 9

COMPETITION AUTHORITIES

Peter Willis, Taylor Wessing

9.1 INTRODUCTION

In contrast to the preceding Chapters, which describe the substantive EU competition rules, this Chapter describes the procedures by which those rules are enforced. Since 1 May 2004, enforcement has been the responsibility of the European Commission, national competition authorities ("NCAs") and national courts in close cooperation, under Regulation 1/2003 on the implementation of the rules on competition laid down in Articles 81 and 82 of the Treaty. NCAs can apply both national and EU competition rules, in the context of a European Competition Network ("ECN") with the Commission at its hub. This Chapter focuses on enforcement by the Commission, but also provides an overview of enforcement by one NCA, the UK's Office of Fair Trading ("OFT"), by way of comparison.

9.2 PRIMACY OF COMMUNITY LAW

It was established over 30 years ago that EU competition rules take precedence over national competition rules.[1] It was clear that national law could not permit an agreement or conduct that was prohibited under EU competition law. It was also established that when a national court rules on an agreement or practice which is already the subject of a Commission Decision, it may not take a Decision running counter to that of the Commission, even if the Commission Decision conflicts with a previous judgment of a national court of first instance.[2]

Regulation 1/2003 codifies some of the earlier case-law in this area, and sets out some general principles.

The key provision of Regulation 1/2003 is Article 3. Where NCAs and courts apply national competition rules to agreements between undertakings which may affect trade between Member States, they must also apply Article

1. Case 14/68, *Walt Wilhelm v. Bundeskartellamt* [1969] ECR 1.
2. Case C-344/98, *Masterfoods v. HB Ice Cream Ltd* [2000] ECR I 11369.

81. Where they apply national rules to unilateral conduct caught by Article 82, they must also apply Article 82.

NCAs and courts may not prohibit, under national law, agreements that affect trade between Member States but do not restrict competition within Article 81 or satisfy the conditions set out in Article 81(3) (either individually or under a block exemption).[3] However, they may apply stricter national rules on unilateral conduct. Member States may also apply national merger rules, and other national rules that predominantly pursue an objective different to that pursued by Articles 81 and 82, such as consumer protection rules.

Article 16 provides that NCAs must not take Decisions that conflict with existing Commission Decisions. In contrast, national courts must avoid conflicts not only with existing Commission Decisions, but also with Decisions contemplated in pending Commission proceedings.

9.3. CASE ALLOCATION AND COORDINATION

Two basic principles are set out in Regulation 1/2003: that cases are to be dealt with "by the most appropriate authorities within the Network"[4] and that "the Commission and [the NCAs] shall apply the Community competition rules in close cooperation".[5] It is important to note that allocation under the modernised regime is not necessarily to one authority only.

Further detail on case allocation is set out in the Joint Statement and Notice on cooperation with the ECN.[6] Cases are to be dealt with by the authorities best able to deal with a case successfully, bearing in mind their ability to gather evidence, bring infringements to an end and apply sanctions. In many cases this will be a single authority. Where more than one Member State is affected, the NCAs concerned should agree between them which is best placed to deal with the case, or at least should designate one authority as the lead enforcer. The Commission will be particularly well placed to deal with the case if three or more Member States are affected, or if the Community interest requires the adoption of a Commission Decision, for example to deal with a new issue.[7]

Case allocation is to be a "predictable process". The competition authorities will endeavour to decide on case allocation swiftly. The first authority to deal with the case will usually remain responsible for it.

NCAs or the Commission may suspend proceedings where another authority is dealing with the case.[8] After the initial period, if a case is being handled by more than one NCA well placed to do so, one of them will take a formal

3. Regulation 1/2003, Article 3(2).
4. *Ibid*, recital 18.
5. *Ibid*, Article 11(1).
6. Joint Statement of the Council of the Commission: http://register.consilium.eu.int, document No 15435/02 ADD1, and Notice on co-operation within the ECN 2004 OJC 101, p 43.
7. See also Notice on cooperation within the ECN, paras 13 and 14.
8. Regulation 1/2003, Article 13(1).

Decision, while the others stay their proceedings.[9] An NCA or the Commission may reject a complaint if another authority has already dealt with the case.[10]

The Commission will provide NCAs with copies of the most important documents gathered in the course of its investigations, and will provide other documents on request. An NCA must inform the Commission before, or without delay after, exercising its powers of investigation. It may also inform other NCAs. It must give 30 days' advance notice to the Commission if it intends to adopt an infringement Decision, a Decision accepting commitments, or a Decision withdrawing the benefit of a block exemption. In addition, it must provide a case summary and its draft Decision and, if requested, copies of relevant documents. It may also provide this information to other NCAs. NCAs and the Commission will also inform each other where they propose to reject complaints or terminate investigations.[11]

If the Commission initiates proceedings[12] with a view to issuing an infringement Decision, an interim measures Decision or a Decision accepting commitments, NCAs lose their power to apply Articles 81 and 82. If an NCA is already acting in a case, the Commission must consult it before initiating proceedings.[13]

Where an NCA which is well placed to do so is already acting, the Commission will not normally initiate proceedings, although there is a short list of cases (eg likely conflict) in which the Commission will take action. Where an NCA is already acting, the Commission will explain to all the NCAs in writing its reasons for taking over the case.

The Commission will not normally (unless the Community interest is at stake) adopt a Decision conflicting with an earlier Decision of an NCA if at the time the NCA circulated the relevant information as outlined above, and the Commission did not take over proceedings.

This is a complex set of case allocation rules. Undoubtedly they are less clear-cut than businesses might wish. Much will depend on how well the NCAs and the Commission observe the underlying principle of cooperation in case handling. In practice, it seems more likely that the result will be a reluctance to investigate on the part of the competition authorities, rather than that there will be widespread duplication of investigations.

9.4 COMPLAINTS

A competition investigation may start following a complaint, on the initiative of the authority itself (for example as a result of its monitoring of price

9. Joint Statement, para 20.
10. Regulation 1/2003, Article 13(2).
11. *Ibid*, Article 11(1)–(5).
12. That is, issues a statement of objections—see 9.9 below.
13. Regulation 1/2003, Article 11(6).

movements in an industry), or following an application for leniency, or "whistle-blowing", exercise. Whistle-blowing is addressed at 9.4.10.2 below. Complaints are briefly described below. The forum for a complaint should be decided by reference to the case allocation criteria outlined above. Complaints will increasingly be directed to NCAs.

A formal complaint that the competition rules have been infringed may be made to the Commission by Member States and by any "natural or legal persons who can show legitimate interest".[14] Any person who suffers, or who is likely to suffer, loss or damage as a result of the alleged infringement will satisfy this requirement, as will consumer groups.[15]

9.4.1 Content

Regulation 773/2004[16] sets out the procedural requirements for making a complaint. A complaint must contain the information set out in Form C—essentially details of the parties, the background, the market definition, and why the complainant has a legitimate interest in making the complaint.

The Commission may grant a dispensation from the requirement to supply part of the information required by Form C. The complainant must provide three paper copies, and, if possible, an electronic copy of the complaint. It must also submit a non-confidential version of the complaint if it claims that any part of the complaint is confidential.

9.4.2 Rights of the complainant

If the Commission considers that there are insufficient grounds for pursuing the complaint, it notifies the complainant of this provisional view. It then sends a formal letter, known as an "Article 7" letter,[17] indicating its intention of rejecting the complaint, and setting a time limit for the complainant to make further representations. An Article 7 letter does not constitute an act of the Commission capable of judicial review under Article 230 of the EU Treaty.[18]

A complainant to the Commission has no right to a Decision on the existence of the alleged infringement.[19] If the complainant makes representations within the time limits specified and the Commission's assessment does not change as a result, the Commission must reject the complaint by a

14. *Ibid*, Article 7(2); Regulation 773/2004, Article 5(1).
15. Case T–114/92, *BEMIM v. Commission* [1995] ECR II 147.
16. 2004 OJ L 123, p 18.
17. From Article 7 of Regulation 773/2004.
18. Case C–282/95P, *Guérin Automobiles v. Commission* [1997] ECR I 1503 (in relation to the corresponding provision of the predecessor of Regulation 773/2004).
19. Case 125/78, *GEMA v. Commission* [1979] ECR 3173.

Decision (which can then be appealed to the Court of First Instance ("CFI")).[20]

If the Commission does pursue a complaint, the complainant has a number of further rights. Under Regulation 1/2003, these are limited to the right to be "associated closely" with the proceedings leading up to the issue of a formal Decision (which may or may not include formal rights to make representations and to participate in hearings). The complainant's rights are more clearly spelt out in Regulation 773/2004, and include the rights to:

— participate in the formal oral hearing; and
— see a non-confidential version of the statement of objections.

These are discussed below.

Rights of complainants to the NCAs may be different, although for example in *Pernod-Ricard and Campbell Distillers v. OFT*,[21] the Competition Appeal Tribunal ("CAT") held that the rights given to complainants under the EU procedure should be imported into the UK regime, so that the OFT should disclose to the complainant a non-confidential version of the statement of objections and should give it the opportunity to submit its views—at least where the investigation was an obviously serious one, which had been going on for some years.

9.5 POWERS OF INVESTIGATION

The Commission has traditionally had wide powers to investigate suspected infringements of the competition rules, including powers to request information and to carry out on-site investigations. These powers have been reinforced in Regulation 1/2003 by the addition of powers to conduct interviews. The decentralised enforcement of the EU competition rules means that NCAs will play a leading role in investigations under the EU rules. However, their powers are not spelt out in Regulation 1/2003 itself. That is left to national legislation.

9.5.1 Grounds for Investigation

Regulation 1/2003 is silent as to the grounds on which the Commission may order an investigation. Exercise of its investigative powers is subject to judicial review by the CFI (in relation to Regulation 17/62). In his opinion issued on 20 September 2001 in, *Roquette Frères SA v. DGCCRF*[22] Mischo AG explained that:

"Review of necessity for the search is a matter for the Court of Justice, and it alone. It is to this court that it falls, when it is seized by the undertaking in question, to verify

20. Regulation 773/2004, Article 7(2).
21. *Pernod-Ricard and Campbell Distillers v. OFT* [2004] CAT 10.
22. Case C–94/00, [2002] ECR I–9011.

scrupulously whether the Commission, before taking its Decision, had before it sufficiently strong indications of the probable existence of an unlawful agreement or concerted practice. The Commission will have to submit to the Community court all such information as may establish that the search was justified. I would repeat that, if it fails to do so, the court will annul the Decision and the Commission will be prohibited from using any documents it has photocopied and also any information it has obtained orally from the undertaking's employees."

In practice, it will always be difficult to challenge the wide discretion given to the Commission in deciding whether to investigate. Only in the case of manifestly unfounded or frivolous investigations would a challenge be likely to succeed.

The grounds on which the OFT may launch an investigation into suspected infringements of Articles 81 and 82 are expressly spelt out—they are the same as those in relation to suspected infringements of the UK rules, namely that the OFT must have "reasonable grounds for suspecting"[23] that there has been an infringement.

9.5.2 Requests for information

The Commission may request "all necessary information" from undertakings and associations of undertakings, either by simple letter (known as an "Article 18 letter") or by Decision (an "Article 18 Decision").[24] Undertakings from which information may be requested need not necessarily be those suspected of an infringement: the Commission frequently sends such requests to undertakings that have notified an agreement, if it requires additional information. It also sends requests to complainants and third parties such as customers and competitors.

There is no penalty for failing to respond to an Article 18 letter within the time limit specified by the Commission, although it is likely to result in the issue of an Article 18 Decision. A failure to respond to an Article 18 Decision, or the provision of incorrect information in response to either a Decision or a letter, may lead to the imposition of a fine, or the imposition of daily penalty payments.[25]

The OFT's powers are broadly similar, although spelt out in more detail. The first power enjoyed by an OFT investigating officer is the power[26] to require any person[27] to provide specified relevant documents or information. The investigating officer may specify where and when the documents or information are to be provided (which will usually be by sending them to the

23. A term interpreted in case law on the powers of investigation of other UK authorities.

24. Regulation 1/2003, Article 18.

25. Up to 1 per cent of annual turnover, or periodic penalty payments of up to 5 per cent of daily turnover.

26. Competition Act 1998, s 26.

27. That is, not just a party to a suspected infringement, but also complainants and other third parties.

OFT, but may involve attending in person[28]), and also in what manner and form they are to be provided (for example, with market shares broken down by year, or by region). This power will be exercised by means of a written request for the documents or information. Both "document" and "information" are defined widely in the Competition Act 1998 ("CA 1998"), allowing the OFT to require the production of all types of information, whether or not recorded, and also to require, for example, computer information to be downloaded and provided in legible form. The OFT can also require the production of estimates and forecasts. If a document is not produced, the investigating officer may require the addressee of the request to state, to the best of his knowledge and belief, where it is.

The OFT has the power to take copies or extracts from any documents produced, and to require present and past officers and employees of the undertaking to provide explanations of any document produced.

9.5.3 Interviews

Regulation 1/2003 introduced a new power for the Commission to interview natural and legal persons in order to collect information relating to the subject-matter of an investigation. The Commission may conduct an interview only if the subject consents,[29] and there is no penalty for refusing to comply, or even for providing incorrect information. The Commission may conduct the interview by telephone or videoconference, and may record the interview in any form, and provide a copy of any recording to the interviewee and give an opportunity to make corrections.[30]

The OFT has no power to carry out interviews in the context of investigations under Articles 81 and 82, or the Competition Act 1998, although it frequently conducts informal voluntary interviews.

9.5.4 On-site investigations

In addition to the "off-site" powers described above, the Commission has the power to conduct on-site investigations, or "dawn raids", on the premises of undertakings.

9.5.4.1 By the Commission

Article 20 of Regulation 1/2003 gives Commission officials the power to conduct "all necessary inspections". As in the case of Article 18, the Commission may proceed on the basis of a mere authorisation, or by binding Decision.

28. A person required to attend the OFT to provide an explanation of a document is entitled to be accompanies by his legal adviser—rule 3(3) of the OFT's rules. The Competition Act 1998 (Office of Fair Trading Rules) (SI 2004 No 2751).

29. Regulation 1/2003, Article 19.

30. Regulation 773/2004, Article 3(1)–(3).

9.5.4 Competition Authorities

Under Article 20(3), the Commission may investigate on the basis of a written authorisation. This type of investigation tends to be used where there is little risk of information being concealed or destroyed. It can also be used where an undertaking is reluctant to be seen to be providing information voluntarily. There is no duty to submit to investigations under Article 20(3), although a refusal is likely to lead to the Commission issuing a Decision ordering an investigation under Article 20(4). The authorisation must specify the subject-matter and purpose of the investigation and the penalties for providing inaccurate or incomplete information.[31]

Alternatively, the Commission may issue a Decision under Article 20(4), ordering an on-site investigation. As in the case of Article 18, there is no need for a previous request under authorisation to have been unsuccessful before the Commission may resort to a Decision. The Commission is likely to proceed by way of a Decision in most cartel cases and other high-profile cases.

A Decision must specify the subject-matter and purpose of the investigation, the date on which it is to begin, the penalties for non-compliance and the provision of incomplete information, and the right to apply to the CFI for review of the Decision.[32]

When conducting an investigation, whether under authorisation (Article 20(3)) or Decision (Article 20(4)), Commission investigators and "other accompanying persons" authorised by the Commission, such as IT experts, have the power to:

- Enter premises, land and means of transport of undertakings and associations of undertakings. The investigators themselves do not have the power to enter by force (although officers of NCAs supporting the Commission investigators may have the power to gain entry by force), nor can they conduct a search unless the undertaking consents.
- Seal premises and records during an investigation with the purpose of preventing undertakings from tampering with records. Seals should not normally be applied for more than 72 hours.[33] Breaking seals carries a penalty of up to 1 per cent of total annual turnover.
- Examine books and other records, irrespective of the medium on which they are stored. This includes all paper and electronic records, such as information stored on computers and reports of fax transmissions.[34] The Commission may not carry out "fishing expeditions", but has a wide discretion to decide what is relevant to its investigation. The undertaking is under a duty to cooperate with the investigators and to produce the documents required.[35]

31. See 9.5.4.4.1 below.
32. Regulation 1/2003, Article 20(4).
33. *Ibid*, recital 25.
34. See 9.5.4.5 below.
35. Case 374/87, *Orkem v. Commission* [1989] ECR 3283.

— Take or obtain in any form copies of or extracts from the books and other records.
— Ask any representative or member of staff of the undertaking for explanations of facts or documents relating to the subject-matter of the inspection and to record the answers. This raises concerns about self-incrimination (see 9.6.3 below). Regulation 1/2003 allows the Commission to ask *any* representative or member of staff for an explanation. The Commission may record such explanations in any form. Where it does, it must provide a copy to the undertaking, and must give an opportunity to make corrections if the interviewee was not authorised to provide the explanation.[36]

Regulation 1/2003 also allows the Commission to order (by Decision) investigations at domestic premises, where "a reasonable suspicion exists that books or other records related to the business and to the subject-matter of the inspection, which may be relevant to prove a serious violation of Article 81 or Article 82", are kept there. It is significant that this power is available only in the case of suspected *serious* infringements (likely to include cartels, resale price maintenance, serious abuses of dominance and obstructing parallel imports). The Commission must consult the relevant NCA before proceeding, and may not execute the Decision without obtaining a court order from the relevant national court. In such cases, the national court may exercise the same supervisory role that it exercises in relation to investigations of business premises, set out below.

When carrying out investigations at domestic premises, Commission officials (and those accompanying them) have the power to enter, examine books and other records and take copies, in the same way as in the case of investigations of business premises. They do not have the power to seal the premises, nor to request explanations of documents or facts. It should also be noted that the Commission itself has no power to penalise failure to submit to such an investigation. In the UK, however, intentional failure to submit to a warrant is an offence.[37]

9.5.4.2 The role of the national courts

The Commission must inform the NCA of the Member State in whose territory the addressee of an Article 18 letter or Decision, or the target of an Article 20 investigation under authorisation, is based. It must consult the national authority in advance where it proposes to order an on-site investigation by Decision. The NCA may offer, or may be invited, to assist in carrying out investigations ordered by Decision. In some cases, this may extend to carrying out investigations on behalf of the Commission.

36. Regulation 773/2004, Article 4(2) and 4(3).
37. Punishable by an unlimited fine and/or imprisonment for up to two years. CA 1998, s 65(2)(b).

9.5.4 Competition Authorities

As established in *Orkem v. Commission*, the undertaking is under a duty to cooperate with the investigators and to produce the documents required.[38] However, an Article 20(4) Decision does not authorise the investigators to enter by force, nor to conduct a search unless the undertaking consents.[39]

Where an undertaking fails to cooperate with an investigation ordered by Decision, the Commission's officials may invoke the assistance of the relevant national authorities. This assistance may include seeking an order from the relevant national court, which may even be sought on a precautionary basis.[40] The CA 1998 provides for the OFT to obtain a warrant from a High Court judge where a Commission investigation ordered by Decision has encountered opposition or is likely to encounter opposition.[41] The national court has a limited power to review such investigations—it may review their execution, but not whether they are necessary.[42]

Once the Commission has obtained the assistance of the NCA, it may then conduct a search for any information necessary for the investigation without the consent of the undertaking.

9.5.4.3 By the OFT

When investigating suspected infringements of EU competition rules or of the CA 1998, the OFT has the power to enter business premises on the basis of an authorisation.[43]

In principle, this power may be exercised only if the inspectors give two working days' notice in writing. However, no notice need be given where the OFT has a reasonable suspicion that the premises are occupied by a party to the agreement or conduct under investigation.

Although the inspectors have no power to enter by force, it is an offence to refuse entry or to withhold documents.

A heavier weapon available to the OFT under the CA 1998 is the power to enter and search under a warrant issued by a judge.[44] This is available only where a previous attempt to gain entry has been unsuccessful, documents have been withheld, or there are reasonable grounds to suspect that documents would otherwise be concealed or destroyed (in practice this latter ground is the one most likely to be invoked).

Regulation 1/2003 also gives NCAs such as the OFT the power to carry out those investigations on behalf of the Commission and other NCAs. In the UK, the CA 1998 provides for the OFT to carry out on-site investigations at the

38. Case 374/87, *Orkem v. Commission* [1989] ECR 3283.
39. Cases 46/87 and 227/88, *Hoechst AG v. Commission* [1989] ECR 2859, at para 31.
40. Regulation 1/2003, Article 20(7). This codifies *Hoechst*; see note 39 above.
41. CA 1998, Part II.
42. Regulation 1/2003, Article 20(8).
43. CA 1998, s 27. Note that, except in section 9.7 below, "Surviving a Dawn Raid", this Chapter does not describe the OFT's powers of investigation in relation to the UK cartel offence under the Enterprise Act 2002, s 188.
44. CA 1998, ss 28(2)(b) and 28A(2)(b).

request of the Commission and other NCAs and off-site requests for information on behalf of other NCAs.

The OFT has also been given powers to carry out certain forms of surveillance in connection with the CA 1998,[45] including:

- "directed surveillance", which is covert but not intrusive, and therefore includes surveillance of business premises and following suspects to ensure that they are in the right office when an investigation starts;
- the use of a "covert human intelligence source" ("CHIS"), ie an informant, which is likely to include the use of a whistle-blower who is required to continue to take part in cartel meetings to gather evidence on the cartel;
- "access to communications data", for example records of telephone numbers dialled (but not records of what was actually said during the telephone conversations).

9.5.4.4 Refusal to submit

9.5.4.4.1 Commission investigations

The Commission may impose penalties not exceeding 1 per cent of worldwide group turnover in the preceding year where an undertaking intentionally or negligently supplies incorrect or misleading information, or fails to comply with an Article 18 or 20 Decision. The Commission may in similar circumstances also impose periodic penalty payments not exceeding 5 per cent of the average daily turnover in the preceding business year per day of non-compliance.[46]

Refusal to submit to an investigation ordered by Decision may also result in NCAs being called to assist. National penalties will then apply to further non-compliance. In the UK, for example, obstruction of the exercise of a warrant issued by a High Court judge in support of an investigation by or on behalf of the Commission is an offence punishable by a fine of up to £5,000 and/or imprisonment of up to two years.

9.5.4.4.2 OFT investigations

The CA 1998 creates a number of offences, including:[47]

- intentional obstruction of an investigation or withholding of a document; or
- knowingly or recklessly providing false information.

45. Regulation of Investigatory Powers (Directed Surveillance and Covert Human Intelligence Sources) Order 2003, SI 2003/3171; Regulation of Investigatory Powers (Communications Data) Order 2003, SI 2003/3172.
46. Regulation 1/2003, Article 24(1).
47. CA 1998, ss 42–44.

Depending on the offence, the maximum penalty is an unlimited fine and/or two years' imprisonment.

There are similar penalties for failure to comply with requirements imposed in the context of investigations conducted by the OFT in support of or on behalf of the Commission, or on behalf of other NCAs.[48]

9.5.4.5 Electronic evidence, relevance and "seize and sift"

The increasing volumes of information stored and transmitted electronically have led competition authorities throughout the world to extend their investigations to personal computers and servers as well as fax and telephone call records. The Commission and OFT have on a number of occasions used e-mails as evidence in infringement Decisions.[49] Search methods used by competition authorities range from use of the search facility built into operating systems such as Windows to specialist forensic software, which can recover apparently deleted files and produce and authenticate an exact image of specific files, or of the entire hard disk and storage of a PC or server.

The Commission is entitled to require an undertaking to produce relevant documents held on the undertaking's computer system and either to copy them onto a disk or print them, so that the Commission can take them away. Regulation 1/2003 allows Commission officials to "examine the books and other records related to the business, *irrespective of the medium on which they are stored*",[50] and similarly to "take or obtain *in any form* copies or extracts"[51] (emphasis added).

Similarly, the use of a word search facility, whether the one incorporated into the undertaking's own software, or one brought along by Commission investigators on their own laptop and applied to the undertaking's computer system, appears also to fall within the scope of Article 20(6) of Regulation 1/2003, where the undertaking fails to cooperate. Full cooperation within the meaning of *Orkem v. Commission* probably also means submitting to the use of investigative software tools.

What is rather more problematic is the practice of taking away an image of an undertaking's entire hard disk or of the results of a search. Although at present the Commission appears generally not to copy entire disk systems, preferring to copy specific files, it does not rule out this approach, and this issue has already caused concern in a number of Member States. The concern is usually twofold: that the competition authority may take away material that is not relevant to its investigation, and that it may take away material subject to legal privilege.

48. CA 1998, ss 65 and 65L.
49. See, for example, *Opel*, 2001 OJ L 59, p 1, at para 18.
50. Regulation 1/2003, Article 20(2)(b).
51. *Ibid*, Article 20(2)(c).

In the UK, investigators (including the OFT) may take documents and review them for relevance off-site.[52] These "seize and sift" powers apply where either it is not practicable for an investigating officer to determine on-site whether something that he has found contains relevant information, or a relevant item cannot be separated from other material on-site.

The German courts considered the issue, in the context of the European Commission's investigations into mobile roaming charges in 2001, and concluded that the Bundeskartellamt (in this instance acting in support of the Commission could:

> "examine business documents on site for their possible relevance to investigations and may take away copies of those documents that it has determined, by on-site examination, to be of possible relevance to the investigation.
>
> However, it may not take away copies of documents determined by on-site examination to be irrelevant, or which have not yet been examined with a view to whether they may be relevant to the investigation. Of course the Commission officials have the power to decide here which documents are relevant and which are irrelevant. However, this Decision-making competence does not relieve the competition officials from carrying out this examination on-site."[53]

For this German court at least, merely applying a keyword search facility did not constitute a sufficient assessment of relevance. However, it seems unlikely that the CFI would conclude that a keyword search was not a sufficient filter for relevance.

In practice, it may be preferable to permit Commission investigators to copy and take away for later analysis a large volume of information, rather than to have them continuing their investigation on-site for some days, possibly sealing premises and computers, and disrupting the undertaking's business with their investigation. In such cases, the undertaking concerned will seek some sort of agreement with the investigators as to the review process and the timetable for the return of material determined to be irrelevant.[54]

However, this approach is less satisfactory where a system may contain a number of individual files covered by legal privilege. In such cases, it may be necessary to arrange for a master copy to be taken and retained securely for the purposes of verifying authenticity of the files, and then for a joint review of the disk image by the investigators and the undertaking's lawyers with a view to agreeing what is privileged, so that those files may be withheld from the investigators. If no agreement can be reached, the process described at 9.6.2.2 below will need to be followed.

52. Part II of the Criminal Justice and Police Act 2001.

53. Amstgericht Bonn/Landgericht Bonn, August/September 2001.

54. The Commission's Notice on the internal rules of procedure for processing requests for access to the file provides for the return of irrelevant material as rapidly as possible after an investigation: 1997 OJ L 23, p 3. Note that the Commission has proposed a revised Notice: 2004 OJ C 259 p 8.

9.5.4 Competition Authorities

Commission investigators may now be accompanied by other persons (such as IT experts).[55] This may make the use of specialist disk-imaging tools more likely.[56]

The Commission's powers do not extend to conducting covert audio or video surveillance.

9.6 RIGHTS OF THE UNDERTAKING UNDER INVESTIGATION

9.6.1 Right to legal advice

In *National Panasonic*,[57] the ECJ held that the Commission had not infringed the fundamental rights of the undertaking where it delayed the start of its investigation for only a short time while waiting for the arrival of the undertaking's solicitors. In practice, both Commission and OFT investigators will usually wait for an hour or so for a lawyer to arrive, provided that the management of the undertaking agrees not to tamper with business records and allows the investigators to enter and occupy the offices of their choice. They will not await the arrival of outside lawyers where the undertaking has in-house lawyers (even if they are not competition specialists).

9.6.2 Legal privilege

Certain advice from an undertaking's lawyers may be privileged, in which case it may be withheld from the investigators.

9.6.2.1 Scope of the privilege

In *AM & S*,[58] the ECJ ruled that legal privilege applies to correspondence between an undertaking and its external lawyer entitled to practise in an EU Member State following the start of formal proceedings by the Commission, or before that date where relating to the subject-matter of the proceedings. Privilege does not extend to advice from in-house lawyers. The Commission has even used advice from in-house lawyers as evidence of an infringement or of intention.[59] In *Hilti*,[60] the CFI ruled that privilege also applied to internal notes confined to reporting the text or content of communications from external lawyers. (This category of privileged documents must be treated by

55. Regulation 1/2003, Article 20(2), (3), (5) and (6); CA 1998, ss 28(3A), 28A(3), 62(5A), 62A(7), 63(5A), 65a(4), 65H(4).

56. See Schaub, "La lutte contre les cartels atteint sa vitesse de croisière en 2001", [2002] *Competition Policy Newsletter*, p 1.

57. See Case 136/79, *National Panasonic (UK) Ltd v. Commission* [1980] ECR 2033.

58. Case 155/79, *AM & S Europe Ltd v. Commission* [1982] ECR 1575.

59. *John Deere*, 1985 OJ L 35, p 38; *London European/Sabena*, 1988 OJ L 317, p 47.

60. Case T–30/89A, *Hilti AG v. Commission* [1990] 4 CMLR 602.

the undertaking receiving it with considerable care: it is suggested that the safest solution is merely to circulate a copy of the advice, or report it verbatim, without commenting on it or attempting to paraphrase it, either of which could lead to a loss of privilege.)

The scope of the privilege, and in particular its limitation to external counsel, has been much criticised. The Commission, faced with a clear judgment of the European Court of Justice ("ECJ"), has, perhaps unsurprisingly, declined to change its position. The opportunity to legislate on this subject offered by the adoption of Regulation 1/2003, was not taken up. With some justification, the Commission also points to the lack of harmonisation at a European level of the status of in-house lawyers. It is possible that the Commission is reluctant to lose a potential target for its investigations.

However, a recent order by the President of the CFI[61] suggests that the court may be prepared to review the rule in *AM & S*. In the course of an investigation carried out in the UK in February 2003 at the premises of Akzo Nobel Chemicals and Akcros Chemicals, Commission investigators took away two groups of documents:

(i) Documents that, although internal, were apparently prepared for the purpose of instructing external counsel. The President held that if the Commission were able to copy working or summary documents prepared solely for the purposes of instructing external counsel, the rights of defence of the undertaking might be irremediably impaired. The documents might therefore be capable of being covered by legal professional privilege.

(ii) Documents that might possibly never have been drafted if the author had not intended to instruct a lawyer, and e-mails between the general manager and an in-house lawyer. In the case of the former, the President held that the application was not wholly unfounded (and should therefore be put before the court). The President acknowledged that the e-mails between the general manager and the in-house lawyer did not fall within the scope of legal privilege as set out in *AM & S*. However, he pointed out that that judgment was based on an interpretation of the principles common to the Member States in 1982. Akzo had produced serious evidence indicating that Community and national law had developed to the extent that an extension of the scope of legal professional privilege to cover communications with employed in-house counsel could not now be ruled out. The key question seems to be whether the in-house lawyer is subject to rules of professional conduct equivalent to those imposed on external counsel. The President therefore concluded that Akzo

61. Cases T–125/03R and T–253/03 R, *Akzo Nobel Chemicals and Akcros Chemicals Ltd v. Commission*, order of 30 October 2003, [2003] ECR II-4771. On appeal, the President of the Court of Justice annulled part of the order of the President of the CFI, but did not dispute the basic principles set out in his order: Case C–7/04P(R), *Commission v. Akzo Nobel Chemicals and Akcros Chemicals Ltd*, order of 27 September 2004, not yet reported.

> had raised "a delicate question of principle, which required a complex legal assessment and must be reserved for the court when it adjudicated on the main application".

Although advice from in-house lawyers may qualify for privilege under some national competition regimes,[62] this recognition should be treated with caution because of the risk that the Commission may investigate.

9.6.2.2 Disputes on privilege

Whether or not a document is subject to legal privilege may be a matter for dispute between the undertaking concerned and the competition authority concerned. In its Decision in *AM & S*, the Court of Justice explained the procedure that should be followed in cases involving the Commission. Essentially, the undertaking must provide the investigators material of such a nature as to demonstrate that the communications are privileged, although it is not bound to reveal the contents of the communications in question. Where the Commission is not satisfied that such evidence has been supplied, it is for the Commission to order production of the communications in question. That Decision can then be appealed to the CFI.

This issue was also raised in *Akzo Nobel Chemicals*[63]—Akzo also argued that the Commission had not followed the procedural principles set out in the *AM & S* judgment.

9.6.3 Privilege against self-incrimination

9.6.3.1 The Orkem principle

The issue of privilege first made an appearance in EU competition law in Case 374/87, *Orkem v Commission.*[64] In view of the subsequent unwillingness of the CFI to depart from the *Orkem* formulation, it is worth examining the judgment in some detail.

The court held, at paragraphs 34 and 35, that:

> "while the Commission is entitled . . . to compel an undertaking to provide all necessary information concerning such facts as may be known to it and to disclose to it, if necessary, such documents relating thereto as are in its possession, even if the latter may be used to establish against it or another undertaking the existence of anti-competitive conduct, it may not, by means of a Decision calling for information, undermine the rights of defence of the undertaking concerned.

62. For example, in the UK: CA 1998, s 30; Enterprise Act 2002, s 196(1). See also generally for the UK position on privilege *Three Rivers District Council and Others v. Governor and Company of the Bank of England* [2004] UKHL 48: legal privilege covers advice not only on an undertaking's legal rights and obligations, but also on the presentation of its case to authorities.

63. See above, n 61.

64. Case 374/87, *Orkem v. Commission* [1989] ECR 3283.

Thus, the Commission may not compel an undertaking to provide it with answers which might involve an admission on its part of the existence of an infringement which it is incumbent on the Commission to prove."

The court then examined the questions posed by the Commission. Applying the principles developed, it concluded that the following questions were permitted:

— questions relating to meetings of producers intended only to secure factual information on the circumstances in which the meetings were held and the capacity in which the participants attended them;
— a requirement to disclose documents relating to those meetings; and
— questions relating to the subject-matter and implementation of measures taken in order to determine and maintain a satisfactory price level.

It concluded that the following questions were not permitted:

— questions relating to the purpose of the action taken and the objectives pursued;
— a request for clarification on every step or concerted measure that may have been envisaged or adopted to support the price initiatives;
— a request for details of any system or method which made it possible to attribute sales targets or quotas to the participants; and
— a request for details of any method facilitating annual monitoring of compliance with any system of targets in terms of volume or quotas.

By this second group of questions, said the court, the Commission was essentially seeking an acknowledgement of Orkem's participation in an infringing agreement.

9.6.3.2 European Court of Human Rights cases

The *Orkem* principle was first called into question by the judgment of the European Court of Human Rights ("ECHR") in *Funke v. France,* in which the ECHR held that the applicant's rights had been infringed by the imposition of a penalty refusing to produce certain documents.[65]

In the light of *Funke*, it is submitted that it is no longer possible to support the ECJ's judgment in *Orkem*. If *Funke* was correctly decided, Article 6 of the European Convention on Human Rights seems to allow an undertaking under investigation by the competition authorities not only to decline to provide directly incriminating information, but also to decline to produce documents and purely factual information.

However, in its subsequent judgment in *Saunders v. UK,*[66] the ECHR distinguished between:

65. *Funke v. France* (1993) 16 EHRR 297.
66. *Saunders v. UK* (1997) 23 EHRR 313.

— material obtained through the use of compulsory powers but "having an existence independent of the will of the accused", which is not covered by the right not to incriminate oneself (this category includes documents seized under a warrant or required to be produced); and
— material obtained through methods of coercion or oppression in defiance of the will of the accused, which *is* covered by the privilege (this would include requirements both to provide explanations of documents produced[67] and to provide information).[68]

Saunders is wider than *Orkem*, in that it permits a person to decline to provide not only directly incriminating information, but also exculpatory remarks and factual information. However, it is narrower than *Funke*, in that it does not entitle a person to withhold documents.[69]

Confusingly, however, the ECHR seems to have reverted to the *Funke* position in *JB v. Switzerland*,[70] a case, like *Funke*, involving the imposition of fines by tax authorities on a taxpayer who refused to provide information on his financial affairs. The ECHR specifically distinguished the documents at issue from the material referred to in *Saunders* as having "an existence independent of the will of the accused" and therefore not obtained "by means of coercion and in defiance of the will of the accused". It held that the repeated requests for information from the tax authorities were oppressive and violated the taxpayer's right not to incriminate himself.

The extent of the right of privilege against self-incrimination following *Orkem*, *Funke* and *Saunders* is, therefore, not entirely clear. What is clear is that, as a matter of Convention law, *Orkem* is no longer good law, whether under *Funke* or *Saunders*.

However, the CFI has since upheld *Orkem*, in *PVC*[71] and again in *Mannesmannrohren-Werke*.[72]

In the latter case, the court dismissed Mannesmann's arguments based on Article 6 of the European Convention on Human Rights, with the following comment:

"As for the arguments that Article 6(1) and (2) of the Convention allow the addressee of a request for information not to reply to questions, even if purely factual, and to refuse to produce documents to the Commission, it is sufficient to note that the applicant may not rely directly on the Convention before the Community courts."

67. Regulation 17/62, Article 20(2)(e).

68. Regulation 1/2003, Article 18.

69. See the dissenting judgment of Judges Martens and Kuris in *Saunders*, inferring from the majority judgment that "contrary to *Funke*, the privilege does not comprise the power to refuse to hand over incriminating documents nor that to prevent the use of such documents, obtained under compulsion, in criminal proceedings".

70. Application No 31827/96, judgment of 3 May 2001.

71. Joined Cases T–305/94, T–306/94, T–307/94, T–313/94, T–314/94, T–315/94, T–316–94, T–318/94, T–325/94, T–328/94, T–329/94 and T–335/94, *Limburgse Vinyl Maatschappij NV and Others v. Commission* [1999] ECR II 931.

72. Case T–112/98, *Mannesmannröhren-Werke AG v. Commission* [2001] ECR II 729.

Whatever the extent of the privilege against self-incrimination, its exercise will be a matter for careful consideration. Excessive use may be counterproductive, by encouraging inspectors to pursue their investigations further, or to draw adverse inferences from documents seized—or, indeed, from the absence of documents.[73] In some situations, the optimum course of action will be to admit the infringement immediately and claim the benefit of one of the Commission's leniency programmes.

9.7 SURVIVING A DAWN RAID

The following section provides some pointers on how to react before, during and after a dawn raid or on-site investigation by the European Commission or Office of Fair Trading, summarised very briefly by the following "investigation checklist":

Do:

- seek legal advice immediately (investigators will usually be prepared to wait a short time before starting the investigation, if you do not have an in-house lawyer);
- consider whether to cooperate fully and claim leniency;
- find out the scope of the investigation from the authorisation documents and make sure that the investigators do not exceed it;
- accompany the investigators during their investigation;
- claim privilege (legal or self-incrimination) where appropriate;
- offer copying facilities;
- take notes of questions and answers;
- keep a copy and list of documents taken; and
- prepare a press response.

Don't:

- infringe the prohibitions (make sure you have a compliance programme);
- panic;
- refuse entry;
- destroy documents;
- obstruct the investigation;
- be hostile; or
- try to give an answer if you're not sure.

Note that, in many EU countries, obstructing an investigation, giving misleading information and withholding documents or information are criminal offences. In the UK, the maximum penalties are unlimited fines and/or imprisonment for up to five years for destroying documents in the context of a cartel

73. Case T–205/94, *Buchmann v. Commission* [1998] ECR II 813. The ECHR has held that Article 6(2) is not necessarily infringed where an adverse inference is drawn from the accused's failure to account for his activities: *Murray v. UK* (1996) 22 EHRR 29.

investigation. Obstructing an investigation may also lead to an increase in the level of any penalty imposed if an infringement of the competition rules is found.

9.7.1 Before the investigation

By their very nature, on-site investigations are usually unannounced and unexpected. They are not the sort of event for which you can easily prepare. However, observing a few basic housekeeping rules may limit the damage caused on the day.

- — Prevention is better than cure—implementing a competition compliance programme reduces the likelihood of infringement in the first place and may be a mitigating factor when any fines are imposed.
- — Make sure that any legal privilege is not lost (see 9.7.2.11 below) and that privileged documents are properly marked. Where possible, file privileged material separately, so as to limit as far as possible the exercise of "seize and sift" powers (see 9.7.2.8 below);
- — Designate one or more members of staff (from the legal department if possible) to act as investigation coordinators.
- — Make sure that staff (particularly receptionists) have instructions to call the investigation coordinators if investigators arrive, and that a coordinator calls outside lawyers (if required) as soon as possible.

Don't: infringe the prohibitions (make sure you have a compliance programme).

9.7.2 During the investigation

9.7.2.1 Advance notice of the investigation

In most cases, the investigators will arrive unannounced. However, Commission investigators acting under authorisation sometimes give notice, and OFT investigators carrying out an investigation without a warrant at premises of a person not suspected of an infringement must give two working days' notice.

In most cases, however, the first warning of an investigation will be when the investigators arrive at reception.

9.7.2.2 The investigators arrive

Commission and OFT investigators will be acting under one of a number of statutory provisions, including Regulation 1/2003 and, in the case of the OFT, the CA 1998 or the Enterprise Act 2002 ("EA 2002"), each of which gives them different, although broadly similar, powers. Major differences are outlined in the text below, but reference may also be made to Table 2, "Know your investigators". This section does not cover investigations by officers of the UK Serious Fraud Office ("SFO"), which also has powers to investigate suspected cartel offences: its powers are very similar to those of the OFT under the EA 2002.

Table 2: Know your investigators

Power	Summary	Type of authorisation	Trigger for investigation	Obligation to submit?	Entry by force?	Search?	Take copies?	Take originals?	Request oral explanations from:	Seize and sift?	Obligation to caution	Right to legal advice
OFT under CA 1998, section 27	OFT on-site investigation at business premises without warrant	Authorisation by OFT	There are reasonable grounds for suspecting an infringement	✓	✗	✗	✓	✗	any person on the premises	✗	✗	✗
OFT under CA 1998, section 28	OFT on-site investigation at business premises with warrant	Warrant issued by High Court judge	As section 27 and reasonable grounds for suspecting that there are on the premises documents which: ● have not been produced as required in response to a written request or under section 27; or ● could be requested in writing but would be destroyed etc; or ● could be required under section 27 but an investigator has been unable to enter.	✓	✓	✓	✓	✓	any person	✓	✗	✗
OFT under CA 1998, section 28A	OFT on-site investigation at domestic premises	Warrant issued by High Court judge	As section 27 and reasonable grounds for suspecting that there are on the premises documents which: ● have not been produced as required in response to a written request; or ● could be requested in writing but would be destroyed etc;	✓	✓	✓	✓	✓	any person	✗	✗	
OFT under CA 1998, section 62 in support of the Commission	OFT on-site investigation at business premises with warrant in support of Commission	Warrant issued by High Court judge	A High Court judge is satisfied that a Commission investigation ordered by decision under Article 20(4) of Regulation 1 is being, or is likely to be, obstructed and that the measures authorized by the warrant are neither arbitrary nor excessive	✓	✓	✓ (may use force)	✓	✗	any representative or member of staff	✗	✗	✗

9.7.2 Competition Authorities

Power	Summary	Type of authorisation	Trigger for investigation	Obligation to submit?	Entry by force?	Search?	Take copies?	Take originals?	Request oral explanations from:	Seize and sift?	Obligation to caution	Right to legal advice
OFT under CA 1998, section 62A in support of the Commission	OFT on-site investigation at non-business premises with warrant in support of Commission	Warrant issued by High Court judge	A High Court judge is satisfied that the Commission has ordered an investigation under Article 21 of Regulation 1 and that the measures authorized by the warrant are neither arbitrary nor excessive	✓	✓	✓ (may use force)	✓	✗	n/a	✗	✗	✗
OFT under CA 1998, section 62B on behalf of the Commission	OFT on-site investigation at business premises on behalf of Commission	Authorisation by OFT	Request of the Commission under Article 22(2) of Regulation 1	✗	✗	✓ only with consent	✓	✗	any representative or member of staff	✗	✗	✗
OFT under CA 1998, section 63 on behalf of the Commission	OFT on-site investigation with warrant at business premises on behalf of Commission	Warrant issued by High Court judge	A High Court judge is satisfied that an OFT investigation at the request of the Commission under Article 22(2) of Regulation 1 in connection with a Commission investigation ordered by decision under Article 20(4) of Regulation 1 is being, or is likely to be, obstructed and that the measures authorized by the warrant are neither arbitrary nor excessive	✓	✓	✓ (may use force)	✓	✗	any representative or member of staff	✗	✗	✗
OFT under CA 1998, sections 65C-65N	OFT on-site investigations on behalf of other NCAs.	Type of authorisation, trigger and powers of investigation corresponding to sections 27 to 28A described above										
OFT under EA 2002, section 193	OFT compulsory interview in cartel case	Notice in writing	Reasonable grounds for suspecting that a cartel offence has been committed	✓	n/a	n/a	✓	✗	the person producing them	n/a	✗ (will give non-statatutory caution)	✗

Power	Summary	Type of authorisation	Trigger for investigation	Obligation to submit?	Entry by force?	Search?	Take copies?	Take originals?	Request oral explanations from:	Seize and sift?	Obligation to caution	Right to legal advice
OFT under EA 2002, section 194	OFT on-site investigation into cartel offence with warrant	Warrant issued by High Court judge	Reasonable grounds for believing that there are on the premises documents which the OFT has power to require to be produced under section 193 and: • have not been produced as required in response to a request under section 193; or • it is not practicable to serve a notice to produce them; or • service of a notice might seriously prejudice the investigation	✓	✓	✓	✗	✓	any person	✓	✗	✗
OFT voluntary interview	Voluntary interview governed by PACE	Consent of interviewee	None specified	✗	n/a	n/a	n/a	n/a	n/a	n/a	✓	✓
Commission under Regulation 1, Article 20(3)	Commission on-site investigation at business premises under authorisation	Commission authorisation	None specified	✗	✗	✓ only with consent of under-taking	✓	✗	any representative or member of staff	✗	✗	✗
Commission under Regulation 1, Article 20(4)	Commission on-site investigation at business premises under decision	Commission decision	None specified	✓	✗	✓ only with consent of under-taking or support of national authority	✓	✗	any representative or member of staff	✗	✗	✗
Commission under Regulation 1, Article 21	Commission on-site investigation at non-business premises under decision	Commission decision, warrant from national court	A reasonable suspicion that relevant books or other records which may be evidence of a serious violation of Article 81 or 82 are on the premises	✓	✗	✓ only with consent of under-taking or support of national authority	✓	✗	✗	✗	✗	✗
Commission under Regulation 1, Article 19	Commission interview	Consent of interviewee	None specified	✗	n/a	n/a	n/a	n/a	n/a	n/a	✗	✗

9.7.2 Competition Authorities

The investigators will typically arrive at around 9.30am if they are acting under civil powers (Regulation 1/2003 or CA 1998) and around 6.30am under criminal powers (EA 2002). When they arrive, the investigators may ask for a named individual, or may ask to see a director or manager. They may immediately say that they are from the OFT or the Commission, and produce their warrant or authorisation, or they may wait until the arrival in reception of the person for whom they have asked before identifying themselves fully. The receptionist should immediately call the person requested.

Once the investigators have identified themselves and produced their authorisation, they must not be refused entry.

Don't: refuse entry.

At the same time, the receptionist should call the investigations coordinator. The investigators will be anxious not to allow any opportunity for documents to be destroyed, and may wish to seal rooms or filing cabinets, and restrict phone calls made or e-mails sent at this stage. If the investigators are from the OFT and have a warrant, they are entitled to do so (or to take other similar steps) if it appears necessary to prevent documents being destroyed. The solution may be to offer to allow one of them to accompany a messenger sent to the coordinator (provided that the coordinator is on-site), so that they can see for themselves that no steps are taken to frustrate the investigation. Under Regulation 1/2003, Commission investigators have the power to seal the premises or business records during an investigation.

Immediately on being informed that investigators have arrived, the coordinator should ask the company's lawyer to come as quickly as possible, and should make any necessary local travel arrangements. It is also vital to consider as early as possible whether to claim leniency and to blow the whistle on any infringement that may have occurred. It may also be necessary to consider whether individuals within the organisation will need separate legal representation, if they have been involved in cartel activities possibly amounting to the UK criminal offence.

Do: seek legal advice immediately.

9.7.2.3 Checking the authorisation

The investigators will now produce their authorisation or warrant, which will set out the purpose and subject of the investigation. It is vital to examine this document very carefully to check that it is in order, and to ascertain the scope of the investigators' powers—see Table 2, "Know your investigators" at 9.7.2.2 above. Although the investigation is limited to what is set out in the authorisation, the investigators have a wide discretion to determine what is relevant to that investigation. The investigators will usually also produce an explanatory note that outlines the rights and duties of the undertaking under investigation and the penalties for non-cooperation. You will probably be asked to acknowledge receipt of the authorisation document. This does not amount to an admission of an infringement and does not prevent you from challenging the scope or the conduct of the investigation in due course. A warrant may impose additional safeguards considered necessary by the judge.

OFT investigators acting under a warrant to investigate suspected infringements of Article 81 or 82 or the Chapter I or Chapter II prohibition of the CA 1998, or investigating a suspected cartel offence under the EA 2002, have the power to use "such force as is reasonably necessary" to enter the premises. This probably means not only entering the front door, but also any internal doors within the premises. "Using force" in this context ranges from breaking a door down to opening a locked door with the key. However, there is no power to use force to conduct the search. So the investigators may not break open locked filing cabinets or desks (although to refuse to open them would be obstruction). They will not use force against persons. In contrast, where they are acting under a warrant in support of the Commission, OFT investigators may use "such force as is reasonably necessary" to search as well as to enter, and may therefore also break open locked briefcases and filing cabinets. Commission investigators acting unsupported by the OFT may not use force at all.

Do: find out the scope of the investigation from the authorisation documents and make sure that the investigators do not exceed it.

9.7.2.4 Waiting for lawyers

The investigators will want to start as soon as possible. Do not try to delay them, for example by offering to show them round the premises. There is no right to postpone the start of the investigation or to refuse entry merely because a particular person is out of the office or unavailable. Nor, it seems, is there an absolute right to legal advice before submitting to an investigation. However, as a matter of practice, investigators will often be prepared to wait for an hour or so to allow a lawyer to arrive before starting. They may wish to impose conditions (such as sealing particular offices or filing cabinets) to prevent interference with potential evidence while they wait. OFT investigators investigating a suspected cartel offence will not wait for legal advisers to arrive, unless they are proposing to take evidence for examination away from the premises using their "seize and sift" powers (see 9.7.2.8 below).

Your lawyer will probably want to speak to the investigators while in transit. He or she will ascertain the type and subject of the investigation and check that it appears to be in order, and will advise you what to do if the investigators are not prepared to wait until his or her arrival. You or your lawyer should seek to agree with the investigators that, as far as possible, requests for oral explanations of documents (see 9.7.2.10 below) and questions of privilege (see 9.7.2.11 below) will not be dealt with until the lawyer arrives.

9.7.2.5 Logistics

The investigators have a job to do. They will probably be with you for at least a day. There is no need either to try to make friends with them or to be discourteous. Offer them refreshments during the day. Remember that it is their investigation; you do not have the right to tell them how to conduct it, although you should check that they stay within their powers and you should challenge and note any irregularity.

Don't: be hostile.

The investigation (and your task of keeping track of what is being inspected) will be made easier if the investigators are given an office to act as their base for the day. It should be a room with ready access to a photocopier.

Do: offer copying facilities.

However, you should not expect to be able to keep the investigators shut in their room and merely pass them documents. They are entitled to be shown particular offices and the contents of relevant filing cabinets. OFT investigators with a warrant can take a more active role and can search for evidence. A coordinator should accompany them throughout. The coordinator should also have access to members of staff with shorthand skills to take verbatim notes of the proceedings, and others able to operate a photocopier and organise and list documents reliably.

Do: accompany the investigators during their investigation.

9.7.2.6 Duty to cooperate

While the investigators are on-site, you must not sit back and let them get on with it, but must cooperate (and you should keep a close eye on their activities anyway). You will be expected to open filing cabinets and desk drawers for them, even if they have the power to search (in the case of OFT investigators with a warrant). If they do not have the power to search, you will similarly be expected to point them to the documents of the type requested, and show them the contents of filing cabinets. If you are not sure what they want, or there are large numbers of documents fitting the description they have given, say so.

Don't: obstruct the investigation.

9.7.2.7 Information held on computers

The investigators have the power to require the production of information held on computers or accessible from the premises. They will usually ask for relevant information to be printed out in hardcopy form. Investigators sometimes bring or use computer software to search for particular words. This should be permitted.

Where other information is recorded in illegible form, the investigators can require a legible copy. This allows them, for example, to obtain printouts of fax transmission reports and telephone records and to require a transcription of tape recordings.

9.7.2.8 "Seize and sift" powers

OFT investigators investigating suspected infringements of UK or EU rules, or under the EA 2002, have the power to take away evidence in order to determine off-site whether it is relevant, if it is not practicable to do so on the premises. This is most likely to be the case where it would take too long to sort and review the evidence on-site. This gives them the right to take away legally privileged material contained within computer systems and other records (although they must return it as soon as they realise that it is privileged). In order to minimise this risk, you should ensure that the process of separating relevant material from irrelevant and privileged material is accomplished as quickly and easily as possible. This might involve holding legally privileged material in separate clearly marked files or computer folders.

The investigators may be prepared for your legal advisers to arrive before taking away evidence in this way. They should also subsequently give you and/ or your advisers the opportunity to be present when they sift the evidence for relevant information.

9.7.2.9 Copying documents

The investigators will want to take away copies of relevant documents, or to produce a computer "image" of relevant files or (if they are OFT investigators exercising their "seize and sift" powers) of the whole or part of specific disks or drives. OFT investigators with a warrant under the CA 1998 have the right to take originals away with them if necessary to preserve them and if they cannot take copies. OFT investigators acting under the criminal cartel powers will usually seek to take originals, as the best evidence. If they propose to take copies, they may wish to do so themselves, or they may be prepared to allow you to do so. Either way, you should ensure that you have your own copy of every document taken or copied. The ideal solution is for three copies of each document to be taken at the same time, numbered for ease of reference and listed on an inventory. One is for the investigators, one for you, and one for your lawyers.

Do: keep a copy and list of documents taken.

9.7.2.10 Oral explanations and interviews

In most cases, the investigators have the right to ask for oral explanations of documents. If you are unable to produce a document, you may be required to state where it may be found. Where possible, you should ensure that answers are given by the coordinator or senior staff. However, you do not necessarily have the right to restrict who can give these explanations—the investigators may want (and are entitled) to ask for explanations from junior employees. You should ensure that the coordinator and/or a member of the legal team is present. Investigators may also ask for explanations of relevant facts. The employee should also be advised not to answer incriminating questions where this privilege is available (see 9.7.2.11 below). The investigators may give some sort of caution, depending on the type of investigation. They must make it clear whether the interviewee is legally required to answer, and the extent to which answers can be used as evidence.

The OFT will not normally conduct compulsory interviews during the course of a search—it is more likely to make an appointment for a later date. However, if it does decide to conduct a formal interview, you are entitled to have a legal adviser present. Similarly, if a person admits involvement in a cartel, or indicates that he wishes to provide information, he will be cautioned and informed of his right to legal advice.

Do: claim privilege against self-incrimination where appropriate.

You should ensure that a detailed note is taken of the questions and answers.

Do: take notes of questions and answers.

The employee concerned should also be told that he or she should not answer a question if he or she is not sure of the answer. You can always offer to come back later with the answer.

Don't: try to give an answer if you're not sure.

9.7.2.11 Privilege

Businesses under investigation enjoy the protection of two types of privilege: legal professional privilege and privilege against self-incrimination.

Legal professional privilege protects *bona fide* advice from a legal adviser and material prepared for the purpose of pending or contemplated litigation. In investigations under the Chapter I and Chapter II prohibitions of the CA 1998, it applies to advice from in-house lawyers as well as external lawyers. In investigations under EU competition law, it applies only to advice from external lawyers qualified to practise in the EU (and not in-house lawyers, non-EU lawyers or accountants). On a number of occasions the Commission has even used advice from in-house lawyers as evidence of an infringement. However, advice from in-house lawyers that merely repeats advice from an external lawyer is privileged. Because the same agreement or conduct can often be investigated under both the CA 1998 and EU law, it can be risky for UK businesses to rely on the wider scope of privilege under the CA 1998.

If you think that a document is privileged, then you should show the investigators enough (for example a "privileged and confidential" heading, the letterhead of a lawyer, or the first few lines of the letter) to allow them to confirm it for themselves. They will of course usually wish to see more! If possible, privilege disputes should be left until your lawyer is present.

If EU investigators do not accept your claim, you should withhold the document and then challenge the Decision ordering production before the CFI. In the case of OFT investigators, you should similarly withhold the document and apply for judicial review. It may be possible to agree with the investigators that an independent third party will determine whether or not a document is privileged. If OFT investigators are exercising their "seize and sift" powers (see 9.7.2.8 above), they may be entitled to take away privileged information, to the extent that it is included in other material and it is not practicable to separate it out before taking it away. It is therefore up to you to seek to identify any privileged information as quickly as possible.

The privilege against self-incrimination is the right not to be required to incriminate oneself by one's testimony. Under the current case law of the ECJ, investigators may ask purely factual questions, such as "who are the persons referred to in the minutes of this meeting?", but not incriminating questions, such as "did you agree to fix prices at that meeting?". As a guideline, Table 3 sets out questions that the ECJ and CFI have ruled[74] to be permitted and not permitted as self-incriminating.

The privilege may in fact be considerably wider than this (possibly extending as far entitling you not to provide even factual answers), in the light of case law of the ECHR. However, before seeking to argue this, careful legal advice and tactical consideration would be required.

Do: claim privilege (legal or self-incrimination) where appropriate.

74. In Case 374/87, *Orkem v. Commission* [1989] ECR 3283 and Case T–112/98, *Mannesmannröhren-Werke AG v. Commission* [2001] ECR II 729.

9.7.2 Competition Authorities

Table 3: The Orkem and Mannesmannröhren-Werke questions

Question	Permitted (✓) or not (✗)
Factual questions relating to the circumstances in which meetings were held and the capacity in which the participants attended them	✓
A requirement to disclose documents relating to those meetings	✓
Questions relating to the subject-matter and implementation of measures taken in order to determine and maintain a satisfactory price level	✓
Dates, places and names of participants in the meetings	✓
Names of the company's participants and copies of the travel documents	✓
Copies of invitations, agendas, minutes, internal memoranda, records and other documents relating to the meetings	✓
In the case of meetings for which no documents can be found, the purpose of the meeting, the decisions adopted and the type of documents received before and after the meeting	✓
Questions relating to the purpose of the action taken and the objectives pursued	✗
A request for clarification on every step or concerted measure that may have been envisaged or adopted to support the price initiatives	✗
A request for details of any system or method that made it possible to attribute sales targets or quotas to the participants	✗
A request for details of any method facilitating annual monitoring of compliance with any system of targets in terms of volume or quotas	✗
What the relationship is between certain agreements and the meetings concerned	✗
To what extent the agreements influenced the decisions adopted at the meetings	✗
To what extent the decisions adopted at the meeting influenced the implementation of the agreements	✗

However, it is important to note that where OFT investigators are exercising their criminal powers of investigation under the EA 2002, the privilege against self-incrimination may not be claimed. The investigators may compel explanations of documents or answers to other questions, even where that would be directly incriminating. The only consolation is that this information may not be used as evidence in a criminal prosecution, and will not be used in CA 1998 against the interviewee's employer.

9.7.3 After the investigation

9.7.3.1 Check information

Before the investigators leave, you should make sure that you have:

- copies of all documents produced by the investigators to authorise the investigation;
- a bundle of copy documents identical to those taken by the investigators, together with a copy of any list or inventory;
- a signed copy of the investigators' official note of any oral explanations given, together with your own notes; and
- notes of any claims of privilege.

9.7.3.2 Post-mortem

Once the investigators have left, you and your lawyers should review the information taken and consider how best to proceed—whether to write to present your arguments, whether to supplement or correct any explanations given or information provided, or whether to offer full cooperation in the hope of qualifying for a reduction in any penalty if the strength of the evidence against you warrants it. You should also consider whether to modify your business conduct. Continuing with an infringement after an investigation has been started is grounds for a significant increase in any penalty.

9.7.3.3 Confidential information

If the OFT or Commission subsequently gives access to the file as part of an infringement procedure, it will withhold business secrets (as well as internal and other confidential information). The authorities will write shortly after conducting an investigation to ask you to identify business secrets contained in the documents taken. You may wish to start work on identifying this information immediately, and preparing non-confidential versions of confidential documents.

9.7.3.4 Managing PR and stock exchange announcements

It is also likely that news of the investigation will find its way to the press. You should work with your PR department and/or advisers to prepare a suitable response. You may also need to consider, with your brokers and lawyers, making a stock exchange announcement.

9.8 EXCHANGES OF INFORMATION AND CONFIDENTIALITY

9.8.1 Exchanges of information within the ECN[75]

8.1.1 Introduction

In order for the modernised regime to work as intended, the authorities need to be able to exchange information with each other: the Commission describes it as "a precondition for efficient and effective allocation and handling of cases".[76] A case may be transferred from one authority to one that is better placed to handle it, requiring transmission to the second authority of evidence gathered by the first. Authorities acting in parallel will need to exchange information. One authority may ask others to investigate on its behalf, and will then wish to use as evidence the information that they produce.

Regulation 1/2003 therefore provides for the exchange of information between authorities, and sets out the circumstances in which that information may be used. As in many other areas of EU competition procedure and enforcement, the Regulation is accompanied by a series of non-statutory Notices. Of particular relevance to the subject of information exchanges is the Commission's Notice on cooperation within the Network of Competition Authorities. Regrettably, however, it perpetuates the tendency of Commission Notices not merely to shed light on the relevant legislation, but also to legislate in their own right. Indeed, on one important issue—the treatment of information contained in leniency applications—the Notice contradicts the Regulation, as explained in greater detail at 9.8.1.9 below.

9.8.1.2 Transmission of information on case allocation and other procedural landmarks

Article 11(2) of Regulation 1/2003 requires the Commission to transmit to the NCAs copies of the most important documents it has collected with a view to making a substantive Decision.

At the request of an NCA, the Commission must also provide it with copies of other existing documents necessary for the assessment of the case. There is no indication of what constitutes a "most important document", what constitutes an "other document" and what documents are "necessary" for the assessment of the case.

Article 11(3) requires NCAs to inform the Commission before, or without delay after, commencing the first formal investigative measure. They *may* also

75. This section is based on the author's article "Transfer of information between authorities in the modernised network" published at [2003] *Competition Law* 1.

76. Notice, n 7 above, at para 26.

inform other NCAs. In practice, information and comments are circulated systematically to all NCAs, as well as to the Commission, by means of a secure extranet.[77]

NCAs must also inform the Commission of their intention at least 30 days before making an infringement decision or a decision withdrawing the benefit of a block exemption, and must provide the Commission with a summary of the case and the proposed decision or the course of action proposed. The NCA must also provide to the Commission copies of relevant documents.

There is no express right to appeal against a Decision by the Commission to disclose or not to disclose a specific document or piece of information. However, an appeal may be possible to the extent that the Decision is capable of affecting the substantive interests of the undertaking concerned.[78]

9.8.1.3 Transmission of information for use as evidence

Whereas Article 11 deals with the exchange of information for the purposes of facilitating case allocation and ensuring consistency as between members of the network, Article 12 deals with the evidential use that may be made of information exchanged. It seems likely that Article 12 will apply equally to information exchanged under Article 11.

9.8.1.4 Types of information exchanged

All documents and other evidence collected by one NCA (or the Commission) may be transmitted to another NCA and used by the recipient as evidence in an infringement Decision under Article 81 or Article 82.

This may include information that the recipient would not have been able to collect itself—for example because it would be privileged under the law of the Member State of the receiving authority. The OFT would therefore be entitled to use as evidence an e-mail from an in-house lawyer, discovered and transmitted to it by the Commission, advising that the conduct concerned is likely to be an abuse of Article 82. Article 12 overrides any conflicting provision of UK law.[79] The Commission confirms this view in its Notice: "the question whether information was gathered in a legal manner by the transmitting authority is governed on the basis of the law applicable to this authority."[80]

Regulation 1/2003 therefore applies a standard based on the lowest common denominator. This is a concern where levels of protection differ significantly between Member States.

77. See the Notice, n 7 above, and the Joint Statement, n 9 above, at para 10.

78. Case 60/81, *IBM v. Commission* [1981] ECR 2639. See also the Order of the President of the CFI in Case T–213/01R, *Österreichische Postsparkasse v. Commission*, 20 December 2001 2001 ECR II-3963 (decision to disclose a copy of the statement of objections).

79. The statement to that effect at para 27 of the Notice, n 7 above, merely reflects the position under Community law.

80. *Ibid.*

9.8.1.5 Use in EU law enforcement only

Both Article 12(1) and 12(2) make it clear that information exchanged under Article 12 may be used for the purposes of applying Articles 81 and 82 only. It may be used only in respect of the subject-matter for which it was collected —in other words, information collected during the course of an investigation into product A may not be used as evidence in proceedings relating to product B.[81]

9.8.1.6 Use in parallel national proceedings

The Commission can of course only apply the EU rules. In contrast, the NCAs will also continue to apply their respective national rules. This adds another dimension to the restrictions on the use of information under Article 12. Article 12 sets out the general rule that, for example, information disclosed to the OFT by the Commission or another NCA under Article 12 may not be used for the purposes of proceedings under the UK competition rules. However, information disclosed to an NCA under Article 12 may be used for the purposes of applying national competition law in the same case in parallel to EU competition law, and provided that it does not lead to a different outcome.

It is likely, for example, that the OFT will be able to use information received from the Commission or another NCA as evidence in proceedings under the Chapter I or Chapter II prohibition of the CA 1998 conducted at the same time as, and in relation to the same undertaking or undertakings as, proceedings under Article 81 or 82. Because the Chapter I and Chapter II prohibitions are based on Articles 81 and 82 and applied in a manner consistent with EU case law, the outcome will rarely differ according to which of these sets of rules the OFT applies.[82]

9.8.1.7 Use of transferred information as "intelligence"

Where the application of Article 12 means that exchanged information cannot be used as evidence, the information does not become entirely worthless. It still has value as intelligence.[83] An NCA receiving from another NCA information that it may not use as evidence may nevertheless use that information in order to launch its own investigation under its own rules.

9.8.1.8 Use of information against individuals

A further exception to the principle of general disclosure in Article 12(1) is found in Article 12(3). This limits the use of disclosed information as evidence

81. As will be seen at 9.8.1.7 below, however, information disclosed in one context may be used as the basis for the launch of an investigation for other purposes under the *Spanish Banks* principle.

82. In contrast, it is unlikely that a criminal prosecution for the cartel offence under EA 2002 would satisfy the Article 12(2) criteria.

83. See, for the underlying principle, *Spanish Banks*: Case C–67/91, *Dirección General de la Defensa de la Competencia v. Asociación Española de Banca Privada* [1992] ECR I 4785.

that may lead to the imposition of sanctions on individuals. Information exchanged under Article 12(1) may be used as the basis for sanctions on individuals only where the law of the transmitting authority also provides for such sanctions for infringement of Article 81 or Article 82. If there is no such consistency, the information may be used only if it has been collected by the transmitting authority in a way that provides the same level of protection of the rights of the individual as that offered by the rules of the receiving authority, although in such cases the receiving authority may not use the information to impose a custodial sentence.

9.8.1.9 Information provided in leniency applications

The Commission and a number of Member States offer either immunity from penalty or a significant reduction in penalty to undertakings that volunteer information on a cartel in accordance with certain conditions.[84]

Paragraph 39 of the Notice creates a very significant exeption to the general rule in Article 12. It explains that information on leniency applications will not be used by other members of the ECN as the basis for starting an investigation, either under national or EU rules. In other words, the NCAs will not rely on their right under *Spanish Banks*.[85] That does not prevent other members of the ECN from opening an investigation into the same alleged cartel on the basis of other information.

Information supplied under a leniency application will be transmitted to other members of the ECN only with the consent of the applicant. Furthermore, information obtained during an investigation that "could not have been carried out except as a result of the leniency application" (ie where the competition authority concerned was unaware of the existence of the cartel before the leniency application) cannot be transmitted to other members of the ECN without the consent of the leniency applicant.[86] Applicants will be "encouraged" to give such consent. It is possible that such encouragement could include treating consent to disclosure as a condition for the grant of leniency.

Paragraph 42 of the Notice states that information relating to cases initiated as a result of a leniency application submitted to the Commission under Article 11(3) of Regulation 1/2003 will be made available only to those NCAs that have committed themselves to respecting the principles set out in the Notice. The commitment is in the form of a statement annexed to the Notice, and will be signed by the NCAs. This is almost certainly sufficient to give rise to a legitimate expectation on the part of undertakings.

84. See http://europa.eu.int/comm/competition/antitrust/legislation/authorities_with_leniency_programme.pdf.
85. See n 83 above.
86. Notice, n 7 above, para 40.

9.8.1.10 Leniency information and consent

Consent to the transmission of leniency information to another authority is not required where:

— the receiving authority has received a leniency application relating to the same infringement from the same applicant, provided that at the time of transmission of the information it was not open to the applicant to withdraw the application to the receiving authority;

— the receiving authority has given a written undertaking that neither the information transmitted to it, nor any information obtained subsequently, will be used by the receiving authority or any other authority to which the information is subsequently transmitted, to impose sanctions on the leniency applicant, any other person covered by the leniency application or any employee or former employee of the applicant or of any other person covered by the application (the leniency applicant will receive a copy of the receiving authority's written undertaking); or

— another member of the ECN carries out an investigation on behalf of the member of the ECN to which the leniency application was submitted; the transmission by the other member of information to the first member does not require the consent of the leniency applicant.

9.8.2 Confidentiality

A fundamental principle is that no infringement may be founded on any document to which the defendant has not had access.[87] This presents the Commission and the OFT with a dilemma, particularly in multi-defendant cartel cases where they wish to rely on a document containing business secrets of one undertaking as evidence against another. However, there are some differences between the position of the Commission and that of the OFT.

Article 28(1) of Regulation 1/2003 provides that, without prejudice to the arrangements for information exchange between member of the ECN, information collected by the Commission and the NCAs may be used only for the purpose for which it was acquired. Article 28(2) provides that, subject to the provisions of Regulation 1/2003 relating to exchanges of information within the ECN and with national courts, and to hearings, the Commission, NCAs and other public authorities and their staff may not disclose confidential business information acquired by them under Regulation 1/2003. This will include most information obtained in competition proceedings. In *Akzo*,[88] the ECJ underlined the "very special protection" afforded to business secrets[89]

87. Case 107/82, *AEG v. Commission* [1983] ECR 3151.

88. Case 53/85, *Akzo Chemie v. Commission* [1986] ECR 1965.

89. Of which it provided a rather circular definition in Case T–353/94, *Postbank v. Commission* [1996] ECR II 921.

and required the Commission to put in place a procedure to give undertakings whose business secrets it proposed to disclose the opportunity to bring a challenge prior to disclosure. Business secrets could never be disclosed to complainants. The Commission's Decision on the terms of reference of hearing officers in certain competition proceedings,[90] codifies this procedure, providing for the Commission to issue a Decision (which may be appealed) if it proposes to disclose business secrets.

Even after the entry into force of Regulation 1/2003, it seems likely that not all information provided to the Commission need be disclosed to the national competition authorities. In *SEP*,[91] the ECJ held that the CFI had been wrong to conclude that the predecessor to Article 28 (Article 20 of Regulation 17/62) necessarily provided sufficient protection against the use of confidential information by national authorities. Article 20 would not avert the irreversible consequences of a national authority that ultimately directed the commercial policy of SEP's main competitor becoming aware of the terms of business accorded to SEP. In such situations, if an undertaking specifically raised the confidential nature of a document, the Commission should follow the *Akzo* procedure of adopting a Decision capable of challenge before the CFI, if it proposed to disclose the documents to a national authority.[92]

This principle is less likely to apply to the use of information by a national authority for the purposes of launching an investigation under national competition law.

9.8.3 EU/US agreement

In 1991, the EU and the US entered into an agreement regarding the application of their competition rules. This provided for the exchange of information between the respective competition authorities. In a subsequent exchange of interpretative letters, the Commission indicated that it could not transmit to the US authorities any information covered by Article 20 of Regulation 17/62 (and now Article 28 of Regulation 1/2003) other than with the consent the undertaking concerned. Although undertakings often give consent for these purposes in order to facilitate transatlantic cooperation (and thereby to speed up clearance) in merger cases, they are less likely to do so in cartel and dominance cases. Information provided to the Commission will therefore not automatically find its way to Washington and form the basis of a criminal prosecution.

Nevertheless, responses to Article 18 letters issued by the Commission may need to be disclosed in US civil proceedings and therefore additional caution may be required in formulating replies to such requests.

90. 2001 OJ L 162, p 21.
91. Case C–36/92, *SEP NV v. Commission* [1994] ECR I 1911.
92. Case 53/85, *Akzo Chemie v. Commission* [1986] ECR 1965.

9.9 FORMAL PROCEEDINGS

Once the Commission has carried out an investigation, and if it proposes to issue a Decision finding that there has been an infringement of the competition rules, it must take a number of formal steps intended to guarantee the rights of the defence, namely:

- — issue a document known as Statement of Objections ("SO"), which sets out its case against the undertaking;
- — give access to its file; and
- — give the undertaking concerned the opportunity to put its case in writing and orally.

The importance of these procedures may be more modest under the CA 1998 than under EU law, because the Competition Appeal Tribunal ("CAT") has the power to review the OFT's Decision in its entirety, and will not be limited, as the CFI is, to a review of the legality of the decision (see 9.11.1 below). Nevertheless, it offers an important opportunity for the parties to ensure that the OFT has taken their views into account.

9.9.1 Statement of objections

Under EU competition law, the purpose of the SO is to give the undertaking concerned all the information necessary to enable it to defend itself properly before the Commission adopts a final Decision.[93] It is a document of vital importance.

The Commission may not include in its final Decision matters in respect of which the undertaking concerned has not been given the opportunity to comment in the SO. The SO must set out the facts, the conclusions the Commission draws from them, a legal assessment, and what the Commission proposes to do. Where the Commission proposes to impose a fine, the SO must set out the duration of the infringement. The Commission need not set out the criteria on which it proposes to calculate the fine, nor the amount of the fine. It is sufficient if it indicates that it is proposing a fine, and gives the main criteria affecting the level of the fine. The SO should also explain how the Commission proposes to apply the principles set out in its fining Guidelines.[94]

Where there are several parties, the Commission may deal with all of them in the same SO, or in individual statements, provided that the case against each party is set out clearly.[95]

93. *Wood Pulp II*: Cases C–89, C–104, C–114, C–116, C–117 and C–125–129/85, *Åhlstrom and Others v. Commission (Re Woodpulp)* [1993] ECR I 1307.
94. See 9.10.4.1 below.
95. Cases T–25, T–26, T–30–32, T–34–39, T–42–46, T–48, T–50–65, T–68–71, T–87, T–88, T–103 and T–104/95, *Cimenteries CBR and Others v. Commission* [2000] ECR II 491.

The Commission must provide a non-confidential version of the statement of objections to any complainant.[96]

Procedure introduced under the CA 1998 largely reflects the procedure developed by the Commission in the light of ECJ and CFI case law, but is set out in rather more detail.

9.9.2 Response to the SO

The undertaking concerned may respond in writing to the SO. In the case of an SO issued by the Commission, it has two months in which to respond, or three in complex cases, although this period may be extended by up to a further month during holiday periods. The OFT generally allows a rather shorter period for responding.

The main thrust of the response to the SO will be in writing, whereby detailed arguments of facts and law can be presented more effectively. The undertaking concerned will wish to refute, as far as possible, the competition authority's findings of fact, the conclusions it has drawn from them and its legal and economic analysis.

9.9.3 Access to the file

Article 27 gives a right of access to the Commission's file, subject to the legitimate interest of undertakings in the protection of their business secrets. The right of access to the file does not extend to confidential information and internal documents of the Commission or the NCAs. In particular, the right of access does not extend to correspondence between the Commission and the NCAs or between NCAs, including documents drawn up pursuant to Articles 11 and 14.

However, it is also clear that failure to give full access to the file will not automatically entail annulment of the Commission's Decision. The mere possibility that there might have been some document on the file that would have exonerated the undertaking concerned will not suffice. In the *Cement* cases, the CFI held that the correct procedure in such cases is for it to examine such documents. If they are unrelated to the case set out against the applicant in the Commission's Decision, the applicant's claim will be rejected. If, on the other hand, there is a link between the document and one of the objections in the Commission's Decision, and the CFI considers that, in the light of the evidence, the document would have had even a small chance of altering the outcome of the procedure if the applicant had been able to rely on it, it will find that the rights of the defence have been infringed.[97]

96. Regulation 773/2004, Article 6.
97. *Cimenteries CBR and Others v. Commission*, n 95 above.

9.9.3 Competition Authorities

In 1997, the Commission issued a notice explaining how it applies its internal rules for file access.[98]

Disputes as to file access are referred to a senior official of the competition authority concerned.

9.9.4 Oral hearing

In Commission infringement proceedings, Regulation 773/2004,[99] gives the prospective addressee of an infringement Decision the right to an oral hearing in addition to its right to respond in writing to the SO.[100] The oral hearing is an opportunity for the parties to present their case to the Commission, although it is advisable not to leave it until this late stage before starting to do so. It is a formal stage of the procedure, conducted by the hearing officer, a senior officer of the Directorate-General for Competition. The oral hearing is not public, but is attended by the parties and interested third parties such as complainants. There is provision for confidential treatment of business secrets at the oral hearing.[101] The Commission may give complainants and other third parties the opportunity to make oral representations if requested. The Commission must prepare a tape recording of the oral hearing, which it provides to the participants.

The Commission's Decision on the terms of reference of hearing officers provides for the hearing officer's report to be made available to the parties and to be published. This is intended to reinforce the value of the oral hearing.

The right to make oral representations under the CA 1998 is more limited. Rule 5(4) of the OFT's Rules provides that the recipient of a statement of objections will be given a reasonable opportunity to make oral representations on the information set out in the statement of objections.

9.10 OUTCOMES

9.10.1 Interim measures

A competition investigation may take a number of years to complete. During that time, the complainant may have suffered significant damage. In 1980, the ECJ ruled in the leading *Camera Care* case[102] that the Commission has the right to order interim measures to preserve the *status quo* pending its investigation, and this has now been codified in Regulation 1/2003. The CA 1998 sets out this right expressly, in section 35.

The conditions for the order of interim measures by the Commission are that:

98. 1997 OJ C 23, p 3.
99. 1998 OJ L 354, p 18.
100. Regulation 773/2004, Article 12.
101. Regulation 773/2004, Article 14.
102. Case 729/79R, *Camera Care Ltd v. Commission* [1980] ECR 119.

— it is likely (there is a *prima facie* case) that there is an infringement of Article 81 or 82;
— relief is required urgently; and
— there is a risk of serious and irreparable damage to competition;

Interim measures will apply for a specified time and may be renewed.[103]

Failure to comply with an interim measures Decision may give rise to a fine of up to 10 per cent of turnover, ie the same level as a fine associated with a definitive Decision.

The conditions for the order of interim measures by the OFT are broadly the same, except that a "reasonable suspicion" of an infringement, rather than a *prima facie* case, will suffice. The threshold under the CA 1998 therefore appears to be rather lower than under EU competition rules.[104]

Interim measures have been ordered in a number of cases since *Camera Care*. In contrast, in *Sea Containers/Stena Sealink*[105] the Commission published an interesting Decision refusing interim measures and setting out the reasons (chiefly that the complainant had accepted terms offered by Stena Sealink and was therefore no longer in a position to show that it would suffer serious and irreparable damage).

In *Camera Care*, the ECJ pointed out that the Commission must still have regard to the legitimate interests of the undertaking against which it proposes to order interim measures. It must therefore give the undertaking a hearing, albeit abbreviated. It must also issue a Decision capable of review before the CFI. Similarly, under the CA 1998, the intended addressee of an interim measures order receives an SO, is given access to the file, and may make oral representations. In its first such case, *Robert Wiseman Dairies plc*, the OFT announced on 25 June 2001 that it proposed to order interim measures and had taken these procedural steps (although it did not subsequently issue a definitive Decision in the case).[106]

Even though interim measures are intended to provide a quick remedy, they can still take a couple of months to order. In cases of greater urgency, the courts may offer a quicker remedy (see Chapter 10).

Failure to comply with an interim measures order is likely to result in an increase in any fine imposed in a definitive Decision.

9.10.2 Commitments (undertakings)

In many cases, the Commission terminates an investigation by accepting undertakings (generally known as "commitments" under the EU rules

103. Regulation 1/2003, Article 9(2).

104. The threshold for ordering interim measures is comparable with the threshold for starting an investigation under s 25. "A reasonable suspicion" arises more readily than a *prima facie* case (cf *Shaabin bin Hussein v. Chang Fook Kam* [1969] 3 All ER 1626).

105. 1994 OJ L 15, p 8.

106. The complainant has since appealed against the OFT's decision not to pursue the case: *Claymore v. OFT* [2003] CAT 3.

because of the existing meaning of the word "undertaking") from the alleged offender.[107] From the point of view of the Commission, such commitments can result in a quicker settlement and reduce the risk of a challenge by the alleged offender, and have no disadvantages where the Commission is not proposing to impose a fine. From the point of view of the alleged offender, making a commitment is likely to result in less adverse publicity, no fine and no formal decision that a complainant could then take to the national courts and use as the basis for a damages claim.

Commitments may also be given in the context of infringement decisions. Where an infringement Decision is appealed to the CFI, the court may also review associated commitments. In *Wood Pulp II*,[108] the Commission's argument that such commitments were unilateral acts, not capable of appeal, was rejected.

Under Regulation 1, the Commission now has the power to make commitments binding as part of its Decision. The Commission may subsequently re-open the case if:

- — there has been a material change in the facts on which the Decision was based;
- — there has been a breach of the commitment; or
- — the Decision was based on incomplete, incorrect or misleading information.

The Commission may impose a fine of up to 10 per cent of annual group turnover for breach of a binding commitment.

9.10.3 Decisions

In the minority of the cases before it, the Commission issues a final Decision. The elimination in Regulation 1/2003 of notifications for exemption will significantly reduce the number of non-infringement Decisions issued. However, the Commission will still be able to issue non-infringement Decisions where it is in the Community public interest to do so. The basis for such Decisions may be either that the agreement or conduct falls outside the Article 81(1) prohibition altogether, or because the conditions of Article 81(3) are satisfied. Most formal Decisions will be infringement Decisions, which may require termination of the infringement and may impose proportionate behavioural remedies or, where behavioural remedies would not be as effective or would be more onerous for the undertaking, structural remedies.

Infringement Decisions typically contain a statement of the background, the facts, a legal analysis and the Commission's conclusions. A Commission

107. A published example is *IBM*, 1984 OJ L 118, p 24; an unpublished commitment was given in *Digital*, Commission Press Release IP/97/868. See also the commentary on *Digital* in the Commission's *Competition Policy Newsletter*, No 1, 1998, at p 26.

108. *Åhlstrom and Others v. Commission (Re Woodpulp)*, n 93 above.

Decision must be adequately reasoned (so that the addressee can understand and, if necessary, challenge the basis on which it was adopted).

9.10.4 Fines and penalties

The headline enforcement weapon of both the Commission and the OFT is their power to impose heavy fines (under the CA 1998, they are referred to as "penalties") for negligent or intentional infringement.[109] In the case of the Commission, the maximum fine is 10 per cent of one year's worldwide group turnover. The largest fine to date was a fine of €497 million imposed on Microsoft for its bundling of Media Player with its Windows operating system and its refusal to disclose interface information to competing manufacturers of server operating systems.

The UK maximum penalty is now also 10 per cent of worldwide turnover.[110] The OFT has so far imposed few penalties under the CA 1998: the highest was a penalty of £17.28 million imposed on Argos in February 2003, for its participation in an alleged agreement to fix the resale prices of Hasbro products.[111]

The fine must be proportionate to both the relevant turnover (ie the turnover of the undertaking derived from the product to which the infringement relates) and the total turnover (ie the turnover for all products).[112]

9.10.4.1 Guidelines on the calculation of fines

The Commission and the OFT have published Guidelines on the method of calculating fines, the Commission in 1997[113] and the OFT in 2000.[114] The intention was to increase transparency, in the hope of reversing the trend of an almost automatic reduction of fines by the CFI on appeal. The Commission's policy seems to have been reasonably successful.

The approach followed in both sets of Guidelines involves calculating the basic amount of the fine according to gravity and duration, and then applying various adjustments (see Table 4). The calculation is done separately for each undertaking, to produce an individual figure. This can result in a wide range of fines in a single case, as can be seen from the *Pre-insulated Pipe Cartel* case, illustrated in Table 5.

109. Regulation 1/2003, Article 23(2); CA 1998, s 36.

110. The method of calculating the cap is set out in detail in the Competition Act 1998 (Determination of Turnover for Penalties) Order 2000, SI 2000/309, as amended by the Competition Act 1998 (Determination of Turnover for Penalties) (Amendment) Order 2004, SI 2004/1259.

111. Reduced on appeal to £15.0 million. *Argos Ltd and Littlewoods Limited v. OFT* [2005] CAT 13.

112. Case T–77/92, *Parker Pen Ltd v. Commission* [1994] ECR II 549.

113. 1998 OJ C 9, p 3.

114. OFT 423, revised in 2004 to reflect the OFT's powers to penalise the infringement of Articles 81 and 82 as well as the UK prohibitions.

Table 4—Commission and OFT fines calculations compared

	Commission's approach	OFT's approach
Calculation of the basic amount	Gravity will be assessed by taking into account the nature of the infringement, its impact on the market and the size of the relevant geographic market. On this basis, infringements will be divided into one of three categories: — Minor infringements with limited market impact. Likely starting point: €1,000 and €1 million. — Serious infringements, with wider market and geographic impact. Likely starting point: between €1 million and €20 million. — Very serious infringements, such as price cartels and clear abuses of dominance by near-monopolists. Likely starting point: in excess of €20 million.	The OFT starts by taking a percentage, up to a maximum of 10 per cent, of the turnover of the undertaking in the relevant market in the last financial year. Within this range, the figure chosen will depend on the gravity of the infringement. Price-fixing and market-sharing agreements and other cartels, and abuses of dominance with a particularly serious effect on competition, will be viewed as serious infringements. The OFT may take into account effects in another Member State if the relevant geographic market for the product concerned is wider than the UK, and if the NCA of the other Member State gives its express consent. The OFT's approach of applying a multiplier to relevant turnover is likely to lead to the automatic imposition of very high starting points on undertakings with large turnovers.
Adjustment for duration	Fines for infringements lasting for between one and five years will generally be increased by up to 50 per cent. Those for longer-term infringements are likely to be increased by up to 10 per cent per annum for each year of the infringement.	The starting point may then be increased by up to 100 per cent per year or part year for infringements lasting more than one year.
Adjustment for deterrence (OFT only)	(The Commission carries out a similar exercise when setting the starting point	The figure may then be increased or decreased, to take account of the OFT's policy objectives,

	Commission's approach	OFT's approach
	and as part of its adjustment for aggravating factors.)	particularly that of deterrence. This adjustment may result in a substantial adjustment of the financial penalty calculated at the earlier steps.
Adjustment for aggravating and mitigating factors	The Commission will then adjust the fine to take account of any aggravating or mitigating circumstances. Aggravating factors include: — repeated infringement; — non-cooperation wih the Commission; — leading or initiating the infringement; — retaliating against other undertakings; and — the need to increase the level of the fine so as to eliminate any gain resulting from the infringement. Examples of mitigating factors include: — playing a purely passive role; — not putting the offending agreement or practice into effect; — termination of the infringement when the Commission investigates; — existence of reasonable doubt on the part of the company that the conduct constitutes an infringement of the rules; — negligent rather than deliberate infringement; and — cooperation with the Commission's investigation.	The OFT may then increase or reduce the penalty to take account of aggravating or mitigating factors. Aggravating factors include: — leading or instigating the infringement; — the involvement of directors or senior management; — retaliatory measures taken against other undertakings; — continuing the infringement after the start of the investigation; — repeated infringement; — infringements committed intentionally rather than aggregately; — retaliation against a leniency applicant. To these might be added obstruction of the OFT's investigation. Mitigating factors include: — participation in the infringement under severe duress or pressure; — genuine uncertainty as to whether the agreement or conduct constituted an infringement; — adequate steps having been taken with a view to ensuring compliance; — termination of the infringement as soon as the OFT intervenes; — cooperation with the OFT's investigation.

	Commission's approach	OFT's approach
Adjustment to avoid exceeding the cap (OFT only)	(The Commission is subject to a 10 per cent cap, as explained above, but this adjustment does not feature formally in its Guidelines.)	The final step is to ensure that the total reached does not exceed the 10 per cent cap referred to above. This adjustment will be made after any reduction made in application of the lieniency policy. The OFT will also take into account any penalty imposed by the Commission or another NCA, in order to avoid double jeopardy.

Name of company	Basic amount of fine (€m)	Total after increase for duration (€m)	Total after aggravating factors (€m)	Total after mitigating factors (€m)	Total after being capped at 10 per cent of turnover)	Total after reduction for cooperation (€m)	Final total (€m)
ABB	**50** Basic amount of €20m, increased by 250 per cent for deterrence, to reflect involvement of the group	70 40 per cent increase	105 an increase of 50 per cent to reflect ABB's role as ringleader, retaliation, and continuation after the investigation	100 reduction of €5m to take account of the payment of compensation to a victim	N/A	70 Provision of significant information *after* the investigation, so a reduction of 30 per cent rather than 50 per cent	**70**
Løgstør	**10** A single-product company	14 40 per cent increase	18.2 An increase of 30 per cent to reflect retaliation and continuation after the investigation	None	12.7	8.9 Provision of significant information, so a reduction of 30 per cent	**8.9**
Tarco	**5** Having regard to its importance on the market	7 40 per cent increase	8.4 Increase of 20 per cent for continuing the infringement after the investigation	None	4.17	3 Provided information and documents establishing the facts, so a reduction of 30 per cent	**3**
Starpipe	**5** As Tarco	7 40 per cent increase	8.4 As Tarco	None	1.84	1.475 Did not contest the allegations, so a reduction of 20 per cent	**1.475**

9.10.4 Competition Authorities

Name of company	Basic amount of fine (€m)	Total after increase for duration (€m)	Total after aggravating factors (€m)	Total after mitigating factors (€m)	Total after being capped at 10 per cent of turnover)	Total after reduction for cooperation (€m)	Final total (€m)
de Henss/Isoplus	5 As Tarco	6.6 33 per cent increase to reflect shorter duration and sporadic nature of involvement	8.125 Increase of 30 per cent for continuing the infringement, playing a leading role in enforcing the cartel and attempting to mislead the Commission	None	4.95	4.95 No reduction: attempted to mislead the Commission	**4.95**
Pan-Isovit	5 As Tarco	6.25 As de Henss/ Ispolus	8 As Tarco	None	1.91	1.5 As Starpipe	**1.5**
Brugg	1 Having regard to its position on the market	1.1 10 per cent increase for 20 months' duration	1.32 As Tarco	None	N/A	0.925 Provided important information and did not contest allegations	**0.925**
KWH	1	1 One year's participation	1.2 As Tarco	1 Refused to participate in boycott	N/A	0.7 As Brugg	**0.7**
Ke-Kelit	1	1.1 10 per cent increase for 15 months	1.32 As Tarco	0.44 Two-thirds reduction for minor role	N/A	035 20 per cent reduction for not contesting SO	**0.36**
Sigma	1	1 One year's participation	1.2 As Tarco	0.4 As Ke-Kelit	N/A	None	**0.4**

9.10.4.2 Leniency for cooperation in cartel cases ("whistle-blower's amnesty")

9.10.4.2.1 Under the EU competition rules

The Commission's Notice on the non-imposition or reduction of fines in cartel cases,[115] sets out a policy intended to improve the detection and termination of secret cartels. It replaces an earlier policy, which had been criticised for failing to offer sufficient incentives to whistle-blowers. It is illustrated in Figure 5.

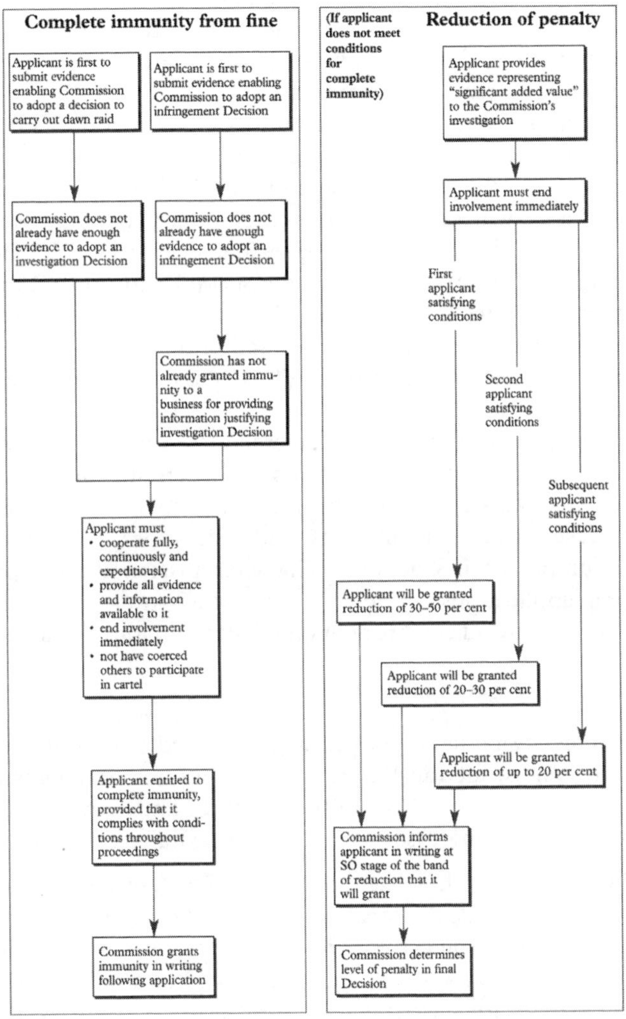

Figure 5: European Commission's cartel leniency programme

115. 2002 OJ C 45, p 3.

It promises immunity to an undertaking that is the first to provide evidence that allows the Commission:

- — to launch an investigation (provided that the Commission did not already have sufficient evidence); or
- — to adopt an infringement Decision (provided that the Commission did not already have sufficient evidence and that no undertaking had been granted immunity at the earlier stage).

In both cases, immunity is conditional on the undertaking cooperating fully throughout the investigation and providing all relevant information, ending its infringement immediately, and not having compelled others to participate in the infringement. The Commission will issue a letter granting conditional immunity when it receives the evidence.

A reduction in fine is available for an undertaking that does not satisfy the conditions for immunity, but which provides evidence representing "significant added value" in the investigation and ends its involvement immediately. The greatest value will be added by contemporary written evidence. The Commission will grant a reduction of 30 to 50 per cent to the first undertaking to come forward, 20 to 30 per cent to the second and up to 20 per cent to subsequent undertakings.

An undertaking that qualifies for a reduction may still appeal against the Commission's Decision, but if it does, the Commission will usually ask the CFI to increase the fine.

One of the major concerns to have emerged from the leniency programme has been the Commission's insistence on a written statement outlining the undertaking's involvement in the infringement. This provides a useful "road map" of the case for potential litigants, and orders for production have been made in a number of US actions. The Commission is now prepared to entertain oral applications for leniency, in which no written statement is submitted, so as to avoid the production of incriminating evidence.

9.10.4.2.2 Under the CA 1998

The OFT's leniency policy is set out in the second part of its guidance on penalties.[116] It is illustrated in Figure 6. Where an undertaking is the first to come forward to provide evidence of the existence and activities of a cartel in either of the two following cases, it will benefit from total immunity:

- — before the OFT has exercised its formal powers of investigation, provided that it does not already have sufficient evidence to establish the existence of the cartel and provided that the undertaking cooperates fully and did not take any steps to coerce another undertaking to participate in the cartel; or

116. See n 114.

— after the OFT has exercised its formal powers of investigation, but has not yet issued an SO, subject to similar conditions as to cooperation and coercion. In this case, the OFT must also be satisfied that the undertaking should benefit from immunity, taking into account the stage at which it comes forward and whether or not the OFT has enough evidence at that stage to make an infringement Decision. By offering immunity even after the start of an investigation, the OFT clearly hopes to provoke a race to provide additional information to assist the speedy collapse of the cartel.

An undertaking that provides evidence of the existence and activities of a cartel before the OFT issues an SO, but is not the first to come forward, or does not meet all the requirements for complete immunity, will be granted a reduction of up to 50 per cent of the penalty that would otherwise be imposed, subject to satisfying similar conditions as to cooperation.

The offer of a reduction is, unlike the offer of complete immunity, not conditional on the undertaking not having coerced other undertakings into participation.

Following the example of the US Department of Justice, the OFT's guidance also offers an additional reduction for cooperation in relation to an investigation into one market if the undertaking at the same time provides evidence of a cartel in a second market, satisfying the conditions for total immunity in relation to that second market ("amnesty plus").

The OFT will issue a letter confirming in advance that the undertaking is eligible for the leniency programme, or indicating the level of any reduction which will be offered.

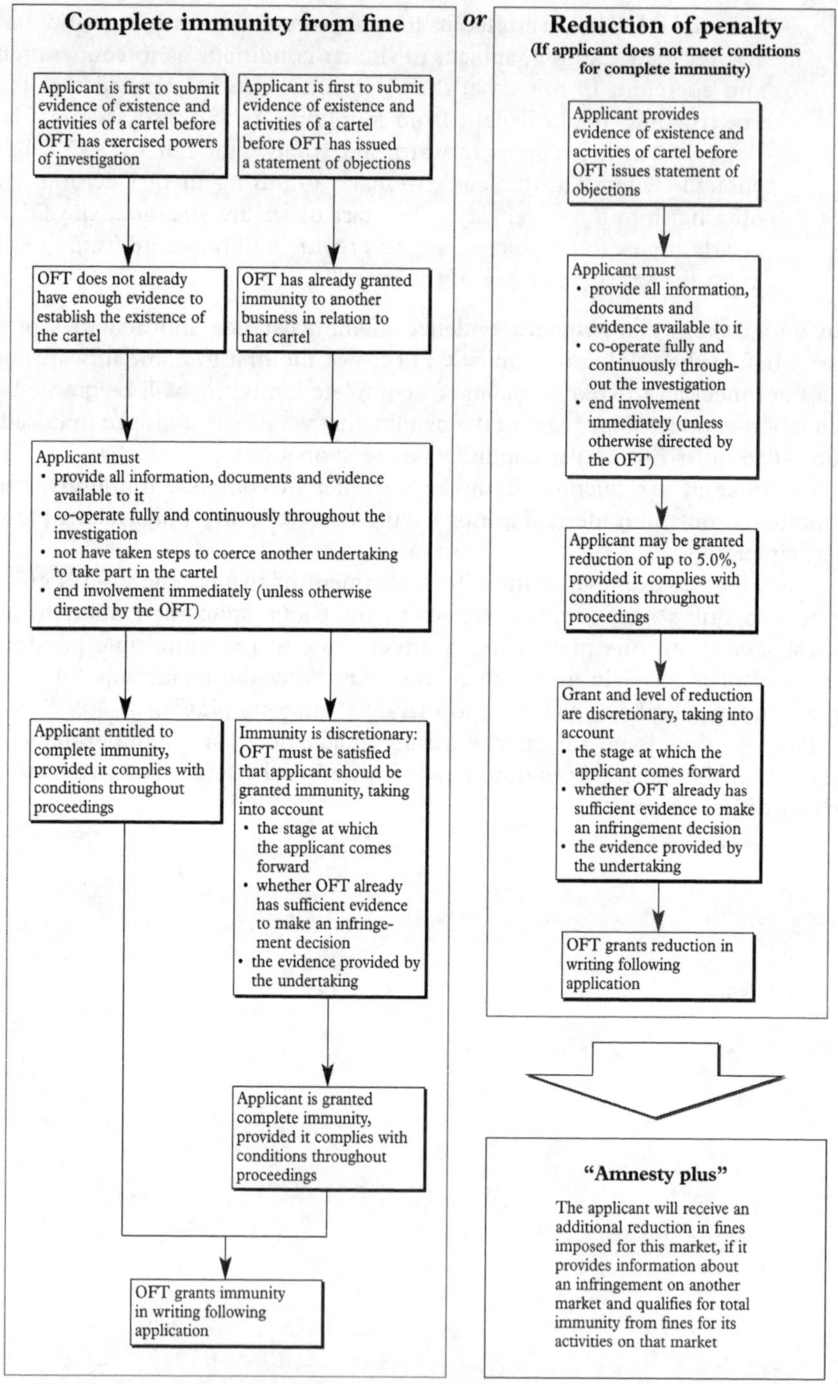

Figure 6: UK cartel leniency programme

9.10.4.3 Leniency and fine reduction strategies

The best way of avoiding a fine is not to infringe, or not to get caught. However, the Commission's and OFT's leniency programmes are intended to increase the detection rate by raising the stakes for any undertaking that does not come forward. This is sometimes known as the "prisoners' dilemma". Accordingly, there can be no certainty that an infringement will not come to light.

Clearly it is better to be the first to come forward than the second. Businesses will therefore need to act very quickly, possibly coordinating applications in a number of jurisdictions around the world within a matter of days. Before deciding whether to claim immunity, however, they will balance the risks. Factors that may lead a business to throw itself on the mercy of the competition authorities, on the grounds that a cartel is likely to be detected in the near future, include:

- an investigation into parallel activities by a competition authority in another jurisdiction;
- a change in the circumstances of the market, such that membership of the cartel loses its attraction for one or more other members;
- acquisition of a cartel member by a business with a developed ethical policy which is likely to discover the cartel and blow the whistle itself; or
- receiving notice that a complaint is likely.

One factor to take into account will be the relative levels of fines and damages claims by victims of price-fixing. Whistle-blowing confers no immunity from the latter.

If it is not possible to gain total immunity by being the first to come forward, considerable reductions can still be gained by full cooperation. Even ABB, a ringleader of the pre-insulated pipe cartel (see 9.10.4.1 above), was given a reduction of 30 per cent for cooperation.

9.10.5 Competition Disqualification Orders and Undertakings

A further weapon available in the UK is the disqualification of directors of companies involved in infringements of UK or EU competition rules. A court must disqualify a director (including a "shadow director" or a person who acts as a director without formally having been appointed as one) from holding certain positions for a period of up to 15 years if:

- an undertaking, which is a company of which that person is a director, has committed a breach of competition law;[117] and

117. Company Directors Disqualification Act 1986, s 9A(2).

— the court considers that the person's conduct as a director makes him or her unfit to be concerned in the management of a company.

In applying the second condition, the court must consider the director's conduct and degree of knowledge of the infringement.

9.10.5.1 Applications for Competition Disqualification Orders

A Competition Disqualification Order ("CDO") may be imposed by any court that convicts an individual of a serious offence[118] in connection with the management of a company, including the cartel offence. Alternatively, the OFT may apply to the High Court to make an order.

In deciding whether to apply for a CDO, the OFT will consider a number of relevant factors, including the extent of the director's responsibility for the breach, and aggravating and mitigating factors similar to those taken into account in calculating the penalty imposed on a company under the UK or EU regimes.[119]

It will also consider whether the company has benefited from leniency under the UK or EU regime. The OFT will not apply for a CDO against any current director of a company that has benefited from leniency in respect of the activities to which that grant of leniency relates. However, where a director has been removed from office because of his or her involvement in the breach of competition law, and/or for opposing the relevant leniency application, the OFT may consider applying for a CDO against that person. This is the case even if the OFT or Commission has subsequently granted granted leniency to that person's former company.

Before applying to the court for a CDO, the OFT must inform the individual concerned, inviting him or her to make representations and/or to offer a Competition Disqualification Undertaking in lieu of having a CDO made.

9.10.5.2 Competition Disqualification Undertakings

As an alternative to seeking a CDO, the OFT may accept a Competition Disqualification Undertaking ("CDU"). Under a CDU, a director undertakes not to assume any of the roles that he or she could be prohibited from holding under a CDO for a maximum period of up to 15 years.[120] Whether or not a CDU will be accepted by the OFT will depend on the period specified and all the facts of the case. For the CDU to be accepted, the OFT must perceive the period offered as "proportionate to the seriousness of the case".[121]

118. An indictable offence.
119. See Table 4 at 9.10.4.1 above.
120. Company Directors Disqualification Act 1986, 9B(5).
121. OFT 510, *Guidance on Competition Disqualification Orders*, at para 3.4.

9.11 APPEALS

9.11.1 Under the EU rules

9.11.1.1 Decisions capable of appeal

An undertaking may appeal against a Decision that is addressed to it or is of "direct and individual concern" to it.[122] Whether an act of the Commission constitutes a Decision depends on whether it is intended to have legal effect. Thus an SO is not capable of appeal.

9.11.1.2 Grounds for appeal

The grounds for an appeal are:

- lack of competence;
- infringement of an essential procedural requirement;
- infringement of the Treaty or of any rule of law relating to its application; or
- misuse of powers.

The CFI also has jurisdiction, under Article 132, to review the Commission's failure to act following a request to do so.

9.11.1.3 Procedure

An appeal is made by lodging a notice of appeal at the Registry of the CFI, within two months of the date of notification of the contested decision. Procedure before the CFI is largely written, and the oral hearing is usually limited to brief argument by each party. A further appeal lies to the ECJ on points of law.

9.11.2 Under the Competition Act 1998

9.11.2.1 Decisions capable of appeal

Where the OFT has made one of the following Decisions, any party to the agreement or conduct in question may appeal to a CAT against that decision:[123]

- infringement or non-infringement of the Chapter I or Chapter II prohibition;

122. Article 230 (formerly Article 173) of the Treaty. See, on the direct and individual concern to a complainant, Case 26/76, *Metro v. Commission* [1977] ECR 1875.

123. The question of what constitutes a decision has been the subject of a number of judgments of the CAT. See, for example, *Bettercare Group Ltd v. Director-General of Fair Trading* [2002] CAT 6, [2002] Comp AR 226; *Freeserve.com v. Director-General of Telecommunications* [2002] CAT 8, [2003] Comp AR 1; *Claymore Dairies Ltd and Express Dairies Ltd v. Director-General of Fair Trading* [2003] CAT 3; *Aquavitae (UK) Ltd v. Director-General of Water Services* [2003] CAT 4.

- — as to whether to grant an individual exemption;
- — on the starting date or duration of, or the conditions or obligations imposed in respect of, an individual exemption, or on its extension or cancellation; and
- — on the imposition or amount of a penalty.

They also include interim and final directions and any other Decision prescribed by order of the Secretary of State.

A third party may also appeal against any of these Decisions, except a Decision on the level of a penalty, provided that it can satisfy the CAT that it has sufficient interest, either individually or in a representative capacity.[124] It will also be possible (in certain circumstances) to apply for judicial review of the actions of the OFT.

Whether an act of the OFT constitutes a Decision is a question of substance, not form, and a question of fact in each case.

9.11.2.2 Grounds for appeal

An appeal may be made on the grounds that the Decision was wrong in fact or in law, or that the OFT exercised its discretion wrongly. It is likely that no appeal will be available purely on the grounds of a procedural irregularity: the irregularity will be required to have rendered the Decision wrong in fact or in law.

9.11.2.3 Procedure

An appeal against a Decision of the OFT is heard by the CAT, usually sitting as a three-member panel. Sir Christopher Bellamy, formerly the British judge at the CFI, is the current President of the CAT.

The CAT must determine the appeal on the merits of the case (ie. not merely on the reasonableness of the original Decision) by reference to the grounds of appeal set out in the notice of appeal. It will determine the appeal on the facts before it. It may confirm or set aside all or part of the Decision under appeal and may remit the matter to the OFT; impose, revoke or vary the amount of a penalty; grant or cancel an individual exemption or vary any conditions or obligations of the exemptions or make any other decision that the OFT could have made, including ordering interim measures and directions. The CAT is therefore not confined to annulling the OFT's decision and leaving it, like the Commission, to adopt a new decision if it wishes to do so. The CAT may substitute its own decision for that of the OFT.

124. CA 1998, s 47, amended by EA 2002, s 17, to remove the requirement to request the OFT to reconsider its decision before being able to appeal to the CAT.

CHAPTER 10

PRIVATE ENFORCEMENT OF EC COMPETITION LAW

Andrew Macnab, Monckton Chambers

10.1 INTRODUCTION

Articles 81 and 82 of the EC Treaty impose obligations on undertakings that give rise to directly effective private rights of action, which individuals and undertakings may enforce in the national courts of the Member States. Competition law rights may be invoked as a shield (ie by way of defence to a claim) and as a sword (ie as a cause of action—eg by way of a claim for an injunction to restrain actual or threatened prohibited conduct or a claim for damages in respect of loss and damage caused by prohibited behaviour).

Recent Community and national measures have sought to make private enforcement of EU competition law rights more easy. This area has been radically overhauled by Regulation 1/2003,[1] with effect from 1 May 2004. National procedural rules, which govern private enforcement before the courts, vary considerably, although as a matter of Community law they are required to guarantee a minimum level of efficacy for claimants under Community law. This Chapter focuses on the private enforcement of the competition rules before the UK courts. In the UK, the Competition Act 1998 ("CA 1998") and court procedural rules[2] have been amended to take account of the changes at the EU level.

At the same time, the CA 1998, which came into force in 2000, has reduced the need for private litigants to rely (solely) on EU competition law rights. The CA 1998 is closely modelled on Articles 81 and 82 of the EC Treaty and is required, so far as possible, to be interpreted consistently with Community law principles. Although UK national competition authorities ("NCAs")[3] and courts are obliged (as a matter of Community law) to apply Community law to a "domestic" situation if the jurisdictional criterion for the application of Community competition law is met (namely where the agreement or conduct

1. Regulation 1/2003 of 16 December 2002 on the implementation of the rules on competition laid down in Articles 81 and 82 of the Treaty, OJ L 1.

2. EU competition law and the CA 1998 apply uniformly throughout the UK. Within the UK, England and Wales, Scotland and Northern Ireland each have their own jurisdictions. In England and Wales, the court having original jurisdiction is the High Court; in Scotland, it is the Court of Session; in Northern Ireland, it is the High Court. In this Chapter, only the law relating to procedure in England and Wales is considered.

3. See Chapter 9 above.

has an appreciable effect on trade between Member States), and must accord precedence to Community rules in the event of a conflict between EU and domestic rules, situations where a conflict exists between the two regimes are likely to be rare. The absence under the CA 1998 of any need to establish an appreciable effect on trade between Member States represents the removal of a hurdle that has tripped up litigants in the past.[4]

Private enforcement of both EU and domestic competition law is increasingly encouraged by the Commission and NCAs. The regulatory authorities' enthusiasm for private enforcement is not necessarily shared by the private sector. Although private claims for breach of EU competition law have been possible for many years, reported cases are few and far between. The recent changes to both EU and UK competition law have made such claims easier to bring—in theory. In practice, the position is somewhat different.

Factors influencing the decision whether to complain to the authorities or to litigate are likely to include the following:[5]

- *Remedies*: complaints procedures are administrative.[6] A decision by the Commission or an NCA does not, in itself, create any private remedy for a third party. On the other hand, litigation has the following advantages, not available through an administrative procedure.
  - *Damages*: litigation is the only means by which a claim for damages (or restitution) may be pursued (either in the High Court or, where section 47A of the CA 1998 applies, the Competition Appeal Tribunal ("CAT")).
  - *Contractual obligations*: national courts may rule on claims for payment or questions of contractual obligation.
  - *Nullity*: it is for the national courts to apply the civil sanction of nullity of Article 81(2) in contractual relationships between individuals and to assess the scope and consequences of the nullity on the agreement as a whole.
  - *Combined claims*: before national courts, it is possible to combine a claim under Community competition law with other claims under national law. An NCA can apply both EU and domestic competition law, but the Commission applies only EU law.
- *Interim remedies*: litigation will usually offer a quicker and more satisfactory means of seeking interim relief (eg an interim injunction to restrain an actual or threatened infringement pending final resolution).
- *Expense*: the Commission or NCA bears the cost of investigating whether an infringement has occurred. By contrast, the litigant must bear the costs of making out the claim, such as legal costs, the costs of

4. For example, the *George Michael* case (*Panayiotou and Others v. Sony Music Entertainment Ltd, The Times,* 30 June 1994, [1994] EMLR 229.

5. See generally Commission Notice on the handling of complaints by the Commission under Articles 81 and 82 of the EC Treaty (2004 OJ C 101, p 05).

6. See Chapter 9 above.

obtaining factual evidence (both witness and documentary) and expert evidence. Article 16 of Regulation 1/2003 and sections 47A and 58A of the CA 1998 can be expected to reduce (if not eliminate) costs in relation to establishing infringement.

— *Expertise*: the Commission and NCAs have much greater experience and expertise in competition law and economics. Following Regulation 1/2003 and the amendments to the Civil Procedure Rules ("CPR"), the national courts are now better placed to seek assistance from the Commission and the NCAs on competition law matters.

— *Control*: the progress of a complaint is dictated by the Commission or the relevant NCA. Litigation is more flexible and a claimant has a greater measure of control over the procedure.

In practice, any prospective litigant would be best advised to see litigation as a last resort. Litigation will be preferable as a first step only in cases of extreme urgency where an interim injunction is required. Otherwise, the prospective litigant will usually prefer—and will be best advised—to complain in the first instance to the Commission or an NCA. A favourable decision may then be used as a platform for a damages claim.

10.2 SOURCES AND NATURE OF EU COMPETITION LAW DUTIES AND RIGHTS

Article 81 and Article 82 have been considered in Chapters 3, 4 and 5 above.

In *BRT v. SABAM*,[7] the Court of Justice of the European Communities ("ECJ") held that both Articles 81(1) and 82 have direct effect in Member States and confer rights and impose obligations on private parties that national courts are required to protect.

As a matter of English law, infringements of Articles 81(1) and 82 are characterised as breaches of statutory duty (ie torts): *Garden Cottage Foods Ltd v. Milk Marketing Board*.[8] *Courage v. Crehan*[9] and the subsequent decision of the Court of Appeal in *Crehan v. Inntrepreneur Pub Company CPC*[10] have established that the statutory duty is owed to everybody: anybody affected by a breach may (for example) sue for damages in accordance with, and subject to, English substantive and procedural rules (eg causation, remoteness and limitation).

Since 1 May 2004, when Regulation 1/2003 took effect, Article 81(3) has also been directly effective and Articles 81 and 82 are now enforceable in their entirety. At the same time, Regulation 1/2003 has sought to ensure that, so far

7. Case 127/73, [1974] ECR 51.
8. [1984] AC 130.
9. Case C–453/99, [2001] ECR I-6297, [2002] QB 507.
10. [2004] EWCA Civ 637.

as possible, EU competition law is applied consistently throughout the common market. Regulation 1/2003 must also be read in conjunction with the Commission Notice on the cooperation between the Commission and the courts of the EU Member States in the application of Articles 81 and 82.[11] The Regulation is directly effective in Member States and the UK has also amended its substantive and procedural law to incorporate the new regime.

10.3 UK COMPETITION LAW

Although this book is about EU competition law, regard must be had to the UK's domestic competition law regime. That regime has had an impact on private enforcement of EU competition claims and should be considered alongside EU competition law.

UK competition law was transformed in 2000, when the CA 1998 came into force. The 1998 Act introduced a competition regime closely modelled on Articles 81 and 82:[12]

- — the "Chapter I prohibition", with certain minor differences, equates to the prohibition in Article 81(1);
- — the "Chapter II prohibition", with certain minor differences, equates to the prohibition in Article 82.

The main difference between Articles 81 and 82 and the Chapter I and II prohibitions is their jurisdictional threshold. Articles 81 and 82 are not engaged unless an agreement, etc, or conduct by a dominant undertaking "may affect trade between Member States".[13] The Chapter I and II prohibitions require only that there be an effect on trade within the UK, which for the purposes of the Act includes part of the UK.[14] Subject to that difference, the Chapter I and II regimes are intended to be consistent with Articles 81 and 82.

10.4 SUBSTANTIVE EFFECTS OF REGULATION 1/2003 IN RELATION TO PRIVATE ENFORCEMENT

10.4.1 Burden of proof in national proceedings

Article 3 of Regulation 1/2003 harmonises and codifies the incidence of the burden of proof. The burden of proving an infringement of Article 81(1) or

11. 2004 OJ C 101/54.

12. The CA 1998 has been subsequently amended by the Enterprise Act 2002 and the Competition Act 1998 and Other Enactments (Amendment) Regulations 2004 (SI 2004/1261).

13. See further Chapters 3 to 5 above and Commission Guidelines on the effect on trade concept contained in Articles 81 and 82 of the Treaty (2004/C101/07).

14. CA 1998, ss 2(1), (7) (Chapter I); ss 18(1), (3) (Chapter II).

Article 82 is on the party alleging the infringement. The burden of proving that the conditions of Article 81(3) are fulfilled is on the undertaking (or association of undertakings) claiming the benefit of Article 81(3).

The Regulation is silent as to the standard of proof. In the CAT and in England and Wales, the civil standard of proof applies, ie the balance of probabilities. The more serious the allegation, the more cogent the evidence required to establish the case on the balance of probabilities.[15] The evidence required to meet the requisite standard will vary from case to case and will depend on the nature of the infringement asserted: it must, however, be sufficient to convince the court or tribunal in the circumstances of the particular case, and to overcome the presumption of innocence to which the undertaking concerned is entitled.[16]

10.4.2 The relationship between Articles 81 and 82 and national competition law

Article 3 of Regulation 1/2003 codifies the relationship between Articles 81 and 82 and national competition laws. It provides for the concurrent application of EU competition law with national competition law and makes plain that the former prevails over inconsistent national law, which must be "disapplied" to the extent necessary to give effect to EU law.[17]

The effect of Article 3(1), coupled with the EU doctrine of the supremacy or primacy of EU law, is to prevent national competition law from excluding the application of EU competition law and to prevent national competition law from upholding agreements etc, or permitting conduct, that would be prohibited under the EU rules. Agreements etc that violate Article 81(1) and do not fulfil the conditions of Article 81(3) cannot be upheld under national law.[18] National courts can apply Articles 81 and 82 without having to apply national competition law in parallel.

Article 3(2) of the Regulation provides that the application of national competition law may not lead to the prohibition of agreements etc that may affect trade between Member States but which do not infringe Article 81(1),[19]

15. See *Napp Pharmaceutical Holdings and Others v. Director-General of Fair Trading* [2002] CAT 1, [2002] CompAR 13, paras 91–113.

16. *JJB Sports plc v. Office of Fair Trading* [2004] CAT 17, para 204.

17. See, eg, Case 106/77, *Simmenthal* [1978] ECR 629; Joined Cases C-10/97 to C-22/97, *Ministero delle Finanze v. IN.CO.GE.'90 srl* [1998] ECR I 6307, paras 18–21. See also *Days Medical Aids Ltd v. Pihsiang Machinery Manufacturing Co Ltd and Others* [2004] EWHC 44 (Comm), in which Langley J held at paras 254–266 that Article 3 codified general EU law and that, where an agreement is compatible with Article 81 but infringes the English law doctrine of restraint of trade, the latter had to be disapplied to the extent necessary to give effect to Community law.

18. Case 14/68, *Walt Wilhelm v. Bundeskartellamt* [1969] ECR 1; Joined Cases 253/78, 1/79–3/79, *Giry and Guerlain* [1980] ECR 2327.

19. See 9.2 above.

or which fulfil the conditions of Article 81(3),[20] or which are covered by a block exemption Regulation.[21]

The Regulation does not preclude Member States from adopting and applying on their territory stricter national laws that prohibit or sanction unilateral conduct engaged in by undertakings.[22] There is therefore no convergence obligation in relation to the parallel application of national competition law and Article 82 in the case of unilateral conduct. However, in case of conflicting provisions, the doctrine of supremacy requires national courts to disapply any provision of national law that contravenes a Community rule.

The foregoing provisions do not apply when a national court is applying national merger control laws. Nor do they preclude the application of provisions of national law that predominantly pursue an objective different from that pursued by Articles 81 and 82.[23]

10.4.3 Uniform application of Community competition law

Article 16(1) of Regulation 1/2003 provides that when a national court rules on any agreement etc under Article 81 or Article 82 that is already the subject of a Commission Decision, it must not take any decision running counter to the Commission's Decision. The national court must also avoid giving a decision that would conflict with a Decision contemplated by the Commission in proceedings initiated by the Commission and, to that effect, the national court "may assess whether it is necessary to stay its proceedings", if necessary also pending final judgment on any appeal against the Commission's Decision in the Community courts, unless it considers that a reference to the ECJ for a preliminary ruling on the validity of the Commission Decision is warranted.[24]

More generally, national courts are bound by the case law of the Community courts as well as by Commission block exemption Regulations.[25] Even where not formally binding, Commission Decisions provide useful guidance. Guidance may also be found in Commission Regulations and in Commission Notices and Guidelines relating to the application of Articles 81 and 82[26] and in the Commission's annual report on competition policy.

20. See 3.3 above.

21. See 3.3.2.2 above.

22. Regulation 1/2003, Article 3(2).

23. Regulation 1/2003, Article 3(3).

24. Regulation 1/2003, Article 16(1); Case C-344/98, *Masterfoods* [2000] ECR I 11369, paras 52–59.

25. Case 63/75, *Fonderies Roubaix* [1976] ECR 111, paras 9–11; Case C-234/89, *Delimitis* [1991] ECR I 935, para 46.

26. Case 66/86, *Ahmed Saeed Flugreisen* [1989] ECR 803, para 27; Case C-234/89, *Delimitis* [1991] ECR I 935, para 50. A list of Commission Guidelines, Notices and Regulations in the field of competition policy, in particular the regulations applying Article 81(3) to certain categories of agreements, decisions or concerted practices, are annexed to the Commission Notice on the cooperation between the Commission and the courts of the EU Member States in the application of Articles 81 and 82 EC (OJ C 101/54). The list is available online on the Commission's website at http://www.europa.eu.int/comm/competition/antitrust/legislation.

10.5 EU COMPETITION LAW AS A DEFENCE

Article 81(2) provides that any agreements or decisions prohibited pursuant to Article 81 "shall be automatically void". The agreement is automatically void as between the parties and cannot be set up against third parties. Similarly, an agreement that offends Article 82 is automatically void and unenforceable as between the parties to the agreement and cannot be set up against third parties. The principle of automatic nullity is capable of having a bearing on all the effects, either past or future, of the agreement or decision concerned.[27]

10.5.1 Severance

Contrary to what might be thought from its wording, Article 81(2) does not render infringing agreements completely and automatically null and void for all purposes. In *Société Technique Minière*[28] the ECJ held that the automatic nullity decreed by Article 81(2) applies only to those contractual provisions that are incompatible with Article 81(1) and not to the wider agreement as a whole. The consequences of such nullity for other parts of the agreement are to be determined by national law. If, therefore, the offending terms can be severed from the remainder of the agreement as a matter of domestic law, the remainder remains valid and enforceable.

Severance is possible under English contract law.[29] The leading authority in relation to Article 81(2) is *Chemidus Wavin*.[30] A licensor sued for sums due under a minimum royalty clause in a patent licence. The Court of Appeal upheld that claim, even though other provisions of the licence arguably infringed Article 81(1), holding that the promise to pay a minimum royalty was an independent promise supported by consideration. If, therefore, the offending provision can be "blue-pencilled"(ie struck out), and if what remains thereafter is a recognisable commercial contract, effect will be given to what remains.

Richard Cound Ltd v. BMW (GB) Ltd[31] is a case where severance was not possible. The Court of Appeal held that, after infringing provisions had been excised from a car distributorship agreement, the remaining agreement was so changed in its character that it was not the sort of contract that the parties had intended to enter into at all and was void in its entirety.

10.5.2 Severance and block exemptions

Agreements in areas covered by block exemptions often contain a number of restrictions that fall within Article 81(1), some of which are exempted under

27. See, eg, Case C-453/99, *Courage Ltd v. Crehan* [2002] QB 507, p 521 (ECJ).
28. *Société Technique Minière v. Maschinenbau Ulm* Case 56/65, [1966] ECR 235.
29. See *Chitty on Contracts*, 29th edn, 2004, paras 16–188–16–197.
30. *Cheuridus Wavin v. TERI* [1978] 3 CMLR 514.
31. [1997] Eu LR 277.

the block exemption and some of which are not. The consequences depend on the terms of the block exemption itself.

In the absence of any specific provision to the contrary in the block exemption, an agreement which contains a restriction that falls within Article 81(1) and which is not exempted by the block exemption falls outside the block exemption in its entirety. The offending restriction may not be severed in order to allow the remaining restrictions to be exempted: *Delimitis*.[32]

Block exemptions do now expressly provide for "excluded" restrictions,[33] ie restrictions within Article 81(1) that are not exempted under Article 81(3), but which may be severed and whose presence in an agreement does not cause the agreement as a whole to fall outside the block exemption.

10.5.3 Temporal effect of nullity

Where an agreement has as its object the prevention, restriction or distortion of competition, that agreement is void *ab initio*. Where infringement of Article 81(1) depends on the agreement's effect, the automatic nullity imposed by Article 81(2) is temporal. An agreement may pass in and out of voidness, depending on its effect on competition at any given time: see *Passmore v. Morland plc*.[34]

10.5.4 Consequences of nullity as between the parties

The consequences of the nullity of an agreement are to be determined by the national court. The extent to which either party may enforce performance of the contract or claim compensation in respect of non-performance will depend on the principles of severance. As a matter of English law, agreements infringing Articles 81 or 82 are not only void but also illegal,[35] since they are expressly prohibited and expose the parties to penalties. In such circumstances, the usual rule is that loss lies where it falls: neither party may recover money paid or property transferred, and neither may sue for damages. That rule did not affect claims (whether for damages or for money had and received) based on Article 82 at the suit of the injured party: *Garden Cottage Foods v. Milk Marketing Board*.[36]

However, as regards parties to an agreement infringing Article 81, the position is now covered by *Courage v. Crehan*.[37] The ECJ held that, in principle, a party to a contract was entitled to rely on a breach of Article 81(1) to

32. Case C-234/89, *Delimitis v. Henninger Brau AG* [1991] ECR I 935, paras 38–42.

33. For example, Regulation 2790/1999 on the application of Article 81(3) of the Treaty to categories of vertical agreements and concerted practices, Article 5; Regulation 772/2004 on the application of Article 81(3) of the Treaty to categories of technology transfer agreements, Article 5. See Chapter 4.

34. [1999] All ER 1005.

35. See *Re Westinghouse Uranium Contract* [1978] AC 547.

36. [1984] AC 130.

37. Case C–453/99, [2001] ECR I 6297, [2002] QB 507.

obtain relief from the other contracting party and could in principle claim damages for loss caused by such a contract. A national rule that barred such a claim on the sole ground that the claimant was a party to the contract was precluded by Article 81. However, having regard to the principle that a litigant should not be permitted to profit from his own unlawful conduct, Community law did not preclude a national rule that barred a party to a contract liable to restrict or distort competition from relying on his own unlawful actions in order to obtain damages, provided however that that party bore significant responsibility for the distortion of competition.

For the purposes of the national court's assessment of a party's degree of responsibility, the matters to be taken into account included the economic and legal context in which the parties found themselves and their respective bargaining power and conduct, and in particular whether the party claiming to have suffered loss was in a markedly weaker position than the other party, so that its freedom to negotiate the terms of the contract and its capacity to avoid or reduce the loss were seriously compromised or even eliminated. The ECJ further indicated that where a contract is contrary to Article 81 only because it is part of a network of similar contracts having a cumulative effect on competition, a party contracting with the person controlling the network cannot bear significant responsibility for the breach of Article 81, particularly where in practice the terms of the contract were imposed on it by the person controlling the network.

10.5.5 Third-party defences

Third parties may rely on the automatic nullity imposed by Article 81(2) or on a breach of Article 82 by way of defence to a claim. There must, however, be some nexus between the alleged infringement of Articles 81(1) or 82 by the claimant and the relief sought by the defendant.

10.6 EU COMPETITION LAW AS A CAUSE OF ACTION: INJUNCTIONS AND DAMAGES

10.6.1 Introduction

The ECJ has stated on many occasions that in the absence of Community rules governing the matter, it is for the domestic legal system of each Member State to designate the courts and tribunals having jurisdiction, and to lay down the detailed procedural rules governing actions for safeguarding directly effective rights that individuals derive from Community law. However, the application of those national provisions must be compatible with general principles of Community law. Thus:

— where there is an infringement of Community law, national law must provide for sanctions that are effective, proportionate and dissuasive;[38]
— where the infringement of Community law causes harm to an individual, the latter should under certain conditions be able to ask the national court for damages. In particular, Community law requires national legal orders to provide a remedy in damages for breach of the competition rules;[39] by parity of reasoning, injunctive relief should also be available;[40]
— national rules on procedures and sanctions to enforce Community law must not be less favourable than the rules applicable to similar domestic actions (the principle of equivalence) and must not render such enforcement virtually impossible or excessively difficult (the principle of effectiveness).

The main civil remedies available in English law in respect of competition law infringements are as follows:

— injunctions to restrain a party from breaching or threatening to breach a relevant prohibition. In some cases, an injunction may be granted to compel a defendant to act in a certain way. Injunctions are available as both a final and an interim remedy;
— damages to compensate a litigant for loss and damage caused by a defendant's breach of competition law.

In principle, restitutionary remedies and declaratory relief are also available.

10.6.2 Injunctions

An injunction may be described as a court order prohibiting a person from doing something (a prohibitory injunction) or requiring a person to do something (a mandatory injunction). Injunctions can be granted by way of both interim and final relief (the latter are also known as "permanent" injunctions). Injunctions may be granted against apprehended or threatened wrongs that have not yet been committed ("*quia timet*" injunctions) as well as to restrain the continuance or repetition of a wrong.

Injunctive relief, both interlocutory and permanent, is available in principle to restrain conduct in breach of, or which threatens to breach, Articles 81 and 82. Such relief is available subject to the usual rules governing the grants of

38. Case 68/88, *Commission v. Greece* [1989] ECR 2965, paras 23–25.
39. C-453/99, *Courage v. Crehan* [2001] ECR I 6297, [2002] QB 507.
40. Opinion of Advocate-General Jacobs in Joined Cases C-246/01, C-306/01, C-354/01 and C-355/01 *AOK Bundesverband*, para 104.

injunctions.[41] Injunctions are equitable remedies; they are discretionary and are not available as of right. An injunction will not ordinarily be granted if damages would be an adequate remedy for a claimant.

The protection conferred by an injunction can be obtained (in effect) through the complaint procedure—the Commission, NCAs and the CAT have power to grant both final and interim relief. In cases of urgency, however, interim injunctive relief is best sought privately.

Indeed, of all the private law remedies, an interim injunction (if granted) is possibly the most useful. An interim injunction puts a stop to actual or threatened conduct at an early stage, pending final determination of the dispute. The principles to be applied in determining whether an interim injunction should be granted are those set out in *American Cyanamid Co v. Ethicon Ltd*:[42]

- Is there a serious question to be tried? If not, an interim injunction should not be granted; unless the material available fails to disclose that the claimant has any real prospect of succeeding in its claim for a permanent injunction at trial, the court should go on to consider whether the balance of convenience lies in favour of granting or refusing the interim injunction.
- Would the claimant be adequately compensated by an award of damages for the loss it would sustain if the interim injunction were not granted until trial? If so, no interim injunction should normally be granted.
- If, however, damages would not provide an adequate remedy for the claimant in the event of its succeeding at the trial, would the defendant be adequately compensated under the claimant's undertaking to pay damages for the loss the defendant would sustain by being subject to an interim injunction until trial? If so, there would be no reason to refuse an interim injunction.

If there is doubt as to the adequacy of the respective remedies in damages, it is necessary to consider the balance of convenience. Where other factors appear to be evenly balanced, the *status quo* will usually be preserved.

English courts have been reluctant to grant interim relief in cases based on Articles 81 and 82 and the Chapter I and Chapter II prohibitions of CA 1998. For an example of a case in which interim relief was granted, see *Network Multimedia Television Ltd v. Jobserve Ltd*,[43] the first and (to date) only case in which an English court has granted an order restraining the actual or threatened breach of the Chapter II prohibition.

41. See eg *Halsbury's Laws of England*, 4th edn, vol 24, para 801 *et seq*; *Meagher, Gummow & Lehane's Equity—Doctrines and Remedies*, 4th edn, 2002, Chapter 21.

42. [1975] AC 396, pp 407–409, *per* Lord Diplock.

43. [2002] UKCLR 184 (Ch D); upheld [2002] UKCLR 814 (CA).

10.6.3 Declarations

Declaratory relief is available in principle. This might be an appropriate form of relief eg for a supplier who wishes to establish that a distribution agreement falls within the terms of a block exemption. It is not necessary for a party to an agreement that is alleged to be void or contain void restrictions to go to court to seek a declaration to that effect. It may simply ignore the restrictions or contract and wait to be sued.

10.6.4 Damages[44]

In English law, "damages in the vast majority of cases are the pecuniary compensation, obtainable by success in an action, for a wrong which is either a tort or a breach of contract, the compensation being in the form of a lump sum awarded at one time, unconditionally and in sterling".[45]

The EC Treaty contains no provision that damages should be available to those who suffer loss because of breaches of Articles 81 or 82, although as a matter of English law it was long assumed that they were available in principle.[46] As stated above, *Courage v. Crehan* has established definitively that damages are, and must be, available in principle for breaches of Articles 81 and 82.

The Court of Appeal's subsequent decision in *Courage v. Crehan*[47] has made it clear that, for the purposes of English law, Articles 81 and 82 create civil causes of action and that any loss suffered by any person is within the scope of the protection conferred by Articles 81 and 82. In order to claim damages, a person must establish (i) a breach of Article 81 or 82; (ii) that the breach caused the loss complained of; and (iii) the amount of that loss. Potential claimants include:

— parties to an infringing agreement (subject to the qualification in *Crehan*);
— direct purchasers (eg those who buy from cartel participants at inflated prices);
— indirect purchasers (eg those who buy from direct purchasers who have increased their prices as a result of having themselves paid inflated prices);
— potential purchasers (eg those who would have bought goods at a competitive price, but did not buy goods at the inflated price);

44. For the English law of damages, see generally *McGregor on Damages*, 17th edn, 2003. In relation to competition law damages, see generally the "Study on the conditions of claims for damages in case of infringement of EC competition rules" prepared by Ashurst for the Commission, 31 August 2004.
45. *McGregor*, *op cit*, n 44 above, para 1–001.
46. See, eg, *Garden Cottage Foods v. Milk Marketing Board* [1984] AC 130.
47. [2004] EWCA Civ 637.

— purchasers from non-participants (eg those who have bought from undertakings not party to a cartel but who have increased their prices in line with the inflated price);
— suppliers (eg those who suffer loss of sales as a result of artificial reductions in output by cartel members);
— competitors (eg those affected by a dominant undertaking's exclusionary conduct);
— end consumers.

The extent, if any, to which any of those persons listed above may recover damages in any given case, and the defences available, remain unresolved.[48] For example, it remains unclear whether or to what extent a "passing-on" defence is open to a cartel member who is sued by a direct purchaser who has in turn passed on the excess price in whole or in part to his customers. It seems likely that Community law permits a passing-on defence, but that a direct purchaser will be able to recover other losses, such as loss of profits by reason of reduced sales.

In this regard, it is established in the field of taxation that a Member State is not required to repay charges levied in breach of Community law where it is established that the person required to pay such charges has actually passed them on in whole or in part to other persons and where reimbursement would amount to unjust enrichment.[49] However, the mere fact that the claimant has passed on the unlawful tax by including it in the price charged to its customers does not mean that the claimant would necessarily be unjustly enriched by reimbursement. "The trader may justly claim that, although the charge has been passed on to the purchaser, the inclusion of that charge in the cost price has, by increasing the price of the goods and reducing sales, caused him damage which excludes, in whole or in part, any unjust enrichment which would otherwise be caused by reimbursement."[50]

10.6.4.1 Liability

The burden of proof rests on a claimant to establish his case on liability (see 10.4.1). That burden will be easy to discharge where the Commission or the OFT has made an infringement decision in relation to the agreement or conduct on which the claim is based: the provisions of Regulation 1/2003 (Article 16) and the CA 1998 (sections 47A and 58A) that enable claimants to "piggy-back" on Commission and NCA infringement decisions are described elsewhere in this Chapter, (see 10.7.2.1 and 10.7.2.3 below).[51]

48. Many of those unresolved issues were due to be addressed by the CAT in *BCL Old Co Ltd and Others v. Aventis SA and Others*, but the case settled before final hearing.

49. See, eg, Joined Cases C-192/95 to C-218/95, *Société Comateb v. Directeur-Général des Douanes et Droits Indirects* [1997] STC 1006, paras 21–33.

50. *Ibid*, para 32.

51. See 10.7.4.5: "evidence" was removed.

10.6.4.2 Quantum[52]

In the absence of any harmonising measure,[53] and subject to the Community law principles of equivalence and effectiveness, the quantum of damages is a matter of domestic law.

In English law, the object of an award of damages is to give the claimant compensation for the loss and damage suffered. The "overriding rule" as to the correct method of assessing damages is that the measure of damages is "that sum of money which will put the party who has been injured, or who has suffered, in the same position as he would have been in if he had not sustained the wrong for which he is now getting his compensation or reparation".[54]

That "overriding rule" is, however, only a starting point. A number of rules cut down a claimant's ability to recover a full indemnity, such as the rules on causation, mitigation and certainty of damage.

10.6.4.2.1 Causation

In English law, a claimant is only entitled to recover damages in respect of a breach of duty if he or she can establish that the breach is the effective or dominant cause of the loss claimed. What is meant by "cause" in this context remains to be determined definitively. At the very least, a remedy in damages should be available where there is a "direct causal link" between the infringement and the claimant's loss.[55] In *Arkin v. Borchard Lines Ltd and Others*[56] Coleman J, citing *Galoo Ltd v. Bright Grahame Murray*,[57] considered (albeit *obiter*)[58] that it was necessary

> " . . . to distinguish between conduct on the part of the defendant which caused the loss and conduct which gave the opportunity for the loss to be sustained. Where the issue is whether there was a break in the chain of causation by conduct on the part of the claimant, that is to say whether the effect of the defendant's conduct was more than to provide the opportunity for the claimant by his own deliberate act to cause himself loss, the approach must be one of common sense, there being in each case an overarching concept that the chain of causation can be broken only if it is concluded that the claimant's own conduct displaced that of the defendant as the predominant cause of the claimant's loss . . . .
>
> Translated into the facts of this case, the issue is essentially whether [the cartel victim's] response to the price setting policies of the [cartel] was so unreasonable that

52. See generally *McGregor op cit,* n 44, above, Chapter 6.

53. The Commission is currently consulting with Member States as to whether, and if so what, Community rules should be introduced.

54. *Livingstone v. Rawyards Coal Co* (1880) 5 App Cas 25, p 39 (Lord Blackburn), cited in *Crehan v. Inntrepreneur Pub Company* [2004] EWCA Civ 637, para 179.

55. By analogy to claims against Member States for breaches of directly effective EU law rights: see, eg, Joined Cases C-46/93 and C-48/93, *Brasserie du Pêcheur and Factortame* [1996] ECR I 1029, para 51.

56. [2003] EWHC 687 (Comm).

57. [1994] 1 WLR 1360.

58. *Ibid,* paras 536–538.

it represented an intervening cause of such losses as may be proved to have been sustained by [the victim]."

10.6.4.2.2 Mitigation[59]

The issue of mitigation of loss is closely related to causation and it is artificial to consider mitigation separately from causation and quantum: see *Arkin*.[60]

10.6.4.2.3 Quantification

The basis on which damages are to be quantified is relatively simple to state. The starting point for any assessment of damages is a comparison between the claimant's actual position and the position in which it would have been if there had been no infringement. Thus, in *Provimi v. Aventis Animal Nutrition SA and Others*,[61] a claim for damages under Article 81, Aikens J considered that "the right question to ask is: what would the situation have been if there had been no cartels?". *Prima facie*, the claimant's loss is the difference between the two positions. In the context of torts involving interference with business relations, to which competition law claims have the nearest similarity, the basic loss tends to be the loss of profits caused by the tort, although that is not an invariable rule. The quantification exercise itself is potentially extremely complex and difficult and may require sophisticated and expensive expert economic and accountancy evidence. The problem is compounded by the speculative nature of the exercise and the need for a claimant to make out its case with a degree of certainty.

An example of the English courts' approach to quantum is provided by *Crehan v. Inntrepreneur* following its return from the ECJ. The High Court held that Mr Crehan, a publican, had failed to make out his case on liability, but also found that, had he done so, damages should have been assessed as at the date of trial and calculated on the following basis:

- first, a sum (£57,121) in respect of the losses actually suffered (including lost profits) during the periods from 11 July 1991 (when he entered into "beer ties" with Inntrepreneur's supplier) until the failure of his business and surrender of his two premises on 4 March and 27 September 1993 respectively, calculated on the basis that, if free of tie, he would have charged less and sold more;
- secondly, a sum (£889,052) in respect of the profits Mr Crehan would have made between 1993 and 2003 (the date of trial) if free of tie;
- thirdly, a sum (£361,500) in respect of the value in 2003 (the date of trial) of the leases Mr Crehan would have owned if free of tie throughout.

59. See generally *McGregor* n 44 above, Chapter 7.
60. [2003] EWHC 687 (Comm), para 536.
61. [2003] EWHC 961.

The Court of Appeal reversed the High Court's decision on liability,[62] but rejected the High Court's method of assessment in part, considering that the second and third heads awarded were simply too speculative and uncertain. The court accepted that damages should be assessed at the dates in 1993 when Mr Crehan gave up possession of the two premises (at which dates Mr Crehan's losses were crystallised[63]) and in addition to his accrued losses (£57,121) awarded him the difference between the value of the leases subject to the ties and free from the ties (£74,215).

10.6.4.6 Impact of fines on damages

There is no reason in principle why damages awarded to a claimant as a result of a competition law infringement should be reduced where a defendant has also been fined by the Commission or an NCA in respect of the infringement.

10.6.4.7 Exemplary damages?

It remains to be determined whether exemplary damages may be awarded to a claimant in respect of an undertaking's breach of competition law. It is submitted, however, that the existence of a system of administrative penalties makes it inappropriate to award damages to a claimant that exceed its personal loss.

10.6.4.8 "Restitutionary damages"

Usually, damages in tort are measured by the claimant's loss, not by the defendant's gain. Recently, however, the English courts have identified the concept of "restitutionary damages",[64] ie damages measured by the defendant's gain. In *Attorney-General v. Blake*[65] it was recognised that damages for torts concerning wrongful interference with another's land, goods and other property (eg patents) have been measured by the defendant's gain and that in such cases the common law generally awarded a sum equivalent to the price or hire that a reasonable person would pay for such use, even if the owner would not himself actually have been using the property. At first sight, there seems little scope for an award of "restitutionary damages" in a competition law claim, but the matter remains open.

10.6.4.9 Identifying defendants: joint and several liability

In principle (although the issue has not yet been decided), parties to an infringing agreement are jointly and severally liable in respect of loss caused by

62. [2004] EWCA Civ 637.
63. *Ibid*, para 173.
64. See *Attorney-General v. Blake* [2001] 1 AC 268 (Lord Nicholls described "restitutionary damages" as an "unhappy expression" which he "[preferred] to avoid"); *Experience Hendrix v. PPX Enterprises Inc* [2003] EWCA Civ 323; *McGregor on Damages* n 44 above, Chapter 12.
65. [2001] 1 AC 268.

the infringing agreement and its implementation. In principle, the claimant may therefore sue one party, more than one party or all parties.

Further, in *Provimi*[66] Aikens J held it to be arguable that a claimant based in Germany could claim damages for breach of Article 81 against defendants based in the UK, even though the defendants were not themselves party to the cartel, but were subsidiaries of cartel members based outside the UK, and even though the claimant had not bought anything from those defendants.

10.6.5 Restitution

"Restitution" is an umbrella term covering a number of common-law and equitable remedies, all of which are based on the principle of unjust enrichment. In essence, a claim for "restitution" is a claim for disgorgement of a benefit unjustly obtained at the expense of another.[67]

The most obvious situation of relevance to competition law claims is where a claimant has paid a sum of money to a defendant pursuant to a void agreement.[68] It can be inferred from the ECJ's reasoning in *Courage v. Crehan* that English law rules on illegality, or any other rule of English law, to the effect that a claimant could not claim repayment of any sum would have to be disapplied if those rules would preclude a properly brought restitutionary claim by a party who does not bear significant responsibility for the distortion of competition.

10.6.6 Defences

10.6.6.1 Limitation

Section 2 of the Limitation Act 1980 provides that an action in tort must be brought within six years of the date on which the cause of action accrued. No cause of action accrues until a claimant suffers relevant loss as a result of the infringement. Loss is not presumed.

Difficult questions may arise in the context of limitation as to whether a breach of duty gives rise to a single cause of action or a series of causes of action. In the competition law context, where the infringement consists of the continuing implementation of an agreement etc that contravenes Article 81, or of conduct infringing Article 82, a new cause of action will accrue every day on which a claimant suffers loss. In those circumstances, a claimant will be able to recover in respect of all loss occurring within six years of the start of a claim, even if the claimant suffered other losses before that date.

Section 32(1) of the Limitation Act 1980 is potentially relevant. It provides (among other things) that where any fact relevant to the claimant's right of

66. [2003] EWHC 961. See 10.6.4.2.3 above.
67. See further Goff & Jones, *The Law of Restitution*, 6th edn, 2002.
68. See 10.5.4 above.

action has been deliberately concealed from him by the defendant, the period of limitation shall not begin to run until the claimant has discovered the concealment or could with reasonable diligence have discovered it. For those purposes, deliberate commission of a breach of duty in circumstances in which it is unlikely to be discovered for some time amounts to deliberate concealment of the facts involved in that breach of duty.

Limitation periods are not applied automatically and must be specifically pleaded by a defendant.

The time limits specified in the Limitation Act 1980 do not apply where the time limits specified by section 47A of the Competition Act 1998 and Rule 31 of the Competition Appeal Tribunal Rules 2003 apply (see 10.7.2.3 below).

10.7 GENERAL POINTS OF PRACTICE, PROCEDURE AND EVIDENCE

10.7.1 Regulation 1/2003

10.7.1.1 Procedural aspects of the application of EU competition rules in national courts

A national court may not apply national rules that are incompatible with the principles set out in 10.6.1 above. Regulation 1/2003 has also introduced directly effective provisions that determine to some extent the conditions in which EU competition rules are enforced and prevail over national law. Because domestic court procedure has been brought in line with the requirements of the Regulation, those provisions are considered in outline only. Again, Regulation 1/2003 must also be read in conjunction with the Commission Notice on the cooperation between the Commission and the courts of the EU Member States in the application of Articles 81 and 82.[69]

10.7.1.2 Cooperation between the Commission and national courts

Article 15 of Regulation 1/2003 provides that in proceedings for the application of Articles 81 or 82, national courts may ask the Commission to transmit to them information in its possession or its opinion on questions concerning the application of the Community competition rules.

10.7.1.3 Transmission of information[70]

A national court may, for example, ask the Commission for documents in its possession or for information of a procedural nature to enable it to discover whether a certain case is pending before the Commission, whether the Commission has initiated a procedure, or whether it has already taken a position.

69. 2004 OJ C 101/54.
70. Regulation 1/2003, paras 21–26.

A national court may also ask the Commission when a Decision is likely to be taken, so as to be able to determine the conditions for any decision to stay proceedings or whether interim measures need to be adopted.

Transmission of information is subject to obligations of secrecy. The Commission may also refuse to transmit information to national courts for overriding reasons relating to the need to safeguard the interests of the Community or to avoid any interference with its functioning and independence. The Commission will not transmit to national courts information voluntarily submitted by a leniency applicant without the consent of that applicant.

10.7.1.4 Requests for opinions[71]

The national court may ask the Commission for its opinion on economic, factual and legal matters.[72] When giving its opinion, the Commission will limit itself to providing the national court with the factual information or the economic or legal clarification asked for, without considering the merits of the case pending before the national court. The opinion of the Commission is not legally binding on the national court.[73]

10.7.1.5 National judgments

Article 15(2) of Regulation 1/2003 requires Member States to forward to the Commission a copy of any written judgment of national courts deciding on the application of Article 81 or 82.

10.7.1.6 Submission of observations to the national court

Article 15(3) of Regulation 1/2003 provides that the Commission and NCAs may submit observations on issues relating to the application of Articles 81 or 82 to a national court that is called upon to apply those provisions. The Article distinguishes between written observations, which the Commission and NCAs may submit on their own initiative, and oral observations, which may only be submitted with the permission of the national court.

The Commission has stated that it will limit its observations under Article 15(3) to an economic and legal analysis of the facts underlying the case pending before the national court.[74]

Article 15(3) also sets out minimum requirements for cooperation between the relevant NCA and the national court. Article 15 is without prejudice to wider powers to make observations before courts conferred on NCAs under domestic law.

71. *Ibid*, paras 27–30.
72. *Ibid*, para 27.
73. *Ibid*, para 29.
74. *Ibid*, para 33; see generally paras 31–35.

10.7.2 England and Wales

In England and Wales, private enforcement of a competition law claim may be brought in two venues:

- A claim for any competition law remedy may be commenced in the Chancery Division of the High Court at the Royal Courts of Justice in London.
- Monetary claims for breaches of EU and UK competition law may be brought in the CAT pursuant to section 47A of the CA 1998.

At this point, it is necessary to refer to the following procedural provisions intended to facilitate private enforcement. They do not affect the substantive law.

10.7.2.1 Competition Act 1998, section 58A

Section 58A of the CA 1998[75] permits a party to "piggy-back" on an OFT infringement decision in order to advance a monetary claim. It applies to proceedings before a domestic court in which damages or any other sum of money[76] is claimed in respect of an infringement of the Chapter I or Chapter II prohibitions of the Act, or Article 81(1) or Article 82. In such proceedings, the court is bound by a decision of the OFT (or a decision of the CAT on appeal from a decision of the OFT) that the Chapter I prohibition, Chapter II prohibition, Article 81(1) or 82 has been infringed, once the relevant period has elapsed (basically, once the appeals procedure has been exhausted).[77] Section 58A came into force on 20 June 2003 and does not apply to decisions made before that date.

The CA 1998 contains no similar provision in relation to Commission Decisions. However, Article 16 of Regulation 1/2003 and the ECJ's decision in *Masterfoods*[78] make it clear that the same rule applies to Commission Decisions.

In effect, therefore, a party can use an infringement decision by the Commission or the OFT to establish the infringement and thus liability (where the infringement causes loss).

10.7.2.2 Competition Act 1998, section 58

Section 58 of the CA 1998 provides that unless the court otherwise directs, a finding of fact made by the OFT in the course of conducting an investigation that is relevant to an issue arising in proceedings brought otherwise than by the OFT in respect of an alleged infringement of the Chapter I or Chapter II prohibitions or Article 81(1) or Article 82 is binding on the parties, after the

75. Inserted by s 20(1) of the Enterprise Act 2002.
76. Section 58A(1) is wide enough to include restitutionary claims, if available. Cf s 47A(1).
77. See ss 58A(2)–(4).
78. Case 344/98, *Masterfoods Ltd v. HB Foods Ltd* [2000] ECR I 11369.

time for appealing to the CAT has expired or the CAT has confirmed the finding on appeal.

10.7.2.3 Competition Act 1998, section 47A

Section 47A of the CA 1998 provides that monetary claims for breaches of EU and UK competition law may be brought in the CAT.[79] The right to make a claim under section 47A is without prejudice to any other right to bring any other proceedings in respect of the claim.[80] Section 47A applies to any claim for damages or any other sum of money that a person who has suffered loss or damage as a result of the infringement of a relevant prohibition may make in civil proceedings brought in any part of the UK.[81] The section applies to claims arising both before and after its commencement.[82] The section covers infringements of the Chapter I and Chapter II prohibitions and Articles 81(1) and 82.[83]

Section 47A(3) provides that, for the purpose of identifying claims that may be made in civil proceedings, any limitation rules that would apply in such proceedings are to be disregarded.[84]

Section 47A(5) provides that no claim may be made under section 47A unless a relevant decision has been made and a specified time has elapsed. Section 47A(6) provides that a relevant decision for these purposes is:

- a decision of the OFT (or, on appeal from such a decision, a decision of the CAT) that the Chapter I or Chapter II prohibition or Article 81(1) or 82 has been infringed; or
- a Decision of the Commission that Article 81(1) or Article 82 of the EC Treaty or Article 65(1) of the European Coal and Steel Community ("ECSC") Treaty has been infringed, or a finding by the Commission under Article 66(7) ECSC.

Section 47A(9) provides that, in determining a claim to which section 47A applies, the CAT is bound by any decision of the OFT, CAT or Commission referred to in section 47A(6) that establishes the infringement.

Section 47A(7) and (8) sets out periods during which proceedings in respect of a claim may not be brought without permission, the intention being to allow the appeals procedure to be exhausted before a claim is pursued.

Rule 31 of the Competition Appeal Tribunal Rules 2003[85] requires a claim for damages (ie a claim under section 47A) to be made within two years of

79. See s 47A(4).
80. See s 47A(10).
81. The wording of s 47A(1) is arguably not wide enough to include a restitutionary claim: cf s 58A.
82. Enterprise Act 2002, s 18(2).
83. Section 47A also applies to infringements of the prohibitions in Articles 65(1) and 66(7) of the Treaty establishing the European Coal and Steel Community Treaty (ECSC).
84. As to limitation generally, see 10.6.6.1 above.
85. SI 2003/1372.

whichever is the later of the end of the period specified in section 47A(7) or (8) and the date on which the cause of action accrued.[86]

10.7.3 The High Court

Procedure in the High Court and county courts in England and Wales is governed by the Civil Procedure Rules ("CPR"). A detailed description of civil procedure is beyond the scope of this book and reference should be made to standard practitioner texts. The following section addresses certain basic issues of procedure and evidence and gives details of specific provisions relating to competition law claims.

10.7.3.1 Competition Law Practice Direction

In England and Wales, the requirements of Articles 15 and 16 of Regulation 1/2003 have been incorporated into the CPR by the insertion of a new rule 30.8 and a new Practice Direction,[87] with effect from 1 May 2004.

10.7.3.2 Which court?

Any proceedings involving any issue relating to the application of Articles 81 or 82, or Chapter I or II, must be commenced in the Chancery Division of the High Court at the Royal Courts of Justice in London.[88] Any party whose statement of case (particulars of claim, defence, reply etc[89]) raises an issue relating to the application of Article 81 or 82, or Chapter I or II, must state that fact in its statement of case and apply for the proceedings to be transferred to the Chancery Division at the Royal Courts of Justice, if they have not been commenced there.[90] If a party's statement of case raises such an issue, that court must transfer the proceedings to the Chancery Division in London.[91] The ordinary rules concerning transfer of proceedings do not apply and the transferring court has no discretion in the matter.

The Chancery Division may transfer the proceedings or any part of the proceedings to another court if the issue relating to the application of Article 81 or 82, or Chapter I or II, has been resolved or the judge considers that the proceedings or part of the proceedings to be transferred does not involve any issue relating to the application of Article 81 or 82, or Chapter I or II.

10.7.3.3 Case management provisions

Any party whose statement of case raises or deals with an issue relating to the application of Article 81 or 82, or Chapter I or II, must serve a copy of the

86. As to which, see 10.6.6.1 above.

87. Practice Direction: Competition Law—Claims Relating to the Application of Articles 81 and 82 of the EC Treaty and Chapters I and II of Part I of the Competition Act 1998.

88. *Ibid*, para 2.1.

89. See generally CPR, r 7.4; Part 15; Part 16.

90. Practice Direction: Competition Law, para 2.2.

91. CPR, rule 30.8.

statement of case on the OFT at the same time as it is served on the other parties to the claim.[92] Paragraph 4 of the Practice Direction contains provisions relating to the Commission's and NCAs' entitlement to make observations in respect of issues relating to Articles 81 and 82 and permits NCAs to make written observations, and apply for permission to make oral observations, on issues relating to the application of Chapter I or II.

10.7.3.4 Avoidance of conflict with Commission Decisions

Paragraph 5 of the Practice Direction requires every party to a claim, and any NCA that has been served with a copy of a party's statement of case, to notify the court at any stage of the proceedings if they are aware that the Commission has adopted, or is contemplating adopting, a Decision in relation to proceedings that it has initiated and the Decision has or would have legal effects in relation to the particular agreement, decision or practice in issue before the court.[93] Where the court is aware that the Commission is contemplating adopting a Decision, it must consider whether to stay the claim pending the Commission's Decision.

10.7.3.5 Judgments

Where any judgment is given that decides on the application of Article 81 or Article 82, the judge shall direct that a copy of the transcript of the judgment shall be sent to the Commission.

10.7.4 General procedure

10.7.4.1 Statements of case

There is no inherent difference between statements of case in a competition case and any other case. The statements of case must contain proper particulars of all the elements necessary to establish the cause of action or defence.[94] In particular, it is necessary to give proper particulars of the factual allegations regarding effect on competition in such terms that it can be seen how the effect complained of flows from the agreement etc or abuse of dominant position. Failure to do so will lead either to a request for further information under CPR Part 18, or an application to strike out the statement of case under CPR rule 3.4 as disclosing no reasonable grounds for bringing or defending the claim.[95] Statements of case must be verified by a statement of truth.[96]

92. Practice Direction: Competition Law, para 3.
93. *Ibid*, para 5.2.
94. See CPR, Part 16.
95. Applications under CPR, r 3.4 are often coupled with applications for summary judgment under r 24.2, as to which see 10.7.4.2 below.
96. CPR, r 22.1. The form of the statement of truth is set out in the Practice Direction supplementing Part 22.

10.7.4.2 Summary judgment

CPR rule 24.2 provides that the court may give summary judgment against a claimant or defendant if certain conditions are met.

10.7.4.3 Interim remedies

The court's power to grant interim injunctions has been described at 10.6.2 above. The procedural rules are set out in CPR Part 25 and Part 23 (which sets out the general rules about applications for court orders).

10.7.4.4 Disclosure and inspection of documents

The CPR provides for the mutual disclosure and inspection of documents (ie anything in which information is recorded). Disclosure in this regard means stating whether a document exists or has existed. A party to whom a document has been disclosed has a right to inspect that document, except where the document is no longer in the control of the party who disclosed it; where the party disclosing the document has a right or a duty to withhold inspection of it; or where permitting inspection would be disproportionate to the issues in the case.[97]

Among the situations where a party has a right to withhold inspection are where documents are privileged from production on grounds of legal advice privilege (confidential communications between a party and his legal advisers for the purpose of giving and receiving legal advice) and litigation privilege (confidential communications between a solicitor and third parties that come into existence after litigation is contemplated and made with a view to such litigation, either for the purpose of obtaining or giving advice in relation to it, or obtaining or collecting evidence, or obtaining or collecting information that may lead to obtaining evidence). Commercial confidentiality is not a ground for withholding inspection, although the court may impose terms, such as restricting inspection to the other party's legal advisers.

Usual practice is to order "standard disclosure", which requires a party to disclose only:

- (a) the documents on which it relies; and
- (b) the documents that:
  - (i) adversely affect its own case;
  - (ii) adversely affect another party's case; or
  - (iii) support another party's case; and
- (c) the documents that it is required to disclose by a relevant Practice Direction.[98]

97. CPR, r 31.3.
98. CPR, r 31.6.

10.7.4.5 Evidence

The party bearing the burden of proof on any given contentious issue must adduce cogent, admissible evidence to support his claim. (A detailed discourse on the English law of evidence is outside the scope of this book, and reference should be made to the standard practitioner texts.) It is at this point that the desirability of a prior infringement decision by the Commission, the OFT or other NCA becomes particularly apparent. A binding infringement decision effectively discharges the burden of proof in establishing liability.

10.7.5 The Competition Appeal Tribunal

The procedural rules governing damages claims in the CAT under section 47A of the 1998 Act are contained in Part IV—as well as Part I, Part II (rules 17 to 24 only) and Part V—of the Competition Appeal Tribunal Rules 2003.[99]

Section 16 of the Enterprise Act 2002 provides for the transfer, subject to rules of court and CAT rules, of section 47A claims between the CAT and (a) the High Court or a county court (in England and Wales or Northern Ireland) or (b) the Court of Session or a sheriff court (in Scotland).

Rule 48 of the CAT rules provides that the CAT may direct that a claim for any sum that may be claimed under section 47A be transferred to a court. Rule 49 provides that a claim that may be made under section 47A may be transferred to the CAT from any court in accordance with rules of court or any Practice Direction.

In England and Wales, the relevant rules (for both the High Court and county courts) are contained in paragraph 8 of the Practice Direction supplementing CPR Part 30. CPR rules 30.1, 30.4 and 30.5 and paragraphs 3 and 6 of that Practice Direction also apply. The High Court or a county court may order the transfer to the CAT of "any part of the proceedings before it which relates to a claim to which section 47A . . . applies". The Practice Direction sets out factors to be taken into account when considering whether to make such an order. Any claim transferred to the High Court by the CAT must be transferred to the Chancery Division of the High Court at the Royal Courts of Justice.

10.7.6 Settlement

The great majority of claims (whether competition law related or otherwise) are settled before trial. A settlement is no different from any other agreement as regards the potential application of EU and UK competition law.

99. SI 2003/1372.

CHAPTER 11

COMPLIANCE

Jane Whittaker and Martin Ballantyne, Macfarlanes

11.1 WHY HAVE A COMPLIANCE POLICY?

11.1.1 Risk management

Competition authorities around the world have made it clear that the task of uncovering cartels (and other price-fixing arrangements) is their highest priority. The escalation in the level of fines imposed on companies who have been found to have acted in breach of competition law demonstrates that this is not an issue that companies can afford to ignore. It is therefore essential that companies ensure that their business is compliant with competition law, and that their employees know what they can and cannot do.

Risk management is a topic that has come increasingly to the fore in companies' thinking, and competition compliance should be a core element of their strategy alongside existing, and often more established, financial, health and safety, regulatory and other procedures.

Take the following scenario: staff have just settled down to work in the morning, when an executive is called by the receptionist who informs him that eight visitors are downstairs, claiming to be officials from the European Commission and the Office of Fair Trading ("OFT"). They are demanding to see a senior representative of the company. The documentation they have with them states that they suspect that the company has been involved in an illegal price-fixing cartel with its competitors, and that the officials are here to investigate.

Such a scenario may be the first time a company (or various employees) comes into contact with competition law. If it had digested the contents of a company compliance programme, the experience of such a "dawn raid" would create considerably less problems for the company and enable it to better protect itself during the dawn raid, which can often have a very significant impact on the subsequent conduct and direction of an investigation by competition authorities. This Chapter seeks to set out how a company can—by sound guidance and management techniques—be best prepared for the day ahead.

11.1.2 Positive benefits

Most companies' aim is to ensure that their business practices are compliant with all relevant laws. The benefits for companies that implement an effective compliance policy are numerous and can be significant:

— *Avoiding fines*: the levels of fines that a company may face for failing to comply with EU and/or national competition rules can be very burdensome.[1] An infringement of Articles 81 or 82 can lead to fines of up to 10 per cent of a company's worldwide turnover. In addition, national competition authorities ("NCAs") are now also able to enforce Articles 81 and 82 as well as their national equivalents. Further, the number of regulators that may be able to impose fines for breaches of competition law has increased considerably over the last few years, as has the associated risk for businesses.

— *Mitigating the level of the fine*: where a company has actively sought to implement a compliance policy, but has nonetheless committed a breach of competition law, the existence of that policy can act as a mitigating factor when the regulator comes to consider the level of fine to be imposed. Merely having a compliance policy set down on paper will not, however, suffice for these purposes. The authorities require some evidence that the company has in good faith actively sought to enforce the policy, but that for some reason a breach has nonetheless occurred. Typically, companies have received reductions of around 10 per cent in the level of fine imposed where they have successfully shown a commitment to compliance.[2] In addition, a company with an effective compliance programme may be able to demonstrate that the breach was due to the actions of a rogue employee rather than a company-wide failing, which in turn may have a mitigating impact on the level of fine.

— *Avoiding invalid agreements*: an understanding of the competition laws will reduce the likelihood of entering into agreements that are invalid from the outset. Further, a competition law audit (a feature of compliance polices) should identify any existing agreements containing provisions that are invalid under competition law. An agreement that infringes Article 81(1) will, in whole or in part, be void and unenforceable. Many national jurisdictions have similar provisions for agreements which are not caught by the EU rules. The unenforceability of certain provisions in an agreement may have significant financial and/or strategic consequences for the parties, particularly if the agreement

1. The Commission imposed fines totalling €1.3 billion in 2003–2004

2. The Commission has taken the establishment of a compliance policy into account as a mitigating factor in several cases including *National Panasonic* 1982 OJ L 354/28; *Fisher-Price/Quaker Oats Ltd-Toyco* 1988 OJ L 49/19; and *Eurofix-Bauco v. Hilti* 1988 OJ L 65/19. The OFT has applied a similar policy, as demonstrated in *Arriva plc/First Group plc*, Decision CA98/9/2002.

forms part of a wider arrangement that cannot operate without the enforceability of the agreement in question.

- *Avoiding potential third-party actions for damages*: third parties who suffer damage as a result of an infringement of EU (and many national) competition laws can seek to recover their losses from those parties involved in the infringement through national courts or equivalent tribunals. While such third party damages actions are still relatively uncommon, a number of countries have recently changed their laws in an attempt to make private enforcement claims easier, in the hope that this move will act as an added deterrent. In the UK, for example, a claimant in a court can rely on a decision of the OFT or the European Commission to establish the fact that a breach of competition law has taken place, and so only needs to demonstrate that the breach caused it some loss. It is anticipated that such damages actions will increase in the future and their potential significance should not be underestimated.[3]
- *Avoiding indirect costs*: companies involved in competition investigations face a number of further, often less obvious, consequences. First, the costs of dealing with an investigation are considerable. There are intangible costs due to lost management time and tangible ones such as external legal costs. Second, when details of the investigation become publicly known, this may have an immediate impact on a public company's share price. Third, the bad publicity surrounding a finding of infringement can have serious knock-on effects for future sales, particularly in the case of branded goods sold direct to the consumer.
- *Triggering a "leniency" application*: an effective compliance policy should result in alerting a company to situations that could prudently give rise to seeking immunity or a reduction in fines under one of the many leniency programmes operated by the various competition authorities.[4]
- *Increasing proactive awareness*: increased awareness among employees of competition law can have a useful proactive effect. A comprehensive compliance policy should educate staff to identify situations where they may be able to use competition law arguments as a "sword", rather than a "shield" (for example where a dominant supplier may be seeking to impose abusive conditions in breach of Article 82, or where a number of customer undertakings may be acting collectively in breach of Article 81(1)).

3. The Commission has published a statement seeking to encourage private enforcement in Member States.

4. If a company finds out about a cartel in which it has been participating but of which senior management had been unaware, it may choose to unilaterally approach the regulators and whistle-blow on the cartel in return for a total or partial reduction in any fine that may ultimately be imposed. See 9.10.4.2.

11.1.2 Compliance

A compliance policy that is inadequately prepared or implemented can, in some circumstances, be worse than having no compliance policy at all. Competition authorities place great emphasis on the proposition that only an "effective" compliance policy will be sufficient to protect a company, and this has manifested itself in a number of cases where companies have had their fine increased because they had a compliance policy in place, but either ignored it or failed to ensure that it was properly implemented.[5]

11.1.3 EU enlargement and cooperation between NCAs

The enlargement of the EU in May 2004 from 15 to 25 Member States has widened the geographical reach of EU competition law and the Commission's corresponding jurisdiction to investigate matters yet further. In addition, a considerable number of further countries, including the US, Canada and Japan, have bilateral agreements with the EU under which they agree to cooperate on competition matters.

Within Europe, the NCAs of the individual Member States and the Commission cooperate through their membership of the European Competition Network ("ECN"), enabling them to exchange certain information on current investigations, increasingly leading to coordinated investigations by a number of NCAs and/or the Commission acting together.

In consequence, companies must ensure that their compliance policy satisfies not only the requirements of EU competition law, but also the national competition laws of Member States and other third countries in which they do business.

In addition, a number of EU Member States, including the UK, Ireland, Germany (for bid-rigging), Austria and France have introduced criminal penalties for individuals who are found guilty of committing certain competition law infringements.

11.2 OVERVIEW OF CONTENTS OF A COMPLIANCE POLICY

The content of the compliance policy must both address the business realities faced by an individual company, and be implemented so as to ensure that it is of practical use on a day-to-day basis.

5. In *British Sugar* 1999 OJ L 76/1, the Commission noted that British Sugar acted in a manner contrary to its compliance policy and breached a promise to ensure that every step it took was in compliance with Community competition law. This, together with the fact that British Sugar was considered an instigator and driving force behind the agreement, resulted in a 75 per cent uplift in its fine. In *John Bruce (UK) Ltd* Decision CA98/12/2002, the OFT reduced Fleet Parts' fine by 10 per cent because it introduced a compliance policy and training programme, whereas Truck and Trailer Components had its fine increased by 10 per cent for breaching of its existing compliance policy.

If a compliance policy is not tailored so as to be suitable for a particular company and is not implemented in an effective way, it may have counter-productive results. For example, the company may be misled into focusing on irrelevant aspects of its business, and therefore pay insufficient attention to those that are most vulnerable to competition law.

A number of NCAs have issued guidance as to what they consider to be to be the basic requisite elements of a compliance policy.[6] Regulators are, however, generally not prepared to authorise companies' individual policies.

When drafting the documentation, it is essential to keep in mind the target audience. While the person responsible for coordinating the policy within the company will often be a member of the in-house legal function, the employees who face situations in which competition law related issues may arise on a daily basis will invariably not be legally trained. In consequence, there is little point in drafting an academic legal treatise on the subject; rather, the text needs to be clear, concise and easy to understand for both management and individuals on the ground.

Companies may assume that a compliance policy can be purchased as an "off-the-shelf" product and that, with a little tinkering, it can be personalised to them, thus enabling them to "tick" the competition compliance "box". While a number of such off the shelf products are available, there is a danger that unless they are very specifically tailored to the company's individual business needs they will, rather like a "make-your-own" will, be more hindrance than help.

11.2.1 Essential elements of the policy

A compliance policy should include:

- *Policy statement from the Board*: it is essential that a compliance policy is endorsed by the management of the company. A statement should therefore be prepared setting out the company's ethos in relation to competition (ie that it believes in free and fair competition), the fact that management takes the matter extremely seriously, and that the onus is on each and every employee in the company to ensure that competition law is adhered to and to report any suspected violations he or she may uncover.
- *The manual itself*: the compliance manual is the centrepiece of the policy. The success or failure of the programme will depend to a significant extent on the drafting of the manual and the methods

6. For example, the OFT has published a guidance leaflet entitled "How your Business can Achieve Compliance"; the US authorities have listed seven essential elements of an effective compliance programme as set out in the "US Sentencing Guidelines"; the Canadian Competition Bureau has published a document entitled "Program of Compliance"; and the Australian Competition and Consumer Commission has stated that compliance programmes should comply with the "Australian Standard on Compliance Programmes" (AS3806).

employed in presenting it to the relevant employees. It is therefore essential that the manual is customised for the relevant everyday situations faced by the individual company. The manual must be written in plain English, and avoid the use of legal terminology.

11.2.1.1 Contents of a manual

A manual should cover the following areas.

11.2.1.1.1 Implementation and enforcement

No compliance policy will be taken seriously by employees unless breaches of the policy carry with them the potential for significant individual consequences. The policy should therefore set out what disciplinary action may be taken against individuals who are found to have acted in breach. The severity of any applicable disciplinary measures is for each company to decide, but ideally this would be dismissal for the most serious of cases.

A balance between sanction and support needs to be established, in that simply threatening employees is of little practical benefit if a company is not also prepared to take steps to help employees to be compliant. The manual should therefore also set out what the company intends to do in terms of training, monitoring and assessment of how the policy is working in practice.

The policy should provide a clear guide as to what employees should do, and whom they should contact, in the event that they suspect that the policy may have been breached. This is a point that needs to be handled sensitively during training sessions, as the notion of a "witch-hunt", or a feeling that employees should become informants against their colleagues, will not be well received. That said, it is essential for an effective procedure to be in place for employees to contact someone (usually the designated compliance officer) in order not only to report suspected violations, but also to seek guidance as to their own actions as and when issues arise.

11.2.1.1.2 The law

A short description of the relevant law is unavoidable, even in a document that needs to be as non-legal as possible. The manual should set out the basic elements of Articles 81 and 82 and the most relevant national law equivalents, together with a reminder of the enforcement powers of the various regulators and the serious consequences of infringement that the company—and in certain circumstances, individuals—may face.

While the essential elements must be covered, this section should be kept as brief as possible. The practical application of the law can be explained far more effectively during face-to-face training sessions; however, it is important that the basic elements are set out in the manual for future reference.

11.2.1.1.3 Guidelines

A section in the manual setting out practical guidelines for employees is likely to be the most important section of the programme. Careful consideration needs to be given to the company's market position and which areas may, in practice, give rise to competition law exposure. There is, for example, little value in setting out a large number of points to note concerning the behaviour of dominant companies if the company concerned has a low market share.

The company's position in the supply chain is also an important factor, as different considerations will be relevant for manufacturers, wholesalers and retailers etc respectively.

Typical areas to cover in this section might include:

- — types of external discussion that will always be prohibited (eg about pricing);
- — guidelines on the type of information that can legitimately be exchanged and what constitutes confidential or commercially sensitive information (bearing in mind that this may vary considerably depending on the nature of the industry);
- — guidelines for the proper conduct of meetings with competitors (or suppliers/customers);
- — guidance on direct and indirect price-fixing (including resale price maintenance where appropriate);
- — guidance on how to deal with complaints from customers and/or suppliers; and
- — guidance for dominant companies on their special obligations in relation to their dealings with customers/suppliers.

The format of the guidance set out above will vary depending on the target audience and the nature of the business and competition law risks faced. Practical examples of "dos and don'ts" which give giving real-life examples from the company's business often prove extremely effective in this context, and a separate, succinct "dos and don'ts" table may be useful, so that staff can have it easily to hand at all times. This should be drawn up with the help of an employee of the company, whether from the legal department or the operational side, to ensure that the examples given reflect the experiences that employees are likely to face or have faced in the course of their work.

11.2.1.2 Investigations and inquiries

A compliance policy should prepare employees for the possibility of investigations by competition authorities. Care needs to be taken at this point to ensure that this is limited to guidance that is relevant to the employees themselves, rather than those who may be responsible for taking the lead in the event of an investigation. The myriad of different procedural rules concerning investigations by the Commission, NCAs, and NCAs acting on behalf of either Commission or other NCAs, is highly complex, and in most cases entirely irrelevant for most of the individuals involved. Of far greater practical importance is a set of guidance notes for receptionists, who will invariably be the first people to have to deal with any inspectors and who therefore need clear guidance on how to act, whom to contact, and what to do with the inspectors standing before them.

In addition, given the investigators' reluctance to wait beyond a short period of time for external lawyers to arrive, senior management need more detailed guidance on what the investigators can and cannot do, and what information individuals can be required to provide.

Finally, all employees will require some general guidance as to their conduct and the level of information that they should divulge. This should also emphasise the importantance of document retention in the event of a dawn raid, as the discovery of "hot" shredders will be deemed suspicious by the investigators and could lead to criminal sanctions being imposed if it can be shown that documentation has been destroyed.[7]

11.2.1.3 Points to note

In addition to considering the target audience of the compliance policy, thought should also be given to the territories in which the policy will have effect. EU competition law has overriding effect in each of the Member States of the EU; however, a number of variations exist at a local level, which may require some elucidation to avoid general statements being relied on in jurisdictions where they are not appropriate.

For example, some Member States' national laws specially prohibit the imposition of maximum pricing,[8] while others do not, and some countries' laws prohibit sales below cost, while others (such as the UK) generally do not.

11.2.2 The role of the compliance officer

At the same time as (or ideally before) the preparation of the compliance policy and the manual, a company should identify an individual to take on the role of compliance officer. The compliance officer will be responsible for the implementation of the compliance policy, as well as acting as the contact person for individuals on a day-to-day basis.

There are no strict rules as to who should take on this role. Companies often decide that a member of the in-house legal function is best placed, while others prefer to have someone directly involved in the commercial aspects of the business in that he or she may have a better grasp of the practical issues which may arise. Either approach can work equally well; essentially, the person selected needs to have a good grasp of the basic law, understand the areas in

7. See 11.2.4.2 below.
8. For example, the imposition of maximum prices is prohibited under the German Act against Restraints of Competition (although at time of writing this is under review).

which the company faces most risk, and have sufficient authority within the company to ensure that the policy is effectively implemented and adhered to. Equally, it is vital that the compliance officer is approachable (and therefore generally available) as the reporting and everyday advice elements of the policy will otherwise be lost.

11.2.3 How can a compliance policy be implemented effectively?

The actual effectiveness of a compliance policy will depend to a significant degree on the quality of its practical implementation. A number of the concepts that need to be understood are not intuitive to non-lawyers and some run contrary to what business people may believe is in the best interests of increasing sales and protecting the financial stability of the company. If a compliance policy is implemented poorly, it will most likely be ignored by those most at risk, either because it is considered to be too complicated to fit in with day-to-day business objectives or because it is simply deemed impractical. Careful preparation of the implementation is therefore essential.

11.2.3.1 Roll-out: preparation

The first task is to ascertain which employees are potentially exposed to competition law risks in the course of their employment, in order to work out who needs to attend compliance training seminars. This will need to be done in conjunction with the designated compliance officer who should have a good understanding of different employees' day-to-day roles.

Those most at risk will usually comprise members of the sales and marketing functions, anyone who has direct contact with competitors (for example at trade association meetings), and anyone involved in the setting-up and operation of distribution or licensing arrangements.

It is vital that senior management also attend compliance training sessions. This is for two reasons: (a) competition law authorities repeatedly make clear that for a compliance policy to be regarded as effective, it must have the backing of senior management; and (b) the compliance policy will be taken more seriously by employees if they know that senior management is receiving the same training.

Having established who needs training, the make-up of the training sessions needs to be determined. Ideally, numbers should be limited to a maximum of 20 per session, as this allows for enough people to generate debate without individuals feeling inhibited from asking questions.

Whether senior management participate in the same training sessions as more junior employees will depend on the nature of the business and the individuals involved. Simultaneous attendance by senior management is not always desirable as, while it clearly demonstrates their support for the training, it can put off more junior staff from asking questions for fear of embarrassment.

If senior managers do not attend the same sessions as others it is, however, essential that a member of senior management is present at the beginning of each session to introduce the training and emphasise its importance.

Consideration needs to be given to the question of who will present each session. This will often comprise one or two external lawyers, possibly in conjunction with the company's in-house counsel, if one is appointed. Larger organisations may have in-house counsel who have competition law expertise and who may therefore wish to conduct the sessions themselves, referring any more difficult questions to outside counsel after the event. In any case, the trainers must have current competition law experience for the policy to have any credibility.

11.2.3.2 Roll-out: format

As with the drafting of the compliance manual, there is no "accepted" format for the presentation of a compliance training session. The nature of the session, and in particular its level of sophistication, will depend on the participants at each session. As with all training, the aim should be to keep participants interested while at the same time imparting the necessary information in a practical manner.

Typical techniques include PowerPoint presentations to cover the basic principles, accompanied by one or more interactive elements such as videos, quizzes, scenarios and role-plays. Each of these elements requires careful preparation to ensure that they address situations relevant to the individual business.

In addition to an outline of the law and how it operates in a company's sphere of operation, an important topic to cover is the use of language in everyday communications. It is no coincidence that one of the first sources that regulators search for in the course of an investigation is backed-up e-mails, as these often contain the prime source of evidence to prove the existence of anti-competitive arrangements. E-mails are invariably retrievable, even after apparent deletion. When read in the wrong context, their language can often easily be misconstrued due to the comparative lack of thought employed (as opposed to the considerations given to drafting, say, a formal letter). Allocating some time in the compliance training session to the significance of the use of careless or ambiguous language in e-mails is therefore advisable, in order to avoid in advance subsequent awkward questions from a competition authority.

11.2.3.3 Roll-out: handouts

The quantity of documentation given to participants at the training sessions will vary depending on how the company decides to disseminate the compliance policy and manual. A balance needs to be struck between providing so much paper that it goes straight into a pile never to be read, and so little that participants have nothing useful to refer to when faced with a question.

Some companies decide to provide everyone with a copy of the full policy and manual, while others place them on their intranet and provide participants at the training sessions with a short crib-sheet to which they should refer when an issue actually arises. We would favour the latter approach, but the decision will clearly depend on the size of the organisation and the nature of the risks it faces.

Perhaps the most important information for participants to take away is contact details of the compliance officer, so that they know who to turn to if an issue arises.

11.2.3.4 Roll-out: declaration of attendance

All participants at a training session should be requested to sign a declaration at the end of the session confirming that they have attended, have received a copy of whatever handouts are produced, and acknowledge that they know of no existing breaches within the company and will undertake to notify the compliance officer of any breaches of which they may become aware in the future.

This achieves two aims: (a) it reinforces the importance of compliance and focuses the minds of the individuals involved; and (b) if anyone is aware of an existing issue then they are likely to raise it at this stage, as they may be reluctant to sign something that they know to be untrue.

11.2.3.5 Ongoing updating

Once introduced, a compliance policy will only work effectively if it is updated on an ongoing basis. Responsibility for ensuring that this is done will usually lie with the designated compliance officer, often in conjunction with any external lawyers who assisted in initially drawing up the policy.

The updating should cover both the written policy/manual and staff training. Changes in the law should be tracked, as should any relevant regulatory decisions or court judgments that affect the company's activities.

Procedures should be put in place to ensure that new joiners receive some form of compliance training as part of their induction. Ideally, all relevant staff should be reminded on a regular basis of the importance of ongoing compliance: this can easily be achieved by means of a quarterly or six-monthly e-mail from senior management, repeating the essential points of the policy and reinforcing the company's commitment to fair competition.

Once the initial training sessions have been conducted, the company should ensure that these are repeated on an ongoing basis (either annually or biannually) to ensure that staff are aware of any significant changes since their last training sessions, and also to serve as a reminder of the essential elements of the policy.

Compliance can also be built into existing staff appraisal procedures, such that employees are regularly asked to sign a form to confirm that they are not aware of any existing compliance breaches. As with the declaration signed at the initial training session, this focuses the minds of employees and should ensure that any potential problems are caught before they escalate.

11.2.3.6 Ongoing evaluation/monitoring

A compliance policy has a dual function: it is an alerting tool for potential or existing risks, but it also provides opportunities to raise competition arguments in a proactive manner in negotiations. In order to realise this function, appropriate processes must be set up to enable staff both to report on both aspects, and to seek advice on situations in which they are unsure how best to act.

11.2.3.6.1 Contact person

As referred to above, the compliance officer will usually be the first contact person for individuals to contact. Line managers should also be briefed to ensure that urgent questions can be dealt with in the compliance officer's absence.

11.2.3.6.2 Confidentiality of reports

In the context of encouraging employees to come forward if they become aware of problems, it is important to acknowledge that some employees may be reluctant to do so unless they receive sufficient comfort that their reports (and identity) will be kept confidential. This is not a simple issue, in that while such a guarantee may increase the number of reports made, it can also hamper the company's ability to take all necessary resulting action, particularly if the employee making the report is personally involved in the alleged infringement. At most, a company should therefore state that it will endeavour to treat reports confidentially, without guaranteeing this in all circumstances.

Other options, such as an anonymous internet chatroom where employees can leave comments or a secure helpline, can also be employed, although the same confidentiality considerations will apply.

The company must decide at an early stage how reports (for example to the designated compliance officer) will be recorded. Again, the interests of the company may diverge here, in that on the one hand it is useful to have a written log of issues that can be referred to should they arise again in the future, while at the same time producing such a log (which is very unlikely to attract any form of legal privilege, even if compiled by an in-house lawyer) can provide an investigating authority with a collated file of evidence that may be unhelpful to the company and of great interest to the investigators.

One way to avoid this is to instruct employees to contact the compliance officer verbally in the first instance, so that the compliance officer can decide what should be documented in order to avoid exposing the company to unnecessary risk. If information is documented, it is important to ensure that any subsequent actions undertaken by the company in relation to the report are also documented, to demonstrate that the issue has not been ignored or tacitly approved.

11.2.3.6.3 Audits

The introduction of a compliance policy should be augmented by carrying out an internal audit of procedures and documents, including e-mails, ideally both at the time of introduction of the policy and then at a later stage to monitor how effectively the policy is working. The nature of any such audit will depend on the size of the company, the way in which it does business (ie mostly written or orally) and the level of risk to which it is exposed. Any audit needs to be strictly focused in order to avoid aimless searching through documents on the off-chance that something may be turned up.

An efficient way of achieving this is to identify those individuals whose are most at risk and to conduct an audit of a "snapshot" of their e-mails on a given day.[9] A list of keywords should be identified, as most e-mail programmes allow for the headings and text of e-mails to be searched for specific words. This exercise should identify any areas in which the company may be facing compliance risks; it can also provide useful examples for future compliance training sessions. To avoid any reluctance to consent or embarrassment on the part of the employees concerned (as well as to ensure confidentiality), it is advisable for such an e-mail audit to be undertaken by a company's external legal advisers.

11.2.3.6.4 Mock dawn raids

Another popular technique for monitoring the effectiveness of a compliance programme is for external advisers to undertake a mock dawn raid to test a company's dawn raid and compliance procedures.

For a mock dawn raid to be effective, it needs to be unannounced. However, a small number of staff will inevitably need to be informed. In addition, while Commission officials can and do interrupt people's working days without compunction, this is likely to be a more sensitive issue in the context of what is effectively a practice rather than the "real thing". In-house counsel who are considering carrying out a mock dawn raid may therefore wish to consider the knock-on effects on relationships this may have for them with the staff who will be involved.

Competition regulators undertaking dawn raids already have a reasonable suspicion that an infringement has taken place and usually have sufficient information to know what kind of information they are looking for. The same will not usually be true for external (or in-house) lawyers undertaking a mock dawn raid, and there is therefore a danger that a search through files ends up being little more than an aimless fishing expedition with little focus. In any

9. Companies must ensure at this stage that all relevant data protection laws are complied with, bearing in mind that these vary considerably in different jurisdictions.

event, it may for a number of reasons be better for "investigators" on a mock dawn raid just to ask for files to be produced rather than actually going through them.

In our view, mock dawn raids are only of real practical value where a company already has a suspicion that infringements in a particular area may be taking place, or knows that certain sections of its business are at particularly high risk.

11.2.4 What else should an undertaking consider?

11.2.4.1 HR policy

A compliance policy linked to a company's HR and disciplinary policy is likely to be more effective than a policy the breach of which results in no individual sanctions on the employees involved. Not only will staff take the issue more seriously if they feel their own employment position may be at stake, but competition regulators also tend to be more inclined to accept that a company has done its best in trying to implement the policy in an effective manner.

While the introduction in some jurisdictions of criminal sanctions for individuals and the potential disqualification of directors for breaches of competition law has already helped to shift the focus onto individuals as well as companies, in practice these will probably only affect very few people. In consequence, tying the compliance policy to existing disciplinary provisions is more persuasive.

This clearly needs to be achieved in compliance with any necessary procedures under local employment legislation, bearing in mind that this may vary in different jurisdictions. Experience shows that different levels of infringement can be dealt with by increasing levels of sanction, resulting ultimately in dismissal for the very worst infringement. As set out at 11.2.3.5 above, the introduction of a competition compliance declaration into employees' regular appraisals also helps to reinforce the importance of the policy.

11.2.4.2 Document retention/destruction policy

The ever-increasing powers of investigation granted to competition authorities have made the question of document retention (or, perhaps more significantly, document destruction) ever more important.[10] Most companies have a policy in place for financial information that must be kept for accounting and tax purposes, and some national jurisdictions require documents such as contracts to be kept for a specified period.

10. See, in particular, the BAT litigation in the UK and Australia; *USA v. Philip Morris and Others* [2004] EWCA Civ 330; *McCabe v. BAT* [2002] VSC 73; and *BAT v. Cowell* [2002] VSCA 197.

Equally, most companies run a back-up of their computer systems each evening to avoid the loss of data in the event of software or hardware failure. As, in order to prove an infringement, competition authorities need to be able to produce sufficient evidence to substantiate their claims, there is an argument that companies should consider the systematic destruction of documents, especially correspondence, as soon as it becomes commercially expedient to do so.

The following factors need to be taken into consideration, as the wholesale shredding of correspondence files may not in practice be in the best interests of the company.

First, the majority of correspondence today is sent electronically. Competition authorities are increasingly sophisticated when it comes to searching for documents, in particular in relation to IT. As the first thing most regulators seek to obtain is copies of old e-mails, some thought should be given to how long back-up e-mails need to be kept for. If back-ups are usually made on a daily basis, there may be no commercial need for a company to keep years' worth of back-up tapes in its archives, ready for little more than inspection by the authorities.

There are, however, also strong arguments in favour of retaining some documentation for future reference. First, a total lack of documentation within a company may appear suspicious to an investigating competition authority, indicating that the company has something to hide and prompting stronger enforcement action.

Second, documents that may on their face appear unhelpful to the company's case are often in fact the very documents that can be used to prove a company's innocence. The wholesale destruction of documents may make a company's defence considerably more difficult to establish if it has nothing in writing to refute the allegations made against it.

Finally, correspondence is notoriously difficult to delete in its entirety. By definition, it has generally been disseminated to a number of different people and there is no guarantee that they will all have deleted it in the same way. This is particularly the case with e-mails, which can very quickly make their way onto the computers of numerous different users, thus taking control of the document away from the originator.

It should also be borne in mind that different jurisdictions have different requirements as regards document retention and so a global policy will need to be tailored to the individual requirements in each jurisdiction in which it is to be implemented.

Any document destruction policy should be put on hold as soon as a competition investigation is commenced, in order to avoid any allegation that the company or individuals have impeded the investigation and so committed a criminal offence. That said, a careful review of the relevant files should be made at this stage to ensure that any files that may come to the investigators' attention do not contain privileged documents.

11.2.4.3 Leniency and whistle-blowing policies

The various leniency regimes now being operated by an increasing number of competition authorities have had a big impact on enforcing the laws against operating cartels. The considerable financial advantages that a company can secure, if it is successful in applying for and obtaining either full immunity or a reduction in any eventual fine, are such that the adoption of some form of company whistle-blowing policy is increasingly attractive.

A whistle-blowing policy has two main aims: (a) to make a swift leniency application if the company discovers that it has been involved in some form of infringing activity; and (b) to alert competition authorities of anti-competitive agreements or acts being perpetrated by third parties to the detriment of the company, in order to protect the company's position in the market.

An effectively functioning compliance policy should bring to a company's attention activities relevant to either aim. The question of how best to act in the circumstances will clearly vary from case to case, and as such a standard set of procedures is unlikely to be of practical use. A whistle-blowing policy will therefore differ from most other policies in that it will act more as a prompt for relevant considerations rather than as a strict set of rules. Equally, given the magnitude of the decision which needs to be taken, it is likely to be limited to senior management alone. In this regard, the compliance officer needs to be fully briefed so as to know when an issue needs to be referred up as appropriate.

Relevant considerations will include:

- the nature and scope of the infringement;
- whether the company is itself involved or merely a victim of the infringing activity;
- the question of which jurisdictions are affected and whether or not leniency policies are available in each jurisdiction;
- the need to act quickly in the event that a leniency application is to be made;
- how best to coordinate simultaneous applications where appropriate;
- how best to deal with any press inquiries or other third-party leaks;
- any knock-on effects of a leniency application, such as third-party damages actions following a finding of infringement.

11.2.4.4 Legal privilege

In evaluating their processes in the context of competition compliance, companies should not forget to consider the thorny issue of which documents in their possession may attract legal privilege and how they wish to store them.

Legal privilege continues to be the subject of considerable debate, with landmark cases going through both the UK and EU courts.[11] Pending the

11. See *Akzo Nobel Chemicals* and *Three Rivers*, discussed at 9.6.2.1 above.

outcome of the *Akzo* case, it remains that advice given by in-house counsel or non-European qualified external counsel is not treated as privileged by the Commission in the course of its investigations. The position varies greatly in other national European jurisdictions: in the UK, for example, the category of privileged documents (including those created by in-house counsel) is relatively wide, whereas Germany takes a far more restrictive approach.

In consequence, companies need to consider the different rules in each jurisdiction in which they operate in order to decide how to obtain, store and file legal advice. In jurisdictions where advice may be privileged, it is advisable to keep it in a separate file, market "legally privileged", so as to seek to avoid having a discussion over each separate document with the investigators during a dawn raid. Where advice is unlikely to attract privilege, a company may decide to receive oral advice only on sensitive competition matters, or to store all copies of the advice at the offices of their outside counsel, who are less likely to be the subject of an investigation.

The question of legal privilege may be determinative when deciding what level of information should be documented by a compliance officer in a log of issues raised with him or her in the course of his or her compliance function. A sensible balance needs to be drawn between providing an investigating authority with a ready-made crib-sheet of potential infringements, and recording enough information to demonstrate that a company has actively implemented its compliance policy and is capable of dealing with issues as and when they arise.

INDEX

Index

Index

Index

Index

Index

Index

Index

Index

Index

Index

Index